BOOTY CAPITALISM

BOOTY CAPITALISM

THE POLITICS
OF BANKING
IN THE
PHILIPPINES

Paul D. Hutchcroft

Cornell University Press

ITHACA AND LONDON

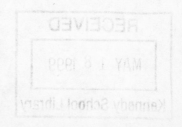

First published 1998 by Cornell University Press

Printed in the United States of America

Cornell University Press strives to use environmentally responsible suppliers and materials to the fullest extent possible in the publishing of its books. Such materials include vegetable-based, low-VOC inks and acid-free papers that are also either recycled, totally chlorine-free, or partly composed of nonwood fibers.

Library of Congress Cataloging-in-Publication Data

Hutchcroft, Paul D. (Paul David)
   Booty capitalism : the politics of banking in the Philippines /
Paul D. Hutchcroft.
      p.   cm.
   Includes index.
   ISBN 0-8014-3428-9 (cloth : alk. paper)
   1. Banks and banking—Philippines. 2. Capitalism. I. Title.
HG3314.H87   1998
332.1'09599—dc21   97-46857

Cloth printing   10 9 8 7 6 5 4 3 2 1

To my mother
and in memory of my father

Contents

Preface

The end of the Cold War has focused increasing attention on variation among capitalist systems. Now that the struggle between communism and capitalism has given way to continual shifts in intra-capitalist rivalry and cooperation, the diversity among "free-market" economies has become more apparent than at any time in the last half century. Nowhere can one find greater variation than in the so-called developing world or Third World (both terms, in their own way, of distinctly Cold War vintage); the astounding growth of newly industrialized countries in East Asia, it is often observed, offers an especially dramatic contrast with the stagnation of much of sub-Saharan Africa.

Unfortunately, modern political economy often provides little guidance in analyzing this variation. Amid today's widespread praise for the "magic of the marketplace," it is not always clear why the tricks of capitalist sorcery vary so enormously from one political setting to another: some states are clearly obstacles to sustained development, while others very successfully guide their economies through the most challenging of externally imposed obstacles. Careful examination of the Philippine political economy, this book demonstrates, offers valuable insights into the relationship between political and economic development in the Third World as a whole. Most of all, analysis of the Philippine experience highlights the centrality of sound political foundations to successful economic development.

My interest in the Philippines significantly predates any particular concern with intra-capitalist variation, government-business relations, or the politics of banking. This work emerges out of a long journey, tracing its origins to my first arrival in the Philippines over fifteen years ago. As part of a church-based program concerned with human rights and development issues, I traveled throughout the archipelago and learned firsthand of the political commitments of a broad range of Filipino society. My ties to the country were further nurtured in other capacities: as a U.S.-based human rights advocate, freelance journalist, intern for an American foundation in Manila, language student, visiting researcher, and scholar of politics. This longstanding association with the Philippines—a combination of extended stays and impatient absences since October 1980—has coincided with the deep crises and popular resistance during the twilight of the Marcos regime, the democratic exuberance of the early Aquino years, the political disenchantment and economic doldrums of the late 1980s and early 1990s, and the new optimism that accompanied the economic upturn under the Ramos administration in the mid-1990s.

Through these years, I have developed an enduring attachment to the archipelago and its people. Although I am an outsider, long association with those seeking change has promoted keen interest in the capacity of the Philippine political system to deliver freedom and prosperity to Filipinos of all social strata. My initial motivation for this study, as discussed below, was to seek an explanation for the country's longstanding difficulties in converting its enormous developmental assets into sustained developmental progress. Analysis of the particular variety of capitalism found in the postwar Philippines—*booty capitalism*—not only yields valuable lessons for students of comparative political economy and political development but will hopefully also be useful to those seeking to promote political and economic transformation in the present-day context. To the extent that my analysis may at times focus excessively on structural obstacles to change, I would like nothing more than to be proved wrong by the many agents of sweeping reform whose work I so deeply admire. I hope, as well, that insights from this book—based on developments up to late 1996—will prove valuable in analyzing the new challenges confronting the Philippines and its neighbors since economic crisis began to rock Asia in mid-1997.

I am grateful to the hundreds of persons who have given generously of their time in assisting the completion of this work, beginning with those who agreed to often-lengthy interviews as well as those who assisted in locating or providing materials essential to my research. It is not possible to list all those who have offered encouragement, support, or helpful ideas since this work was first conceived in 1989, but I must highlight the contributions of Patricio Abinales, Jose Almonte, the late Chester Babst, Coeli Barry, Cynthia and Germelino Bautista, Emil Bolongaita, Robin Broad, Gerald Burns, Alexander Calata, Sheila Coronel, Nick Cullather, Emmanuel Esguerra, Armand Fabella, Raul Fabella, Jaime Faustino, Antonio Gatmaitan (an especially insightful and encouraging early informant), Terence George, James Goodno, Gary Hawes, Eva-Lotta Hedman, Carolina Hernandez, John Humphreys, Erik Jensen, Joseph Lim, Victor Limlingan, the late Charles Lindsey, Lawrence MacDonald, Alex Magno, Lorna Makil, Roberto Millena, Matt Miller, Kay Mohlman, Resil Mojares,

Fr. Theodore Murnane, Yoshiko Nagano, Vitaliano Nañagas, Lin Neumann, Romulo Neri, Ramon Orosa, Esther Pacheco, Emerito Ramos, Noet Ravalo, Cooper Resabal, Temario Rivera, Sixto K. Roxas, James Rush and Asuncion Benitez-Rush, Sheila Samonte, Steven Solnick, Filomeno Sta. Ana, Edita Tan, Rigoberto Tiglao, David Timberman, Ramon Tiaoqui, Carlota Valenzuela, Jeffrey Winters, David Wurfel, and Josef Yap. Particular thanks to Antonio Abad, Emmanuel de Dios, Donald Emmerson, Barbara Goldoftas, Amado Mendoza, Joel Rocamora, Mark Thompson, and the anonymous readers of Cornell University Press and Ateneo de Manila University Press for providing comments on some or all portions of earlier drafts of the manuscript, as well as to Roger Haydon of Cornell University Press for valuable guidance throughout the process of revision. Any errors, of course, are mine alone.

Additional thanks to Philippine institutions that have, at various points, offered refuge and assistance: both the Third World Studies Center and the School of Economics at the University of the Philippines–Diliman, the Philippine-American Educational Foundation, the Philippine Social Science Council, the Philippine Center for Policy Studies, and the University of San Carlos in Cebu City. Also much appreciated is the assistance provided by the staffs of the libraries of the Ateneo de Manila University; *Business World;* the Central Bank of the Philippines; Ibon Databank; the Lopez Museum; Sycip, Gorres & Velayo; and the University of the Philippines (particularly at the School of Economics). Valuable research assistance has been provided by many persons, most notably Gina Benemerito, Ben Endriga, and Edgar Jovero. *Maraming salamat sa inyong lahat!*

In the United States, heartfelt debts of gratitude extend back to prefieldwork graduate student days in New Haven, where Kay Mansfield of the Yale Council on Southeast Asia provided "matron-client" nurture to us all, Edita Baradi kindly polished our Tagalog, and Charles Bryant guided us through Stirling Library's fine Southeast Asian collection. After returning from field research, I benefited enormously from the collegial and supportive environment of the Harvard Academy for International and Area Studies. Most recently, a host of colleagues at the Department of Political Science and the Center for Southeast Asian Studies of the University of Wisconsin–Madison—in particular Donald Emmerson, Edward Friedman, Herbert Kritzer, T. J. Pempel, Virginia Sapiro, Michael Schatzberg, Bernard Yack, Crawford Young, Michael Cullinane, Daniel Doeppers, and Alfred McCoy—have offered hearty encouragement and much useful advice toward the completion of this work. Carmel Capati and Gwendolyn Bevis provided excellent research assistance in the final stages of this work.

I gratefully acknowledge the generous financial support I have received at various stages, most of all from the U.S. Department of Education Fulbright–Hays Doctoral Dissertation Research Abroad Program, the Social Science Research Council and the American Council of Learned Societies (with funds provided by the William and Flora Hewlett Foundation), the Harvard Academy, and the University of Wisconsin–Madison Graduate School Research Committee. A collaborative research project of the East-West Center provided an opportunity to gain valuable insights on the politics of finance from Stephan Haggard, Manuel Montes, Andrew MacIntyre, Richard Doner, and others; panel presentations at various conferences, moreover, have elicited further useful ideas from a range of scholars.

Readers seeking greater detail on various aspects of this work—including bank ownership, selective credit allocation, total year-end assets, and protracted legal battles—are referred to my Yale Ph.D. thesis, "Predatory Oligarchy, Patrimonial State: The Politics of Private Domestic Banking in the Philippines," available from UMI dissertation services. All those who provided extensive comments and encouragement on that work have assisted in providing a stronger foundation for this book, including my professors, Margaret Keck and Sylvia Maxfield, and my ever-insightful *kumpadre* John Sidel. Benedict Anderson has encouraged and assisted me in countless ways, from the time we overlapped in Quezon City in 1989 and 1990 to the present. My greatest intellectual debts are to James Scott, a mentor who has the rare ability to simultaneously provide his students with the encouragement to go on and the challenge to do better. His straightforward, demystifying, and humanistic approach to scholarship is a goal toward which I will continuously aim.

Throughout this project I have depended heavily on the support of family. Trinidad and Zosimo Labra in Cebu City always provided welcome respite for Manila-weary souls, and the clan compound was the best possible venue for experiencing the extraordinarily uplifting spirit of Philippine holiday celebrations (where else but the Philippines can one see a statue of the Risen Lord regaled with John Philip Sousa marches at 1:30 a.m. Easter morn?). My parents, Charles and Etha Hutchcroft, enthusiastically supported my entire sojourn into the Philippines. It is to my mother and in memory of my father that I dedicate this work; together, they taught me the best of what I know.

Most of all, heartfelt thanks to Edna Labra Hutchcroft, my loving companion, whose keen insights helped shape this book in countless ways. Her quiet confidence and quick wit sustained me—and endured amid all the *sakripisyo ng pamilya* this work brought forth. I am forever grateful to her, to Anna, and to Ian for sharing all the joys of life together. Blest be the ties that bind.

PAUL D. HUTCHCROFT

Madison, Wisconsin

List of Abbreviations

ADFU	Apex Development Finance Unit
APEC	Asia-Pacific Economic Cooperation
AFTA	ASEAN Free Trade Area
APT	Asset Privatization Trust
AWSJ	Asian Wall Street Journal
ASEAN	Association of Southeast Asian Nations
BF	Banco Filipino
Bancom	Bancom Development Corporation
BAP	Bankers Association of the Philippines
BOI	Board of Investments
BIR	Bureau of Internal Revenue
BPI	Bank of the Philippine Islands
BSP	Bangko Sentral ng Pilipinas
CB, CBP	Central Bank of the Philippines
CDCP	Construction Development Corporation of the Philippines
CLUP	Civil Liberties Union of the Philippines
CMA	central monetary authority
Combank	Commercial Bank of Manila
DBP	Development Bank of the Philippines
DOSRI	Directors, officers, stockholders, and related interests (used in connection with bank loans to these persons and firms)
ECB	expanded commercial bank
E.O.	Executive Order
FEER	*Far Eastern Economic Review*
GATT	General Agreement on Trade and Tariffs
GDP	Gross Domestic Product
GNP	Gross National Product
Genbank	General Bank and Trust Company

G.O.	General Order
GSIS	Government Service Insurance System
Herdis group	the diversified conglomerate of Herminio Disini
IBAA	Insular Bank of Asia and America
IMF	International Monetary Fund
Interbank	International Corporate Bank
ISI	import-substitution industrialization
KBL	*Kilusang Bagong Lipunan* (New Society Movement)
LBP	Land Bank of the Philippines
LCs	letters of credit
L.O.I.	Letter of Instruction
LP	Liberal Party
Manilabank	Manila Banking Corporation
MHS	Ministry of Human Settlements
Overseas, OBM	Overseas Bank of Manila
NISA	National Intelligence Security Agency
NDC	National Development Corporation
NEDA	National Economic Development Authority
NICs	newly industrializing countries
NP	*Nacionalista* Party
OBUs	Overseas Banking Units
PBC, PBCommerce	Philippine Bank of Commerce
PCA	Philippine Coconut Authority
PCIB, PCIBank	Philippine Commercial and Industrial Bank; after 1983, Philippine Commercial and International Bank
PCCI	Philippine Chamber of Commerce and Industry
PCGG	Philippine Commission on Good Government
P.D.	Presidential Decree
PDIC	Philippine Deposit Insurance Corporation
PDCP	Private Development Corporation of the Philippines
Philexport	Philippine Exporters Confederation
Philfinance	Philippine Underwriters Finance Corporation
Philsucom	Philippine Sugar Commission
Philtrust, PTC	Philippine Trust Company
PNB	Philippine National Bank
R.A.	Republic Act
SCB	*Studies of Commercial Banks*
SEC	Securities and Exchange Commission
SES	Supervision and Examination Sector (of the Central Bank)
SGV	Sycip, Gorres & Velayo (a prominent Manila accounting firm)
SSS	Social Security System
UCPB	United Coconut Planters Bank
unibank	universal bank
USAID	U.S. Agency for International Development
VTA	voting trust agreement

BOOTY CAPITALISM

Introduction

When this book first began to take shape in 1989 and 1990, my primary goal was to explain the Philippines' longstanding "developmental bog."[1] In contrast to its booming neighbors, the country was plagued by very low—and occasionally even negative—rates of economic growth. The 1980s provided an especially glaring contrast: whereas the so-called Asian tigers and tiger cubs grew on average by 6.9 percent per year, the Philippines lagged far behind with average annual growth rates of only 0.9 percent. Real per capita income declined by 7.2 percent from 1980 to 1992.[2] By almost any measure of economic growth, the country was in a quagmire; despite tremendous human and natural resources, the Philippine political economy displayed a particularly strong resistance to fundamental change.

From a historical perspective, it is curious that such a question would even be posed. In the early postwar years, the Philippines had distinct advantages over many of its neighbors (for example, large quantities of U.S. aid and a population with high educational levels and a remarkable facility for English); within the region, only Japan exceeded its standard of living. Thirty and forty years ago, a scholar in my position would probably have asked an entirely different question: What is it about the Philippines that makes it work so well? Unlike many of its neighbors, the country not only had very impressive rates of manufacturing growth, but was also achieving political stability (with regular elections and a relatively unpoliticized military). Did something go wrong, or were there funda-

---

[1] This term is borrowed from Ruth McVey, "The Materialization of the Southeast Asian Entrepreneur," in *Southeast Asian Capitalists,* ed. McVey (Ithaca, N.Y.: Cornell Southeast Asia Program, 1992), 22.

[2] World Bank, *The Philippines: An Opening for Sustained Growth,* Report No. 11061-PH (Washington, D.C.: World Bank, 1993), i, 1.

1

mental—and partially submerged—problems present even in the heyday of Philippine industrialization in the 1950s?

Not surprisingly, answers to this question have varied across time. In 1970, as both democratic institutions and economic growth were wearing thin, many perceived a trade-off between the two that needed to be resolved in favor of economic growth. The economy may be faltering, many would have argued, but its problems could easily be resolved by a dose of authoritarianism. Without an obstructionist Congress, technocrats could take charge of economic policy and bring on long-delayed and sorely needed reform. Indeed, when President Ferdinand E. Marcos declared martial law in 1972, he promised that his authoritarian regime would defeat the "old oligarchy" and bring new economic opportunity to the people.

By 1980, however, few could continue to place hope in authoritarianism, Marcos-style. Cronyism ran rampant, a new oligarchy had emerged, and the primary engine of economic growth was foreign debt. As the initial economic successes of the martial law years lost steam, a scholar would probably begin to note basic structural problems in the Philippine political economy, but might expect them to be resolved—if only the dictatorship could be deposed and the influence of its foreign backers curbed. Given the enormous reliance of the Marcos regime on external support, one might at that time have adopted the "dependency" framework, and blamed the country's problems primarily on the self-serving meddling of outside forces: the former colonial power and current military superpower, the United States, and multilateral institutions such as the World Bank and the International Monetary Fund (IMF).

From the vantage point of the late 1980s, as similarly dependent countries managed to carve out stronger roles for themselves, it became necessary to explore whether the Philippines might face much more fundamental obstacles to sustained development. Many basic patterns of domestic politics endured even after the dramatic restoration of democracy in 1986, and sporadic initiatives for economic reform under President Corazon Aquino were generally overwhelmed by the opposition of those who had long enriched themselves through special privileges, protectionism, and restrictions on competition. As a reform-minded secretary of finance readily acknowledged, "the base for crony capitalism" survived the downfall of Marcos.[3]

The experiences of the mid-1990s have lifted expectations once again. Upon taking office in 1992, President Fidel V. Ramos expressed a clear sense of the country's weakness in competing effectively in the international economy, and undertook an ambitious reform program to "bring down the old economic order." The political dominance of "oligarchic

---

[3] *Manila Chronicle,* June 2, 1990.

groups" able to "bend the State to do their will," he explained, "has distorted our economy and rendered government ineffectual. This is the reason why the Philippines has lagged so far behind the East Asian Tigers." In the new development strategy, declared Ramos, "We shall insist that our business and political elites commit themselves unequivocally to the common good."[4] Thanks in large part to the reform program, the country's annual growth rates climbed to 5 percent to 7 percent by mid-decade—still modest and short-lived in comparison to many Southeast Asian neighbors, but a tremendous improvement over the rock-bottom growth of earlier years.

Despite the clear achievements of a reform program committed to liberalization, privatization, and the dismantling of "cartels and monopolies," one of its premier architects acknowledged in 1996 that accomplishments to date represent the "easy" reforms. As "hard" reforms requiring greater administrative capacity were being attempted, explained Presidential Security Adviser Jose Almonte, "the weaknesses of the Philippine State are starting to show." The government has yet to "free itself from the influence of [the] oligarchy," he explained, and there is no assurance that it can succeed in doing so. "Unless the Philippine State becomes stronger and more efficient," he concluded, "it will not be able to deal with our long-standing problems.[5] Indeed, the Ramos administration has been far more successful in removing the state from obstructive roles than in building up its capacity to achieve constructive tasks. It is far easier, for example, to liberalize imports than to promote high value-added exports; less troublesome to dismantle a system of preferential fiscal incentives than to create a revenue system able to sustain the long-term infrastructural needs of development; and (as analyzed in Chapter Nine) much simpler to give out new bank licenses than to assure the "prudential regulation" of the financial system. For all that has been done in the realm of economic reform, a concerted program of political and institutional reform will be required if the Philippine state is to contribute effectively to developmental goals. Not surprisingly, many question the political sustainability of economic reforms into future years.

Political Obstacles, Perennial Aspirations

This book asserts that a major source of obstacles to sustained development in the Philippines lies in the political sphere, and that these obstacles

[4] Fidel V. Ramos, "Philippines 2000: Our Development Strategy," a speech to the First Multisectoral Forum on Science and Technology, Metro Manila, January 21, 1993; State of the Nation Address, July 26, 1993, quoted in Joel Rocamora, *Breaking Through* (Metro Manila: Anvil Publishers, 1994), 174.

[5] Jose T. Almonte, "Building State Capacity for Reform," a speech to the Philippine Economic Society, Metro Manila, February 9, 1996.

are revealed through careful examination of relations between the state and dominant economic interests. In other words, successful *economic* development has been constrained to a large extent by weaknesses of *political* development. This is a simple conclusion, but one that is all too often forgotten in an era in which markets are widely praised and governments routinely reviled. Classical institutional perspectives provide many insights into the importance of understanding the political foundations of capitalist development, and highlight the bureaucratic foundations of advanced capitalism. While the end of the Cold War has clearly exposed the enormous variation that exists among capitalist systems, modern political economy provides few guideposts for analyzing such variation within the Third World. Careful examination of the Philippine polity and economy not only demonstrates how different types of states help to nurture different types of capitalism, but also how deficiencies in the political sphere can obstruct capitalist development. While clearer understanding of the country's lackluster developmental experience served as the initial major goal of this work, a second question has emerged in the course of comparative reflection: what does this experience teach us about the necessary political foundations of advanced forms of capitalism in the modern Third World?

By most counts, the Philippines should have all the ingredients necessary for developmental success: tremendous entrepreneurial talents, an enormously talented and well-educated workforce (readily conversant in the dominant language of international business), a rich endowment of natural resources, and a vibrant community of economists and development specialists. A 1993 World Bank study on the economic success of most of the country's capitalist neighbors (South Korea, Taiwan, Hong Kong, Singapore, Malaysia, Thailand, and Indonesia) dismisses the Philippines as a "perennial aspirant" to the ranks of the newly industrializing economies, "not able to combine enough positive factors from among macroeconomic stability, strong technocratic bureaucracy, export competitiveness, political stability, and policy consistency." Similarly, one veteran journalist lamented in 1991 that "the Philippines adds up to less than the sum of its parts."[6] A central explanation for the faulty arithmetic, I argue, can be traced to longstanding deficiencies in the Philippine political sphere. The Philippines may seem to have everything going for it, but for most of the postwar period the country has been unable to go very far very fast. As such, it can be treated as a limiting case, one that greatly illuminates larger issues of the relationship between political and economic development in the modern Third World.

[6] Danny M. Leipziger and Vinod Thomas, *Lessons of East Asia: An Overview of Country Experience* (Washington, D.C.: The World Bank, 1993), 5, 10; Interview, A. Lin Neumann, former president of the Foreign Correspondents Association of the Philippines, January 30, 1991.

The third major question that motivates this work also emerged from comparative analysis, as I reflected on the process by which the Philippines could eventually begin to convert its considerable developmental assets into sustained developmental success. How might this process of change compare with other experiences of political and economic transformation? By the mid-1990s, these questions have become increasingly relevant. The 1992 withdrawal of U.S. bases has greatly altered the country's external environment, promoted new perceptions of the Philippines' place in the world, and encouraged the important measures of economic reform pursued under Ramos's leadership. The question of whether the reforms will succeed in initiating a fundamental transformation of the political economy is analyzed further in the concluding chapter; the ultimate outcome promises to be of broad comparative interest to those concerned with issues of political and economic change in less-developed nations.

Analyzing Booty Capitalism

In addressing the three major questions of this study, I draw upon the historically based analyses of Max Weber and others, who demonstrate that "bringing political arbitrariness to heel" is a critical (but often overlooked) prerequisite for the development of advanced forms of capitalist accumulation. Where patrimonial features are strong, Weber argues, "modern rational capitalism" will not prosper; conversely, "capitalism in its modern stages of development depends upon the bureaucracy."[7] The first two chapters develop this theoretical framework, and provide a broad overview of the historical development and present-day nature of relations between state and oligarchy in the Philippines. To place Philippine polity, society, and economy in comparative perspective, I develop a broad cross-national typology of variations in Third World capitalist systems—and variations in the political systems that undergird them. The Philippines provides a clear-cut example of what kinds of obstacles to capitalist development can result when the power of an oligarchic private sector is never tamed, and there is no concerted effort to promote the development of the public sector. Chapter Three compares polities that exhibit strong patrimonial features, and argues that the Philippines' patrimonial *oligarchic* state (as compared to a Thai-or Indonesian-style patrimonial *administrative* state, where a bureaucratic elite traditionally predominates) presents particu-

[7] E. L. Jones, *The European Miracle: Environments, Economies, and Geopolitics in the History of Europe and Asia* (Cambridge: Cambridge University Press, 1981), 236; Max Weber, *Economy and Society* (Berkeley: University of California Press, 1978), I: 224. "The patrimonial office," writes Weber, "lacks above all the bureaucratic separation of the 'private' and the 'official' sphere" (II: 1028).

larly obstinate structural barriers to the demise of patrimonial features and the creation of a more rational-legal state.

The theoretical and comparative assertions of this work are based on a detailed analysis of relations between state and oligarchy in the private domestic commercial banking sector. Chapter Four provides historical background on the development of the overall banking system, and Chapters Five through Nine concentrate attention on the relationship between the Central Bank and the commercial banks (particularly the private domestic banks) between the years 1960 and 1995. The concluding chapter summarizes both the overall argument and the lessons derived from the banking sector, and examines possibilities for transformation of the system of booty capitalism into a political economic order more responsive to the developmental needs of the nation as a whole.

The Politics of Banking

Why banking? First, within the banking arena, one finds the most important of the state economic policymaking agencies and many of the most powerful of the oligarchic extended families (those that have diversified into commercial banking). As we shall see, the Central Bank has been unable to defend itself from the legal attacks of bankers, unable to enforce regulations that will prevent oligarchs from looting the loan portfolios of their banks, and unwilling to challenge the cartel practices within the industry. Just as important, however, when the Central Bank *does* flex its muscle, one is more likely to find decisions made on the basis of personalistic criteria than on the basis of clear institutional interests.

Second, because banking is an arena where one might expect to find relatively more modern and institutionalized patterns of interaction, it is of particular significance to be able to demonstrate the persistence of patrimonial features. The Central Bank—and its successor institution, the Bangko Sentral—have often enjoyed high ratings from the business sector for generally keeping inflation at low levels and defending the value of the peso; since the 1950s, in fact, these goals have been broadly shared by both monetary authorities and the diversified family conglomerates that dominate the economy. Because the central monetary authority is consistently the most highly regarded of the economic policymaking agencies, it is especially revealing to demonstrate a high degree of arbitrariness and weakness in its relations with the banking sector.[8]

[8] A 1989 survey found that bankers were "quite happy" with the Central Bank's role in fiscal and monetary policy, but thought that Central Bank examiners lacked the "sophistication" and training to monitor bank risk and detect insider abuse. Sycip, Gorres, Velayo & Co. and Bankers Association of the Philippines, *Banking in the Philippines: A Vision for the 1990s*

Third, even advocates of a minimalist state generally acknowledge the need for firm and consistent "prudential regulation" of the financial sector. As a critic of imprudent liberalization once noted, banks are not butcher shops. Deterioration of trust in a bank, unlike trust in a butcher shop, can have major consequences for the larger economy; moreover, the banker's dealings with customers are far more complex than those of a butcher. While the butcher engages in spot transactions (meat for money), the banker borrows funds and lends them out to persons whose creditworthiness must be verified.[9] To the extent that the Philippine state is unable to provide quality regulation of its banks, I will suggest, it shows itself to be incapable of providing a firm political foundation for "laissez-faire" capitalism—not to mention, of course, those forms of developmental capitalism requiring a far more competent state apparatus.

The major focus of this work is two arenas that offer particular insights into the nature of relations between state and oligarchy in the banking system: bank supervision and selective credit allocation. "Banking," observes one former bank president, "is a prism through which to understand power politics in the Philippines."[10] A study of the banking system highlights larger patterns at work within the political economy: how a predatory oligarchy extracts privilege from a patrimonial state, and how developmental policy objectives are continually choked out by a clamor of particularistic demands made by those who currently enjoy proximity to the political machinery. Likewise, the retarded development and poor performance of the banking sector can be treated as a microcosm of larger problems in the economy as a whole.

There are two overarching characteristics of the Philippine banking system, both of which have endured despite regime change, repeated attempts at reform, and circumstances that one might initially expect to have been conducive to building more effective mechanisms of state regulation. First is rampant favoritism, reflecting the patrimonial character of

---

(Manila: SGV, 1989), 17–18. In a 1995 survey of businesspersons, the Bangko Sentral received the highest performance rating of all government agencies. *Philippine Daily Inquirer,* September 13, 1995. Weber, in fact, anticipates that the realms of credit and banking will have a more "rational" character; see "Author's Introduction," in *The Protestant Ethic and the Spirit of Capitalism* (New York: Charles Scribner's Sons, 1958), 20.

[9] World Bank, *World Development Report 1991* (New York: Oxford University Press, 1991), 136; Carlos Diaz-Alejandro, "Good-Bye Financial Repression, Hello Financial Crash," *Journal of Development Economics* 19 (1985): 1–24, at 2. He further notes that "the credibility of a government commitment to a truly laissez-faire domestic financial system is very low. . . . '[P]ublic opinion,' including generals and their aunts, simply does not believe that the state would (or could) allow most depositors to be wiped out by the failure of banks and financial intermediaries." Moreover, "foreign financial agents will not accept a separation of private and public debts when a crisis arrives" (pp. 17–18).

[10] Interview, Antonio P. Gatmaitan, former president of Commercial Bank of Manila, September 18, 1989.

the state. The favor or disfavor of those oligarchs currently holding state office is a major determinant of the relative success or failure of particular banks. The Central Bank's allocation of valuable privileges—whether they be bank licenses, government deposits, emergency bailouts, or loans—are rarely made on the basis of clear-cut, objective rules that apply to all players. Although the type of favors extracted from the state may have changed through the years, one can note parallels between how sugar interests raided the newly formed Philippine National Bank after World War I, how exchange controls were obtained in the 1950s, how banks bribed officials for government deposits in the 1960s, how the Marcos regime raided state financial institutions for "behest loans" during the martial law years, and how the large banks have harvested windfall profits by investing government deposits in government securities in the late 1980s. Favored treatment, it should be noted, is not imperative to the success of a commercial bank; certain institutions, by adopting a conserva-tive lending policy and striving for steady growth, seem to do reasonably well without any obvious special treatment by the Central Bank or the Palace. But in instances where banks have enjoyed meteoric growth, one is nearly sure to find special favors, granted through special relations with prominent officials.

The second overarching characteristic is the largely ineffectual state regulation of the banking sector, reflecting both the patrimonial character of the state and the weakness of the state apparatus in relation to the powerful social forces that are concentrated in the banking sector. Despite three major financial reform efforts, two of which specifically targeted problems of bank supervision, the Central Bank remains largely ineffectual in systematically disciplining banks that violate Central Bank regulations— *even* those regulations related to abuse of loan portfolios, violations of which have contributed to four major episodes of bank instability in a twenty-five-year period. This weakness becomes especially apparent in ex-amining legal actions lodged against Central Bank personnel; in the Phil-ippines, bank supervisors are more likely to be intimidated than to intimi-date. A 1988 World Bank report recommends that "in the future the CBP [Central Bank of the Philippines] should consider adopting a firmer ap-proach in dealing with banks which violate its rules and regulations." At the same time, they acknowledge that because of the many suits filed against Central Bank personnel in the wake of recent bank failures, the "CBP staff . . . feel personally vulnerable to suits brought against them for their official acts, and this is now affecting their performance."[11]

Even when the Central Bank has acted against those who milked their

---

[11] World Bank, *Philippine Financial Sector Study,* Report No. 7177-H (Washington, D.C.: World Bank, 1988), viii, x.

banks, former bank owners have been known to use personal connections, even up to the Supreme Court, to confound Central Bank discipline. Former Governor Jaime Laya noted that even martial law "didn't seem to stop the lawsuits against Central Bank personnel." He actually laughed as he told me how the Central Bank legal office has "never won a case." But the former head of the bank supervision sector, who has herself been sued, doesn't find it a laughing matter: "Why only in this country," she exclaimed, "do the regulators go to jail, and the bankers go scot-free?"[12]

If the system genuinely worked for the greater good, perhaps rampant favoritism and weak state regulation could be overlooked. But there are five major areas in which the Philippine financial system has historically performed poorly, all of which have hampered larger developmental objectives. First, the banking system has a pitiful record of mobilizing savings, a key element in almost any successful program of economic development. In part because real savings deposit rates have generally been negative over the past two decades, the Philippines has by far the worst record of promoting financial intermediation in all of ASEAN. Rates of financial intermediation (the ratio of the sum of demand, savings, and time deposits to gross national product) have been very weak across time, hovering in the range of 20 percent to 30 percent since 1970 while Malaysia and Thailand have climbed from roughly 25 percent to 80 percent in the same period.[13] The failure to mobilize more funds domestically has contributed to the country's considerable reliance on foreign savings.

Second, a review of the postwar commercial banking system (which dominates the financial system as a whole)[14] shows that political factors greatly hinder the efficient allocation of credit. There have been three major types of commercial banks: patronage-infested government banks (most important, the Philippine National Bank, but formerly two smaller banks as well); a large number of private banks, most of which are family-

---

[12] Interviews, Jaime C. Laya, former governor of the Central Bank (1981–1984), May 21, 1990, and Carlota P. Valenzuela, former deputy governor, Supervision and Examination Sector, Central Bank, March 22, 1990.

[13] Indonesia, meanwhile, jumped from roughly 10 percent to 50 percent rates of financial intermediation between the early 1980s and early 1990s. See Edita A. Tan, "Bank Concentration and the Structure of Interest," Discussion Paper No. 8915, University of the Philippines School of Economics (Quezon City, 1989), 3; and Carlos C. Bautista, Roy C. Ybañez, and Gerardo Agulto Jr., "A Study on the Philippine Financial System: Focus on the Commercial Banking Industry," (Quezon City: unpublished ms., 1995), 6, 33–35.

[14] The commercial banks have held a majority of the system's total assets (excluding Central Bank assets) throughout the postwar era, and if one adds their resources to those of (1) specialized government banks, the Development Bank of the Philippines (DBP) and the Land Bank of the Philippines (LBP), and (2) government insurance companies, the Social Security System (SSS) and Government Service Insurance System (GSIS), one can account for over three-quarters of all financial assets. Even when the investment houses (merchant banks) were at the height of their strength, in the mid-1970s, the combined assets of commercial banks were eleven times those of investment houses.

dominated; and four highly profitable branches of foreign banks, all of which have been in operation since at least the late 1940s.[15] First priority in loan allocation by government banks generally goes to those with greatest proximity to the political machinery. Within private domestic banks, the historical pattern is for related enterprises of the extended family (or families) owning the bank to enjoy first priority on loans. The basic building blocks of the Philippine business community are extended family conglomerates, and among the surest means for such groups to secure credit is through ownership (or partial ownership) of a commercial bank.

These loan abuses, in which families milk their banks to support related enterprises, are compounded by other types of distortion in credit allocation. Bankers often use their powers of loan allocation to bolster their patronage networks and to strengthen ties with political allies who could reciprocate in some way at a later time. A banker "dispenses largesse and favors," explains one former bank president. "To be given a loan [is] to be given a great favor," and builds on the "reciprocity [that] is a part of the fabric of Philippine life."[16] Because bank ownership also advances familial interests by yielding a wealth of useful information about political and economic developments, it is commonly referred to as "the next best thing to tapping into a confessional booth."

Third, the banking system has created a high degree of financial instability, the root cause of which is regulators' inability to curb the milking of loan portfolios by bank owners, directors, and officers for related family enterprises. As early as 1970, one economist noted that the Philippines "has probably had more financial scandals or financial institutions in distress than any other Southeast Asian country."[17] Problems later intensified, with major episodes of bank failure in the mid-1970s, the early 1980s, and the mid-1980s. Banking reforms have been largely unsuccessful either in curbing these loan abuses or in altering the ownership patterns that encourage them.

Fourth, the banking system provides enormous profits to those banks that are primarily in the business of banking for the sake of banking profits (and not for the sake of financing related family enterprises). According to the World Bank, pretax profit margins in the Philippines in the late 1980s were roughly 300 percent higher than the average of such margins in eight other countries.[18] Bankers enjoy oligopolistic power that is unchallenged by the Central Bank, and prices for important banking services

---

[15] By year-end 1995, as discussed in Chapter Nine, PNB was more than 50 percent privatized and ten new foreign banks were allowed to open branches in the country.

[16] Interview, Ramon S. Orosa, former president of Philippine Commercial and Industrial Bank and former chairman of International Corporate Bank, April 30, 1990.

[17] Robert F. Emery, *The Financial Institutions of Southeast Asia: A Country-by-Country Study* (New York: Praeger, 1970), 482.

[18] World Bank, *Philippine Financial Sector* (1988), iii, 73.

seem to be set by the actions of a cartel. Large spreads between interest rates for loans and deposits (initially enforced by regulation, but more recently maintained, it seems, through collusive actions) guarantee high levels of profitability for those banks whose loan portfolios are less flagrantly milked by their directors, officers, and stockholders. As a result, the four foreign banks have found profits from their Philippine branches to be among the highest in their entire international branch network.[19]

Finally, continual raids of oligarchs and cronies on the resources of the state seriously depleted the national treasury and killed the Central Bank. Throughout the postwar era—but particularly in the years when international credit was easiest to obtain—the Central Bank handed out extraordinarily generous gifts to public and private financial institutions, including the allocation of large quantities of foreign loans, the assumption of foreign exchange risk on certain types of financial operations, and the disbursement of a wide array of other instruments of selective credit.[20] While one might initially expect that the distribution of such largesse would strengthen the hand of the Central Bank in bank supervision and reform implementation, the benefits of such patronage accrued far more to Palace and Central Bank favorites than to the Central Bank as an institution. The legacy of the Central Bank's exceeding generosity was its untimely death, in 1993, at the age of forty-four. In summary, the banking system produces enormous particularistic advantage amid rampant waste of domestic savings and squandering of foreign resources.

Because of the patently unimpressive performance of the postwar Philippine banking sector, one can easily make the argument that the deficiencies of this sector hinder developmental progress. This is entirely true, and not an unimportant assertion. In this book, however, I make an even more fundamental argument: the deficiencies of the political sphere are central to explaining the country's longstanding "developmental bog." The banking sector provides a prism through which to understand better the nature of relations between the state and dominant economic interests, and the inadequate development of the political sphere. No doubt other case studies would yield similar understandings, but the most comprehensive analysis of all can be achieved by examining the banking sector.

In short, this book asserts, the Philippines' developmental quagmire can be traced in large degree to the endurance of a predatory oligarchy and a patrimonial state. Together, the distinctive features of state-oligarchy relations in the Philippines make up the system of booty capitalism. Throughout modern Philippine history, one finds far more oligarchy building than

[19] Anonymous interview, international economist, May 1990.
[20] The vast bulk of selective credit allocation (rediscounting, foreign loan allocations by the Central Bank, foreign exchange swaps, specialized credit programs, placements of government deposits, and so on) has been channeled through the commercial banks.

state building: the oligarchic families have had ample opportunities, historically, to consolidate their power with the support of external forces, while the state has remained woefully underdeveloped. As a result, the state apparatus continues to be easy prey to a powerful oligarchic class that enjoys an independent economic base outside the state, yet depends upon particularistic access to the political machinery as the major avenue to private accumulation. Until there is greater development of the state apparatus, I argue, the Philippines will be unable to achieve sustained economic success.

CHAPTER ONE

The Political Foundations of
Booty Capitalism in the Philippines

States are not standardized commodities. They come in a wide array of sizes, shapes, and styles. That incumbents sometimes use the state apparatus to extract and distribute unproductive rents is undeniable. That all states perform certain functions indispensable to economic transformation is equally so. That both characteristics are randomly distributed across states is very unlikely, yet we have only a hazy sense of the range of variation, to say nothing of its causes.
>   —Peter Evans, "Predatory, Developmental, and Other Apparatuses: A Comparative Political Economy Perspective on the Third World State," 1989

In the reality of political systems, patrimonial and legal elements are mixed, though all societies have patrimonial traces while some have only a few legal ones.
>   —Daniel S. Lev, "Judicial Authority and the Struggle for an Indonesian Rechtsstaat," 1978

A scholar of the Philippines once noted that "business is born, and flourishes or fails, not so much in the market place as in the halls of the legislature or in the administrative offices of the government."[1] Although this observation was made in 1959, it could have been repeated with equal validity in subsequent decades. Whether in the pre–martial law years (1946–1972), martial law years (1972–1986), or post-Marcos years (after 1986), one finds remarkable continuity in basic patterns of interaction between the Philippine state and dominant economic interests. Even as it is often incapable of meeting even the most basic infrastructural needs of the economy, the Philippine state is nonetheless central to any comprehensive analysis of the country's political economy. Access to the state apparatus has been the major avenue to private accumulation, as the quest for "rent-seeking" opportunities brings a stampede of favored elites and would-be favored elites to the gates of Malacañang Palace. The state apparatus has repeatedly been choked by an anarchy of particularistic demands from, and particularistic actions on behalf of, those oligarchs and cronies

---

[1] Thomas R. McHale, "An Econecological Approach to Economic Development" (Ph.D. dissertation, Harvard University, 1959), 217.

who are currently most favored by its top officials: one will obtain a highly coveted loan or import license, another will enjoy a stake in a cartelized industry protected by highly discretionary state regulations.[2]

Because of the weak institutionalization of the state, the personal favor and disfavor of those currently in power is a critical determinant of business success and failure. Political administration in the Philippines is often treated as a personal affair, and one can find many parallels between the modern Philippine polity and Weber's description of patrimonial states: "In general, the notion of an *objectively defined* official duty is unknown to the office that is based purely upon personal relations of subordination. . . . Instead of bureaucratic impartiality and of the ideal—based on the abstract validity of one objective law for all—of administrating without respect of persons, the opposite principle prevails. Practically everything depends explicitly upon the personal considerations: upon the attitude toward the concrete applicant and his concrete request and upon purely personal connections, favors, promises, and privileges."[3] It is not enough to say that the state lacks significant autonomy and capacity; in fact, to paraphrase Weber, the conceptual separation of the state from all personal authority of individuals is often remote from Philippine "structures of authority."[4]

While all states possess patrimonial features to some degree, it is clear that there is a particularly large gap between the Philippine state and the archetypal bureaucratic state.[5] The patrimonial framework helps us to

[2] *Rents* are created when the state restricts the operations of the market. The processes of rationing foreign exchange, curbing free trade, and licensing some aspect of economic activity—to give just a few examples—serve to create "rent havens" that can be captured by some combination of well-placed businesspersons and bureaucrats. See Peter Evans, *Embedded Autonomy: States and Industrial Transformation* (Princeton: Princeton University Press, 1995), 23–24.

[3] Max Weber, *Economy and Society,* (Berkeley: University of California Press, 1981), II: 1041. For a related discussion of the applicability of the patrimonial framework to the Philippine case, see Paul D. Hutchcroft, "Oligarchs and Cronies in the Philippine State: The Politics of Patrimonial Plunder," *World Politics* 43, no. 3 (1991): 414–450.

[4] Weber, *Economy and Society,* II: 998. Skocpol defines state autonomy as situations in which "states conceived as organizations claiming control over territories and people may formulate and pursue goals that are not simply reflective of the demands or interests of social groups, classes, or society." Theda Skocpol, "Bringing the State Back In: Strategies of Analysis in Current Research," in *Bringing the State Back In,* ed. Peter B. Evans et al. (Cambridge: Cambridge University Press, 1985), 9. In polities with strong patrimonial features, there is by definition a weak separation between the private and the official sphere, and therefore a particularly weak degree of autonomy. See Weber, *Economy and Society,* II: 1028.

"State capacity," explains Sikkink," involves the administrative and coercive abilities of the state apparatus to implement official goals." Kathryn Sikkink, *Ideas and Institutions: Developmentalism in Brazil and Argentina* (Ithaca, N.Y.: Cornell University Press, 1991), 11. In polities with strong patrimonial features, allegiance to official goals is commonly swamped by allegiance to personal goals.

[5] Weber develops pure categories, and then permits hybrid characterizations of his historical cases. When he compares various historical examples of bureaucracies, he creates a

understand two important elements of government-business relations in the Philippines that are not necessarily inherent in a state that displays a weak degree of autonomy: (1) the high degree of favoritism, as when oligarchs and cronies plunder the state apparatus for particularistic advantage—a feature some have characterized as "rent-seeking gone wild"; and (2) the capacity of those oligarchs currently holding official position to inflict punishment on their enemies. Because personal considerations are the primary basis for extracting favors from the state, or for meting out punishment on one's enemies, it is important to devote significant attention to the patrimonial features that persist within the postwar Philippine state.

Faced with the myriad particularistic demands of powerful elite interests, the Philippine state has rarely displayed the capacity to formulate or implement a coherent policy of economic development. Indeed, the Philippines presents a stark example of a state that has failed to effect the kind of economic change found among the East Asian newly industrializing countries (NICs). The statist model, successful though it has been in East Asian settings, is not a viable option for a state with such a highly fractured and ineffective bureaucracy. Unlike the Korean and Taiwanese states, which at certain crucial historical junctures enjoyed considerable autonomy from dominant economic interests, the Philippine state is so lacking in autonomy from dominant economic interests that even the most basic regulation of capital is continuously frustrated. Peter Evans notes that the bureaucratic capacity of the "developmentalist states" of East Asia can only be understood as part of a long historical experience; similarly, Haggard and Cheng note that "development models are not simple packages of policies; they are configurations of political, institutional, and historical events." In the Philippines, this long historical project has yet to produce anything resembling a developmentalist state. Gershenkron may be correct that successful strategies of late industrialization require far more than laissez-faire policies, but the Philippines lacks the state apparatus to effect such a far-reaching process of economic transformation.[6]

---

continuum that contains those with "strong patrimonial elements" at one end, those with "patrimonial admixtures" somewhere in the middle, and the purest examples of rational bureaucracy at the opposite end. (*Economy and Society,* II: 964.) It is in this spirit that I use the term "patrimonial features."

[6] Evans describes Korea and Taiwan as "developmentalist states" enjoying "embedded autonomy," and explains that "the combination of historically accumulated bureaucratic capacity and conjuncturally generated state autonomy put these state apparatuses in a very exceptional position." Peter B. Evans, "Predatory, Developmental, and Other Apparatuses: A Comparative Political Economy Perspective on the Third World State," *Sociological Forum* 4, no. 4 (1989): 561–587, at 575; Stephan Haggard and Tun-jen Cheng, "State and Capital in the East Asian NICs," in *The Political Economy of the New Asian Industrialism,* ed. Frederic C. Deyo (Ithaca, N.Y.: Cornell University Press, 1987), 128; and Alexander Gershenkron, *Economic Backwardness in Historical Perspective* (Cambridge: Harvard University Press, 1962).

Enforcing Laissez-Faire

The limitations of the Philippine state apparatus, however, go far deeper. Not only is it incapable of replicating the kind of interventionist capacity of its East Asian neighbors, it is also incapable of providing the even more basic legal and administrative underpinnings necessary for "free-market" capitalism. It is commonly presumed that laissez-faire is truly laissez-faire; that is, without state involvement in the economy, the "magic of the marketplace" will naturally take hold. If only the public sector can be shrunk to a minimum, some radical free-marketeers proclaim, capitalism will flourish. On the contrary, the Philippines presents an insightful case study of precisely what kinds of economic problems can result from the *insufficient development* of the state apparatus.

Even advocates of a relatively minimalist role for the state, such as the World Bank, emphasize that "governments need to do more in those areas where markets alone cannot be relied upon. Above all, this means investing in education, health, nutrition, family planning, and poverty alleviation; building social, physical, administrative, regulatory, and legal infrastructure of better quality; mobilizing resources to finance public expenditures; and providing a stable macroeconomic foundation, without which little can be achieved."[7] In the Philippines, the major issue is not the virtues or demerits of capable state interventions in the economy. With few exceptions, strategies often considered developmentally effective elsewhere (such as "picking winners" in industry through selective credit allocation and a strategic reliance on state-owned enterprises) have been developmental disasters in the Philippines. Rather, the major issue is the capacity of the state to carry out even the most minimally defined functions. The Philippine state has displayed strained capacity, to say the least, in its ability to provide adequate electricity and other infrastructure and to provide the basic regulation and administrative services that even neoclassical analysts consider essential to the proper workings of a capitalist economy. In the following pages, there will be a detailed examination of the inability of the Philippine state to provide effective political foundations for an arena universally viewed as central to the success of any modern economy: the banking industry.

Examination of the political foundations of development in the Philippines reveals enormous contrasts with those found in the newly industrializing countries of East Asia and Latin America. Haggard notes that the four large countries covered in his study (South Korea, Taiwan, Mexico, and Brazil) have all experienced significant levels of state building, and possess relatively cohesive, centralized, capable, and autonomous states. In Mexico, for example, "institutional change (beginning in the wake of the

---

[7] World Bank, *World Development Report 1991* (Oxford: Oxford University Press, 1991), 9.

Revolution) was a crucial prerequisite for policy change, *indeed, for any 'policy' at all.*" Patrimonial states, including Zaire and Haiti, "have proved incapable of pursuing any coherent policy at all." Robert Wade portrays Taiwan as an "extreme example" of economic corporatism, with a "hard state" able "not only to resist private demands but actively to shape economy and society." He provides a lengthy list of prescriptions for the rest of the Third World, but explicitly confines his treatment to countries with "benign political leaders, whose concerns go beyond using state power to support the affluence of a small group."[8]

These analysts of the most successful examples of Third World capitalism are thus suggesting that the experience of such places as Taiwan and South Korea probably have limited relevance to countries that remain far from achieving their degree of political and institutional development. Indeed, many scholars have noted that notions of policy and policymaking common to relatively more advanced countries require major modification when applied to states with strong patrimonial features. "The essential business of a state Minister" in India, writes Robert Wade, "is not to make policy. It is to modify the application of rules and regulations on a particularistic basis, in return for money and/or loyalty." Within most Black African states, observes Goran Hyden, "individuals and organizations do not engage in politics to . . . influence a government's policies within an overall and legitimate framework of agreed-upon rules."[9] Similarly, Lucian Pye observed in 1960 that "the transitional societies of Southeast Asia have not fully incorporated the view common to rational-legal systems of authority that the appropriate goal of politics is the production of public policy in the form of laws"; rather, "power and prestige" are often treated as "values to be fully enjoyed for their own sake and not rationalized into mere means to achieve policy goals." This is echoed both in Harold Crouch's analysis of the early years of Indonesia's New Order, where "political competition among the elite did not involve policy, but power and the distribution of spoils," and in David Wurfel's 1967 analysis of Philippine policymaking, which begins with a necessary distinction between government actions with generalized impact and those with more particularized application.[10]

---

[8] Stephan Haggard, *Pathways from the Periphery: The Politics of Growth in the Newly Industrializing Countries* (Ithaca, N.Y.: Cornell University Press, 1990), 168, 263 (emphasis added); Robert Wade, *Governing the Market: Economic Theory and the Role of Government in East Asian Industrialization* (Princeton: Princeton University Press, 1990), 294–95, 337, 350; see also 108.

[9] Robert Wade, "The Market for Public Office: Why the Indian State Is Not Better at Development," *World Development* 13 (1985): 467–497, at 480; Goran Hyden, *No Shortcuts to Progress: African Development Management in Perspective* (Berkeley: University of California Press, 1983), 35. See also James C. Scott, *Comparative Political Corruption* (Englewood Cliffs, N.J.: Prentice-Hall, 1972), 23.

[10] Lucian W. Pye, "The Politics of Southeast Asia," in *The Politics of the Developing Areas*, ed. Gabriel A. Almond and James S. Coleman (Princeton: Princeton University Press, 1960), 142–43; Harold Crouch, "Patrimonialism and Military Rule in Indonesia," *World Politics* 31

While such observations seem obvious to those familiar with power and politics in many Third World settings, it is in fact strikingly common for many analysts (both economists and political scientists) to treat promulgated policy as the key variable, and largely ignore the enormous variation that exists in the institutions responsible for implementing and enforcing the policies. In the words of Joel Migdal, social scientists become "preoccupied with details of recipes [and neglect] to taste the finished dishes."[11]

In historical perspective, it should come as no surprise that many of the world's states find it difficult to carry out even the most fundamental tasks. Karl Polanyi reminds us that in the development of capitalism in England, there "was nothing natural about *laissez-faire;* free markets could never have come into being merely by allowing things to take their course." Rather, "*laissez-faire* itself was enforced by the state," and its historical development required "an enormous increase in the administrative functions of the state." Weber explains that "capitalism in its modern stages of development requires the bureaucracy"; above all, advanced forms of capitalism require an administrative and legal structure able to promote "political and procedural predictability. . . . [M]odern rational capitalism has need, not only of the technical means of production, but of a calculable legal system and of administration in terms of formal rules. Without it adventurous and speculative trading capitalism and all sorts of politically determined capitalisms are possible, but no rational enterprise under individual initiative, with fixed capital and certainty of calculations."[12]

Categorizing Capitalist Systems

Where bureaucratic actions are often highly arbitrary, Weber argues, only certain types of "politically determined capitalisms" are able to thrive. Such forms of capitalism "often reach a very high level of development,"

(July): 571–87 (at 578); David Wurfel, "Individuals and Groups in the Philippine Policy Process," in *Foundations and Dynamics of Filipino Government and Politics,* ed. Jose Veloso Abueva and Raul P. De Guzman (Manila: Bookmark, 1967), 209. See also Laothamatas's description of businesspersons' "particularistic" impact on policymaking in Thailand's former bureaucratic polity, where "the effect was felt in the implementation stage rather than in the formulation stage of policy." Anek Laothamatas, *Business Associations and the New Political Economy of Thailand: From Bureaucratic Polity to Liberal Corporatism* (Boulder: Westview Press, 1992), 149–50.

[11] Joel Migdal, *Strong Societies and Weak States* (Princeton: Princeton University Press, 1988), 11. While Migdal was referring to the formalistic-legalistic approaches of early postwar political science, his characterization unfortunately retains much truth today.

[12] Karl Polanyi, *The Great Transformation: The Political and Economic Origins of Our Time* (Boston: Beacon Press, 1944), 139; Weber, *Economy and Society,* I: 224, II: 1095; Weber, "Author's Introduction," in *The Protestant Ethic and the Spirit of Capitalism* (New York: Charles Scribner's Sons, 1958), 25.

according to Weber, but the absence of calculability in the political sphere ultimately inhibits the development of more advanced forms of capitalist accumulation. Because all capitalism is in some sense "politically determined," I prefer to use *rent capitalism* as the overarching term to describe systems in which "money is invested in arrangements for appropriating wealth which has already been produced rather than in [arrangements for actually] producing it."[13] Rent capitalism can be distinguished from *production-oriented capitalism* according to the relative dominance of rent-seeking and production-oriented behavior. It is important to note, however, that no real capitalist system belongs purely in one category or the other, and that the lines between the two categories are often blurred: a system of rent capitalism may register significant levels of production, and a system of production-oriented capitalism may display a fair degree of rent-seeking.

More broadly, it is necessary to rethink the standard categorization of capitalist systems in developing countries. Economies are commonly expected to fall somewhere along a continuum between laissez-faire and statist models. The Philippines highlights the basic inadequacy of this popular typology, precisely because its economy does not exhibit key characteristics of *either* laissez-faire or statist capitalism. Although the system is primarily driven by private sector initiative, one finds little evidence of the dominance of market forces. And while access to the state machinery is the major avenue to capitalist accumulation, the Philippine state has been so swamped by the particularistic demands of powerful oligarchic forces that it has rarely been able to play a coherent role in guiding economic development. Because the Philippines does not properly fit anywhere along the standard continuum, it suggests the need for typologies that can begin to encompass the enormous variation that exists in modern capitalist systems.

The laissez-faire versus statist continuum generally highlights only one vital dimension of intra-capitalist variation: the relative strengths of state apparatuses and business interests. A second dimension, however, is just as vital: variation among state apparatuses, many of which exhibit strong patrimonial features. For heuristic purposes, these two elements of capitalist variation can be displayed on a simple matrix:

[13] Stanislav Andreski, ed., *Max Weber on Capitalism, Bureaucracy and Religion* (Boston: George Allen and Unwin, 1983), 9; Weber, I: 240, II: 1091, quote at 240. My definition of "rent capitalism" is taken from Andreski's definition of "political capitalism." This definition has clear parallels with those that define rent seeking as "directly unproductive profit-seeking (DUP) activity." David C. Colander, ed., *Neoclassical Political Economy: The Analysis of Rent-Seeking and DUP Activities* (Cambridge, Mass.: Ballinger Publishing Company, 1984), 6. It also corresponds broadly with the popular term *crony capitalism*, used to describe a system in which Marcos favorites were accorded special treatment without being required to make productive contributions to the national economy.

	State apparatus relatively stronger vis-à-vis business interests	State apparatus relatively weaker vis-à-vis business interests
Relatively more "rational-legal" state	Statist Capitalism (developmental state)	Laissez-faire Capitalism (regulatory state)
Relatively more patrimonial state	"Bureaucratic" Capitalism (patrimonial administrative state)	Booty Capitalism (patrimonial oligarchic state)

Combining these two dimensions enables us to go beyond simple generalizations about government-business relations, and more fully explore the political foundations of contrasting forms of capitalism—including those of many developing countries. The two familiar forms of production-oriented capitalism—differentiated according to the relative strengths of state apparatuses and business interests—are located on the upper portion of the matrix. On the lower portion, it is useful to distinguish between two major subtypes of rent capitalism (that is, systems in which rent-seeking behavior predominates), both of which have their foundations in a relatively patrimonial state. They can be differentiated along a continuum that reflects the relative strength of state apparatuses and business interests and the predominant direction of rent extraction: in *bureaucratic capitalism,* a bureaucratic elite extracts privilege from a weak business class, while in *booty capitalism* a powerful business class extracts privilege from a largely incoherent bureaucracy. As will be explained in Chapter Three, bureaucratic capitalism is built on the foundations of the patrimonial administrative state, while booty capitalism arises out of the political foundations of the patrimonial oligarchic state. While this analysis does not presume to capture all variations of capitalism within these two dimensions, it does aim to achieve a more accurate characterization of Philippine capitalism and to highlight the need to think more critically about the great variation that exists across capitalist systems.[14]

Montes is entirely correct to characterize the Philippine economy as a rent-seeking economy, and to contrast its operations with "'profit-seeking,' or productivity-improving economic activities. . . . In a 'profit-seeking' economic structure, assets and income are won and lost on the basis of the ability of the business owner to develop the property. . . .

[14] Within the matrix, it must be emphasized, both axes represent continua along which capitalist systems can be placed. Despite the presence of lines separating the different types of polities and capitalist systems, there is in reality no clear demarcation among categories. The horizontal axis, moreover, is not a measure of state autonomy. Because patrimonial states by definition lack a clear separation between the private and the official spheres, they cannot be considered autonomous. Matrix is reprinted, with permission, from Paul D. Hutchcroft, "Booty Capitalism: An Analysis of Business-Government Relations in the Philippines," in *Business and Government in Industrializing East and Southeast Asia,* ed. Andrew MacIntyre (Sydney: Allen & Unwin, and Ithaca, N.Y.: Cornell University Press, 1994), p. 221.

[O]perations must be organized to produce a surplus and surpluses earned in the operation must be correctly reinvested. In a 'rent-seeking' society, ownership of property alone guarantees the access to wealth. . . . [and] the operations of the state determine the assignment of and the continued enjoyment of economic advantages."[15]

But it is important to go one step further, and focus clearly on *who* has the greatest "enjoyment of economic advantages" within capitalist systems dominated by rent-seeking behavior. In other words, it is important to specify the primary direction of extraction in rent capitalism. Within booty capitalism, a group with an economic base *outside* the state is plundering the state for particularistic resources.[16]

The Logic of Booty Capitalism

For reasons that we shall explore later, oligarchic collectors of booty in the Philippines are well organized at the level of the family conglomerate, but very poorly organized at any broader level of aggregation. There is little separation between the enterprise and the household, and it is often difficult to discern larger segments of capital divided along coherent sectoral lines. In creating and responding to opportunities for enrichment provided by favorable access to the state machinery, the major families have created highly diversified conglomerates, and few have any strong loyalty to specific sectors of the economy. Because particularistic access to the state apparatus plays such a central role in the creation of wealth, the most enduring division among capital is that of the "ins" versus the "outs."

For those families who find themselves on the right side of this ever-shifting line, the spoils are legion. As one former presidential adviser explains, "every administration in this country has spawned its own mil-

---

[15] In the Philippines this "property" can include "protection from competition through quotas, tariffs, and measured capacities, subsidized credit, access to foreign reparations, loans, and grants." Those who gain such property need not develop it; rather, "they only need to maintain their influence over people in the government machinery to maintain and expand their ownership of economic advantages." The "internal efficiencies and investments" of their firms become a secondary concern. Manuel F. Montes, "The Business Sector and Development Policy," in *National Development Policies and the Business Sector in the Philippines* (Tokyo: Institute of Developing Economies, 1988), 64–66; and "Financing Development: The 'Democratic' versus the 'Corporatist' Approach in the Philippines," in *The Political Economy of Fiscal Policy*, ed. Miguel Urrutia, Shinichi Ichimura, and Setsuko Yukawa (Tokyo: The United Nations University, 1989), 135.

[16] My use of the term *booty capitalism* to describe a subtype of rent capitalism is not unlike Weber's use of the term to describe a subtype of "politically determined" capitalism. While he seemingly used "booty capitalism" to describe the gains of war, however, I am using the term to describe the plunder of state resources by social forces with a firm economic base outside the state. Although my use of the term *booty* probably involves a more systematic source of gain than Weber had in mind, it is certainly not inconsistent with the Random House dictionary's definition: "1. loot or plunder seized in war or by robbery. 2. any prize or gain." The term is made even more appropriate by the fact that competition for booty sometimes involves the use of violence.

lionaires." There is, in fact, a certain social mobility at the helm of Philippine society, as new families appear out of nowhere and some of the old families fall by the wayside. This steady creation of nouveaux riches makes it impossible to reduce the Philippine oligarchy to a certain number of old families. As new faces gain favorable access to the state apparatus, they too can achieve big-time success in Philippine business. This social mobility highlights the appropriateness of the term *oligarchy* for analysis of the Philippine political economy. We find in the Philippines not a fixed aristocracy, but rather a social group that is based on wealth and that changes over time. As Aristotle wrote, "where men rule because of the possession of wealth, whether their number be large or small, that is oligarchy." Unlike an aristocracy, an oligarchy has little stability in its composition; there is a constant stream of new entrants as new wealth is created. As a system of government, oligarchy is rule "for the benefit of the men of means" not rule for the "common good."[17]

It is indeed paradoxical that a state so thoroughly overrun by the particularistic demands of the oligarchy should nonetheless remain a central subject of analysis. The state's important role seems to derive primarily from responsibilities it has necessarily assumed in handling the country's *external* economic relations: it disburses aid and loans received from abroad and it sets policies on foreign exchange, trade, and investment. Not coincidentally, the state agency generally most influential in economic policymaking, the Central Bank, is also the agency with the greatest responsibility in external economic relations. Throughout the postwar era, the country's geopolitical importance has brought in huge quantities of external resources, which have been funneled through the central government in Manila and become ripe pickings for private interests.

External forces play a key role in maintaining both the physical and economic viability of the state, despite the constant diversion of incoming resources to interests other than those of the state. Indeed, as will be discussed further in the next chapter, one cannot understand either the formation or the endurance of the Philippine state without considering the critical role of external forces. Most important, the country's role as host of the U.S. military bases has helped ensure repeated rescue from the

---

[17] Interview, Adrian Cristobal, former special assistant for special studies (to President Marcos), June 19, 1989; Aristotle, *The Politics,* trans. T. A. Sinclair, ed. Trevor J. Saunders (Harmondsworth: Penguin Books, 1985), 192, 190. See also 252–60. Thanks to Jim Nolt for introducing me to basic elements of Aristotelian thought. Moreover, the fluid composition of the upper reaches of Philippine society displays how "patrimonial" is far more appropriate than "feudal" in describing important characteristics of the Philippine political economy. As Weber explains: "Patriarchal patrimonialism is much more tolerant than feudalism toward social mobility and the acquisition of wealth. The patrimonial ruler does not like independent economic and social powers. . . . but he also does not support status barriers." Weber, *Economy and Society,* II: 1102.

balance-of-payments crises that have plagued the postwar economy. Because of the country's geopolitical importance, these bailouts have commonly proceeded even when "conditionalities" attached by foreign aid missions and multilateral agencies failed to be met.

This combination of a poorly developed state apparatus, a powerful oligarchy, and ready support from an external military power has left the Philippines with a booty capitalism that endures to the present day. As President Fidel Ramos noted in his 1992 inaugural address, the Philippine economic system "rewards people who do not produce at the expense of those who do . . . [and] enables persons with political influence to extract wealth without effort from the economy." Within this system, a kind of "private sector initiative" overwhelms an externally stocked but nonetheless weak state in the quest for particularistic resources. This type of capitalism, however, is not self-sustaining; ultimately, it depends on the international dole. As discussed further below, the withdrawal of U.S. military bases has brought increasing pressure to begin to orient the system toward more internationally competitive modes of operation.

In summary, the case of the Philippines highlights important political underpinnings to the development of more advanced forms of capitalism. Not only is the Philippine state incapable of guiding the process of late, late industrialization via the statist model; it is, even more fundamentally, incapable of providing the administrative and legal apparatus necessary for the development of free-market capitalism. The economy does not properly belong on the standard laissez-faire versus statist continuum, and can only be properly characterized through careful examination of both the relative strengths of the state apparatus and business interests and the nature of the state. Without greater development of the state apparatus, this book asserts, oligarchic-dominated booty capitalism will continue to stunt the development of the Philippine economy.

State and Oligarchy in Historical Perspective

A major puzzle in understanding the Philippine political economy is _why_ the power of the oligarchy so clearly overwhelms the power of the state. Even the most cursory comparative view of Third World political economies reveals, quite clearly, enormous variation among states and great diversity in the character of government-business relations. Comparative historical analysis is the logical starting point for better understanding these critical cross-national differences.[18]

[18] As Evans suggests, to explain critical differences among state apparatuses it is necessary to understand the "historical traditions [and] specific class configurations out of which they

Looking across the scope of modern Philippine history, one finds a striking absence of any sustained effort at state building. In their initial colonization in the sixteenth and seventeenth centuries, the Spanish encountered very localized political units. Except in the Muslim areas of the south (regions that were never effectively subjugated by the central government in Manila until the early twentieth century), there existed no political units that could even begin to compare with the large precolonial kingdoms found elsewhere in the region. The central state that the Spanish created was so woefully understaffed that the civil authorities had to rely heavily upon ecclesiastical personnel to extend their reach throughout the archipelago.[19] Even when Spaniards could be attracted to the colony, their attention was focused on the galleon trade with Mexico, which ran from 1565 to 1815; few developed strong ties to agricultural or other ventures based in the local economy. Unlike much of Latin America, where a much stronger and deeper Spanish presence left behind a clear organic-statist tradition, the legacy of Spanish secular authority in the Philippines was neither particularly organic nor statist.[20]

With the process of agricultural commercialization that swept the world in the nineteenth century, the Spanish colonial administration in Manila was largely upstaged by other forces that were able to respond more effectively to new opportunities: British and American trading houses, Chinese traders, and an increasingly powerful landed elite, dominated by Chinese mestizos. "From the commercial point of view," one observer noted in 1879, "the Philippines is an Anglo-Chinese colony flying the Spanish flag." Manila was no longer the single entrepôt it had been during the years of the galleon trade; rather, regional economies each had their own separate ties with the world market. This, writes Alfred McCoy, encouraged "strong centrifugal forces that weakened the emerging nation." Only in a few areas (most notably the tobacco monopoly) "did the colonial government . . . control the new commercial agriculture." Unlike Thailand and Indonesia, explains Harold Crouch, where "bureaucratic-aristocratic" elites (descended from precolonial kingdoms) were strengthened by the nine-

---

arise." Evans, "Third World State," 562, 583. Many scholars, of course, are currently demonstrating certain advantages to examining the microfoundations of politics, and in the process are employing the analytical equivalent of a telescopic lens. If the objective is to understand broad macro-level variation, however, it is necessary to use the wide-angle lens intrinsic to a comparative historical approach.

[19] Phelan explains that "the conquest was facilitated by the fragmentation of Philippine society," and "the occupation of the Philippines was essentially a missionary enterprise." In fact, "the vast majority of Filipinos in the provinces seldom saw any Spaniard except the local priest." See John Leddy Phelan, *The Hispanization of the Philippines: Spanish Aims and Filipino Responses, 1565–1700* (Madison: The University of Wisconsin Press, 1967), 13, 15, 131.

[20] See William Lytle Schurz, *The Manila Galleon* (New York: E.P. Dutton & Co., Inc., 1959). On the "organic-statist" tradition in Latin America, see Alfred Stepan, *The State and Society: Peru in Comparative Perspective* (Princeton: Princeton University Press, 1978), 26–45.

teenth-century commercialization of agriculture, the Philippines found that the same process "gave rise to a new class of . . . landowners who were quite separate from the bureaucracy."[21] Their economic base was firmly *outside* the central state.

This group of relatively autonomous landowners formed the primary social base for the first Republic of the Philippines, established in 1899. As Benedict Anderson explains, however, the Republic was fragile, "with more than a few similarities to Bolivar's abortive Gran Colombia." Large chunks of territory were outside its control, and many of its generals "began to follow the pattern of their American forebears, by setting themselves up as independent caudillos. Had it not been for William McKinley, one might almost say, the Philippines in the early twentieth century could have fractured into three weak caudillo-ridden states with the internal politics of nineteenth-century Venezuela or Ecuador."[22]

The "benevolent assimilation" of these very powerful local forces became an important element of American efforts to win the war that its bloody conquest had provoked. But while the Americans successfully coopted local caciques into newly formed political institutions, they never effectively undercut their base of power at the local level. In effect, American colonialism aborted what might have been a more "natural," Latin-American-style *caudillo* route to state formation, and superimposed a weak central state over a polity of quite autonomous local centers of power.

American colonial rule, in fact, actually reinforced the decentralized nature of the Philippines by concentrating far less on the creation of a central bureaucracy than on the introduction of representative institutions. Anderson explains that "unlike all the other modern colonial regimes in twentieth century Southeast Asia, which operated through huge, autocratic, white-run bureaucracies, the American authorities in Manila, once assured of the mestizos' self-interested loyalty to the motherland, created only a minimal civil service, and quickly turned over most of its component positions to the natives." The representative institutions enabled local caciques to consolidate their hold on the national state, and fostered the creation of "a solid, visible 'national oligarchy.'" The oligarchy took advantage of its own base of power and came to exercise

---

[21] Carlos Recur, quoted in Benito Fernandez Legarda, "Foreign Trade, Economic Change, and Entrepreneurship in the Nineteenth Century Philippines" (Ph.D. dissertation, Harvard University, 1955), 171; Alfred W. McCoy, "Introduction: The Social History of an Archipelago," in *Philippine Social History: Global Trade and Local Transformations*, ed. Alfred W. McCoy and Ed. C. De Jesus (Quezon City: Ateneo de Manila University Press, 1982), 8; and Harold Crouch, *Economic Change, Social Structure and the Political System in Southeast Asia: Philippine Development Compared with the Other ASEAN Countries* (Singapore: Institute of Southeast Asian Studies, 1985), 10–18, quote at 10. See also Vicente B. Valdepeñas Jr., and Ge[r]melino M. Bautista, *The Emergence of the Philippine Economy*, (Manila: Papyrus Press, 1977), 86–109.

[22] See Benedict Anderson, "Cacique Democracy and the Philippines: Origins and Dreams," *New Left Review* no. 169 (May/June 1988), 3–33, at 9–10.

powerful—yet particularistic—control over elements of the state apparatus through a spoils system that had become well entrenched at the national level early in the century. "Civil servants frequently owed their employment to legislator patrons, and up to the end of the American period the civilian machinery of state remained weak and divided." This control of the bureaucracy, it must be emphasized, was exercised from a strong societal base: while the oligarchy dominated the legislature, it showed little interest in directly assuming bureaucratic posts. Despite growth in the bureaucracy, a bureaucratic elite never emerged.[23]

Indeed, the contrast between the historical development of the Philippine bureaucracy and that of the Thai bureaucratic elite is instructive. Doeppers explains that widespread Filipinization of the bureaucracy, in only the second decade of American rule, created opportunities for social mobility that resulted in "the formation of an indigenous bureaucratic middle class." But access to public education and the examination system "ensured that the civil service did not swiftly become a self-perpetuating class," as it had in Thailand—where entrance to government posts was greatly restricted by the bureaucratic elite that consolidated its hold over the state machinery in the wake of the 1932 revolution. Moreover, because there were many more opportunities *outside* the bureaucracy in Manila than in Bangkok, there were certain periods in the prewar era in which many middle-class Filipinos actually left the bureaucracy for jobs in business. Most significantly, the old oligarchy showed little interest in moving into bureaucratic ventures: a mere handful of the highest ranking bureaucrats in 1931, writes Doeppers, were drawn from the landowning class.[24] There was little need: the oligarchy already had a firm economic base outside the bureaucracy, absolute control of representative institutions, and—through the latter—thorough penetration of the administrative departments of government. If in Thailand we find an elite traditionally based in the bureaucracy, in the Philippines we find a bureaucracy long subordinated to particularistic elite interests.

In short, the legacy of U.S. colonialism was considerable oligarchy building, but very little in the way of state building. Under the American regime, the oligarchy consolidated itself into a national force, took control of the central government in Manila, and responded to countless new oppor-

[23] As Anderson explains, their "economic base lay in hacienda agriculture, not in the capital city." Anderson, 11–12; Onofre D. Corpuz, *The Bureaucracy in the Philippines* (Manila: University of the Philippines Institute of Public Administration, 1957), 249.

[24] Daniel F. Doeppers, *Manila, 1900–1941: Social Change in a Late Colonial Metropolis*, Yale University Southeast Asia Studies Monograph Series No. 27 (New Haven, 1984), 2, 62, 139–40, 72 (quotes from 2, 62); Hans-Dieter Evers, "The Formation of a Social Class Structure: Urbanization, Bureaucratization and Social Mobility in Thailand," *American Sociological Review* 31 (1966): 480–88.

tunities for enrichment. One source of largesse came in the form of preferential access for Philippine agricultural products in American markets. In the quarter century after the passage of the Payne-Aldrich tariff act of 1909, establishing free trade between the United States and the Philippines, sugar exports increased almost sevenfold. Sugar planters, enjoying the protection of U.S. tariff laws, had little need to bring production costs down to internationally competitive levels. Similarly, explains Gary Hawes, "U.S. tariff and commercial policy was the most important factor in stimulating the expansion of the Philippine coconut industry," which enjoyed a "tremendous advantage" over other producers.[25]

A second source of largesse came from effective manipulation of the growing colonial state apparatus. Under the administration of the Democratic governor-general, Francis Burton Harrison (1913–1921), Filipino elites began to control both houses of Congress, and enjoy considerable influence within the executive branch through a Council of State comprising the governor-general, the speaker of the House, the president of the Senate, and members of the Cabinet. Moreover, it was during this period that the bureaucracy was substantially Filipinized, and a wide range of state enterprises were created. Simultaneous to the expansion in the role of the state in the economy, then, was an expansion in the oligarchy's control over the state. As discussed in Chapter Four, by far the richest new source of booty for the emerging "national oligarchy" was the Philippine National Bank. Within five years, the newly empowered landed oligarchs—particularly those from the sugar bloc—had plundered its coffers so thoroughly that not only the bank but also the public treasury and the currency system nearly collapsed.

On the eve of the Pacific War, Philippine oligarchs so enjoyed the arrangements provided by the American colonial regime that they were loath to make the transition to independence. "Though the caciques could not decently say so in public," explains Anderson, "independence was the last thing they desired, precisely because it threatened the source of their huge wealth: access to the American market." When independence did come, in 1946, it was accompanied by provisions that were clearly advantageous to the landed oligarchy that controlled the state. First, a bilateral free trade agreement ensured continuing dependence on the American market. Second, a new source of riches came in the form of $620 million in U.S. rehabilitation assistance for war damages, which

[25] Valdepeñas and Bautista, 114–15; Alfred W. McCoy, "'In Extreme Unction': The Philippine Sugar Industry," in *Political Economy of Philippine Commodities* (Quezon City: Third World Studies Center, University of the Philippines, 1983) 135–79; and Gary Hawes, *The Philippine State and the Marcos Regime: The Politics of Export* (Ithaca, N.Y.: Cornell University Press, 1987), 60–61, 86–89 (quotes from 61, 60).

helped finance "conspicuous consumption of luxuries and non-essentials by the high-income groups."[26]

While the consolidation of the national oligarchy occurred under American colonial sponsorship, even in the postcolonial era the oligarchs have remained highly dependent upon U.S. aid, investment, and counterinsurgency support. Only three years after independence, the Philippine state nearly collapsed. Rehabilitation assistance was plundered by the oligarchs to pay for duty-free imports of consumer durables, and the government lacked the means to stem the hemorrhage of foreign exchange. The military and economic rescue operation was coordinated by Washington. As Frank Golay explains, "By the end of 1949 the government seemed willing to let the military go unpaid and the educational system wither for want of funds, and even to succumb to the Huk rebellion, rather than face up to minimum responsibility for governmental functions. . . . [There was] mounting evidence that the body politic was incapable of action in the interests of all Filipinos. It is a depressing commentary that the reforms, when they did come, were to a considerable extent installed from the outside as a result of [a U.S. mission that]. . . . made far-reaching recommendations in the areas of fiscal policy, agricultural development, and social and administrative reform."[27]

In part because the grantor of independence was a rising superpower—not a declining European power, as elsewhere in Southeast Asia—it was especially difficult for the Philippines to emerge as a truly sovereign nation. Throughout the postwar years, oligarchs have needed external support to sustain an unjust, inefficient, and graft-ridden political and economic structure; Washington, in turn, received unrestricted access to two of its most important overseas military installations.

After independence, there was seemingly a strengthening of patrimonial features, or a blurring of the distinction between "official" and "private spheres." First, within the central bureaucracy, personal contacts became even more important for entrance to the bureaucracy, and the role of competitive examination became relatively marginal. Wurfel re-

---

[26] Anderson, 12; Joint Philippine-American Finance Commission, "Report and Recommendations of the Joint Philippine-American Finance Commission" (Washington, D.C.: Government Printing Office, 1947), 3. The report noted that despite "heavy physical devastation" and "the low output of several basic industries," a high level of U.S. government spending and assistance enabled the country to enjoy "abundant dollar resources, a stable currency, and a flow of imports which is unrestricted and in greater volume than ever before in its history."

[27] Frank H. Golay, *The Philippines: Public Policy and National Economic Development* (Ithaca, N.Y.: Cornell University Press, 1961), 71–72, 80. The near-collapse of the state came not only from its inability to extract revenue from the oligarchy, but also from its lack of tariff autonomy vis-à-vis the former colonial power. To acquire postwar rehabilitation assistance and safeguard their access to the protected American market, the oligarchs bargained away fundamental chunks of the country's economic sovereignty. See Hawes, 28–30, 89–90.

ports that congressmen actually felt they were spending "most of their time
. . . running an employment agency." The bureaucracy expanded rapidly,
especially at election time.[28] One episode is illustrative of the degree to
which the loyalties of individual bureaucrats were tied to extrabureaucratic
forces. In 1959, the Palace and Congress worked out the so-called *50–50
agreement,* in which responsibility for filling new bureaucratic posts would
be divided equally between the president and the House of Representatives. While bureau directors complained about the requirement that they
bring unqualified personnel into their units, they lacked the power to
stand up to external pressures.[29]

Second, in the countryside, patron-client relations were undergoing
significant changes. Patrons, historically reliant on their own local resources, found expanded opportunities in obtaining external and office-
based resources. This did not diminish the power of local oligarchs vis-à-vis
the central state, but merely increased the role of state resources *within*
longstanding patron-client relationships.[30] In the context of a national
electoral system, these local oligarchs retained enormous power to milk
the central state's "particularistic distributive capacity."[31] Third, the broad-

[28] David Wurfel, *Filipino Politics: Development and Decay* (Ithaca, N.Y.: Cornell University
Press, 1988), 80–85.

[29] As one bureau director remarked, "I have no real control over a man who owes his
loyalty to a congressman . . . discipline breaks down now. The man who gets his first job
through a congressman will also try to get a promotion the same way. Most of those we have to
accommodate aren't even eligible." Another bureau director explained that the budget of
his agency "cannot exist if we don't cooperate with congressmen. If you tell them 'NO'
outright, by golly, they will tear you to shreds in the next budget hearing." See Gregorio A.
Francisco Jr. and Raul P. De Guzman, "The '50–50 Agreement,'" in *Patterns in Decision-
Making: Case Studies in Philippine Public Administration,* ed. Raul P. De Guzman (Manila:
Graduate School of Public Administration, 1963), 91–120 (quotes at 109, 112, 116); Dante
Simbulan, "A Study of the Socio-Economic Elite in Philippine Politics and Government"
(Ph.D. dissertation, Australian National University, Research School of Social Science, 1965),
267.

[30] Nowak and Snyder explain that the "growing penetration of national bureaucratic
institutions into local areas heightens the dependence of the local elite upon office-based
resources." See Thomas C. Nowak and Kay A. Snyder, "Clientelist Politics in the Philippines:
Integration or Instability," *American Political Science Review* 68 (1974), 1147–1170, at 1151.
See also Fegan's discussion of how the closing of the land frontier made civil service positions
a more important element of patron-client largesse in the postwar years—and led to a
process of "bureaucratic involution" on the national level (Brian Fegan, "The Social History
of a Central Luzon Barrio," in *Philippine Social History,* ed. McCoy and De Jesus, 119–24). An
influential early work on patron-client relations in the Philippines is Carl H.Landé, *Leaders,
Factions, and Parties: The Structure of Philippine Politics,* Yale University Southeast Asia Studies
Monograph Series No. 6 (New Haven, 1966).

[31] James C. Scott, "Patron-Client Politics and Political Change in Southeast Asia," in
Friends, Followers and Factions, ed. Steffen W. Schmidt et al. (Berkeley: University of California
Press, 1977), 123–46, at 137 and 143 (quote from 143). Sidel rejects the patron-client
framework (in large part due to its inadequate attention to violence), and describes how
legislators and local officials used the state apparatus and coercion to wield power at the local
level throughout the postwar era. His alternative framework, bossism, analyzes how "para-
statal *mafias,* small-town mayors, congressmen, and provincial governors . . . have emerged,

ened responsibilities of the postcolonial state created new economic opportunities for those with favorable political connections. Oligarchs both
responded to and created new sources of booty that could be tapped
through access to the state machinery, and their economic interests became much more diversified (beyond agriculture, to include commerce,
manufacturing, and finance). When, for example, import and exchange
controls were imposed in response to the 1949 balance-of-payments crisis,
rent-seeking entrepreneurs flooded the halls of the Central Bank in search
of the dollar allocations that would enable them to reap windfall profits in
producing for a protected domestic market.

These developments—in the central bureaucracy and local patron-
client relations, as well as in the expansion of governmental economic
responsibilities—highlight the seeming strengthening of patrimonial features within the postcolonial Philippine state. Because these patterns became more pronounced in recent times, as access to the state began to be
more important for securing patronage and rents, the term *neopatrimonial*
helps to capture the historical sequence. These postwar developments
occurred in the midst of important continuity in the relative strengths of
state and oligarchy: whether colonial or postcolonial, the civilian state
apparatus remained "weak and divided" in the face of powerful oligarchic
interests. Moreover, even as raids on state resources increased in importance, the oligarchy retained its firm economic base outside the state.

In summary, the combination of historical factors bequeathed to the
postcolonial Philippines provided fertile ground for booty capitalism. The
state apparatus remained woefully underdeveloped, easy prey for a powerful oligarchic class that had been able to consolidate its power under
American colonial rule. Even as it was plundered by these oligarchs, however, the perpetuation of the state was ultimately assured by ready support
from the former colonial power. Despite changes in regime, basic patterns
persisted throughout the first forty-five years of the postwar era: while the
state was plundered internally, it was repeatedly rescued externally. As
shall be analyzed further in Chapter Ten, the withdrawal of U.S. military
bases in 1992 seems to have provided an important stimulus for initiating
a program intended to transform many basic aspects of the operation of
the Philippine political economy. While the process can be expected to be
long and arduous, one element of a hopeful scenario is that new perceptions of the country's position in the world encourage increasing attention
to the need for fundamental reform.

---

entrenched themselves, and retained monopolistic control over coercive and economic
resources within their respective bailiwicks." John Thayer Sidel, "Coercion, Capital, and the
Post-Colonial State: Bossism in the Postwar Philippines" (Ph.D. dissertation, Cornell University, 1995), 49.

CHAPTER TWO

The Foundations of Modern,
Rational Capitalism: "Bringing
Political Arbitrariness to Heel"

The notion of an *underdeveloped* state apparatus is, to be sure, anti-thetical to the ideological bias that has often dominated political discourse in recent years, both in the 1980s (the decade of Reagan and Thatcher) and the 1990s (as deep suspicions of the efficacy of government action endure in often more intense form). States are commonly seen as inherently obstructive to the process of economic growth; at best, they are entities whose role must be confined to the most basic of tasks: protection of property rights, external defense, infrastructural development, and so on. Many theorists of our age, Peter Evans points out, begin with the attitude that "The only good bureaucracy is a dead bureaucracy." Most advocates of rent-seeking theories, observes Margaret Levi, "are obsessed with demonstrating the negative impact of government on the economy. They view competitive markets as the most socially efficient means to produce goods and services . . . [and] do not treat the effects of government intervention as variable, sometimes reducing and sometimes stimulating social waste."[1]

Blinded by the excesses of many modern states, perhaps, antistatist theorists seem to have forgotten—or taken for granted—the necessary role that bureaucracy has played in the historical development of capitalism. Long before there was "a reasonable fear that bureaucracies might become Parkinsonian," writes E. L. Jones, state action was able "to extend the market farther and faster than its evident attractions could do unaided. . . . The attainment of minimum stability conditions for economic growth lies so far back in the history of the developed world that we all now

[1] Peter B. Evans, "Predatory, Developmental, and Other Apparatuses: A Comparative Political Economy Perspective on the Third World State," *Sociological Forum* 4, no. 4 (1989): 561–587, at 566; Margaret Levi, *Of Rule and Revenue* (Berkeley: University of California Press, 1988), 24.

take it for granted." The development of the market economy, he argues further, depended critically upon "progress in bringing political arbitrariness to heel."[2]

Because of the careful historical grounding of his work, Weber provides a necessary corrective to those who forget the central role of the state in the creation of laissez-faire political economy, and place excessive faith in the "magic of the marketplace." Radical free-marketeers often make the facile argument that the best thing for capitalism is for the state to "get off the backs of the private sector." The Philippines, on the contrary, presents a living example of what kinds of obstacles to capitalist development can result when the power of an oligarchic private sector is never tamed, and there is no concerted effort to promote the development of the public sector. By highlighting the political foundations of capitalist development, a Weberian analysis helps us to understand cases such as the Philippines that lack fundamental political prerequisites to the development of modern capitalist economies.

This chapter begins by examining Weber's theory of capitalist development. The second section discusses how the weak degree of calculability in the political sphere hinders the development of more advanced forms of capitalism in the Philippines. The third section provides necessary caveats to applying the patrimonial framework to the modern Philippine political economy, and puts particular emphasis on the contrast between the external factors that shape the Philippine polity and the external environment in which Weber's patrimonial polities existed.

Weber's Theory of Capitalist Development

Weber's analysis has particular relevance for students of Third World political economy, since it is primarily a theory of capitalist development rather than a theory of the workings of mature capitalism. Because advanced capitalism is still in formation in many parts of the Third World, a theory of the *rise of capitalism* is of particular value in explaining current realities. Collins points out, with some exaggeration, that "Marx and most of his followers have devoted their attention to showing the dynamics of capitalism, not to the preconditions for its emergence. Weber's concerns

---

[2] See E. L. Jones, *The European Miracle: Environments, Economies, and Geopolitics in the History of Europe and Asia* (Cambridge: Cambridge University Press, 1981), 93–95, 236–37 (quotes from 93, 236). "Arbitrary behavior includes irregular levies, confiscations, forced loans, debt repudiation, debasements, expulsions, and judicial murder, all of them productive of uncertainty, to say the least. . . . We now take [security for persons and property] so much for granted that we seldom trace out how it was first satisfied" (p. 93).

were almost entirely the reverse. Hence, it is possible that the two analyses could be complementary, Marx's taking up where Weber's leaves off."[3]

While there is no clear demarcation, of course, as to where one leaves off and the other takes up, it is clear that each framework brings enormous insight to the analysis of capitalism. One of Weber's primary achievements was to focus attention on the political preconditions of capitalist development; a major lesson in Marx, on the other hand, is the need to highlight the role of class in the political conflicts of capitalist societies.[4]

Weber's "mature theory of the development of capitalism" was basically an *institutional* theory of capitalist development that went beyond his earlier, more idealist, conceptions of the origins of capitalism.[5] Within this often-complex theory, "The key term is *calculability;* it occurs over and over again in those pages. What is distinctive about modern, large-scale, 'rational' capitalism—in contrast to earlier, partial forms—is that it is methodical and predictable, reducing all areas of production and distribution as much as possible to routine. This is also Weber's criterion for calling bureaucracy the most 'rational' form of organization."[6]

The conditions that facilitate this calculability are found both at the level of "the production process itself" and at the level of "the legal and administrative environment,"[7] but Weber generally seems to treat calcula-

[3] Randall Collins, "Weber's Last Theory of Capitalism: A Systematization," *American Sociological Review* 45 (1980): 925–42, at 937–38.

[4] Collins further explains that "the main Weberian criticism of the Marxian tradition, even in its present form, is that it does not yet recognize the set of institutional forms, especially as grounded in the legal system, upon which capitalism has rested" (p. 940). Weber highlights how variations in state structure can be explained by both economic and noneconomic factors, and how these varying state structures, in turn, shape different types of capitalist systems. In other words, Weber shows us that lines of causation run in two directions: not only from the economic sphere to the political sphere, but also from the political sphere to the economic sphere.

[5] As Collins explains, "Weber's last word on the subject of capitalism" is found in the *General Economic History.* There, the idealist focus of earlier work (particularly evident in *The Protestant Ethic and the Spirit of Capitalism*) occupies "a relatively small place in his overall scheme." While "[t]he state is the factor most often overlooked in Weber's theory of capitalism. . . . it is the factor to which he gave the most attention." In addition to *General Economic History,* Collins also draws on "the building blocks presented in *Economy and Society.*" See Collins, 925–27, 931–32.

[6] Max Weber, *General Economic History* (New Brunswick, N.J.: Transaction Books, 1981); Collins, 927. In his analysis, Weber distinguishes between two types of rationality: "formal rationality refers primarily to *calculability of means and procedures,* substantive rationality primarily to the *value* (from some explicitly defined standpoint) *of ends or results.*" The first is "a matter of fact," while the latter is "a matter of value." For example, while Weber considered modern capitalism formally rational, he was nonetheless "sympathetic to socialist criticism of the substantive irrationality of capitalism." See Brubaker, 4–5, 10, 35–43 (quotes at 36, 38); Max Weber, *Economy and Society* (Berkeley: University of California Press, 1978), I: 85, 109, 138.

[7] Rogers Brubaker, *The Limits of Rationality: An Essay on the Social and Moral Thought of Max Weber* (Boston: George Allen & Unwin, 1984), 12. Weber lists six conditions of modern,

bility in the latter as the *prerequisite* for calculability in the former. Legal and administrative predictability is not just another precondition for capitalist development; it is the most basic precondition of all: "'[P]rogress' toward the bureaucratic state, adjudicating and administering according to rationally established law and regulation, is nowadays very closely related to the modern capitalist development. The modern capitalist enterprise rests primarily on *calculation* and presupposes a legal and administrative system, whose functioning can be rationally predicted, at least in principle, by virtue of its fixed general norms, *just like the expected performance of a machine.*" Elsewhere, he notes that "the capitalistic form of industrial organization, if it is to operate rationally, must be able to depend upon calculable adjudication and administration."[8]

Political Arbitrariness and Philippine Capitalism

If one uses Weber's theory as a guide for evaluating the nature of capitalism in the Philippines today, it is clear that capitalist structures are an integral part of the process of production.[9] The reasons for this measure of

---

rational capitalism that relate to the *production process:* (1) industrial enterprises have appropriated all the means of production; (2) there are no "irrational limitations on trading in the market"; (3) "rational technology, . . . [is] reduced to calculation to the largest possible degree, which implies mechanization"; (4) labor is at the same time legally free yet "economically compelled" to sell its services; (5) there is "commercialization of economic life," meaning "the general use of commercial instruments to represent share rights in enterprise, and also in property ownership"; and (6) the enterprise is separated from the household budget and household property. The first five characteristics are found in *General Economic History*. The sixth "principal condition" is found in other works. "It is particularly important," writes Weber, "that the capital at the disposal of the enterprise should be clearly distinguished from the private wealth of the owners." See *General Economic History*, 276–78; *Economy and Society*, I: 161–62; and "Author's Introduction," *The Protestant Ethic and the Spirit of Capitalism* (New York: Charles Scribner's Sons, 1958), 21–22 (this introduction, published in 1920–21—just after his death and more than fifteen years after *The Protestant Ethic* itself—contributes to Weber's later, institutional theory of capitalist development).

  [8] *Economy and Society* II: 1394 (second emphasis added); *General Economic History*, 277. See also *Economy and Society* I: 92, 161–62. In their interpretative remarks on Weber's theory of capitalism, both Brubaker and Collins treat calculability in the political sphere as a basic prerequisite for the "rationalization" of economic life. See Brubaker, 15; and Collins, 928. Beyond this, however, it is important to note that Weber's analysis does not provide clear answers to at least three important questions. As Callaghy explains, Weber "does not show how modern capitalism emerges out of the slow and uneven emergence of . . . 'preconditions'. . . . How much of a given factor must exist? What mixture of the partial presence of several factors is sufficient? What relationship exists between the various factors that facilitates their emergence?" See Thomas M. Callaghy, "The State and the Development of Capitalism in Africa: Theoretical, Historical, and Comparative Reflections," *The Precarious Balance: State and Society in Africa*, ed. Donald Rothchild and Naomi Chazan (Boulder: Westview Press, 1988), 94.

  [9] A cursory examination of the political economy reveals the general presence of five out of six conditions of modern, rational capitalism that relate to the production process: entre-

capitalist development are beyond the scope of this work, but the most obvious explanation lies in the economic transformation of the Philippines that took place under Spanish and especially American colonial rule: capitalist enterprises were created, domestic and foreign trade was widely expanded, technology was imported (and refined to fit local conditions), slavery was prohibited, and capitalist methods of property ownership formalized.

Despite the obvious presence of capitalist structures, however, one finds on closer examination that the Philippine political economy lacks certain attributes that Weber considered essential to the development of modern, rational capitalism. First and most fundamentally, there is weak degree of calculability in the legal and administrative sphere. The Philippine economy is capitalist, to be sure, but its capitalism is of the "politically determined" variety. As discussed earlier, the colonial heritage included a state apparatus unable to "bring political arbitrariness to heel" and foster the emergence of more advanced forms of capitalist accumulation. To the limited extent that rational-legal political structures were created in the colonial years, they quickly deteriorated to a more neopatrimonial character in the postcolonial years. The patrimonial character of this state yields a harvest of "unpredictability and inconsistency," as state officials "variously [display both] benevolence and disfavor. . . . It is quite possible that a private individual, by skillfully taking advantage of the given circumstances and of personal relations, obtains a privileged position which offers him nearly unlimited acquisitive opportunities. . . . [But] [i]ndustrial capitalism must be able to count on the continuity, trustworthiness and objectivity of the legal order, and on the rational, predictable functioning of legal and administrative agencies."[10]

Second, the weak degree of calculability in the political and legal sphere inhibits the fuller development of calculability in the sphere of production—particularly by impeding the clear separation of the household and the enterprise, one of Weber's six conditions of modern, rational capitalism that relate to the production process. Indeed, the prevalence of political arbitrariness plays a major role in shaping the most basic organization of business enterprises in the Philippines. Because the success of the enterprise depends to such a large extent on the political connections of the

---

preneurs have appropriated the means of production, noneconomic restrictions on the movement of goods have been minimized, modern technologies are widely dispersed, labor is formally free, and economic life is largely commercialized. The Philippines, moreover, meets Weber's criterion for proper use of the term "capitalistic." Such a designation can be made, he writes, when "the provision for wants is capitalistically organized to such a predominant degree that if we imagine this form of organization taken away the whole economic system must collapse." *General Economic History,* 276.

[10] *Economy and Society,* II: 1095.

household, it has been foolish for Philippine entrepreneurs to try to force a clear separation between the two. In fact, enterprise and household are mutually beneficial: the household provides the privileged opportunities to the enterprise, while the enterprise helps maintain the economic and political viability of the household. The success of an enterprise cannot be measured merely by the profits that it funnels to family coffers; success must also be measured by the patronage networks that it supports and the inside information that it collects.[11] It should come as no surprise, then, that intra-and interfamily feuds are regular occurrences in the corporate boardrooms of the Philippines. Nor is it surprising that families generally have been—until very recently—loath to raise significant amounts of capital via public offerings, since such a strategy threatens to reduce the degree of family control over an enterprise.[12]

As noted, the ultimate prerequisite of the development of modern capitalism is the need for calculability in the political sphere: the legal and administrative system should, ideally, approximate "the expected performance of a machine." In the Philippines, political arbitrariness exercises a negative influence on the development of more rational capitalism both directly (by continually generating uncertainties in the entire range of government-business relations) and indirectly through the sphere of production (by perpetuating the weak separation of enterprise and household).

The relative weakness of legal and administrative calculability shapes not only the family-based organization of Philippine business, but also the primary strategies of wealth accumulation that these families employ. First, Philippine enterprises have devoted an inordinate amount of resources to trying to ensure that they either gain or protect "a privileged position . . . [offering] unlimited acquisitive opportunities." When the form of patrimonialism is decentralized, as in the pre-Marcos and post-Marcos years, electoral competition is a key means by which the oligarchs gain access to the state machinery, and divide up the spoils among themselves; traditionally, these contests are decided by the best mobilization of "gold, goons, and guns." When, on the other hand, the form of patrimonialism is relatively more centralized, as during the Marcos dictatorship, the means

[11] As noted earlier, ownership (or part-ownership) of a bank is particularly important to the major oligarchic families, since it can simultaneously generate profits, provide a ready source of funds to other family enterprises, dispense patronage (in the form of bank loans), and generate valuable information.

[12] As Weber writes, it is in modern, rational capitalism (not "politically oriented capitalism") "that we find . . . the 'going public' of business enterprises." *Economy and Society,* I: 166. Although Philippine capital markets are among the oldest in Asia (thanks to the American colonial heritage), they were until very recently "one of the smallest and least admired." *Far Eastern Economic Review* (hereafter *FEER*), August 1, 1991, 64. Post-1993 changes in Philippine capital markets are discussed below.

of gaining and protecting access to the state included the declaration of martial law and a subsequent combination of repression and patronage. As economist Emmanuel de Dios explains, "politics . . . is itself a major form of organization of the economy. Political violence may be viewed simply as one form of *investment,* and corruption as a form of *return.*"[13] Whether the regime is democratic or authoritarian, oligarchs know that the best way to accumulate wealth is to gain and maintain favorable access to the trough of state. Families cannot rely on an impersonal state to provide the conditions favorable to capital accumulation; rather, they need to *create* these conditions for themselves.

The weak degree of calculability in the political sphere also helps us to understand a second major strategy of Philippine business: the broad diversification of family conglomerates into many sectors of the economy. In any capitalist economy, of course, business conglomerates diversify in response to perceived market risks. Twenty years ago, Nowak and Snyder explained that "diversification of familial economic power decreases susceptibility to fluctuations in world prices, potential loss of privileges in the U.S. market, and local policy chances such as devaluation, which hurt some sectors more than others."[14] In an economy in which wealth depends to such a large degree on access to the state machinery, however, *political* risks are an additional and particularly compelling motivation for diversification. There is a strong desire to guard against the uncertainties of change in political leadership: a family can't depend exclusively on investments assisted by current friends in the Palace, for example, because in the next administration those investments may be jeopardized by a lack of necessary connections in key government offices. Access to the state in one administration is used to strengthen more independent economic foundations *outside the state* in subsequent administrations. Although more detailed sociological case studies of individual family conglomerates are necessary in order to explain strategies of diversification fully, they should be seen as a rational response of Philippine families—not only to the usual array of market and macroeconomic risks, but also to political risks imposed by the patrimonial character of the state.[15]

[13] Emmanuel S. de Dios, "A Political Economy of Philippine Policy-Making," *Economic Policy-Making in the Asia-Pacific Region,* ed. John W. Langford and K. Lorne Brownsey (Halifax, Nova Scotia: The Institute for Research on Public Policy, 1990) 109–47, at 111.

[14] Thomas C. Nowak and Kay A. Snyder, "Clientelist Politics in the Philippines: Integration or Instability," *American Political Science Review* 68 (1974), 1147–1170, at 1148–49. They also note the important—but often neglected—role of urban real estate in diversification strategies.

[15] De Dios suggests that economic diversification by groups may often be quite inefficient from the standpoint of the larger economy (contrary to those who argue that internalization over a broad front will probably result in net gains in efficiency). Groups hesitate to open up to outside equity because many of their interests are determined by access to "idiosyncratic partisan government patronage." See Emmanuel S. de Dios, "Resource Mobilisation and

Beginning in the 1950s and 1960s, the closely held conglomerates of the major oligarchic families became highly diversified units, commonly combining manufacturing, finance, agriculture, commerce, services, urban real estate, and so on, all under one roof. Until the present, in fact, these diversified family conglomerates remain the single dominant segment of capital within the Philippine economy. As Temario Rivera explains, this process of diversification has produced "an inherently self-contradictory set of interests," since one element of a particular conglomerate may be favored by policies detrimental to another element of the very same conglomerate. But because of certain features of business-government relations in the Philippines, these intraconglomerate contradictions are not as problematic as they might at first seem. It became common—through the process of diversification in the 1950s and especially the 1960s—for major families to combine many different types of ventures within one conglomerate. As a result, they collectively came to share a certain homogeneity of interests on broad issues of macro-economic policy; in short, there was a simultaneous diversification and homogenization of familial interests.[16] Moreover, capitalists in the Philippines strategize more toward the acquisition of particularistic favors than the realization of generalized shifts in policy. A high degree of dependence upon the political machinery for such benefits as foreign exchange licenses, access to foreign markets, government loans, and foreign assistance means that participation in the political process is as likely to be motivated by a search for booty as by larger issues of economic policy.

While this scramble for privilege is rational from the standpoint of individual family conglomerates, it often brings chaos at the level of national developmental objectives. Because of the weakness of state-building in Philippine history, it is rare to find any center of gravity to guide the process of economic development along more coherent lines. The family conglomerates respond to—and create—new sources of largesse: protected markets for agricultural produce overseas, loans from state banks,

---

Industrial Organisation," in *Resource Mobilization and Resource Use in the Philippines,* ed. Raul V. Fabella and Hideyoshi Sakai (Tokyo: Institute of Developing Economies, 1994), 71.

[16] Temario C. Rivera, *Landlords and Capitalists: Class, Family, and State in Philippine Manufacturing* (Quezon City: University of the Philippines Press, 1994), 51. In analyzing elite structures in the Philippines in the early 1970s, Nowak and Snyder also observed this simultaneous process of diversification and homogenization. Because of the diversification of interests within family groups, they note, conflicts between industrial and agrarian elites do not seem imminent (*contra* Barrington Moore's observations about "the process of industrialization in Western Europe and the United States"). Instead, they note "a basic homogeneity of interest" within the elite (p. 1148). On one very prominent family's diversification of interests, see Alfred W. McCoy, "Rent-Seeking Families and the Philippine State: A History of the Lopez Family," in *An Anarchy of Families: State and Family in the Philippines,* ed. McCoy (Madison: University of Wisconsin Center for Southeast Asian Studies, 1993), 429–536.

foreign aid and reparations, foreign exchange licenses, natural resource exploitation, incentives to start up private commercial banks, and so on.[17] Having diversified according to available opportunities, families then expect policy to accommodate their varied interests. Development policies commonly lack any real direction, but family conglomerates are able to move in many directions simultaneously, and thus to protect themselves against the vicissitudes of Philippine politics. From an economic standpoint, there is a vicious cycle breeding developmental stagnation; from the standpoint of family conglomerates, on the other hand, there exists rather virtuous protection against the gales of political change.

Third, in addition to diversifying economic interests, it is also common for families to diversify their political networks to guard against changes in political leadership. If one's major political allies suddenly fall from power, it is advantageous to have alternative routes of access to the political machinery. The phenomenon of *namamangka sa dalawang ilog* (rowing one's boat in two rivers) is greatly facilitated by the very fluid nature of mainstream political parties and factions, which have long displayed a weak degree of institutionalization and an even weaker devotion to any clear ideology. Switching parties (referred to as *turncoatism*) is thus a common phenomenon, as politicians seek to ally with those who have the greatest potential to dispense patronage resources;[18] after Marcos was deposed, those who were most opportunistic in suddenly shifting allegiance to the Aquino administration were labeled *balimbing*, in honor of a star-shaped fruit that appears to be the same no matter from which side it is viewed. Those least public in their political affiliations, of course, are most adept at cultivating ties across political divides and adjusting to changing political fortunes. Chinese-Filipino entrepreneurs, historically more vulnerable to exactions and more reliant on extrafamilial links to the political machin-

[17] While this book concentrates on the banking sector, careful studies of other sectors of the political economy include Belinda A. Aquino, *Politics of Plunder: The Philippines Under Marcos* (Quezon City: Great Books Trading and the University of the Philippines College of Public Administration, 1987); Jaime Faustino, "Mining the State: Dominant Forces, Marcos and Aquino" (M.A. thesis, University of the Philippines, 1992); Gary Hawes, *The Philippine State and the Marcos Regime: The Politics of Export* (Ithaca, N.Y.: Cornell University Press, 1987); James Putzel, *A Captive Land: The Politics of Agrarian Reform in the Philippines* (Quezon City: Ateneo de Manila University Press, 1992); Jeffrey M. Riedinger, *Agrarian Reform in the Philippines: Democratic Transitions and Redistributive Reform* (Stanford, Calif.: Stanford University Press, 1995); Rivera, *Landlords and Capitalists;* John Thayer Sidel, "Coercion, Capital, and the Post-Colonial State: Bossism in the Postwar Philippines" (Ph.D. dissertation, Cornell University, 1995); Third World Studies Program, *Political Economy of Philippine Commodities* (Quezon City: Third World Studies Center, University of the Philippines, 1983); and Marites Dañguilan Vitug, *Power from the Forest: The Politics of Logging* (Metro Manila: Philippine Center for Investigative Journalism, 1993).

[18] See David Wurfel, *Filipino Politics: Development and Decay* (Ithaca, N.Y.: Cornell University Press, 1988), 96–97. Thanks to John Sidel for emphasizing the importance of strategies of political diversification.

ery, have earned a particular reputation for their ability to cultivate ties with more than one side in any political contest.

This book highlights the tremendous arbitrariness of state action in a sector generally considered the apex of a modern economy: the banking sector. It is important to emphasize, however, that the weak degree of calculability in the political sphere is manifest throughout the Philippine political economy, from the towering heights of national financial policy all the way down to the simplest of tasks. Minor functionaries may have the discretionary power to decide whether (and for how much) they will register a vehicle, and firefighters may have the discretionary power to decide whether (and for how much) they will turn on the hoses and put out a fire.[19]

Not surprisingly, the high degree of arbitrariness in the political sphere is readily apparent in the fiscal realm: entrepreneurs cannot predict the level of exactions, official and unofficial, that will be demanded of them by the state and its officials. The amount of tax paid to the state is negotiable, and therefore highly dependent upon the current strength of one's political connections. Given the highly politicized nature of the Bureau of Internal Revenue and the Bureau of Customs, it is not coincidental that both are controlled by the Office of the President—even though they are technically part of the Department of Finance. As business journalist Rigoberto Tiglao explains, the president's power to appoint the heads of the bureaus of internal revenue and customs have ensured that "these two major tax-collecting organisations are weapons that could be used to harass a ruling party's enemies and at the same time . . . [generate] the president's personal stash (through bribery by tax evaders) or . . . [dispense] favors to allies."[20] Similarly, there is great variability in the under-the-table unofficial "taxes" that businesses must commonly pay to get results from state functionaries. Needless to say, this variability quite dramatically inhibits the development of rational capital accounting at the level of the enterprise.

[19] It is for this reason that those with the most vulnerable access to the political machinery—the Chinese-Filipino entrepreneurs—have often established their own private firefighting units. They cannot rely on the state to put out fires, so they have to provide that service for themselves.

[20] Rigoberto Tiglao, "The Dilemmas of Economic Policymaking in a 'People Power' State," in *The Politics of Economic Reform in Southeast Asia,* ed. David G. Timberman (Metro Manila: Asian Institute of Management, 1992), 77–89, at 85. Revenue maximization is not the strong suit of the Philippine state; in fact, the country continues to have the lowest tax effort in capitalist Southeast Asia. In 1989, only 36 percent of potential taxpayers even bothered to file income-tax returns, and a mere 2.5 percent of these persons actually paid taxes. Among corporate enterprises, only 33 percent of those who filed returns actually paid taxes. *FEER,* March 26, 1992, 50–51; see also Manuel F. Montes, "Financing Development: The 'Democratic' versus the 'Corporatist' Approach in the Philippines," *The Political Economy of Fiscal Policy,* ed. Miguel Urrutia, Shinichi Ichimura, and Setsuko Yukawa (Tokyo: The United Nations University, 1989).

What is striking about many patrimonial states, Weber reminds us, is not the prevalence of corruption per se, but the great variability of corruption. Bribery and corruption have "the least serious effect" when they are calculable, and become most onerous when fees are "highly variable" and "settled from case to case with every individual official." In this analysis, corruption per se is not incompatible with advanced capitalism; indeed, one can think of myriad examples where the two thrive simultaneously. Rather, it is highly variable corruption that most impedes "the development of rational economic activity."[21]

In summary, the weak degree of calculability in the legal and administrative sphere (that is, political arbitrariness) hinders the fuller development of calculability in the productive sphere; moreover, political arbitrariness hinders the separation "of the enterprise and its conditions of success and failure from the household." Families must devote enormous resources to the task of gaining and maintaining access to the political machinery, and they must diversify their investments across many sectors to protect themselves against the gales of political change.

The Patrimonial Framework and the Modern Philippine Political Economy

A focus on patrimonial aspects of the state, I argue, promotes clearer understanding of important characteristics of the Philippine political economy, and highlights critical obstacles to the development of more advanced forms of capitalism. As Weber wrote, "the patrimonial state lacks the political and procedural *predictability,* indispensable for capitalist development, which is provided by the rational rules of modern bureaucratic administration."[22] In employing the patrimonial framework, however, it is important not to obscure four critical differences between the postcolonial Philippines and the economies, societies, and polities analyzed by Weber many decades ago.

First, except during the Marcos years, the postwar Philippines has not had the clearly identifiable central ruler that Weber expected to see in patrimonial polities. Instead, a nominally strong president of relatively short tenure must make major accommodations to "local patrimonial lords" who possess economic power and assume quasi-military and quasi-judicial functions in their localities, and are represented at the national level in a powerful legislature. Even under Marcos's relatively more centralized form of patrimonialism, the entrenched power of the oligarchy

21 Weber, *Economy and Society,* I: 240, 162, 161.
22 Weber, *Economy and Society,* II: 1095.

greatly limited his scope of action.[23] Second, Weber would not have imagined the strengthening of patrimonial features in a modernizing economy. Particularly strange, from his standpoint, would be the existence of a decentralized form of patrimonialism in the midst of a money economy well integrated by trade and modern communications.[24] Third, Weber's notion of historical progression does not anticipate the "neopatrimonialism" that comes in the wake of a more "rational-legal" colonial state. He probably would have considered it especially anomalous to find patrimonial features in the ex-colony of the world's most advanced industrial power. As discussed earlier, patrimonial features appear to have become more pronounced after independence in 1946.[25]

The fourth difference is the most fundamental one, and is closely related to the other three caveats as well. Simply put, Weber's patrimonial polities were far more self-contained than the postcolonial Philippine polity.[26] Marcos's own personal strategies, for example, cannot be understood except in a world of Swiss banks and Manhattan real estate. On a deeper level, however, one can say that the major reason that patrimonial features in the Philippines diverge to such an extent from those features found in Weber's polities lies in the contrast between the external factors that shape the Philippine polity and the external environment in which Weber's polities existed. One cannot begin to explain the perpetuation and maintenance of the Philippine state without a careful examination of the particularities of its colonial heritage and postwar international environment. Precisely because Weber did not anticipate the colonial and postcolonial conditions that help perpetuate the existence of weak states, he would not have anticipated anything quite like the postcolonial Philippine state.

Indeed, the Philippine state does not even fit Weber's basic definition of a *state:* it lacks an effective monopoly over violence and taxation, and it is too weak to maintain control over much of its territory. As Jackson and Rosberg point out, the perpetuation of many modern Third World states

23 Wurfel, *Filipino Politics,* 76–88. On the limits of Marcos's power vis-à-vis the "old oligarchy," see Hutchcroft, "Oligarchs and Cronies in the Philippine State: The Politics of Patrimonial Plunder," *World Politics* 43, no. 3 (1991): 414–450, at 442–45.

24 Weber, *Economy and Society,* II: 1091–92; see also 1014.

25 This parallels Roth's discussion of a "detraditionalized" patrimonialism that "becomes the dominant form of government" in "some of the newer states." See Guenther Roth, "Personal Rulership, Patrimonialism, and Empire-Building in the New States," *World Politics* 20 (1968): 194–206, at 196, 199. Weber discusses the historical "march of bureaucracy" in *Economy and Society,* II: 1002–3.

26 Weber does, indeed, speak of foreign trade as a critical element of the development of centralized patrimonial bureaucracies, and mentions power competition among patrimonial states as a factor determining the ruler's attitudes to "mobile money capital." See *Economy and Society,* II: 1092, 1103. But as discussed below, such international ties are qualitatively different from those found in the Third World today.

cannot be understood unless one considers external factors, and distinguishes between an empirical and juridical definition of the state. Many Third World states, they point out, do not fit within Weber's classic *empirical definition* of the state ("a corporate group that has compulsory jurisdiction, exercises continuous organization, and claims a monopoly of force over a territory and its population, including 'all action taking place in the area of its jurisdiction'"). They do, however, meet the *juridical definition* of statehood, that which is recognized by the "international society of states." In Europe, they argue, "empirical statehood preceded juridical statehood or was concurrent with it"; in Black Africa and other parts of the Third World, however, there has been a very different sort of state-building process: "external factors are more likely than internal factors to provide an adequate explanation of the formation and persistence of states." In short, a "political system may possess some or all of the empirical qualifications of statehood, but without the [internationally recognized] juridical attributes of territory and independence it is not a state."[27]

In the Philippines, as well, one cannot understand the state's persistence without an examination of external factors—during both the colonial and the postcolonial periods. As noted earlier, it is entirely possible that the central state of the Philippines would not have survived into the twentieth century without colonial intervention. Only by looking at this colonial heritage can we understand the formation and persistence of a central state that is unable to effectively exert authority over "local lords."

Moreover, one can say that if the postwar "international society of states" helps ensure the survival of central states that cannot, empirically, claim control over much of their territories, the "special relationship" between superpower United States and client Philippines provided quite an exceptional external guarantee of survival to a state that lacked many attributes of empirical statehood. The Philippines' status as an ex-colony and postcolonial client of the United States ensured the survival of the central state in the Philippines, wrapping it in a cocoon that insulated it both from

[27] Robert H. Jackson and Carl G. Rosberg, "Why Africa's Weak States Persist: The Empirical and the Juridical in Statehood," *World Politics* 13, no. 1 (1982): 1–24, at 2, 3, 23, 13. They further point out that "*international society is at least partly responsible for perpetuating the underdevelopment of the empirical state* in Africa by providing resources to incompetent or corrupt governments without being permitted to ensure that these resources are effectively and properly used" (pp. 22–23, emphasis added). This is an important point, but unfortunately they give it little emphasis and fail to develop it further. The turbulent, conflictual process by which empirical statehood is obtained may, in certain cases, be actively obstructed by external forces, which (for larger geopolitical objectives) intervene to prop up dominant social forces and quash their potential rivals. In this way, a domestic social imbalance may be effectively guaranteed by external actors. The former colonial power in the Philippines has played a central role in propping up the oligarchy and ensuring the continued weakness of countervailing social forces (especially popular forces); the perpetuation of social imbalance, in turn, reduces the likelihood of fundamental transformation of the political sphere.

the need to guard against external threat and (because of a steady flow of external resources) from the need to develop a self-sustaining economy. Only by looking at this postcolonial international environment can we understand how the central state persisted despite its inability to tame the power of "local patrimonial lords"; how a decentralized form of patrimonialism persisted amid a modernizing economy; and how neo-patrimonialism arose in the wake of a relatively more "rational-legal" colonial state. In effect, client relations with the United States created and sustained a hothouse within which patrimonial features have flourished.

In summary, it is unlikely that Weber would ever have imagined anything quite approximating the Philippine political economy, since the perpetuation of its weak central state is a phenomenon seemingly unique to the colonial and postcolonial period. In describing the Philippines as a polity with strong patrimonial features, therefore, it is important not to forget that we are transplanting Weber's framework into a setting that he did not anticipate.

CHAPTER THREE

Patrimonial States and Rent Capitalism: The Philippines in Comparative Perspective

How does the Philippines compare with other Third World polities that exhibit strong patrimonial features? Clearly, the Philippines provides only one example of a polity that has been unable to bring "political arbitrariness to heel," and only one example of how capitalism can be "politically oriented." Weber devotes great effort to analyzing variation among patrimonial structures, and explains that some are more advanced than others in developing "bureaucratic features with increasing functional division and rationalization" and operating "according to definitive procedures." Moreover, he suggests that some patrimonial polities provide a clearer distinction between the "'state'" and the "personal authority of individuals" than others, and thus begin to approximate certain aspects of the modern bureaucratic state. In other words, the ease by which an individual bureaucrat can "squirm out of the state apparatus into which he has been harnessed" (and pursue individual, rather than corporate, goals) varies greatly even among patrimonial polities. Some display far more internal cohesion than others.[1]

In addition, Weber employs many terms to describe capitalist systems that are hampered by the weak degree of calculability in the political sphere, and distinguishes among various forms of (not fully rational) capitalist activity according to whether their "sources of gain" originate in

---

[1] Max Weber, *Economy and Society* (Berkeley: University of California Press, 1978), II: 1028, 1089, 998, 987–88. While Weber's complex treatment of variation among patrimonial polities is beyond the scope of this work, he focuses on such criteria as whether (1) the ruler's powers are relatively more stereotyped or arbitrary (see, for example, *Economy and Society* I: 232, II: 1038, 1040, and 1070); (2) polities are relatively more centralized or decentralized (see I: 235, II: 1025, 1031–32, 1040); and (3) the patrimonial bureaucracy is confronted by or relatively free of countervailing social pressures (see II: 1045 and 1047).

"trade, war, politics, or administration."[2] Moreover, Weber writes that "politically oriented capitalism, just as capitalist wholesale trade, is very much compatible with patrimonialism."[3] Central to his analysis, of course, is a focus on the political foundations of variation among capitalist systems.

It is useful to extend Weber's broad categories to a discussion of the variation that exists within modern-day patrimonial polities and capitalist systems, and place the Philippine political economy in larger comparative context. In doing so, we return to a consideration of the two dimensions of capitalist variation that were introduced in Chapter One, and combine our focus on the nature of the state with a discussion of the relative strengths of state apparatuses and business interests. Certain patrimonial polities, I argue, seem to evolve much more readily than others, and Weber's theory of capitalist development offers clues as to why.

The first section of this chapter compares the Philippine polity with other states that have strong patrimonial features, and Philippine-style capitalism with other forms of rent capitalism. The second section argues the need for a more differentiated view of state apparatuses and capitalist systems, and the third section provides an initial framework in which to understand better why patrimonial features are more likely to evolve in some settings and persist in others.

Comparing Patrimonial Polities

For the purposes of present analysis, we can confine the discussion to two broad types of patrimonial polities.[4] First, there is the *patrimonial administrative state,* exemplified by such diverse examples as the former

---

[2] Weber, "Author's Introduction," in *The Protestant Ethic and the Spirit of Capitalism* (New York: Charles Scribner's Sons, 1958), 23–24. Callaghy lists the wide array of terms found in Weber's texts: "commercial capitalism," "political capitalism," "booty capitalism," "adventurers' capitalism," "traditional capitalism," and "patrimonial capitalism." Thomas M. Callaghy, "The State and the Development of Capitalism in Africa: Theoretical, Historical, and Comparative Reflections," in *The Precarious Balance: State and Society in Africa,* ed. Donald Rothchild and Naomi Chazan (Boulder: Westview Press, 1988), 69. From a historical standpoint, Weber considers these forms of capitalism the rule, and modern rational capitalism the exception. Because the "capitalistic adventurer . . . has existed everywhere" and across history, with widely varying sources of enrichment, Weber seems not at all surprised to encounter such enormous variation in "politically oriented capitalism." There has long been capitalist activity of diverse kinds; for him, what is "peculiar" is the "modern form of capitalism." "Author's Introduction," 20, 23–24. See also *Economy and Society,* II: 1395.

[3] This is not, however, a deterministic relationship. As Weber writes, "Patrimonialism is compatible with household and market economy, petty-bourgeois and manorial agriculture, absence and presence of capitalist economy." *Economy and Society,* I: 1091.

[4] The comparative analysis in this section expands upon my "Booty Capitalism: An Analysis of Business-Government Relations in the Philippines," in *Business and Government in Industrializing East and Southeast Asia,* ed. Andrew MacIntyre (Sydney: Allen & Unwin, and Ithaca, N.Y.: Cornell University Press, 1994).

"bureaucratic polity" of Thailand (dominant in the years 1932–1973), the New Order of Indonesia (most clearly during the earlier years of Suharto's rule), and Mobutu Sese Seko's Zaire (prior to the regime's disintegration in the mid-1990s). In these political systems, the dominant social force is a bureaucratic elite or "political aristocracy," and countervailing social forces are strikingly weak. The Thai bureaucratic polity, writes Laothamatas, was notable for the "weakness of extra-bureaucratic forces, be they governmental actors (such as the monarchy, the judiciary, and the legislature) or nongovernmental actors"; the business class displayed "political passivity." In Indonesia, explains Crouch, "the most important political competition took place within the military elite," while the masses were forcibly depoliticized and industrialists mere clients of the patrimonial officialdom. Although Zaire does not have a bureaucratic elite as historically rooted as those of Thailand and Indonesia, there are nonetheless parallels in the imbalance of forces inside and outside the state. As Callaghy described Zaire in the mid-1980s, "Politics is highly personalized, and . . . a political aristocracy . . . is consolidating its power within the structures of the state while the stratification gap between the rulers and the ruled grows. . . . [Mobutu] has maintained tight control over the emerging commercial elite which he has created to a large extent." Weber discusses broadly comparable examples of centralized patrimonial officialdoms, and notes that in certain cases officials were "the only major privileged strata confronting the masses."[5]

The type of "politically determined" or rent capitalism that one generally finds in the patrimonial administrative state reflects—not surprisingly—the relative strengths of the state apparatus and business interests. In his classic work on the Thai bureaucratic polity, Riggs explains that government service provided "the greatest opportunities for combining high income with security, prestige, and power," and those unable to gain admission to the bureaucracy had to settle for entrepreneurship. Because businesspersons lacked political access, Riggs calls them "pariah entrepreneurs." The political environment offered them little security, and in order to engage in business at all they had to contribute "financially to the private income of [influential] protectors and patrons in the government." Since the major beneficiaries of the process of rent extraction were

[5] Anek Laothamatas, *Business Associations and the New Political Economy of Thailand: From Bureaucratic Polity to Liberal Corporatism,* (Boulder: Westview Press, 1992), 2 (see also 149–50); Harold Crouch, "Patrimonialism and Military Rule in Indonesia," *World Politics* 31 (1979), 571–87, at 578–79; and Thomas M. Callaghy, *The State-Society Struggle: Zaire in Comparative Perspective* (New York: Columbia University Press, 1984), 6, 30; Weber, *Economy and Society,* II: 1044–51, at 1045. The term "patrimonial administrative state" comes from Callaghy, chapter 1. Crouch and Callaghy offer excellent, historically based analyses of patrimonial dynamics in other postcolonial settings, and it was through their work that I first became interested in applying Weberian insights to the study of the Philippine political economy.

based in the administrative apparatus of the state, this form of rent capitalism can be characterized as *bureaucratic capitalism.*[6]

A quarter century ago, Riggs quite pessimistically asserted that pariah entrepreneurs would be unable to alter an environment that threatens the security of long-term investments and foster the emergence of economic institutions more conducive to private enterprise and a free-market system. He anticipated that governmental careers would remain the major avenues to prestige, power, and economic opportunity, and that the authority of the bureaucratic elite would perpetuate itself. Recent history, however, has contradicted Riggs's pessimism, and shown that bureaucratic capitalism may carry the seeds of its own destruction. "From our present vantage-point," Ruth McVey says of Thailand and Indonesia, "the features of the bureaucratic polity . . . *have less the aspect of a developmental bog than of a container for fundamental transformation.*"

How does this sweeping change take place? Perhaps the best analysis of the dynamics of this ongoing transformation is Crouch's analysis of Indonesia—an analysis that is equally relevant to understanding the process of change in Thailand. Drawing on Weber, Crouch explains, "In the early stages, a patrimonial political structure need not be an obstacle to capitalist economic development. By placing themselves as clients under the protection and patronage of powerful members of the ruler's court, industrialists can acquire the security and predictability they need. But as a modern economy grows and becomes increasingly complex, industrialists require more than informal understandings with officials to assure them of the safety of their investments." Over time, although many powerful military and bureaucratic officials will resist giving up their special privileges, one may see a fitful process in which business enterprises require (and demand) some greater measure of regularization and bureaucratization.

There seem to be two major sources of regularization and bureaucratization: (1) piecemeal reforms, instituted from above; and (2) far more sweeping reforms, forced by the emergence of new social forces that challenge the prevailing order. In the first type of reform, the state leaders may support selective measures of economic reform in an effort to satisfy the political imperatives of regime preservation and/or enhance the country's

---

[6] Fred W. Riggs, *Thailand: The Modernization of a Bureaucratic Polity*, (Honolulu: East-West Center Press, 1966), 250–51. The term *bureaucratic capitalism* is meant to correspond with Riggs's widely used term, "bureaucratic polity." It must be emphasized, however, that neither category has any resemblance to Weber's notions of how modern bureaucracy or modern capitalism should operate. Riggs might more properly have used the term "administrative polity" (just as Callaghy uses the term "patrimonial administrative state" to describe Zaire), but since his "bureaucratic polity" is so deeply etched in the analysis of Southeast Asian political economy, I regretfully perpetuate the inappropriate terminology in describing its economic system.

position internationally. Suharto and his generals, for example, were acutely aware of the fact that hyperinflation had contributed to popular discontent with the Sukarno regime, and that the long-term viability of the New Order depended on creating "an expanding pool of available resources, not only for patrimonial distribution within the elite, but also for the pre-emption of potential opposition from outside." In the late 1970s, writes Crouch, the major pressures for regularization and bureaucratization in Indonesia came from "sections of the army concerned about the long-term legitimacy of military rule."[7] In both Thailand and Indonesia, the success of top-down reforms was greatly enhanced by the presence of a few relatively well-insulated agencies with high levels of technocratic expertise.

The second type of reform is much more extensive, and results from the emergence of new social forces able to effectively challenge the (patrimonially based) power of the bureaucratic and military elites. The basis for such conflict—fundamental shifts in the distribution of power among contending social forces—has been forming in recent decades in both Indonesia and Thailand. Possible dynamics of an optimistic scenario of long-term change can be summarized (and greatly simplified) as follows. First, there is substantial economic growth, encouraged not only by conducive policy but also by substantial contributions of foreign capital, foreign aid, and exports. (Indonesia initially relied heavily on booming oil exports, and Thailand on "capital injected into the country by the United States in connection with the Vietnam war").[8] Second, in the process of economic growth, a more assertive business class emerges. Third, elements of this business class may demand a certain regularization of relations between the government and business interests—signs of which have been more apparent in Thailand than in Indonesia. In many cases, notes McVey, "foreign interests have helped to protect domestic capital from the state," and have been "a powerful ally in lobbying against policies and practices hostile to business."[9] The hegemony of the bureaucratic and military elites

[7] Ruth McVey, "The Materialization of the Southeast Asian Entrepreneur," in *Southeast Asian Capitalists,* ed. McVey (Ithaca, N.Y.: Cornell Southeast Asia Program, 1992), 22; Crouch, 579, 582–83 (quotes from 579, 582).

[8] Both Crouch and McVey emphasize the centrality of externally generated resources in bringing about the emergence of more modern and complex economies. "In contrast to traditional patrimonial states, which acquired funds largely through the exploitation of the peasantry and through wholesale trade, the New Order has depended on a rapidly expanding modern economy financed by foreign aid, foreign investment, and rising oil prices" (Crouch, 579).

[9] McVey, 29–30. External firms, of course, cannot always be counted on to support the regularization of relations between government and business. Just like domestic capital, foreign capital can purchase a "viable calculability nexus" (Callaghy, 1988, 76) with a patrimonial state by cultivating relations with the proper officials, and if this nexus is working quite suitably (and remains essentially undisturbed by regime change) there is little reason

is challenged, and the long-term result may be, fourth, the gradual and fitful creation of a political environment that provides a more congenial foundation to the development of advanced forms of capitalist accumulation. Out of societal conflict emerges fundamental change in the political sphere, which in turn facilitates the eventual emergence of more rational forms of capitalism. In short, economic expansion has the capacity not only to line the pockets of the patrimonial officialdom and to enhance the political viability of patrimonial regimes; it can *also,* over the long run (and despite the best efforts of the officialdom), promote social changes so profound as to effectively challenge the very foundations of the patrimonial administrative state.

Indeed, recent works focus on the increasing assertiveness of the Indonesian and Thai bourgeoisies, and the May 1992 tumult in Thailand—with the strong role played by businesspersons and the middle class—confirms that new social forces have burst onto the political stage. In the process of social conflict, there is a relative diminution of the (patrimonially based) powers of the Thai bureaucratic elite.[10] The increasing strength of the Indonesian and Thai bourgeoisies has parallels to a process that took place in the development of European capitalism, when domination by the political level gradually gave way to domination by the economic level. As Callaghy explains, the rising bourgeoisie began to demand less "special protection and favor," and "slowly and unevenly" to rely more on the "generalized presence" of Weber's preconditions to capitalist development. "As this shift took place over time, key bourgeois elements began to *expect* a viable calculability nexus without having to 'pay' for it each time via patron-client ties and patrimonial administration, and they increasingly demanded it as their class weight, presence and power accumulated. As Weber indicated, this is the difference between the presence of some of the contextualizing factors of modern capitalism and their

---

for outsiders to use their influence to challenge the patrimonial political order. Because a more nearly bureaucratic political order is much more likely to provide a calculable environment to the investments of individual firms, however, one can expect that foreign capital, in general, will support (although rarely lead the charge in promoting) the regularization of relations between government and business.

[10] Examples of works charting the increasing assertiveness of the bourgeoisie in Thailand and Indonesia include Richard Robison, *The Rise of Capital* (Sydney: Allen & Unwin, 1986); Andrew MacIntyre, *Business and Politics in Indonesia* (Sydney: Allen & Unwin, 1990); Kevin Hewison, *Bankers and Bureaucrats: Capital and the Role of the State in Thailand,* Monograph No. 34, Yale University Southeast Asia Studies (New Haven, 1989); and Laothamatas. In addition, while Lev deals little with the business class *per se,* he offers an excellent analysis of "efforts to establish an Indonesian 'law state' in the context of middle-class assaults on patrimonial assumptions of political order" (Daniel S. Lev, "Judicial Authority and the Struggle for an Indonesian Rechtsstaat," *Law and Society Review* 13, no. 1 (1978): 37–71, at 37). The events of May 1992 and their aftermath are chronicled in Surin Maisrikrod, *Thailand's Two General Elections in 1992: Democracy Sustained,* Research Notes and Discussion Paper No. 75 (Singapore: Institute of Southeast Asian Studies, 1992)

becoming the dominant elements of a [modern, rational] capitalist *system*."[11]

At the same time, one finds evidence of important change even within the bureaucratic elite itself. Particularly in Thailand, it seems that elements of the old bureaucratic elite are beginning to be absorbed into the ranks of the bourgeoisie; as McVey points out, bureaucratic elites may become ever less reliant on the milking of office-based privileges, as they (and even more important, their children) have begun "taking a serious and active role in business." In effect, individual members of an old social force (the bureaucratic elite) may respond to changed structural conditions by gradually incorporating themselves and their children into a new social force (the rising bourgeoisie). In an optimistic scenario, this means that entrepreneurship based on rent-seeking behavior becomes less important relative to entrepreneurship based on productive activity. While the recent nature of the change makes it difficult to discern the strength of this trend, McVey sees "signs of the gradual crystallization of entrepreneurial attitudes, a shift in weight from bureaucratic and political to business values, and the emergence of more long-term commitment."[12]

Unfortunately, the story of the patrimonial administrative state in Zaire gives little cause for optimism even over the long term. First, even at its peak the Mobutu regime attempted few selective liberalization measures; whereas Suharto and the Thai bureaucratic elite were generally determined to promote an economic expansion whose benefits would be realized fairly widely among the population, the Zairian political aristocracy "demonstrated a notably feeble commitment to increasing the standard of living of the masses over whom it rules." The country's strategic importance, moreover, often undercut the efforts of international financial institutions to impose reform conditionality to aid flows. Like Marcos, Mobutu was a master in knowing how to "take the money and run." External resources seem to have done little but consolidate the position of the political ruling class. Second, reform pressures from below are greatly muted by the failure of new social forces to emerge. Mobutu seems to have been far more anxious to stunt the growth of an autonomous bourgeoisie than were his counterparts in the bureaucratic polities of Southeast Asia; in any case, the much weaker cohesion of the Zairian bureaucracy provided a far less congenial political environment in which a new business class might emerge. There are probably few political economies in the world that provide worse political foundations for capitalist accumulation than Mobutu's Zaire, where (in Mobutu's own words) "holding any slice of public power constitutes a veritable exchange instrument." In summary,

[11] Callaghy, "The State and the Development of Capitalism," 76; see also Crouch, "Patrimonialism and Military Rule," 582.

[12] McVey, 23–24, 26.

while the emergence of a more assertive business class is beginning to be apparent in Indonesia, and is far more evident in Thailand, it is by no means inevitable that a patrimonial administrative state will undergo this process of self-destruction. In Zaire (as in most of Africa), Callaghy asserted in the 1980s, "the political level is still clearly dominant," and bourgeois elements are not yet strong enough to effectively challenge the patrimonially based power of the political aristocracy.[13] More recently, prospects for serious reform seem to have all but vanished, as accelerating post–Cold War decay of political structures has shifted the focus from transformation of the patrimonial state to the very survival of the state itself.[14]

The second type of patrimonial polity is the *patrimonial oligarchic state,* exemplified here by the Philippines. In this polity, the dominant social force has an economic base largely independent of the state apparatus, but the state nonetheless plays a central role in the process of wealth accumulation. As in all patrimonial polities, there is weak separation between the official and the private sphere; unlike the patrimonial administrative state, however, the influence of extrabureaucratic forces swamps the influence of the bureaucracy, and major power resides not in a class of officeholders but rather in the private sector. To the extent there is a central ruler, that person "stands as one landlord . . . above other *landlords.*"[15]

The type of rent capitalism that corresponds with the patrimonial oligarchic state reflects the relative power of the state apparatus and business interests. In contrast to bureaucratic capitalism, where the major beneficiaries of rent extraction are based within the administrative apparatus, the principal direction of rent extraction is reversed: a powerful oligarchic business class extracts privilege from a largely incoherent bureaucracy. As noted, we can call this *booty capitalism* and distinguish it from the bureaucratic capitalism found in patrimonial administrative states.

In specifying the principal direction of rent extraction, I am not denying that civilian and military officials in the Philippines regularly participate in the process of rent seeking. Indeed, customs officials often extract bribes from smugglers, just as their higher-ups in the bureaucracy can extract "consideration" from industrialists seeking more formalized (but still par-

[13] Thomas M. Callaghy, "External Actors and the Relative Autonomy of the Political Aristocracy in Zaire," *Journal of Commonwealth and Comparative Politics* 11 (1983): 61–83, at 68, 80, 70; Callaghy, "The State and the Development of Capitalism," 76.

[14] See Crawford Young, "Zaire: The Shattered Illusion of the Integral State," *The Journal of Modern African Studies* 32 (1994): 247–263; and Herbert Weiss, "Zaire: Collapsed Society, Surviving State, Future Polity," in *Collapsed States: The Disintegration and Restoration of Legitimate Authority,* ed. I. William Zartman (Boulder: Lynne Reinner Publishers, 1995).

[15] As Weber writes, where local administrators are able to develop their own "military and economic power," it "soon tended to encourage the administrator's disengagement from the central authority." Local landowners could also gain relative autonomy within their area of control, and become "local patrimonial lords" with their own arbitrary powers over their subjects. *Economy and Society,* II: 1055, 1044, 1059; see, in general, 1051–59.

ticularistic) benefits such as protection from competition through import quotas. Other examples abound, whether in the allocation of logging concessions or in the allocation of selective credit. But the major beneficiaries of rent capitalism in the Philippines are not the bureaucrats who push the papers; they are rather the oligarchs who (from their extrabureaucratic perch) cause them to be pushed. Bureaucratic officials have never constituted a bureaucratic elite or political aristocracy, and have never become a powerful social force in their own right. In postwar Thailand and Indonesia, one finds many examples of the military—as a coherent bureaucratic entity—grabbing control of major enterprises (plantations, airlines, banks, and so on); in the Philippines, major advantages tend to be grabbed by familial interests with a clear base outside the state.

The weakness and incoherence of the postwar Philippine bureaucracy begins with the process by which bureaucrats are hired. Because the primary loyalty of government employees often remains with the patrons who got them the job in the first place, agency heads have little ability to command the obedience of their subordinates. The formal lines of demarcation among agencies are greatly undercut by the informal—yet powerful—ties of loyalty between political patrons and their clients in the bureaucracy. As a result, the bureaucracy is highly splintered, and even coherent agency-based factions are often difficult to discern. In short, the Philippine bureaucracy not only lacks coherence among its various parts (a common malady of the clique-ridden bureaucratic polity); more fundamentally, it also lacks coherence *within* its various parts.

The patrimonial oligarchic state is more resistant to reform than the patrimonial administrative state in two respects. First, piecemeal reforms are often inhibited both by the lack of bureaucratic coherence and by the tremendous power of oligarchic interests. Although there are clearly instances when regimes might benefit by selective measures of reform, there has been little assurance that the weak bureaucracy (even if bolstered by infusions of technocratic expertise) can implement them over the objections of various entrenched interests long accustomed to particularistic plunder of the state apparatus. The relative ease with which Suharto and his generals can achieve selective liberalization contrasts greatly with the enormous obstacles to similar types of reforms in the Philippines. As we shall see, even when Marcos placed technocrats at the helm of key economic policymaking agencies during martial law, the political logic of cronyism placed major obstacles in the path of serious reform. While technocrats helped the regime to secure funding from multilateral agencies, their advice was commonly ignored at home.[16]

---

[16] On a comparative basis, it seems that Suharto found it easier to force through liberalization measures than did his counterparts in Thailand, and the Thai bureaucrats found it

Second and more important, because it often discourages the emergence of new social forces able to challenge the patrimonial basis of power, booty capitalism is much more resistant to fundamental transformation than bureaucratic capitalism is. Even when external forces help finance the growth of a more modern and complex economy, there is little impact on the distribution of power within the polity. The Philippines received an even greater (and much earlier) external stimulus to its economy than either Indonesia or Thailand did, as foreign aid and foreign investment streamed into the country in the early decades of the postwar era. But this stimulus fell upon the rocky soil of the patrimonial oligarchic polity, and did not foster the emergence of new social forces. The major reason, quite simply, is that economic growth in this form of polity tends merely to strengthen the oligarchic social forces that are already the major beneficiaries of patrimonial largesse. Unlike the patrimonial administrative state, it is far less likely to encourage the creation of increasingly assertive new social forces.

In the midst of increasing economic complexity, no countervailing social force has yet emerged to provide a strong challenge to either the patrimonial features of the political economy or the longstanding dominance of the oligarchy. Nonoligarchic social forces never seem to achieve the "critical mass" necessary to force major overhaul of the system. First, small-and medium-scale capitalists are hard-hit by frequent balance-of-payments crises, and are therefore a weak constituency for the export-oriented, free-market economic reforms pushed by local technocrats and multilateral institutions.[17] Second, the potency of reformist zeal that might be found within the Philippine middle class is curbed by the huge exodus of skilled technicians to foreign lands. Third, revolutionary forces have been hobbled by internal divisions, occasionally effective counterinsurgency drives, and weak external support.

Moreover, there has been little incentive for oligarchs themselves to press for a more predictable political order, because their major preoc-

---

easier to force through liberalization measures than did their counterparts in the Philippines. As Doner and Laothamatas show, it is important to differentiate between the Thai and Indonesian cases, because efforts at selective liberalization undertaken by political elites in Thailand have had to contend with a much stronger private sector than exists in Indonesia. See Richard F. Doner and Anek Laothamatas, "The Political Economy of Structural Adjustment in Thailand," World Bank Working Paper, 1993. The weakness of Marcos-era technocrats is further analyzed in subsequent chapters.

[17] Emmanuel S. de Dios, "A Political Economy of Philippine Policy-Making," in *Economic Policy-Making in the Asia-Pacific Region,* ed. John W. Langford and K. Lorne Brownsey (Halifax, Nova Scotia: The Institute for Research on Public Policy, 1990), 140–41. World Bank analysts speak of the "missing middle," meaning "an industrial structure with heavy concentration among the largest firms, a preponderance of small firms, and very few medium-sized firms." See World Bank, "The Philippines: An Opening for Sustained Growth," Report No. 11061-PH (Washington, D.C., 1993), 32.

cupation is the need to gain or maintain favorable proximity to the political machinery. Even those oligarchs temporarily on the outs with the regime exert far more effort in trying to get back into favor than in demanding profound structural change. Far from being a "container for fundamental transformation," the patrimonial oligarchic state and the booty capitalism that it engenders are a "developmental bog" into which the postwar Philippine economy has—despite its enormous resources and talents—so often become mired. As discussed further below, however, one must not discount the potential for future change—especially as recent shifts in the country's external situation promote greater attention to the need for reform.

Toward a Typology of State Apparatuses and Capitalism

Building on this discussion of variation among patrimonial polities, it is now possible to propose initial steps that might help to encourage a more differentiated view of state apparatuses and to explore intra-capitalist variation. The recent demise of most communist states has focused increasing attention on the need to understand the enormous variance found among capitalist systems. Because the central international divide is no longer communism versus capitalism but rather tensions among major capitalist powers, the diversity of capitalist systems has become more apparent than at any time in the last half century.[18]

Within the Third World today, it is more obvious than ever that states vary, and that some are better suited than others to promoting capitalist development and economic transformation: contrast the explosion of growth in the newly industrialized countries of East Asia, for example, with the stagnation of much of sub-Saharan Africa. Some states are clearly obstructive to the development of modern capitalism, while others have succeeded in overcoming major externally imposed obstacles. From our current vantage point, older theories based on the conception of a generic Third World state and a generic Third World society—whether modern-

---

[18] As economist William Cline explains, amid the dominance of capitalist systems (all of which are premised on common notions of the right to private ownership and the centrality of private initiative) there is nonetheless competition and "debate between the Japanese model which gives a bigger role to government planning, the U.S. model which is essentially laissez-faire and the European model which gives more emphasis on social welfare." *New York Times*, April 29, 1992. Major capitalist powers also debate which forms of capitalism should be peddled to developing countries. Japanese officials, for example, have challenged the dominance of American ideological biases within the World Bank—arguing that the institution places "undue faith in market mechanisms" and urging that the Bank "should focus on increasing the institutional and technological capabilities of developing economies in order to intervene more effectively within the market." *FEER*, March 12, 1992.

ization theory, dependency theory, or ruminations on the essential nature of the postcolonial state—are perhaps of more interest to intellectual historians than to theorists of modern political economy.

Despite the fact that scholars of Third World political economy are clearly confronted by vastly different types of state apparatuses and capitalist systems, there is often a tendency to ignore or overlook this variation so as to achieve more parsimonious comparability of cases across national boundaries. A Weberian analysis provides a necessary corrective, both because it highlights the tremendous variation that does in fact exist, and because it points to the need to examine carefully the political foundations upon which varying capitalist systems are based. As argued in Chapter One, it is important to consider both the relative strengths of state apparatuses and business interests and the nature of the state. While the present analysis does not presume to capture all variations of capitalism within these two dimensions, it does attempt to take analysis beyond the usual laissez-faire versus statist continuum which, as discussed earlier, fails to capture adequately the wide variation found in capitalist systems throughout the developing world.

By focusing on cross-national differences such as those found in the matrix shown on page 20, it is possible to understand better why rent-seeking behavior predominates in some settings, yet is far more constrained in others. Economists who theorize about rent seeking generally confine their discussions to micro-level behavior within "the rent-seeking *society*," and have very little to say about the *state* structures in which this behavior most thrives. To the extent that rent-seeking theorists do examine cross-national differences, they tend to make the mistake of presuming that the degree of rent seeking is dependent on one simple variable: the more government intervention in the economy, the more rent seeking. As Buchanan writes, "Rent-seeking activity is directly related to the scope and range of governmental activity in the economy, and to the relative size of the public sector."[19]

If one were to rely on this framework, it would be hard to fathom how the actions of developmental states have often been very successful in guiding the process of economic transformation. Moreover, laissez-faire prescriptions for patrimonial states would probably do little to address their basic deficiencies; it is of little value to preach the virtues of a freer market and the evils of government intervention when what is needed is a

---

[19] James M. Buchanan, "Rent Seeking and Profit Seeking," in *Toward A Theory of the Rent-Seeking Society*, ed. James M. Buchanan, Robert D. Tollison, and Gordon Tullock (College Station, Texas: Texas A&M Press, 1980), 9. Similarly, Krueger seems to assert that the greater the presence of government-imposed restrictions on the economy, the more "all-pervasive" one can expect rent-seeking behavior to become. Anne O. Krueger, "The Political Economy of the Rent-Seeking Society," *The American Economic Review* 64, no. 3 (1974): 291–303, at 302.

state apparatus that can finally provide the calculability necessary to support more advanced forms of capitalism. Careful examination of the political foundations of capitalist systems not only strengthens our understanding of cross-national variation in the prevalence and character of rent-seeking behavior, but also helps us to analyze the social dynamics by which rent capitalisms may be transformed.

Peter Evans has provided an important critique of "neo-utilitarian" approaches to political economy, highlighting the need to examine variation among state apparatuses. The expectation among utilitarians "that a state run by an undisciplined collection of individually maximizing incumbents will tend to become a predatory monster are plausible, but it is patently false that some natural law of human behavior dictates that states are invariably constructed on this basis"; some states are actually "corporately coherent organizations" that do more to promote economic transformation than to obstruct it. "A differentiated view of Third World states," Evans concludes, "suggests . . . that the construction of a 'real' bureaucratic apparatus (as opposed to a pseudobureaucratic patrimonial apparatus) is a crucial developmental task." When prescribing solutions for economies hobbled by rent-seeking behavior, in other words, state bashing should give way to state building.

In his analysis, Evans classifies state apparatuses along a continuum of "predatory" (à la Mobutu's Zaire) to "developmental" (à la the East Asian NICs and Japan). Most Third World states, he explains, fall somewhere between these two extremes (and are dubbed "intermediate states"). In focusing attention on variation among developmental states and intermediate states, however, Evans has overlooked important elements of variation among patrimonial polities. In particular, by presenting Zaire as his archetypal example of a state that fails to promote development, he does not consider other cases that would also be patrimonial but be properly placed elsewhere according to the relative strengths of state apparatuses and business interests (that is, along the horizontal axis of the matrix presented on page 20).[20] The Philippines is not plagued by the overpowering strength of a predatory state but rather by the overpowering strength of a predatory oligarchy; as discussed earlier, the primary direction of rent

[20] Peter B. Evans, "Predatory, Developmental, and Other Apparatuses: A Comparative Political Economy Perspective on the Third World State," *Sociological Forum* 4, no. 4 (1989): 561–587, at 565–582. Evans's continuum basically confines itself to the left side of my matrix. He not only fails to incorporate the patrimonial oligarchic state; it is also unclear where he would place the minimalist regulatory state associated with laissez-faire capitalism. In fairness, however, Evans's focus on variations among developmental and intermediate states (rather than patrimonial states) is entirely consistent with his overall interest in the role played by states in industrial transformation. The fullest exposition of his excellent thesis is *Embedded Autonomy: States and Industrial Transformation* (Princeton: Princeton University Press, 1995).

extraction in the Philippines is the opposite of that in Zaire. Few would dispute President Ramos's observation that the "Filipino State has historically required extraordinarily little of its citizens"; in fact, the overriding concern is how a few of its citizens can so systematically plunder the state for private ends.[21] The distinction between the "patrimonial administrative state" and the "patrimonial oligarchic state" highlights at least one key difference in types of predation obstructive to capitalist growth.

Nonetheless, Evans very clearly points analysis in the right direction, beyond the minutiae of individual bureaucratic behavior and toward a focus on the enormous cross-national variation that exists among the institutional contexts in which bureaucrats act. It is correct to presume rational actors, in other words, but a big mistake to presume the presence of a rational-legal state. Such recognition is a critical initial step for the Philippines—and many other Third World nations—to overcome long-standing obstacles to sustained developmental success. The next section further examines the possible paths by which states might begin to climb from the lower to the upper portion of the matrix, that is, be transformed into relatively more rational-legal structures.

Prospects for the Evolution of Patrimonial Features

One of the leading scholars of patrimonial features in modern Third World states, Thomas Callaghy, readily acknowledges that "no theory exists about how . . . shifts [from personalized to bureaucratic administration] occur." This section does not attempt to create such a theory, but seeks rather to offer an initial comparative framework in which to analyze certain possibilities for transformation. In doing so, one must heed Callaghy's caveat to both scholars and policymakers: "Change is usually slow, incremental, uneven, often contradictory from a given analytical or policy point of view, and dependent on the outcome of unpredictable socioeconomic and political struggles. We cannot afford to stop looking for changes or trying to bring them about, but we must retain a sense of the historical complexity involved."[22]

[21] Inaugural speech of President Ramos, June 30, 1992, in *Philippine News*, July 8–14, 1992. Certain senators in the Aquino era actually considered plunder of the state such an enduring plague upon the land that they introduced a measure declaring it punishable by death. Any persons amassing $2.3 million or $4.6 million in "ill-gotten wealth"—the sponsors were in disagreement as to the proper threshold—would be executed by the state they had sacked. *Manila Chronicle*, June 11, 1989.

[22] Thomas M. Callaghy, "Toward State Capability and Embedded Liberalism in the Third World: Lessons for Adjustment," in *Fragile Coalitions: The Politics of Economic Adjustment*, ed. Joan M. Nelson (New Brunswick: Transaction Books, 1989), 132.

Complexity notwithstanding, certain broad patterns are worth exploring. Our analysis begins by returning to the basic distinction between two major sources of regularization and bureaucratization: selective measures introduced from above, and far more sweeping reforms pushed from below by increasingly assertive new social forces. The politico-military leadership in Thailand initiated major programs of top-down reform as early as the late 1950s, but only in the subsequent process of economic growth did new social forces emerge demanding at least some measure of regularization of relations between the government and business interests. Motivated by the legitimacy that comes from successful pursuit of economic development, a sufficiently capable state—able to implement measures of selective reform—encouraged the emergence of a stronger bourgeoisie, thus laying the basis for substantial conflict among contending forces. In the process, of course, the character of the state was challenged by a process that it had itself initiated.

Insights into the process of bottom-up reform can be found in Weber's theory of capitalist development, which Collins sees as a "conflict theory" focusing on "the crucial role of balances and tensions between opposing elements. . . . [T]he creation of a calculable, open-market economy depends upon a continuous balance of power among differently organized groups. The formal egalitarianism of the law depends upon balances among competing citizens and among competing jurisdictions. . . . The open-market system is a situation of institutionalized strife. Its essence is struggle, in an expanded version of the Marxian sense, but with the qualification that this could go on continuously, and indeed must, if the system is to survive. . . . The possibility for follower-societies of the non-Western world to acquire the dynamism of industrial capitalism depends upon there being a balance among class forces, and among competing political forces and cultural forces as well." It is difficult to imagine a more forceful image of this conflict than the May 1992 showdown in Bangkok, when Thai businesspersons and their allies—armed with cellular phones—openly confronted an intransigent military leadership on the streets of the city. In the wake of this conflict, military prerogatives were challenged on many fronts. Even if subsequent contention over new forms of corruption (now centered on corporate groups and rural "godfathers") could be a factor in bringing the army to power once again, there remains a far greater balance among forces now than in previous decades.[23] Recent

---

[23] Randall Collins, "Weber's Last Theory of Capitalism: A Systematization," *American Sociological Review* 45 (1980): 925–42, at 936; Clark D. Neher, "Thailand's Politics as Usual," *Current History*, December 1995, 436, 438. Indeed, a major factor behind Thai economic problems of the mid-1990s seems to be the disintegration of technocratic capacity amid this decline in the traditional power of bureaucratic elites. The economy continues to require a highly competent Bank of Thailand and Ministry of Finance, but current regulatory mishaps

economic travails, similarly, do not reverse the longer-term trend toward a relative diminution of the power of bureaucratic and military elites in favor of a stronger role for business interests.

In other settings, on the other hand, a greater degree of balance has yet to emerge. The "rise of capital" is evident in Indonesia, but programs of economic deregulation proceed very much on the regime's terms; as Jeffrey Winters observed in 1995, Suharto has been able to respond to "demands for reform in a highly focused and partial manner." Not unlike Indonesia, China is a patrimonial administrative state in which the power of officialdom swamps that of civil society. In the analysis of Barrett McCormick, the absence of social balance hobbles the development of a more rational-legal state—and the very strength of the Party relative to society actually "makes extensive patrimonialism inevitable." To the extent that rational-legal rulership is present, it is imposed from above rather than emerging from a "vigorous civil society." Such form of law "is not nearly as attractive to society as contract law in a market setting and will not result in a similar rationalization of social relations. Instead, many individuals are likely to seek and gain particularistic exceptions, and the overall effectiveness of rational-legal rulership from above is likely to be limited."[24]

Over the long term, however, to the extent that rapid economic growth arising from two decades of liberalization creates increasingly assertive new social forces, one should not be surprised to see sweeping change pushed from below. The specific expression of conflict will surely vary from case to case, and will quite probably be along different lines from those found in Thailand in 1992. Change in Indonesia could as likely emerge from popular discontent, as the middle class clings to the regime out of fear; change in China could as likely be expressed in terms of center versus province tensions. The key point is that the emergence of countervailing power—of some variety—may promote far more sweeping change than that which has already occurred through top-down reform. Over the long term, such societal conflict may encourage the creation of political and

---

suggest significant institutional deterioration even in these formerly highly regarded agencies. A key challenge will be crafting mechanisms that ensure basic levels of competence in the Thai bureaucracy even after the recent reconfigurations of power in society as a whole. Possible dynamics of an optimistic scenario of long-term change are highlighted above; in a pessimistic scenario, on the other hand, the historic power shifts of modern Thailand (a more assertive business class and a less influential military-bureaucratic elite) could potentially result in little more than the replacement of the patrimonial administrative state with a patrimonial oligarchic state (in terms of the matrix presented in Chapter One, minimal movement upward toward a more "rational-legal" state).

[24] Jeffrey A. Winters, "Suharto's Indonesia: Prosperity and Freedom for the Few," *Current History*, December 1995, 424. Barrett L. McCormick, *Political Reform in Post-Mao China: Democracy and Bureaucracy in a Leninist State* (Berkeley: University of California Press, 1990), 7, 21, 20.

institutional foundations better able to sustain the rapid growth that both countries have experienced in recent years.

Zaire has also displayed far less scope for the development of the sort of societal conflict discussed by Collins. Mobutu actively opposed the emergence of an autonomous bourgeoisie, and sustained an overwhelming imbalance among societal forces; as Callaghy observed in the early 1980s: "although other classes and protoclasses exist in Zaire, the political aristocracy does not have any serious *internal class competitors* for control of the state." Speculation about the emergence of an autonomous business class has been overtaken by speculation about the sustainability of the state itself. While the case of Zaire is a particularly dramatic example, many African political economies highlight the stagnation that can result when there are both weak reform tendencies from above and weak societal pressures from below.

Goran Hyden argues that the "softness" of the African state "is the inevitable product of a situation where no class is really in control and dominant enough to ensure the reproduction of a given macro-economic system."[25] In the Philippines, however, a soft state endures despite (indeed, to a large extent *because of*) the ability of a particular class to control, dominate, and reproduce itself. If the Philippines is any guide, one should not expect the creation of a strong bourgeoisie, in and of itself, to strengthen the African state. Collins's exposition of Weber's "conflict theory" suggests that the most critical factor in strengthening the political foundations of capitalist development is probably not the existence of any particular concentration of power (either in the state or in society), but rather the balance that exists among various forces.

In the Philippines, the configuration of forces remains grossly imbalanced—but the imbalance is the mirror image of that found in either Zaire or China or the traditional Thai and Indonesian bureaucratic polities. The power of civil society overshadows that of officialdom, not vice versa. The oligarchy does not face "any serious internal class competitors for control of the state," and there is little prospect of any such forces emerging in the near future. As noted, external resources and economic growth have done far more to strengthen the oligarchy's hegemony than to encourage the growth of social forces that might challenge it. New faces appear, but the common pattern is their ready incorporation into the dominant social force.

Because the imbalance of social forces in the Philippines endures, there has been little sustained pressure for changes in the patrimonial nature of the state. Indeed, the Philippine state is not formed (or reformed) out of a

[25] Callaghy, "The Political Aristocracy in Zaire," 71; Goran Hyden, *No Shortcuts to Progress* (Berkeley: University of California Press, 1983), 63.

contract with its citizenry, but a colonial creation that has withered on the vine. The legal and administrative system imposed in colonial times was long ago distorted to conform to the prevailing imbalance of power within society; it is not, to be sure, based on any internally generated contract among contending forces. Until there exists some sort of balance among contending forces, the rule of law will probably remain weak and the political foundations for advanced capitalism will be very difficult to construct. Moreover, to return to the insights of Jackson and Rosberg, the definitional basis of the state will remain far more juridical than empirical in nature.

Is such conflict always a necessary element of the development of advanced capitalism? The cases of South Korea and Taiwan suggest that top-down, selective reforms may be sufficient in and of themselves to promote rapid capitalist development. Both are paradigmatic examples of top-down transformation, where military elites pushed rapid economic growth out of a desire both to confront external threats and build domestic legitimacy. Jung-en Woo shows that—at least until the 1980s—the Korean state was not challenged by "countervailing social power," and in fact initiated its rapid capitalist development "without the capitalist class." She convincingly argues the inseparability of security issues and economic growth in the South Korean experience, and describes how military leaders forcefully harnessed business leaders in the launching of "Korea, Inc." Slowly but surely, the patrimonial features of the Rhee regime came to be replaced with a more regularized system of government-business relations. Similarly, Wade notes how the presence of external military threat provided an imperative for the Taiwanese state to mold society and economy, while other factors provided both opportunity and means.[26]

Over time, however, even South Korea and Taiwan have experienced major bottom-up pressures as well. As Peter Evans argues, the systems of "embedded autonomy" that characterize state-business relations in South Korea and Taiwan become their "own gravedigger. . . . As private capital has become less dependent on the resources provided by the state, the state's relative dominance has diminished." The result in Korea, Woo explains, is an assertion of power by the large conglomerates, or chaebol: "In an age of 'deepening' finance and maturing capitalism . . . the chaebol eschewed a capricious political order that so casually mixed benevolence with terror; it came to desire greater stability and the rule of law, even if

[26] Jung-en Woo, *Race to the Swift: State and Finance in Korean Industrialization* (New York: Columbia University Press, 1991), 14, 83–85; Robert Wade, *Governing the Market: Economic Theory and the Role of Government in East Asian Industrialization* (Princeton: Princeton University Press, 1990), 337–39. This analysis accords broadly with Haggard's conclusion that "international pressures are the most powerful stimulus to policy reform" in newly industrializing countries. Stephan Haggard, *Pathways from the Periphery: The Politics of Growth in the Newly Industrializing Countries* (Ithaca, N.Y.: Cornell University Press, 1990), 28.

that meant liberal democracy (*especially* if that meant 'liberal democracy' along Japanese lines)."[27] Their enthusiasm for liberal democracy probably waned in 1995, when two former Korean presidents were prosecuted for accepting bribes from chaebol; nonetheless, the episode dramatically demonstrated the degree to which the forces that initiated top-down reforms in the early postwar period eventually came to face major challenges from the system they had created.

Thus even in the most successful postwar Third World political economies, where major reforms were first initiated from above by strong military governments, one finds a dual process of top-down and bottom-up reform. While South Korea and Taiwan show that state leaders have been able to initiate successful, dynamic capitalist growth primarily through top-down measures, the emergence of new social forces—and conflict among contending forces—is eventually likely to become an essential element of modern industrial capitalism even when actively avoided by authoritarian leaders. As Collins concludes, "in the highly industrialized societies also, the continuation of capitalism depends on the continuation of the same conflicts [among competing forces]. The victory of any one side would spell the doom of the system."

This brief survey of several highly divergent Third World political economies suggests that one must look at both top-down and bottom-up processes of change to see how obstructive social and political structures might be transformed into environments more conducive to the development of advanced forms of capitalism. Where top-down reforms are absent, as in Zaire, bottom-up pressures are unlikely to emerge with any great strength; on the other hand, the transformative impact of top-down reform alone is generally limited by the weakness of sustained bottom-up pressures. Exceptional external shocks or threats did contribute enormously to the dirigiste push for rapid capitalist growth in South Korea and Taiwan, but even in these cases fuller transformation awaited the emergence of stronger societal pressures from below. In short, some measure of top-down reform is probably necessary to help initiate politico-economic transformation; sustaining and deepening the process, however, relies on "a continuous balance of power"—and ongoing conflict—"among differently organized groups."

While scholarship unfortunately provides few general clues as to how patrimonial polities are transformed into bureaucratic states, it is clear that any attempt to assess the possibilities of—or to promote—such an enormous shift must begin with careful attention to particular national circumstances arising from particular historical legacies. Comparative analysis

[27] Peter Evans, "The State as Problem and Solution: Predation, Embedded Autonomy, and Structural Change," in *The Politics of Economic Adjustment,* ed. Stephan Haggard and Robert R. Kaufman (Princeton: Princeton University Press, 1992), 165; Woo, 201.

heightens understanding of the enormous cross-national variation that exists in political and economic development, but each country must ultimately chart its own path in these fitful processes; predictions that one country's experience will be replicated by another often do more to confuse than to clarify the tasks ahead. Awareness of history not only creates a keener sense of current possibilities but also a clearer road map for achieving future potential; moreover, it guards against unrealistic expectations of change that inevitably create unnecessary disappointments and demoralization. Goran Hyden's observations on Africa are relevant to many other settings as well: "[There must be] a greater willingness to place the African development problematic in its proper historical context, and accept that the structures which presuppose macro development are not in place in most African countries and need first to be effectively institutionalized. . . . The sooner Africa, and the rest of the world, comes to grips with [the complex developmental task needing to be done], its difficulties as well as its opportunities, the quicker we may be able to see a way out of the present impasse." While historical awareness is the starting point, such analysis is by no means determinative of future possibilities. In the end, as Gerschenkron counsels, "No past experience, however rich, and no historical research, however thorough, can save the living generation the creative task of finding their own answers and shaping their own future."[28]

In the Philippines as well, developmental assessments often ignore the particular challenges presented by the country's historical legacy. Drawing on insights from the past, these introductory chapters have argued that without fundamental change in the nature of the state, the country will have difficulty sustaining either a statist or laissez-faire approach to economic development. If Weber's "conflict theory" is correct, the emergence of modern, rational capitalism will probably depend on a prolonged, turbulent process of breaking down the oligarchy's domination of the state apparatus and building up a state able to provide some greater measure of calculable adjudication and administration. Possibilities for thoroughgoing transformation of the present-day Philippine political economy—through both top-down and bottom-up processes—are analyzed in greater detail in Chapter Ten. While inducements for change are now heightened, I argue, obstacles to change remain formidable.

---

[28] Hyden, 213; Alexander Gershenkron, *Economic Backwardness in Historical Perspective* (Cambridge, Mass.: Harvard University Press, 1962), 6.

CHAPTER FOUR

Private Interests and Public Resources: The Historical Development of the Philippine Banking System

In Philippine-style oligarchic patrimonialism, dominant social forces have an independent economic base outside the state but nonetheless rely upon access to the state as the major avenue of accumulation. The most comprehensive analysis of the dynamics of booty capitalism can be derived from an examination of the politics of banking, a sector in which the most important state economic policymaking agency, the Central Bank, interacts with the largest collection of oligarchic families. This chapter provides brief historical background on the banking system prior to 1960. The first section surveys the American colonial period and the immediate postindependence years, while the second and third sections examine two key developments in the first decade after the birth of the Central Bank in 1949: the imposition of import and exchange controls, and changes in the structure of the banking industry. While the specific mechanisms of plunder have varied through the years, clear and dramatic patterns of particularistic raids on public resources can be traced by examining the history of Philippine banking from the American colonial period to the present.

The American Colonial Period: Banking on the Public Trough

Upon assuming power in the Philippines at the turn of the century, American colonial officials encountered a financial system clearly unsuited to the needs of the country's agricultural development. Two British banks dominated the system, confining the bulk of their business to financing foreign trade. An American bank followed this pattern "like a tail to a kite," and the fourth major bank, largely owned by the Church, had limited resources to devote to promoting agricultural growth.[1] In 1904, only about 3 percent of total loans were secured by agricultural land, even though agriculture was the major occupation among the country's roughly eight million inhabitants. An early governor-general told the U.S. Congress in 1906, "I have never been in a province in the islands . . . where the municipal and provincial officials have been gathered together when the first thing that they have presented to my attention was not the need for an agricultural bank."[2]

The response to this need came, somewhat ironically, from a colonial regime noted for its minimalist approach to government. U.S. congressional efforts to form a privately controlled agricultural bank in 1907 failed for lack of private interest, and the following year a government-owned bank was formed. The bank's modest resources were enjoyed primarily by sugar planters and larger farmers, and replenished with government deposits in 1912.[3] By 1916, as the bank's resources were again nearly exhausted and the wartime economic boom led to even greater demand for credit, Democratic Governor-General Francis Burton Harrison recommended the creation of a much larger, multipurpose national bank "capable of sustaining all the government's developmental efforts." The establishment of the Philippine National Bank, we shall see, marked a dramatic new chapter in state involvement in the financial sector.[4]

As discussed in Chapter One, the Harrison administration not only promoted the formation of a range of state enterprises, but also pushed for the Filipino control of both houses of Congress that began in 1916.[5] Simultaneous to the expansion in the role of the state, then, was an expansion in the oligarchy's control over that state. Two Republican-appointed

---

[1] Francis Burton Harrison (governor-general of the Philippine Islands from 1913 to 1921), *The Cornerstone of Philippine Independence* (New York: The Century Co., 1922), 262. The two British banks were the Chartered Bank of India, China, and Australia and the Hongkong and Shanghai Banking Corporation, both of which opened Philippine branches in the 1870s. The American bank was the International Banking Corporation, which began Philippine operations in 1904 and whose branch was taken over by the National City Bank of New York in 1914. The ecclesiastical bank is Bank of the Philippine Islands, established in 1851 as the Banco Espanol Filipino de Isabel II.

[2] E. W. Kemmerer, "An Agricultural Bank for the Philippines," *Yale Review*, November 1907, 264 and 267 (quoting Governor-General Henry C. Ide).

[3] Kemmerer, 270; H. Parker Willis, "The Philippine National Bank," *Journal of Political Economy*, May 1917, 412; Peter W. Stanley, *A Nation in the Making: The Philippines and the United States, 1899–1921* (Cambridge: Harvard University Press, 1974), 234–35; and Leonard F. Giesecke, *History of American Economic Policy in the Philippines During the American Colonial Period, 1900–1935* (New York: Garland Publishing, Inc., 1987), 113–14.

[4] Stanley, 235. "It is for the United States a new form of government activity in the business field," noted its first president. Willis, 409.

[5] See Harrison, 257–261. Besides PNB, the government became involved in managing the railroad, a coal company, and a cement company. It also created the Public Utility Commission, the Government Sugar Central Board, and the National Development Company (the latter of which has remained an important government corporation).

governors-general later noted that 1916 was the year in which legislation "becomes increasingly radical in its . . . government interference in business."[6] More precisely, because state institutions were overwhelmed by the power of the increasingly assertive national oligarchy, the legislation opened broad new fields for oligarchic plunder. By far the largest business venture of the government—and the richest new source of booty for the emerging national oligarchy—was the Philippine National Bank. Within five years, the newly empowered landed oligarchs had plundered the bank so thoroughly that not only the bank but also the government and its currency system were threatened by "utter breakdown." The Republican governors-general considered "[t]he story of the Philippine National Bank . . . one of the most unfortunate and darkest pages of Philippine history."[7] This story reveals certain basic patterns of interaction between a predatory oligarchy and a patrimonial state that have continued to plague the postwar Philippine financial sector—despite increasing levels of complexity in both the economy and the structure of the state.

The bank's first chairman and president was H. Parker Willis, former secretary of the Board of Governors of the U.S. Federal Reserve, who felt that the Philippines' potential for agricultural development was being hampered by the "exorbitant rates" of interest in the countryside.[8] From the start, however, Willis's efforts to create a prudent, conservative bank were thwarted. When his draft bill for the bank emerged from the legislature, the PNB was an institution that "ambiguously combined elements of central, developmental, speculative, and wildcat banking." The government was to provide P10 million in capitalization, and required to deposit all of its funds in the new bank. PNB was given the power to issue notes and to conduct exchange operations for the government. The bank's top officers were able to make loans without consultation, and the upper limit on loans was pegged at a level much higher than what Willis advised. He resigned less than a year after the bank's formation, as his more cautious approach was repeatedly undermined.

Under new leadership, credit expanded wildly out of control, and the loan portfolio bulged with favors to well-connected agricultural families. The Bank "grew like Jack's beanstalk in the fairy story," boasted Harrison,

[6] Leonard Wood and W. Cameron Forbes, "Report of the Special Mission of Investigation to the Philippine Islands," October 8, 1921. Reprinted in *Report of the Governor General Philippine Islands . . . For the Fiscal Year Ended December 31, 1921* (Washington: Government Printing Office, 1922), 41. Both Harrison and leaders of the ruling Nacionalista Party, Stanley explains, believed that "the funds of the insular government and the management of its developmental programs should be in the hands of a public, Filipino institution, not a private, American one" (p. 236).

[7] Stanley, 247; Wood-Forbes report, 37.

[8] Willis, 409–11, 417–18, 430. Stanley describes Willis as an "anti-imperialist economist" (p. 236).

and by 1918 held almost two-thirds of total assets of the Philippine banking system.[9] "Minimum precaution in regard to security was taken," an official report noted, and banking laws were flagrantly violated. Moreover, bank examiners found "[l]arge loans were made to directors, or to interests controlled by directors, involving heavy losses."[10] When the basic source of bank funds—government deposits—proved insufficient, the bank not only began printing money but also made a "systematic raid" on the currency reserve fund in New York, snatching $41,500,000 to lend out in the Philippines![11] By 1921, an accounting firm determined that PNB had squandered the entire capital stock contributed by the government, as well as half of all government deposits in the bank. It declared the bank "hopelessly insolvent," and accused it of violating "every principle which prudence, intelligence, or even honesty, dictate." The devastation went beyond the bank to affect the entire economy: by 1921, the currency was in a shambles, and the government nearly broke.[12]

In broader perspective, one can say that the newly reorganized colonial state was plundered by the national oligarchy it had spawned. Prior to the arrival of the Americans, provincial elites had limited contact with Manila; in creating representative institutions, U.S. colonials created an arena in which these forces vied for national-level office and power, interacting with each other in the capital city. While Philippine elites faced major divisions in the initial years after the American conquest—as contending forces staked out contrasting positions on how to relate to the new colonial power—there was increasing unanimity in favor of similar modes of collaboration by 1905. As Michael Cullinane explains, an "ideological consensus" emerged in which both established Manila *ilustrados* and rising provincial elites publicly favored "immediate, complete, and absolute independence" at the same time they were working closely behind the scenes with colonial authorities. Leading politicians "were far less eager for immediate independence than Harrison," notes David Steinberg, "since what they privately wanted was the benefits of self-rule without the liabilities of ultimate authority."[13]

[9] Stanley, 236, 240–41; *The Independent* (Manila), January 1, 1925, 6–7; Wood-Forbes report, 37; Harrison, 261; George F. Luthringer, *The Gold-Exchange Standard in the Philippines* (Princeton: Princeton University Press, 1934), 94.

[10] Wood-Forbes, 37; Luthringer, 156. Collateral was often wildly overvalued, and violations of the terms of the loans were often "frankly admitted" by borrowers. Stanley, 241. Of the P40 million lent to sugar centrals, reports Luthringer, estimated losses were P15 million.

[11] Stanley, 246–47; Wood-Forbes report, 37. After this "systematic raid," notes a bank examiner, funds were invested "in long time, non-liquid, and doubtful loans. . . . to the shame of the American officials who were responsible. . . . The stupidity of the transaction is almost unequaled in the annals of finance." Luthringer, 121n.

[12] Luthringer, 155; Wood-Forbes, 37–38; Stanley, 247.

[13] Michael Cullinane, "Ilustrado Politics: The Response of the Filipino Educated Elite to American Colonial Rule, 1898–1907" (Ph.D. dissertation, University of Michigan, 1989),

Once the ideological consensus had been established, the major task of politics was merely to fight over the spoils available to those with most favorable access to the political machinery. As a former associate of President Manuel L. Quezon explained, there were few philosophical differences within the Philippine elite from the emergence of the *Nacionalista* Party in 1907 until the end of the American colonial regime. "The political battles of [Quezon's] time," he said, "were fought . . . upon the rivalry, more or less concealed, for factional power and personal leadership. In those circumstances a political philosophy was unnecessary; it might even be a disadvantage."[14]

Although the Philippine National Bank operated on a greatly reduced scale after it was reorganized in 1924, its loan portfolio continued to be a rich source of patronage for top officials. In later years, under the more centralized regime of Quezon (the first president of the Philippine Commonwealth, created in 1935), the Palace was able to manipulate powerful groups "by means of the loan-giving and loan-denying power of the Philippine National Bank." In effect, the state bank was swamped by the power of oligarchs and oligarchic regimes, and its resources largely dissipated through plunder and patronage, to the benefit of the landholding elite— particularly those families in the sugar industry.[15]

The PNB was not the only new commercial bank in the Philippine financial sector in the American colonial period, although it remained by far the largest bank. A Japanese bank set up a branch during the World

---

515–18; David Joel Steinberg, *In Search of Southeast Asia: A Modern History* (Honolulu: University of Hawaii Press, 1987), 279.

[14] Claro M. Recto, "The Political Philosophy of Manuel L. Quezon," a speech delivered on the seventy-fifth birthday anniversary of President Quezon, August 19, 1953, reprinted as an appendix to *Quezon: Paladin of Philippine Freedom,* ed. Carlos Quirino (Manila: Filipiana Book Guild, 1971) 391–403, at 392.

[15] Philippine National Bank, *Philippine National Bank, 60th Anniversary: July 22, 1916–76* (n.p., n.d. [Manila, 1976?]), 10; Recto, 394. See also Joseph Ralston Hayden, *The Philippines: A Study in National Development* (New York: The MacMillan Company, 1942), 327; and Alfred W. McCoy, "Quezon's Commonwealth: The Emergence of Philippine Authoritarianism," in *Philippine Colonial History,* ed. Ruby R. Paredes, Yale University Southeast Asia Studies Monograph No. 32 (New Haven, 1989), 114–160, at 121–22, 135.

Historically, the degree to which the PNB is either raided by outside forces or used as a tool of patronage by powerful politicians in Manila depends critically upon the balance of power, center versus periphery, in the larger political arena. Quezon, the first leader able to centralize a greater degree of power at the top of the political system, at the same time centralized access to PNB loans through his regime. In the postwar years, as we shall see, a comparable level of regime centralization was achieved by Ferdinand Marcos. While Quezon and Marcos were never successful in taming the decentralized power of the landed oligarchy—and did not by any means create a centralized bureaucratic officialdom—their regimes were certainly more centralized than other modern Philippine regimes. The Quezon-Marcos comparison is very skillfully presented in McCoy, "Quezon's Commonwealth," 117–18; for a discussion of Marcos's attempt to move from a decentralized to a centralized patrimonial polity, see Hutchcroft, "Oligarchs and Cronies in the Philippine State: The Politics of Patrimonial Plunder," *World Politics* 43, no. 3 (1991): 414–450, at 442–47.

War I boom, and three banks were established by local American and Chinese-Filipino investors in the 1920s.[16] By the formation of the Philippine Commonwealth in 1935, there were nine commercial banks and two savings banks in the Philippines—all of which were controlled by the government, foreign banks, the Church, Americans, or Chinese. Unlike the pre-PNB days, however, foreign banks no longer dominated the system: their total resources in the period 1916–1934 were only 21 percent to 32 percent of the country's total banking resources.

To better supervise this expanding sector, the Bureau of Banking (part of the Finance Department) was established in 1929, taking over the task of bank supervision from the Insular Treasurer.[17] Five new banks were established in the early Commonwealth years, including the first privately owned Filipino bank (Philippine Bank of Commerce) in 1938 and a government-owned Agriculture and Industrial Bank in 1939.[18] These banks had barely gotten off the ground, however, when the Japanese Occupation wreaked havoc on the Philippine banking and currency system. Four Filipino banks remained open through much of the war, but by 1945 both inflation and wartime destruction had so devalued the assets of the banks that concerted government assistance was necessary for their postwar rehabilitation.[19]

Six months after the country was granted its independence on July 4, 1946, the administration of President Manuel Roxas created a new government bank. The Rehabilitation Finance Corporation absorbed the Agricultural and Industrial Bank and was given the specific mandate of assist-

[16] Yokohama Specie Bank was set up in 1918; the three domestic banks are Philippine Trust Co. (which became a commercial bank in 1920); Peoples Bank and Trust Company (1926); and China Banking Corporation (1920). Other banks were established but did not endure. Nicanor Tomas, "Banking in the Philippines from 1925–1950," *The Fookien Times Yearbook 1951*, 71; *FEER*, August 4, 1978, 32; Maria Teresa Colayco, *A Tradition of Leadership: Bank of the Philippine Islands* (Manila: Bank of the Philippine Islands, 1984), 91, 127n.

[17] Philippine Economic Association, *Economic Problems of the Philippines* (Manila: Bureau of Printing, 1934), 214–215; Colayco, 101; Luthringer, 87n.

[18] Tomas, "Banking in the Philippines," 72; *Central Bank of the Philippines: January 3, 1949—January 3, 1974* (Manila: Central Bank of the Philippines, 1974), 114. Two were foreign banks (Nederlandsch Indische Handelsbank and Bank of Taiwan); another was a bank with ties to China's Chiang Kai-shek regime (Philippine Bank of Communications). The new government bank, designed to provide long-term mortgage credit, had 9 percent of the total resources of commercial and savings banks on the eve of the war. Nicanor Tomas, "The Banking System and the Philippine Economy," *The Fookien Times Yearbook, 1955*, 81; Joint Philippine-American Finance Commission, *Report and Recommendations of the Joint Philippine-American Finance Commission* (Washington: Government Printing Office, 1947), 57.

[19] See Tomas, "Banking in the Philippines," 173; Colayco, 115–149; Licaros, 111–12; and A.V.H. Hartendorp, *Short History of Industry and Trade of the Philippines: From Pre-Spanish Times to the End of the Roxas Administration* (Manila: American Chamber of Commerce of the Philippines, Inc., 1953), 194–97. Besides the Bank of Taiwan and the Yokohama Specie Bank, the banks remaining open were PNB, the Philippine Bank of Commerce, the Bank of the Philippine Islands, and Philippine Trust Company. Seven foreign and Chinese-Filipino banks were declared "enemy" banks, and liquidated. Colayco, 118; Hartendorp, 71.

ing with postwar rehabilitation. From the start, however, it suffered from a shortage of funds, since it was largely dependent on the proceeds from the sale of surplus American war matériel. The disposition of this matériel was handled so corruptly that it yielded less than 15 percent of what had been expected from it, and the bank "never had the funds to become the massive agency that Roxas had envisioned." Most of its initial paid-in capital was committed within months, and the proportion of residential to both industrial and agricultural loans was far higher than originally planned.[20]

New Bank, New Booty: The Central Bank and Import and Exchange Controls

The formation of the Central Bank of the Philippines, in 1949, marks the beginning of the modern era of the Philippine financial system. Although the major focus of this book is on the Central Bank's responsibility for supervising and nurturing the country's financial sector, it is important to point out that the institution was initially established primarily as a means of ending colonial-era restrictions on the country's currency. Influential Filipinos had called for the creation of a central bank since at least 1934, and in 1939 the Commonwealth Legislature approved a bill drafted by then Secretary of Finance Manuel Roxas that would do so.[21] But President Franklin D. Roosevelt did not approve the bill, and it was not until after the Joint Philippine-American Finance Commission's 1947 recommendation in favor of a central bank that earlier plans could become a reality. With its creation, the country was to acquire control over the domestic money supply in accordance with the economy's internal needs; in signing the Central Bank bill in mid-1948, President Elpidio Quirino proclaimed it "a charter of our economic sovereignty."[22]

In fact, important restrictions remained on Filipino sovereignty within the financial sphere, including the 1946 Bell Trade Act's prohibition on any change in the dollar-peso exchange rate without the permission of the

[20] Ronald King Edgerton, "The Politics of Reconstruction in the Philippines, 1945–1948" (Ph.D. dissertation, University of Michigan, 1975), 378–382 (quote from 380). By May 26, 1947—not yet five months after the bank had opened its doors—P18.5 million had been committed to residential loans, far in excess of the intended P10 million. Joint Philippine-American Finance Commission, 57–58.

[21] Philippine Economic Association, 219–220; *Central Bank of the Philippines*, 36.

[22] Shirley Jenkins, *American Economic Policy Toward the Philippines* (Palo Alto, Calif.: Stanford University Press, 1954), 127; Joint Philippine-American Finance Commission, 46–47; *Central Bank of the Philippines*, 36. See also Nick Cullather, *Illusions of Influence: The Political Economy of United States-Philippines Relations, 1942–1960* (Stanford, Calif.: Stanford University Press, 1994).

U.S. president. As Jenkins writes, this provision "served as a kind of guaranty to [American] investors . . . in the possible event of capital withdrawals." Golay further points out that the Philippines was "the only country suffering extensive capital destruction in World War II which has chosen to defend its prewar exchange rate." The decision to maintain the prewar currency parity of the peso (at P2 to $1) led to chronic postwar balance-of-payment problems.[23]

As noted in Chapter One, the first major balance-of-payments crisis hit in 1949, just as the Central Bank opened its doors. The new institution soon found itself consumed with the task of helping to administer the import and exchange controls instituted as a means of overcoming the crisis. The first Central Bank governor, Miguel Cuaderno Sr., had been co-chair of the Joint Commission and shared the Americans' firm commitment to hold down inflation and defend the value of the peso. As Golay explains, Cuaderno and the Monetary Board that he dominated derived power "from the decision to defend the pre-war parity of the peso and the intense external disequilibrium arising out of that decision. Major aspects of economic policy are circumscribed by the availability of foreign exchange. . . . Exchange and import controls have created strong vested interests that can be depended upon to support the Monetary Board. Moreover, strong official support from the United States as well as the backing of the influential American Chamber of Commerce has contributed to [its] influence."[24] This American support was critical in enabling Cuaderno to withstand pressures (particularly from the powerful sugar bloc) for devaluation and an end to the system of import and exchange controls.[25]

The controls remained in force throughout the 1950s, and—contrary to initial expectations of how the Central Bank would wield its influence—became the dominant tool in both regulating the money supply and allocating selective credit. In an economy dominated by the system of controls, Filipino entrepreneurs preferred to take their loans in foreign exchange, and success in obtaining a loan from the bank generally depended upon success in obtaining an exchange license. Banks carried high levels of excess reserves, Golay notes, and the Central Bank relied

[23] Jenkins, 111; Frank H. Golay, *The Philippines: Public Policy and National Economic Development* (Ithaca, N.Y.: Cornell University Press, 1961), 117, 119 (quote from 119).

[24] The Monetary Board was the governing body of the Central Bank. Under the controls, which started being effective in curbing imports in 1950, a license to import automatically constituted a foreign exchange license. Golay, 163–64, 239, 412 (quote at 412).

[25] In the process of this struggle against proponents of a weaker peso and looser money, Cuaderno won widespread international respect for the conservative approach that he adopted (accolades of his own performance, in fact, are readily cited in his book). See Golay, 20, 85, 227; and Miguel Cuaderno Sr. *Problems of Economic Development* (n.p., 1964), 131–32, 138, 144–46 (quote at 146).

upon "management of the international reserve [as] a pervasive, powerful technique of monetary control."[26]

The allocation of licenses was rife with corruption, and several scandals erupted in the course of the decade over particularly favorable allotments provided to those with the best political connections. The controls were first administered by a separate Import Control Board (on which the Central Bank was represented) but "anomalies in the operation of controls [became] a nationwide scandal." Coquia reports that the board gained a reputation for "suspicious deals" in which import licenses "were easily procured at 10% commission" by those "close to high ranking officials."[27] In 1953, the Central Bank took over the administration of the controls. Although major responsibility for allocating foreign exchange licenses resided with the Monetary Board, private banks were deputized—as "authorized agent banks"—to assist in the allocation efforts. As early as 1955, Central Bank officials were anxious to assert greater control over the allocation process and to terminate the granting of exchange quotas to the private banks. Gregorio S. Licaros, special assistant to Governor Cuaderno, proposed the formation of a "CB import-export committee," chaired by himself, to allocate foreign exchange for imports.[28]

In subsequent years, the Central Bank was itself accused of corruption in its allocation of foreign exchange. In 1955, three members of the Monetary Board resigned after being accused of fraud in the allocation of import licenses. Strong criticism was again made during the November 1957 elections, when incumbent President Carlos Garcia "exerted heavy pressure on the Monetary Board to make liberal exchange allocations." Because the allocation of exchange provided windfall profits to recipients, the distribution of licenses was an effective means of rewarding campaign supporters and assisting political favorites.[29] Windfall profits also bred

[26] Golay, 237. On further dynamics of the system, see also Golay, pp. 222–24 and 233 and Miguel Cuaderno Sr. "The Central Bank and Economic Planning," in *Planning for Progress: The Administration of Economic Planning in the Philippines,* ed. R. S. Milne (Manila: Institute of Public Administration and Institute of Economic Development and Research, 1960), 104–05.

[27] Golay, 163–68. See also Carlos Quirino, *Apo Lakay: The Biography of President Elpidio Quirino of the Philippines* (Metro Manila: Total Book World, 1987), 112; and Jorge R. Coquia, *The Presidential Election of 1953* (Manila: University Publishing Co., 1955), 102–03.

[28] *CB News Digest,* September 13, 1955, 13–14. Banks used the exchange quotas as a "come-on" to expand their clientele, one veteran banker explained. Interviews, Chester G. Babst, former president of the Bankers Association of the Philippines, April 27 and May 3, 1990.

[29] Frank H. Golay, "The Philippine Monetary Policy Debate," *Pacific Affairs* 29, no. 3 (1956): 253–64, at 261–62; Golay, *The Philippines,* 92, 95 (quote at 92). Golay argues that while the Central Bank did a better job than the Import Control Board in administering the controls, criticisms of Central Bank corruption nonetheless mounted, and "reached a peak of intensity in the winter of 1955, rapidly undermin[ing] public confidence in the bank." Golay, *The Philippines,* 85n. Cuaderno acknowledges criticism of the Central Bank's allocation of licenses in a December 1955 speech published in *Problems of Economic Development,* 171, 173.

fierce competition among potential recipients, and manufacturers "considered effort at the Central Bank as important as at their plants." One (perhaps apocryphal) incident quite effectively symbolizes the plunderous manner in which licenses were sometimes obtained: in the late 1950s, it is said, Congressman Ferdinand Marcos "burst into [the] office" of a Central Bank official who had refused to license the imports of "a well-heeled Chinese businessman," and pointed a revolver at the head of the official until "the documents were signed and turned over to him."[30]

Although initially an ad hoc response to crisis, the controls—by placing severe limits on the quantities of imports—became an important impetus for industrialization: manufacturing increased as a proportion of net domestic product from 10.7 percent in 1948 to 17.9 percent in 1960. On the whole, however, the power to allocate foreign exchange licenses was used haphazardly, and many opportunities were squandered. The selection "of both commodities imported as well as individuals rewarded the windfall frequently involve[d] economically irrational criteria," explains Golay, and the most successful industries "tended to be ones using large quantities of imported raw materials, the finished products of which were subject to exclusion." When efforts at more coherent industrial planning did begin, in 1958, they were hampered by intra-agency squabbles and inadequate Central Bank capacity to audit firms.[31]

In historical context, the period of controls can be seen as one more source of booty for an oligarchy whose strategies of capital accumulation had long depended on favorable access to the state apparatus. Given the weak capacity of the state apparatus, it is not surprising that the controls were far less a tool of state industrial planning than an object of oligarchic plunder. As a rule, what the oligarchs grabbed from the state was theirs to keep; not only was there massive corruption in the allocation of licenses, but the beneficiaries of the system had no obligation to make even the most minimal contribution to larger developmental objectives. In some cases, so-called industrialists requested a foreign exchange license to support manufacturing ventures and then diverted the proceeds to import finished goods.

[30] Golay, *The Philippines*, pp. 92, 95, 168, 178–79; Laurence Davis Stifel, *The Textile Industry: A Case Study of Industrial Development in the Philippines*, Southeast Asia Program, Cornell University, Data Paper No. 49 (Ithaca, 1963), 104. The Marcos incident is reported in Sterling Seagrave, *The Marcos Dynasty*, (New York: Harper and Row, 1988), 162; a similar story is found in Primitivo Mijares, *The Conjugal Dictatorship of Ferdinand and Imelda Marcos I* (San Francisco: Union Square Publications, 1986 [first printed in 1976]), 262.

[31] Robert E. Baldwin, *Foreign Trade Regimes and Economic Development: The Philippines* (New York: National Bureau of Economic Research, 1975), 2; Golay, *The Philippines*, 141, 163–64, 239. Stifel's study of the textile industry concludes that the "opportunity which the Central Bank had to plan a balanced growth of the industry was delayed until development had progressed so far that optimum firm integration patterns were no longer feasible." Stifel, 70, 74, 80 (quote from 70).

Given the government's obvious weakness vis-à-vis business, neither agroexporters nor industrialists had to worry much about being taxed on their windfall profits: just as there were no export taxes on sugar, there were minimal taxes on the sale of foreign exchange to industrialists. In the early years of the controls, in fact, the government failed to collect any of the windfall arising from the import restrictions through taxing the sales of exchange; *all* the benefits of the system were grabbed by the recipients of the licenses. As Golay points out, "the search for revenues on the part of the government is not aggressive, and the pressures to divert to the government the windfall arising out of import restrictions are minimized." One side was aggressive, the other was not: quite clearly, these episodes reveal a state that is more plundered than plunderer.[32]

While developmental opportunities were generally squandered, the priority often given to Filipino importers and producers in the allocation of foreign exchange was successful in encouraging the creation of a group of Filipino manufacturing entrepreneurs. What were the origins of these entrepreneurs? Rivera concludes that landed families with a firm "tradition of political control over the state" made out especially well in the competition for licenses. "Through their longstanding economic and political power rooted in land ownership and lucrative export commercial agriculture," landed elites "entrenched themselves as the dominant segment of the postwar local manufacturing class."[33]

But new faces appeared as well. Rivera calls them "non-landed nouveau capitalists," and notes that because of their lack of capital, many "established and expanded their firms after gaining access to government credit and licenses, as well as government-administered foreign aid and loans, and by forging various links with foreign partners." The entrée of these "new rich" highlights the dynamism in oligarchic composition in the Philippines, as discussed in Chapter One.

Third, as the anecdote about Congressman Marcos illustrates, many Chinese-Filipino entrepreneurs also did very well in securing exchange licenses—often with the help of politicians. The anti-Chinese Retail Nationalization Act, Yoshihara explains, forced many Chinese-Filipinos to move out of commerce and into manufacturing. Rivera's study shows that 45 percent of today's top manufacturing firms are controlled by Chinese-Filipino families, and that most of them were established in the 1950s and 1960s.[34]

---

[32] Golay, *The Philippines*, 152–3, 178–82 (quote at 182).

[33] Temario Campos Rivera, "Class, the State, and Foreign Capital: The Politics of Philippine Industrialization, 1950–1986" (Ph.D. dissertation, University of Wisconsin-Madison, 1991), 101. A similar conclusion is reached in John J. Carroll, *The Filipino Manufacturing Entrepreneur: Agent and Product of Change* (Ithaca, N.Y.: Cornell University Press, 1965), 100.

[34] Yoshihara Kunio, *Philippine Industrialization: Foreign and Domestic Capital* (Singapore: Oxford University Press, 1985), 82–107, at 86; Rivera, 110. Rivera also notes that Chinese-Filipino capitalists long "had to work through dummies and political patrons to enhance

Finally, foreign manufacturers must be counted as major beneficiaries of the controls, since many firms were able to "reap monopoly profits by investing in assembly and finishing plants" in a protected import-substitution industrialization (ISI) market. The linkages between foreign capital and leading Filipino families provided windfall profits to each side, and led to the creation of a powerful "enduring coalition" for the perpetuation of the protectionist system.[35]

In short, the period of controls created a new source of riches for many of the landed oligarchs, at the same time that it provided an important avenue for new faces to make it to the top. Familial economic interests began to change, away from an overarching concern with agriculture and toward a more diversified mix of interests—most notably ISI and agriculture. As we shall see, this process of diversification—begun in the 1950s and continuing in later decades—is central to understanding the configuration of oligarchic economic interests up to the present.

The diversification of family conglomerates, however, did not occur overnight. While there was a clear trend toward major families combining agricultural interests with newer manufacturing ventures, in the shorter term there was a fissure within the ranks of the elite between the sugar bloc and other agroexporters on one side, and emerging industrial interests on the other. Prior to the 1950s, agricultural export was essentially the only game around. While oligarchs fought among themselves for particularistic advantage, there was a high degree of consensus on economic policy: the premier goal, of course, was to maintain access to the American market. Moreover, as discussed earlier, there had been broad ideological consensus within the elite since roughly 1905; even during the war years, this consensus endured as the bulk of the Philippine elite worked out a similar stance of collaborating with the Japanese. Disputes within the elite were generally motivated by longstanding political feuds rather than ideological differences.[36]

By the mid-1950s, however, an intra-elite rift became especially evident in a major "monetary policy debate" that pitted Central Bank Governor

---

their political connections and access to state funds and licenses" (p. 136).

[35] Sylvia Maxfield and James H. Nolt, "Protectionism and the Internationalization of Capital: U.S. Sponsorship of Import Substitution Industrialization in the Philippines, Turkey and Argentina," *International Studies Quarterly* 34 (1990): 49–81, at 64, 67 (quote from 64); Charles W. Lindsey, "The Philippine State and Transnational Investment," *Bulletin of Concerned Asian Scholars* 19, 2 (1987): 24–41, at 25, 27; Rivera, 182, 156. Lindsey shows (p. 28) that by 1970, 57.7 percent of foreign investment was in the manufacturing sector, while only 10.7 percent was in commerce. Within manufacturing, 58.9 percent of all equity was Filipino-owned, and 41.1 percent foreign-owned.

[36] See David Joel Steinberg, *Philippine Collaboration in World War II* (Ann Arbor: University of Michigan Press, 1967) and Alfred W. McCoy, "'Politics By Other Means': World War II in the Western Visayas, Philippines," in *Southeast Asia Under Japanese Occupation*, ed. McCoy (New Haven: Yale University Southeast Asia Studies Monograph Series Number 22, 1980).

Miguel Cuaderno and his allies against leading members of the sugar bloc. Cuaderno sought to maintain conservative monetary and fiscal policies, retain the system of controls, and oppose devaluation of the peso. The agroexporters advocated greatly expanded government borrowing as well as relaxation of exchange controls in order that they might retain half of their foreign exchange earnings.

In 1956, the agroexporters were temporarily vanquished when Cuaderno returned from the United States with $85 million in official and private credits—concrete evidence of continuing American support.[37] But the agroexporters continued to oppose the system and both legally and illicitly increase the amount of foreign exchange earnings that they could retain. The allocation of exchange licenses was increasingly tarnished by the corruption that it generated.[38] As foreign exchange difficulties mounted, and the major external backer of the system—the United States—began to reassess its support for the controls, it was only a matter of time before the system would be dismantled. By 1960, the seemingly unavoidable decontrol process had finally begun; two years later, the peso was devalued by roughly 50 percent.[39]

The Banking System Under Cuaderno, 1949–1960

Although Cuaderno's Central Bank was largely preoccupied with administering the controls and heading off the impact of government deficit financing, the 1950s was also a period in which the financial system experienced both significant growth and reconfiguration. Beginning in 1954, a major factor in the growth of the system was the issue of government bonds by the Ramon Magsaysay administration—against Cuaderno's advice.[40]

[37] On the overall monetary policy debate, see Cuaderno, *Problems of Economic Development*, 55, 134–36; Golay, *The Philippines*, 229–230; and Golay, "Philippine Monetary Policy," 253–64. On the active U.S. role in sponsoring Philippine ISI, see Maxfield and Nolt, 62–68.

[38] Golay discusses several legal and illicit means of evading and exploiting the control system (by both exporters and industrialists). See *The Philippines*, 151–56, 167–68.

[39] Golay (*The Philippines*, p. 240) remarks that as foreign exchange problems increased in the 1950s, the country "resumed an earlier postwar policy of mendicancy." The most comprehensive account of the decontrol process is found in Baldwin, 50–64. At some point in the late 1950s, the United States reversed its support for the system of controls, and Cuaderno could no longer rely on official U.S. backing. See Cuaderno, *Problems of Economic Development*, 71–77; and Cheryl Payer, *The Debt Trap: The International Monetary Fund and the Third World* (New York: Monthly Review Press, 1974), 60–61.

[40] Cuaderno, *Problems of Economic Development*, 120, 55; Golay, *The Philippines*, 91, 229, 236. Total assets of the banking system grew at an average rate of 16.3 percent between 1954 and 1959, compared to an annual average growth rate of only 4.3 percent between 1949 and 1954. Data derived from reports of the Central Bank, Philippine National Bank, and Sycip, Gorres & Velayo. See also Andres K. Roxas, "The Commercial Banking System: Past and Future," in "Top 100 Corporations," a special report in the *Manila Chronicle*, September 22, 1969, p. 20.

In 1949, the only private Filipino bank was the Philippine Bank of Commerce (established in 1938 with Cuaderno as its first president). Of the ten other commercial banks, one was government-owned (the Philippine National Bank, the largest of all banks), four were branches of foreign banks, two were controlled by the Manila Archdiocese, and three were Philippine-chartered banks controlled by American or Chinese interests. In remarks that parallel those made by American observers earlier in the century, the Philippine-American Finance Commission reported in 1947 that many felt the "foreign banks were not using their resources, derived in large measure from local deposits, to promote the growth of the national economy."[41]

By 1960, there were three major changes in the shape of the commercial banking system: the role of the four foreign banks declined relative to Filipino-chartered banks, private banks controlled by *anakbayan* families—families of Filipino heritage—assumed increasing importance relative to those controlled by Chinese-Filipino families, and private banks became more important relative to government banks. Just as the system of import and exchange controls and other measures in the 1950s helped to promote the Filipinization of retail and import trade and manufacturing, there were also important efforts to promote the Filipinization of the private banking sector. By requiring at least 60 percent Filipino ownership for newly established banks, the 1948 General Banking Act froze at four the number of foreign banks able to operate wholly owned subsidiaries in the Philippines. The four foreign banks were prohibited from opening new branches within the Philippines, barred from accepting government deposits, and rarely able to rediscount with the Central Bank. Between 1950 and 1960, the proportion of total assets held by foreign banks declined from roughly 30 percent to 15 percent.[42]

Second, in 1957, the Monetary Board tightened the 1948 provisions by requiring that all new banks have 100 percent Filipino ownership. Quite clearly, the measure targeted aspiring Chinese-Filipino bank owners.[43]

[41] Joint Philippine-American Finance Commission, 55. Two foreign banks were British and two American: Standard Chartered Bank, Hongkong and Shanghai Bank, National City Bank, and Bank of America. As discussed earlier, the first three banks had a long tenure in the Philippines. The Bank of America, on the other hand, did not establish a branch in the Philippines until 1947, when it absorbed the branch of the Netherlandsch Indische Handlesbank. Miguel Cuaderno, "Philippine Banking," 155. The Church's banks were the Bank of the Philippine Islands and Philippine Trust Co. (acquired prior to World War II). People's Bank was controlled by resident American interests, China Banking Corporation by Filipino-Chinese, and the Philippine Bank of Communications by the Bank of Communications in China.

[42] See Appendix 1. Strangely enough, the Cuaderno Papers contain practically no mention of promoting Filipino financial institutions. Miguel Cuaderno Sr. Papers, 1934–1973, University of the Philippines–Diliman Library.

[43] Frank H. Golay et al., *Underdevelopment and Economic Nationalism in Southeast Asia* (Ithaca, N.Y.: Cornell University Press, 1969), 47–48, 90–92; Miguel Cuaderno Sr. "Philippine Banking: Its Achievements and the Challenge Ahead," in *Banking and National Development* [a

During Cuaderno's twelve-year tenure, there were nine new private domestic commercial banks, of which seven were established by families that would popularly be labeled Filipino, and two by families generally considered Chinese-Filipino. Ownership links to new industrial ventures probably contributed to marked increases in the percentage of total credit allocated by private commercial banks to industry, from 9.5 percent in 1954 to 26 percent in 1959.[44]

Third, private domestic banks emerged as a much more central element of the banking system even as government banks remained major players. In 1955, Congress increased the authorized capital of the PNB—the first such increase since 1924. Increases in capitalization were supported by government bonds, and further support came both from Central Bank rediscounting and from placements of government deposits. The Rehabilitation Finance Corporation, which had long suffered from limited resources, was transformed into the better-capitalized Development Bank of the Philippines in 1958. Fresh infusions of funds came from Japanese reparations and the government insurance systems.[45] Despite these changes, the importance of government banks declined relative to that of private banks: by 1958, the total assets of private domestic banks began to exceed the total assets of the largest government financial institution, the PNB.[46] As will be discussed in the following chapter, the experience of the first Philippine-owned private domestic bank, the Philippine Bank of Commerce, provides the earliest insights into deeply divisive interfamily and intrafamily feuds that have often hampered the operations of private banks throughout the postwar era.

Conclusion

As we have seen, the prewar banking system was dominated by foreign banks, government banks (especially PNB), ecclesiastical banks, and local

---

compilation of speeches from a 1963 seminar] (n.p., n.d.), 172. During this time, one finds no reports of foreign investors seeking to own 40 percent of a Philippine-chartered bank, as permitted by the 1948 law. In fact, the regulation specifically targeted naturalized Filipinos (the vast bulk of whom were of Chinese descent) by stipulating that "the ownership of banks established thereafter be limited to *natural-born* citizens" (Golay et al., 48, emphasis added). The 1957 regulation was promulgated about one year prior to the advent of the "Filipino First" movement of President Garcia.

44 Edita A. Tan, "Philippine Monetary Policy and Aspects of the Financial Market: A Review of the Literature," in *PIDS Survey of Development Research I* (Metro Manila: Philippine Institute for Development Studies, 1980), 181.

45 *Philippine National Bank,* 14; Cuaderno, *Problems of Economic Development,* 41; Golay, *The Philippines,* 246.

46 Extrapolated from Central Bank and Sycip Gorres, & Velayo (hereafter SGV) data. By the end of 1959, "the total loans of the private domestic banking sector for the first time exceeded those of the Philippine National Bank as a percentage of total loans outstanding." Jose B. Fernandez Jr., "Banking Trends in 1960," *Progress,* 1960: 42–46.

banks controlled by American or Chinese interests. No bank experienced a more rapid rise, nor a more rapid fall, than the PNB. During the first five years of its existence, in particular, its resources were flagrantly milked by a national oligarchy that was largely unrestrained in its plunder of newly established state institutions. The PNB debacle, which drained government coffers and nearly destroyed the currency system, remains a powerful image of the degree to which a predatory oligarchy can ride roughshod over a weak patrimonial state.

The allocation of import and exchange controls by the newly opened Central Bank provided a new source of riches after 1949, and promoted the diversification of familial economic interests into industrial ventures. Further diversification is evident in the increasingly central role of locally owned private commercial banks throughout the course of the 1950s. Even greater change, however, was yet to come: by the early 1960s, as nearly all major families expanded their interests into financial ventures, bank ownership opened up new possibilities for private plunder of the public trough.

CHAPTER FIVE

"Open Sesame": The Emergence of Private Domestic Commercial Banks, 1960–1972

Late in the tenure of Central Bank Governor Miguel Cuaderno (1949–1960), as we have seen, private domestic banks became the dominant element of the Philippine commercial banking sector. The rate of expansion of private domestic banks under Cuaderno, however, was dwarfed by their rapid proliferation under his successor, Andres V. Castillo (1961–1967). Within the space of only four years, nearly every major family diversified into banking, and the number of private domestic commercial banks ballooned from thirteen at year-end 1960 to thirty-three in February 1965. While Cuaderno had been relatively reluctant to hand out bank licenses, notes one prominent banker, Castillo "made an open sesame."[1] Castillo, writing in 1964, observed that "[b]anking today appears to be a 'popular' venture among investment-conscious and business-minded people," no longer the "exclusive club" it had been prior to the creation of the Central Bank in 1949.[2]

This chapter begins by examining the impact of the lifting of import and exchange controls on the Philippine political economy, and proceeds in the second section to an analysis of the major causes of the mushrooming of banks in the early 1960s, the process by which government rediscounts and deposits were allocated, and the families who received the bank licenses. The third section analyzes two contrasting examples of bank failure: Republic Bank, owned by a family with good political connections, and Overseas Bank of Manila, owned by a family with much shakier access

[1] Interview, Jose Fernandez Jr., April 6, 1990. Cuaderno had been "very careful in his choice of people he gifted with the license," according to Fernandez (himself a recipient of the last Cuaderno-granted license, when he established Far East Bank in April 1960).

[2] Andres V. Castillo, "Bankers and Their Responsibilities," in *The Fookien Times Yearbook 1964*, 141–42, 178, at 141. While gross national product increased by 176 percent between 1949 and 1963, he notes, total resources of the commercial banking system expanded by 427 percent.

to the political machinery. Fourth, I examine a bank that was the exception to the rule: the Far East Bank and Trust Company, which compensated for the absence of effective state regulation by practicing a kind of "self-regulation" within the confines of its own board of directors. The fifth section examines Central Bank efforts to regulate the banking sector more effectively, and the conclusion analyzes why these attempts were ultimately unsuccessful within the larger context of relations between a predatory oligarchy and a patrimonial state. In earlier eras, loans from the Philippine National Bank and exchange licenses from the Central Bank had dominated the oligarchs' quest for the booty of state; beginning in the early 1960s, ownership of a private bank became a new and central element of Philippine-style booty capitalism.

Diversification and Homogenization: The 1950s and 1960s

As explained in the previous chapter, the process of decontrol began in 1960 and culminated in the devaluation of the peso in 1962. The import and exchange controls provided the Philippine oligarchy a new source of riches to tap from the political machinery, and promoted a process of import-substitution industrialization (ISI) as many families diversified into manufacturing ventures. In the short term, this led to the tentative creation of a sectoral distinction between agroexporters and industrialists, best evidenced by the monetary policy debate of the mid-1950s. With the continuing diversification of major family conglomerates in later years, however, sectoral distinctions became an increasingly inaccurate way of describing the configuration of oligarchic economic interests. The more the family conglomerates put their eggs into several baskets, the more consensus existed within the elite on broader issues of economic policy, and the less pressing were sectoral disputes. Most significantly, since the 1960s there has been no intra-elite dispute approaching the magnitude of the Cuaderno–sugar bloc monetary policy debate. If those battle lines had still been drawn in the 1960s, it is likely that there would have been a repeat performance of similar intra-elite debates over such issues as monetary policy, exchange rate policy, and so on. While there are tentative signs that such fissures may in fact be developing in the 1990s (as will be discussed in Chapter Ten), one generally finds strong elite consensus over major issues of economic policy in the 1960s, 1970s, and 1980s.

In his analysis of "economic diversification within single families," David Wurfel concludes that "the occasional policy conflicts between industry and export agriculture" are "muted by family ties." Because of the "complicated kinship dimension," it is difficult to find "rational policy debates based on clear conceptions of group interest." Philippine firms tend to be closely held within diversified family groups, many of which—especially since the 1960s—include a bank whose loan portfolio can be milked by family enterprises. Loyalty is primarily to the family grouping, not to any of its agricultural, industrial, commercial, real estate, or financial elements. In the 1950s, certain sector-based business organizations gained in prominence, but they were often "greatly torn by conflicting interests." These groups never became powerful political forces in their own right, as families found it far more advantageous to use their influence to gain particularistic favors than to seek generalized policy change.[3] Even in the 1950s, it was quite conceivable that the same conglomerate could simultaneously search out a foreign exchange license to pay for raw materials at a manufacturing plant and support measures that left more foreign exchange in the hands of agricultural exporters.

The process of decontrol in the early 1960s brought strikingly little sense of direction to the country's economic policy. Economists saw a plethora of contradictions: while the 1962 devaluation boosted agricultural exports—and spurred the growth of raw material exports, especially copper and logs—it was accompanied by tariff measures that provided continuing protection to emerging industries. By 1966, the impact of the devaluation began to be eroded by inflation—thus assisting import-dependent manufacturing firms and inhibiting the fuller development of the export sector. Nonetheless, ISI continued to stagnate, and in the late 1960s the government enacted measures to promote export-led growth. But as Montes explains, these measures were only a "half-hearted flirtation." From an economist's standpoint, the country lacked any clear developmental policy.[4]

From the perspective of a diversified Philippine family conglomerate, things probably didn't look so grim—especially if favorable access to the political machinery provided opportunities for a range of particularistic privileges: loans from state banks, special favors for their own banks, logging and mining concessions, preferential tax exemptions, advantageous treatment on tax assessment and payments, special tariff walls or exemp-

---

[3] David Wurfel, "Elites of Wealth and Elites of Power, The Changing Dynamic: A Philippine Case Study," in *Southeast Asian Affairs 1979* (Singapore: Institute for Southeast Asian Studies, 1979), 244; and Wurfel, "Individuals and Groups in the Philippine Policy Process," in *Foundations and Dynamics of Filipino Government and Politics,* ed. Jose Veloso Abueva and Raul P. De Guzman (Manila: Bookmark, 1967) 208–23, at 215.

[4] Gonzalo M. Jurado, "Foreign Trade and External Debt," in *Philippine Economic Problems in Perspective,* ed. José Encarnación Jr. (Quezon City: University of the Philippines School of Economics, 1976), 274; Manuel F. Montes, *The Philippines: Stabilization and Adjustment Policies and Programmes* (Helsinki: World Institute for Development Economics Research, 1987), 2; Robert E. Baldwin, *Foreign Trade Regimes and Economic Development: The Philippines* (New York: National Bureau of Economic Research, 1975), 62. A similar argument is found in John H. Power and Gerardo P. Sicat, *The Philippines: Industrialization and Trade Policies* (New York: Oxford University Press, 1971), 42.

tions, favorable arrangements with the Bureau of Customs, and so on. Precisely because the overall policy regime was so lacking in direction, families could move in many directions in pursuit of greater wealth. Exports of sugar, logs, and copper were propelled by devaluation, while manufacturing firms were accommodated by a new form of protection (through tariffs rather than exchange controls). Although incoherent from an economic standpoint, macroeconomic policies seem to have been a quite coherent means of serving the economic interests of the diversified family conglomerates that dominated the political economy. The absence of clear debate over economic strategy suggests that family conglomerates were well served by policies that simultaneously protected ISI firms and promoted agricultural exports.

In short, beginning in the 1950s but becoming ever more obvious since the 1960s, there has been a simultaneous process of diversification and homogenization: because it is so common for family conglomerates to combine ventures in agriculture, import substitution, banking, commerce, and urban real estate under one roof, major families have come to share a certain homogeneity of interest on major issues of economic policy. As in prewar years, there has been substantial consensus on big issues, and political battles are fought more exclusively over factional and personal issues that arise in the quest for the booty of state. One dominant segment of capital emerged and remains hegemonic to the present: the diversified conglomerates of oligarchic families.

Understanding the "Bank Rush" of 1960–1965

If the period of controls was characterized by diversification of major families into industrial ventures, the early 1960s was the time for diversification into financial ventures. The first major impetus for this diversification was generous incentives, in particular government deposits, rediscounting, and continued low minimum capitalization requirements; as Patrick and Moreno write, "the monetary authorities in effect subsidized the banks." Government deposits began to be placed in private banks in late 1960, and remained an important source of funds for several banks until the mid-1960s.[5] Rediscounting (in which the Central Bank pur-

[5] Central Bank of the Philippines, *Annual Report, 1960* (Manila: Central Bank of the Philippines), 122 and various later issues of the *Annual Report;* Hugh Patrick and Honorata A. Moreno, "Philippine Private Domestic Commercial Banking, 1946–80, in the Light of Japanese Experience," in *Japan and the Developing Countries: A Comparative Analysis,* ed. Kazushi Ohkawa and Gustav Ranis (New York: Basil Blackwell, 1985), 311–65, at 326. The term "bank rush" comes from Virginia Benitez Licuanan, *Money in the Bank: The Story of Money and Banking in the Philippines and the PCIBank Story* (Manila: PCIBank Human Resources Development Foundation, 1985), 126. According to one banker, there were actually government

chases a bank's assets at a discount and thereby augments the bank's resources for additional lending) had been monopolized by the PNB prior to 1957, and did not become important to private banks until the early 1960s (when loan rates increased relative to the rediscount rates, creating a substantial profit margin, banks sought as much cheap credit as they could from the Central Bank).[6] There were seemingly no minimum capitalization requirements from 1949 to 1966, except for an implicit rule that each new bank exceed the initial capitalization of the previous licensee.[7]

Just as the allocation of exchange licenses in the previous decade was overwhelmed by corruption and favoritism to those with the best political connections, similar factors governed the allocation of new forms of selective credit to the rapidly expanding private domestic commercial banking sector in the early 1960s. Access to the rediscounting window, which over time became the most important means of selective credit allocation, was to be determined by sectoral priorities specified by the Central Bank between 1959 and 1962. These categories, however, were so broadly construed as to undermine any serious attempt at the targeting of specific sectors or specific investment priorities. Not until June 1966 did the Central Bank make its first effort to outline priorities more comprehensively—so comprehensively, in fact, that (at least on paper) nearly every entrepreneur in the Philippines was a potential recipient of Central Bank largesse.[8] Given the utter absence of selectivity in the guidelines, one can surmise that other—noneconomic—criteria were of predominant importance. In the 1960s as in subsequent years, decisions were based much more in terms of particularistic criteria (allocation to particular banks and individuals) than in terms of developmental goals (allocation to specific industries and investment priorities).

---

deposits in private banks prior to 1960, albeit on an unofficial basis: government funds in the PNB and DBP would be redeposited in Chinese-Filipino banks in exchange for "hidden encouragement" paid to PNB and DBP officials. Anonymous interview, 1990.

[6] Edita A. Tan, "Philippine Monetary Policy and Aspects of the Financial Market: A Review of the Literature," in *PIDS Survey of Development Research I* (Manila: Philippine Institute for Development Studies, 1980), 177; and Edita A. Tan, "Conduct of Monetary Policy and Quantitative Control of Credit," University of the Philippines School of Economics, Discussion Paper No. 73-8 (Quezon City, 1973), 14.

[7] Interview, Carlota P. Valenzuela, former deputy governor, Supervision and Examination Sector, March 22, 1990. Although Castillo says that a September 1963 regulation required newly established banks to have initial paid-in capital of P20 million, this regulation seems not to have been strictly enforced. Castillo, "Bankers and Their Responsibilities," 178.

[8] "Priority I" classification was given to extremely broad categories (for example, agricultural products or industrial products), but if these categories weren't sufficient one could still hope to fall under such "Priority II" categories as (a) any production and distribution that doesn't qualify under Priority I and (b) "other non-productive and speculative activities"! Edita A. Tan, "Central Banking and Credit Policies in the Philippines," University of the Philippines School of Economics, Discussion Paper 72-20 (Quezon City, 1972), p. III.26; Tan, "Philippine Monetary Policy," 176; Central Bank Circulars 223 and 227 (June 25 and August 15, 1966, respectively); Republic Act 265 ("The Central Bank Act"), Section 87.

In comparative perspective, there is nothing surprising about corruption and favoritism in the allocation of selective credit; what is significant, however, is the failure of the Philippine state either to guide sectoral allocation or to enforce performance criteria on the recipients of government largesse. Unlike their counterparts in South Korea and Taiwan, Philippine entrepreneurs could quite easily take the money and run; there was little sense of quid pro quo to a state so utterly incapable of promoting long-run developmental objectives.[9]

The banks' other major source of booty in the early 1960s was government deposits. It was not uncommon for banks to offer government officials under-the-table payments or high interest rates (in violation of interest rate ceilings) in exchange for government deposits; bankers with strong connections got the government deposits. A few institutions enjoyed particularly favorable placements between 1960 and 1966, the years in which the Central Bank permitted public monies to be placed in private banks. In 1962, an average of one-quarter of all bank deposits came from the government, and a handful of banks obtained 30 percent to 48 percent of deposits from the public sector.[10]

The second major reason for diversification into the banking sector was the credit crunch faced by many family conglomerates amid the lifting of exchange controls and accompanying devaluation between 1960 and 1962. In the 1950s, as discussed earlier, banks tended to base loan decisions on the ability of entrepreneurs to obtain an exchange license from the Central Bank. Bankers were anxious to facilitate such foreign exchange transactions, explains Jose B. Fernandez, since they provided "almost certain profits" with very little credit risk. Indeed, the high profitability of ISI firms of the 1950s had far less to do with manufacturing prowess than with favorable access to subsidized foreign exchange: some of the industries were called "beauty parlor" industries because all they did was "cut and curl" imported manufactures. Confined to basic tasks of assembly and packaging, the modest credit needs of ISI firms were quite readily met by the existing financial system. Vicente Paterno explains that families could obtain the minimal equity requirements from their own resources (often landholdings), long-term loans from the Development

[9] See, for example, Jung-en Woo, *Race to the Swift: State and Finance in Korean Industrialization* (New York: Columbia University Press, 1991); Robert Wade, *Governing the Market: Economic Theory and the Role of Government in East Asian Industrialization* (Princeton: Princeton University Press, 1990); and relevant chapters of Stephan Haggard, Chung H. Lee, and Sylvia Maxfield, eds., *The Politics of Finance in Developing Countries* (Ithaca, N.Y.: Cornell University Press, 1993).

[10] Interview, Chester Babst, May 3, 1990. On banks most favored in the allocation of government deposits, see Paul D. Hutchcroft, "Predatory Oligarchy, Patrimonial State: The Politics of Private Domestic Commercial Banking in the Philippines" (Ph.D. dissertation, Yale University, 1993), 262. As noted in the Preface, readers seeking more comprehensive data on ownership, selective credit allocation, total assets, and so on are referred to this work.

Bank of the Philippines, and short-term credit (for raw materials and supplies) from commercial banks.

When the period of decontrol began, however, many businesses (especially those most dependent on imports) were scrambling for credit. The devaluation increased the peso costs of paying for inputs and servicing external debts, Paterno further explains, and "the wrenching pressure on financial institutions" encouraged the Central Bank to begin to license many more new commercial banks. Because the best way to obtain credit for family enterprises was to diversify into banking, most prominent families set out to obtain bank licenses, if they had not already done so. The industry became a something of a fad.[11]

Third, the banking business was becoming more profitable than ever. High credit demand pushed up interest rates, while the cost of funds was kept down by cheap credit from the Central Bank, ceilings on savings deposit rates, and government deposits. In addition, after decontrol "everybody wanted to get into the import and export business." Banks made hefty profits both through opening letters of credit (LCs), and through lending funds to businesses that were unable to put up the required 30 percent margin deposit on LCs. As veteran banker Chester Babst recalls: "It was some kind of a racket." At a time when some other business was not doing well, "banking was the most profitable and the safest" investment. According to economists Hooley and Moreno, the spread between lending and deposit rates of interest was so large during this period that banks were able "to obtain as much as one-fourth to one-third of new capital from retained earnings." They find this spread "remarkable" and seemingly "unique" to the Philippines.[12]

In summary, there are three reasons why banking became a more attractive venture than ever: government incentives (cheap credit, government deposits, and low minimum capitalization requirements), the credit needs of related family enterprises (particularly fledgling industrial ventures), and high profitability. The question remains, however, as to why the banking system expanded in the manner in which it did. The Central Bank might have encouraged established banks to become bigger, stronger, and more efficient; instead, however, Governor Castillo declared the country

[11] Jose B. Fernandez Jr., "Banking Trends in 1960," *Progress*, 1960: 42–46, at 44; Licuanan, 136; Vicente T. Paterno (secretary of industry during the Marcos years), "Financial Markets and Industrial Development," *CB Review*, August 12, 1975, 7–9, at 8. In the Philippines, complains the former president of a bank licensed in the 1950s, "when a line of undertaking proves good, everybody jumps in and the whole damn thing goes down." Interview, Babst, April 27, 1990.

[12] Interview, Babst, May 3, 1990; Central Bank, *Annual Report, 1962*, 46; Richard W. Hooley and Honorata A. Moreno, "A Study of Financial Flows in the Philippines," University of the Philippines School of Economics, Discussion Paper No. 76-10 (Quezon City, 1976), 134–35.

"underbanked" and favored increasing the number of banks. Jose Fernandez explains the policy choice in terms of the personal preferences of Cuaderno and Castillo, and notes that both Castillo and President Diosdado Macapagal "came on with a more liberal policy in general"—not only in supporting decontrol, but also in liberalizing bank licensing.[13]

It is likely, however, that there were larger structural forces at work in determining this choice. As the Central Bank set out to expand available commercial bank credit, it actually seems to have preferred a system of fewer, larger banks to the proliferation of weak, small banks—but lacked the power to shape the banking sector in such a way. A 1963 Central Bank study concluded that the economy would not be well served by "the operation of additional small banking units." As Castillo explained, businesses were expanding in size, business risks had increased since decontrol, commercial banks had limited managerial resources, and the Central Bank would face a "proportionate increase in supervisory difficulties as the number of units to be supervised increases." Overall, "there would be little need for new institutions if the existing banks increased their capitalization." (Indeed, many aspiring bank owners borrowed funds from other banks to obtain the capital to start up their own banks. The creation of more banks, therefore, did not automatically mobilize greater capital for the banking system as a whole.)[14]

If the Central Bank actually preferred a banking system with a few large banks, why did Castillo continue to dole out bank licenses at such an unprecedented rate? To answer this, it is necessary to examine once again the familial basis of the Philippine political economy. Any attempt to require high levels of capitalization of the private banks would probably have been undermined by the strong desire of most families to maintain clear control over their enterprises. Increased levels of capitalization would, in general, mean that each bank was pooling the resources of many more families. The more families involved in any given bank, the less control any particular family would have over bank management. The less control a family had over the management of a bank, the less able it would be to tap the bank's loan portfolio for related family enterprises—which was of course a primary incentive for getting into the banking business in the first place.

Castillo noted the many shortcomings of banks with a small ownership base, and feared that some banks would "overstretch themselves . . . in a manner disproportionate to their capital base" yet avoid expanding that base so as to preserve control "by an individual, a family, or a distinct group." The "logical development in Philippine banking," he explained

[13] Licuanan, 126; *CB News Digest,* May 7, 1963, 21; Interview, Fernandez, April 6, 1990.
[14] Castillo, "Bankers and Their Responsibilities," 178; Interview, Amado Castro, Central Bank Professor of monetary economics, University of the Philippines School of Economics and former governor of the Development Bank of the Philippines, February 14, 1990.

further, "would be the merger of some of the small banks into big institutions in order to take care of the increasing demands of their clients, strengthen their liquidity position, and maintain greater stability of the banking system. *This is more of a hope at this time than a plea for immediate implementation because the present ownership of the banks which are controlled by a few families militate against its early realization.*"[15]

In short, Castillo recognized the dangers of too many small banks but also understood the limits of Central Bank power. Because it was contrary to the interests of most family conglomerates to establish high levels of minimum capitalization, Castillo dared not even make a plea for them to submit to such an idea. The interests of the diversified family conglomerates reigned supreme over the logic of the banking system as a whole, and Castillo ended up expanding the number of banks rather than expanding the size of the banks.

As we shall see, the Central Bank and its officialdom were by no means losers in this game of handing out a large number of bank licenses. Central Bank officials had long enjoyed a central role in the discretionary manner by which exchange licenses were doled out, and the process of decontrol was taking away an important pillar of their power. While the major beneficiaries of the allocation of this state booty remained those with a firm base outside the state, those inside the state apparatus were often able to reserve a slice of the rents for their own benefit, as well. For many officials of the Central Bank, it was probably fortuitous that just as the Bank was losing its central role in the allocation of exchange licenses, an important new role was being created in the discretionary manner by which bank licenses, selective credit, branch licenses, and other privileges were allocated. It seems likely that the more players there were in the system, the more opportunities there were for Central Bank officials to enjoy these discretionary powers.

The families that flocked to banking included both those of old landed wealth and those (of old and new wealth) that had been involved in the import-substitution industries of the 1950s. As one observer notes, "banking was such a profitable business . . . that it seemed logical for most business clans with large accumulations of family wealth to climax their financial activities by forming a bank."[16] In the midst of this "bank rush," however, there were at least two major families—both from prominent old Spanish clans—that did not establish their own banks: the Sorianos (who controlled the San Miguel Corporation) and the Elizaldes (who had diversified interests in sugar milling, distilling, rope making, and so on). The Sorianos were heavy borrowers, but San Miguel's status as the country's premier firm gave them ready access to loans. The head of the family, it is

---

[15] Castillo, "Bankers and Their Responsibilities," 178 (emphasis added).
[16] Licuanan, 127. Appendix 2 lists the years in which new banks were opened.

said, felt he had little to gain by being identified with one bank; in any case, the Sorianos had familial relations with the Ayalas, who took over control of the Bank of the Philippine Islands from the Archdiocese in 1969. The Elizaldes were also heavy borrowers with ready access to loans, and felt little advantage in identifying with any one bank. In sum, one might almost say that these two families were so well established that they had little need to set up their own banks.[17]

The previous chapter discusses the longstanding involvement of Chinese-Filipinos in the Philippine banking industry, and new barriers to entry imposed in the late 1950s. By 1965, however, the restrictive regulations were relaxed somewhat, and banks established after 1957 were allowed 20 percent to 30 percent ownership by naturalized Filipinos.[18] While the overall impact of these regulations may have been to obstruct greater Chinese-Filipino involvement in the banking sector temporarily, entrepreneurs from this community nonetheless continued to enjoy a major stake in the banking system. First, despite the 1957 regulation, families generally considered Chinese-Filipino were involved in the formation of such new banks as Metropolitan Bank, Rizal Commercial Banking Corporation, and General Bank. Combined with those Chinese-Filipino banks earlier established (China Banking Corporation and Philippine Bank of Communications in the prewar years, and Equitable Bank and Pacific Bank in the 1950s), Chinese-Filipinos remained a major element of the Philippine banking sector.[19] Second, in subsequent years many Chinese-Filipino entrepreneurs were able to acquire significant ownership stakes in already existing commercial banks. Finally, as I discuss in the next chapter, the restrictions of the 1950s and 1960s were to a large extent counteracted by acts of clear favoritism toward certain Chinese-Filipino banks in the 1970s.

Two Ashes, One Phoenix: Republic Bank and Overseas Bank of Manila

In the course of the 1960s, the rapidly evolving banking sector was rocked by two major episodes of bank failure, Republic Bank in 1964 and

[17] Licuanan, 127; anonymous interview, former senior Central Bank official, 1990. The Sorianos acquired a stake in Asian Savings Bank in 1984, soon after major a rift with the Ayalas; by 1990, the institution became a commercial bank (renamed AsianBank). Given the marked decline of the fortunes of the Elizalde family over the past three decades, one could—in hindsight—view their failure to go into banking as a major strategic error. On their decline, see *Philippine Daily Inquirer,* October 24, 1995.

[18] Banks established prior to 1957 were never included in the restrictions. Frank H. Golay et al., *Underdevelopment and Economic Nationalism in Southeast Asia* (Ithaca, N.Y.: Cornell University Press, 1969), 47–48, 91.

[19] These banks, moreover, play a key role in the strong informal networks commonly found in Chinese-Filipino communities. Outsiders frequently remark at how large banking transactions are traditionally forged merely through such informal means as a handshake.

Overseas Bank of Manila in 1968. On one level, these cases reveal common patterns of failure: although both banks benefited from the capture of large quantities of government deposits, they were nonetheless gravely weakened by excessive plunder from the related enterprises of the families that owned them. On another level, the experience of these banks diverged greatly. The family controlling Republic Bank was in the end very successful in using favorable connections to augment bank resources and fend off challenges to the bank's continued existence. By contrast, the political connections of the owner of the Overseas Bank of Manila were less favorable and the outcome unenviable. Their stories highlight how banking success in the Philippines is often strongly tied to favorable access to the political apparatus.

Republic Bank, first established as a savings bank in 1953, came under the firm control of Pablo R. Roman in September 1960 after a protracted fight for control with another bank founder, Damaso Perez; each accused the other of booking excessive and "irregular" loans for themselves. Roman, a Bataan businessman with distillery and lumber interests, was soon thereafter granted the first commercial bank license handed out by incoming Governor Castillo, on his second day in office.[20] The subsequent fortunes of the bank can seemingly be correlated quite closely to Roman's relationship to the political machinery. He was on the outs during the last year of Nacionalista Party (NP) President Carlos P. Garcia's term in 1961, and well connected early in the term of Liberal Party (LP) President Diosdado Macapagal (whom he had supported in the 1961 elections). By early 1964, however, he seems to have had a falling out with the Macapagal administration and its LP allies in Congress, and subsequently supported NP candidate Ferdinand Marcos (an erstwhile LP member) in the 1965 presidential election. Roman also switched over to the Nacionalistas in 1965, and won a congressional seat from his home province of Bataan at the same time that Marcos was elected president. From that point on, he quite clearly enjoyed close ties to the Palace.[21]

Not surprisingly, then, Republic Bank did not figure among the favored banks in the competition for these deposits in 1961 (the first full year in which government deposits were legally placed in private banks), but by 1962 nearly half of the bank's deposits came from public funds. At the end of the year, one-quarter of all government deposits in private commercial banks were held by Roman's bank. The bank registered rapid gains in total

[20] Pablo R. Roman, *The Power of Human Trust: Selected Speeches of Pablo R. Roman* (Quezon City: Phoenix Press, Inc., 1965), 8, 48–51; *Manila Times*, February 20, 1963; and *Daily Mirror,* February 20, 1963. According to one insider, "some clouds" surround the circumstances by which Roman acquired the bank. Anonymous interview, 1990.

[21] *Manila Times*, June 3, 1967. Roman reportedly financed the 1965 publication of Marcos's campaign biography, *For Every Tear a Victory,* written by Hartzell Spence and best remembered for its wild glorification of Marcos's war record.

assets, and jumped from eleventh-largest private commercial bank at year-end 1961 to third-largest at year-end 1963.[22]

As the bank was registering meteoric growth, however, NP congresspersons began to attack Roman for "the biggest banking frauds in history." They hinted that the bank was paying kickbacks in return for the huge placements of government deposits, charged that the Central Bank had in 1959 discovered some P2 million ($1 million) in loans granted to "fictitious persons" and "dummies" of Roman, and revealed that Roman employed the brother of the superintendent of banks as manager of an important branch of the bank. These allegations helped precipitate a run on a provincial branch of the bank, an event which was contained by prompt assurances of support by Castillo. In May, however, a committee headed by LP Congressman Floro Crisologo cleared Roman of any responsibility for irregular loans in 1958 and 1959.[23]

In addition to his ties to the Palace, Roman enjoyed excellent connections with the Central Bank. First, as noted earlier, he employed the bank superintendent's brother. Second, the chairman of Republic Bank, Bienvenido Y. Dizon, was a member of the Monetary Board (and immediate past president of the Philippine National Bank). Third, in May 1963 he employed former Governor Cuaderno as consultant to the bank at a reported monthly salary of P12,500 (worth roughly $3,200 in devalued pesos). Roman's old rival, Damaso Perez, complained that Castillo was "tending to cover up" for Roman, and that Cuaderno had failed, as Central Bank governor, to enforce a 1959 Monetary Board resolution calling for the replacement of Republic Bank's officers. Castillo confirmed past irregularities at Republic Savings Bank, but blamed the "past administration" for condoning them.[24]

On January 16, 1964, however, the Central Bank finally began a serious

---

[22] *Manila Times,* February 21, 1963, and *Daily Mirror,* February 23, 1963; SGV data.

[23] *Manila Times,* February 20, February 21, and May 25, 1963. "Resolute and calm," explains the introduction to his book, "Don Pablo weathered the storm of conspiracy against the proven principles of banking he holds and believe [*sic*] in." *Power of Human Trust,* 9.

[24] *Daily Mirror,* May 29, 1963; *Manila Times,* February 23, March 1, and May 14, 1963. It is not known if Castillo was pinning blame on the Cuaderno administration of the Central Bank, or the Garcia administration of the Republic. Castillo had formerly acted as deputy governor of the Central Bank under Cuaderno (1954–1960), but there seems to have been new tension developing between the two men during this period. Cuaderno backed Marcos in the November 1965 elections, and Castillo was known to be close to Macapagal. At that time, Cuaderno declared that "[w]hat has been done is done, but let it not be said that those of us who fought very hard to maintain the good name of the Central Bank do not despair of the shameful subservience the present authorities of this institution have shown to an unfortunate Chief of State on this matter." Cuaderno, "Philippine Banking," 157–60; Cuaderno, unpublished paper written for the Study Group for President-Elect Marcos, November 27, 1965; and Cuaderno, "The Central Bank (1962–1965)," unpublished manuscript, May 15, 1966. Miguel Cuaderno Sr., Papers, 1934–1973, University of the Philippines–Diliman Library.

investigation of abuses within the bank (in the wake of which the bank suffered another mild run). Four days later, Castillo wrote to Roman to list the bank's specific violations of the law, and Roman meanwhile requested emergency assistance. Apparently in exchange for Central Bank emergency loans of P13 million, Roman resigned as president of the bank and assigned voting rights on his stocks (80 percent of total shareholdings) to a board of trustees that included Cuaderno. In addition, the Monetary Board rescinded the bank's authority to accept additional government deposits.

Nacionalista congresspersons, however, were not appeased, and called for Castillo's ouster for the "CB-RB mess." Out of P160 million in loans granted without sufficient collateral, they charged, P78 million were granted to members of the bank's board of directors. Although lending operations were supposed to have been frozen, a P500,000 loan to Mrs. Roman had just been renewed. Government deposits of P100 million in the bank, he said, exceeded the bank's capitalization ten times.[25] In February—seemingly in response to these charges—the Macapagal administration reported that the reserves of Republic Bank were deficient and that the bank was accepting overvalued collateral in exchange for huge loans to its directors and officers and their relatives. The Finance Secretary said Central Bank ceilings on government deposits were being violated, and the Central Bank was guilty of violating its own rules on government deposits.

The Crisologo committee, which had earlier defended Roman and his bank, now urged criminal prosecution of top Central Bank and Republic Bank officials, and called on the Central Bank to extend emergency loans to rehabilitate the bank and secure the government deposits placed there. Crisologo noted Cuaderno's large earnings and charged that most of the bank's irregularities had occurred under his watch. Alfonso Calalang, former deputy governor of the Central Bank, complained that the Central Bank was too lax in its supervision of the private banks. NP Senator Jose W. Diokno called for court action against Republic Bank officials, and suggested that the bank was "being used as a funnel for government deposits to be converted into loans to persons influential with the administration."[26] Castillo defended the Central Bank, but responded to criticism in

[25] *Daily Mirror,* January 17, 1964; *Manila Times* January 18, 22, 23, and 30, 1964 and February 4, 1964; Vicente T. Tan, "The Uneven Hand: The Exercise of Central Bank Powers to Close Banking Institutions" (Ph.D. dissertation, University of Santo Tomas, 1982), 71–74, 84–85.

[26] *Daily Mirror,* February 7, 1964; *Manila Times,* February 13, 1964, March 3 and 4, 1964. Diokno's allegations were confirmed by a former high-level official of the Central Bank, as well as by a prominent banker (interviews, mid-1990). Calalang was at the time chairman of Filipinas Bank; in 1968, he succeeded Castillo as Central Bank governor.

March 1964 by dissolving the earlier board of trustees (of which Cuaderno was a member) and asking PNB to take over control of the bank.[27]

As the wheels of Philippine politics continued to turn, however, Pablo Roman rehabilitated his fortunes and climbed from the outs back up to a firmly inside position. In 1965—as a candidate for Congress who had just lost his bank—he authored a collection of speeches that introduced him as "a leader who is beyond reproach, a man whose best asset is goodwill and whose humility in a materialistic and unreasonable world seems totally strange." The story of Republic's closing is recast in terms of a valiant struggle for Philippine-controlled development: "Unique among the citizens of this country are those who can see no threats from foreign banking community [*sic*], but are instead concentrating on the affairs of their countrymen with the intent of harassing them. This colonial attitude must be smashed. . . . I regard [Republic Bank] as the unfailing ally of the Filipino businessman."[28]

By 1967, with Roman in Congress (and chairman of the House Committee on Banks, Currency, and Corporations!), a judge ordered that PNB could no longer continue to manage Republic Bank. As the *Manila Times* reported, "Roman was congratulated by his colleagues in the House as he distributed copies of the court order." The Central Bank tried to convince the courts that PNB should continue to manage the bank, but to no avail; Roman resumed the presidency of the bank in March 1968. In the meantime, Roman chalked up other important legal victories: in 1967, the Supreme Court threw out Damaso Perez's petition to have Roman prosecuted, and in 1970 an appeals court faulted the Central Bank both for its failure to investigate Republic Bank "in a discreet manner" in 1964, and for its subsequent adoption of "repressive measures which could only end in the liquidation" of the bank. In the view of the court, the Central Bank had a clear responsibility to rehabilitate Republic Bank (no matter, it seems, what its past sins may have been). At the same time that its halting efforts at bank supervision were being bashed by judiciary, the Central Bank could find little solace from the executive branch. In various ceremonies through the late 1960s and early 1970s, President Marcos called Republic Bank "one of the leading commercial banks in the country

---

[27] See Castillo, "Bankers and Their Responsibilities," 178. Castillo explained that individual government agencies, not the Central Bank, determined where they would deposit their funds. Nonetheless, the monetary authorities clearly failed to discharge properly even the limited responsibility of prescribing maximum limits on placements of government deposits in individual banks.

[28] *Power of Trust*, 2, 24, 53–54. In his book, "*Don* Pablo R. Roman" repeatedly invokes the name of Claro M. Recto, the senator who first gave inspiration to the nationalist cause. The introduction to his book proclaims Roman a "living legend to his people, in the same manner" as was the late Recto (p. 1). Roman was on the board of the Claro M. Recto Memorial Foundation.

today," and praised Roman as "a highly respected member of the banking community."[29]

The story of Emerito Ramos's Overseas Bank of Manila (OBM) offers a striking contrast to that of Roman's Republic Bank. Ramos—who presided over a family conglomerate with interests in such diverse ventures as urban real estate, mining, lumber, fishing, agribusiness, filmmaking, and trading with Japan—established his bank as a closed family corporation in January 1964 using money borrowed from a bank partially owned by a friend. His plans for further expansion had been constrained by a shortage of credit, he explained. "I thought that with a bank, my liquidity needs would be eased." Unfortunately for Ramos, however, he found that even with a bank he was unable to meet the demand for loans generated both by his own companies and by others who were "itching to start their own businesses." By the second year of the bank's operations, the total of all loans was more than twice that of all deposits. In 1965, the Central Bank suspended OBM's lending operations four times for chronic reserve deficiency, and began to charge high rates of interest on its chronic debts to the Central Bank's clearing house.

Despite the Central Bank's efforts to curb lending by the bank, however, Ramos continued to pursue a different course. By the end of 1964, he explains, he began "campaigning" for deposits to increase the bank's resources—first by offering hefty kickbacks to government officials to encourage them to deposit funds in his bank, and later (after the 1966 prohibition on the deposit of government funds in private banks) by offering similar incentives to private depositors. "Many depositors," he said, "got more in kickbacks than the value of their deposits." From his standpoint, the annual kickbacks of 22 percent to 26 percent plus 6 percent interest he paid to depositors was cheaper than the 36 percent penalty rate that the Central Bank charged for reserve deficiencies.[30]

Meanwhile, Ramos kept two sets of books so that the bank would not be caught for his various violations of Central Bank regulations, including "liquidity floor" requirements of banks holding government deposits. Creative bookkeeping, however, merely delayed further bank distress. Although he admits that the kickbacks "compounded" the bank's liquidity

[29] *Manila Times,* June 3, 14, and 21, 1967, July 8, 1967, and June 20, 1971; Tan, "The Uneven Hand," 81–83 (citing court opinions). The "repressive measures" cited by the court included high interest rates on emergency loans and restrictions on the scope of Republic Bank's business.

[30] Anonymous [said to be authored by the lawyers of Emerito M. Ramos Sr.], "The Story of the Overseas Bank of Manila (or Combank, now Boston Bank of the Philippines)," unpublished manuscript, n.d. [1987?], 1–3; Interviews, Emerito M. Ramos Sr., former chairman of Overseas Bank, February 24 and March 17, 1990; Norma B. Ong, "A Case Study of the Overseas Bank of Manila" (B.S.B.A. thesis, University of the Philippines College of Business Administration, 1969), 30–31; *Manila Times,* October 13, 1971.

problems, Ramos blames his bank's problems in large part on the Central Bank's failure to bail him out of his troubles with emergency funds.[31]

Unlike Roman, however, Ramos lacked effective inside connections with either the Palace or the Central Bank. Ramos had supported Macapagal rather than Marcos in the 1965 elections, and by his own description relations with the President were not good: *"hindi kami magka-vibes"* (we [Marcos and I] didn't have good vibes). As his debts mounted, those upon whom he was dependent for assistance eventually lost patience with the way he was mismanaging his bank—and ever more fearful of the consequences a bank failure might have on the rest of the banking system. In September 1967 President Marcos called Ramos and Governor Castillo to the Palace to discuss the problems of the bank. According to Ramos, after Marcos "said that he did not want to see any bank closed under his administration," the parties negotiated an agreement under which "the CB shall rehabilitate, normalize and stabilize OBM" in exchange for Ramos mortgaging two pieces of real estate as security for the Central Bank advances.[32] Castillo told Ramos that he had to execute the agreement "to stave off liquidation."

A Central Bank team (consisting of PNB and DBP officials) took over management of the bank in December, and soon asked incoming Central Bank Governor Alfonso Calalang for a P20 million emergency loan. But the Central Bank, which had already provided assistance of P49 million, coughed up (after much delay) only P13 million more. The new management publicly denounced what they considered an inadequate response, and in later years complained that "eight months of indecision made depositors lose faith and as a result, we were faced with more court suits and withdrawals than ever before."[33] It is not known why the Central Bank did not offer greater support to the new management, but one can speculate that once they obtained full access to all the bank's records they realized what a hopeless mess Ramos had created. According to the Superintendent of Banks, Overseas Bank "needed at least P206 million [at low interest rates] in order to merely reach a break-even point in its operations." With better supervisory capacity and strength, it is likely that they would have realized this much earlier—and not waited until 1967 and

[31] Interviews, Ramos, February 24 and March 17, 1990; "The Story of the Overseas Bank," 3, 12; *Manila Times,* August 28, 1968 and May 8, 1969. Ramos also blames the tight credit situation that developed in 1967; short-term credit, he points out, was being invested in long-term projects, and borrowers could not meet their obligations (p. 3).

[32] "The Story of the Overseas Bank," 4. According to Ramos, Pablo Roman had advised him not to submit to a VTA (since Roman felt that the PNB had taken advantage of Republic Bank) but Ramos apparently felt that he had no choice. Interviews, Ramos, February 24 and March 17, 1990. See also "The Story of the Overseas Bank," p. 7.

[33] *Manila Times,* August 15 and 21, 1968 and October 13, 1971; "Ramos vs. Central Bank of the Philippines," *Supreme Court Reports Annotated,* vol. 41, October 4, 1971, 579–80.

1. President Ferdinand E. Marcos confers with Central Bank Governor Alfonso Calalang (1968–1970), February 1968. Photo credit: From the Lopez Museum collection.

1968 to act against a bank that had already shown major problems as early as 1964 and 1965. By late July and early August the Monetary Board (apparently with President Marcos's support) passed resolutions excluding Overseas Bank from its clearing operations, suspending the bank's operations, and ordering the liquidation of the bank. Central Bank officials at the same time began to publicize their charges against Ramos: P35 million worth of unrecorded deposits; P33.2 million in loans to the Ramos family or enterprises and other bank officers and directors (an amount equal to 47.3 percent of the bank's total loan portfolio and 184 percent of paid-in capital); and a special internal slush fund into which deposits and loan repayments had frequently been diverted.[34]

[34] *Manila Times*, August 11, 15, 21, and 28, 1968; Ong, 60. Ramos, however, is adamant that his own obligations to Overseas Bank were P20 million (not P33 million)—plus an additional debt of P25 million formerly owed to the banks of friends (including Pablo Roman as well as Cardinal Santos, whose Archdiocese owned Philippine Trust) but later consolidated (at Central Bank urging) with the debts to his own bank. In Ramos's calculation, then, total debt to OBM equaled P45 million. Interviews, Ramos, February 24 and March 17, 1990. Despite all these loans, Ramos says that his liquidity needs were not met. It is quite likely that, just as he was borrowing from good friends' banks, good friends were also borrowing from Overseas Bank.

2. Bank run, October 1968. Among the banks facing serious problems at this time was Overseas Bank of Manila. Photo credit: From the Lopez Museum collection.

Although he lacked "good vibes" with the President, Ramos was by no means powerless in his dealings with the Palace. In one of the many strange twists that confirms the centrality of personalistic ties to Philippine politics, Ramos was close friends with influential newspaper columnist Teodoro F. Valencia, one of the regime's closest allies in the media. "Valencia," explains Ramos, "shielded me from the onslaughts of Marcos. That was the role that he performed." The connection was not strong enough "to get things from Marcos for me," says Ramos, "except defensive things." Valencia continued to run interference for Ramos as the OBM case simmered in the courts until the 1980s.[35]

Ramos's second source of defensive connections, he quite openly acknowledges, was good ties with members of the Supreme Court. At least two justices were friends through membership in the Civil Liberties Union

[35] "The Story of the Overseas Bank," 3, 25; Interviews, Ramos, February 24 and March 17, 1990. The connection continued to be useful after the declaration of martial law, in 1972, when Ramos was especially in need of a defender. As he explains, he had to sell off many of his businesses to survive. "Our business with Japan was shattered already. We couldn't get government approvals." When the regime began to go after his insurance company, Ramos asked Valencia to become president of the insurance firm. With Valencia there "to defend us against the Insurance Commission, the BIR [Bureau of Internal Revenue], and the Bureau of Customs," Ramos said, "they could not move on us."

3. Angry depositors of a savings bank demonstrate outside the old Central Bank building in June 1969, demanding that bank officials return their savings (earned by "blood and sweat"), and warning depositors of other institutions that they may be the next victims of fraud by thieving bank officials. Photo credit: From the Lopez Museum collection.

of the Philippines (CLUP), an organization that has been the strongest and most consistent exponent of the "nationalist" cause throughout much of the postwar era. Within two weeks after the unfavorable 1968 Monetary Board resolutions, Ramos obtained a restraining order from the Supreme Court halting liquidation proceedings. In September, the Senate initiated an investigation into the condition of the banking sector, and in the process helped bring on the first major bank run since the war. The damage was contained, as the Central Bank backed up depositors of all banks except Overseas Bank and a savings bank. But even in the wake of the bank run, Central Bank officials discounted the possibilities of rehabilitating Overseas Bank. "Like the chastity of a fallen woman," Governor Calalang told the press, "a fallen bank would be impossible to restore."[36] If Ramos had enjoyed better connections inside the Central Bank, one might specu-

[36] *Manila Times*, August 15 and September 14, 1968; *Central Bank of the Philippines*, 123, 231; Interviews, Ramos, February 24 and March 17, 1990. Even in its fallen state, Overseas Bank provided lucrative opportunities to some of the new management and some bank supervisors. According to one insider, bank depositors could sometimes withdraw their funds from the moribund banks at a discount (of roughly 10 percent); the discount was then pocketed by the official who had arranged the withdrawal. Anonymous interview, 1990.

4. Concerned depositors crowd a bank lobby in an October 1968 bank run. Photo credit: From the Lopez Museum collection.

late that there might have been a much earlier and much more concerted effort to restore the "chastity" of his bank; but since Ramos was on the outs with both the Central Bank and the Marcos administration, the chances of a full-scale rescue were slight. Unlike Roman, Ramos was never to get his bank back.

Like Roman, however, Ramos found the courts a most hospitable venue in which to continue to press his claims and beat back the efforts of the bank supervisors. A 1971 Supreme Court ruling castigated the Central Bank for its victimization of Ramos, drawing on the precedent of Roman's bank. Since "the CB had advanced funds to rehabilitate [Republic Bank] and allow it to resume operating," so was it committed to ensuring that Overseas Bank, as well, would be able to resume operation once again. At certain points, the decision suggests that no matter how much the bank violated Central Bank rules, the blame for the bank's sorry condition was to be borne by the Central Bank because it had (1) penalized the bank for violating its regulations and (2) given insufficient and delayed support to the bank in subsequent years. The Central Bank's order of liquidation was annulled, and Ramos scored a major victory over those who (in his view) had the audacity not to provide unlimited funds toward the rehabilitation of his bank.[37] The Central Bank was exasperated to be publicly humiliated by someone who had (in their view) so brazenly abused his own bank. As one former regulator recalled: "We had very clear evidences [*sic*], but there was nothing we could do. He was very influential with the Supreme Court." After Ramos won the 1971 case before the high tribunal, the official recalled, he had a "big party" to which the justices were invited.

When the Congress threatened to investigate the Central Bank's role in the case, Governor Gregorio Licaros (who succeeded Governor Calalang in January 1970) highlighted the degree of insider abuse and urged Overseas depositors to file claims against the bank.[38] Neither he nor Marcos seem to have had any liking for Ramos, and together they ignored the Supreme Court's order of rehabilitation. The result was a stalemate in which Ramos was as effective in frustrating the regulatory authority of the Central Bank as Licaros and other regulatory officials were in frustrating— often by extralegal means—Ramos's goal of regaining his bank and his valuable real estate properties. The bank did not reopen for business until Ramos sold out to a renowned Marcos crony, Herminio Disini, in 1980.

The cases of Republic Bank and Overseas Bank highlight certain important patterns in the politics of bank failures that have endured into subsequent years. Common political dynamics can be summarized as follows: (1) Banks are milked of loans by their owners to support related family enterprises. (2) After encountering liquidity problems, the bank owners expect unlimited help from the public treasury, and compare their own (insufficient) bailout to larger bailout packages in the past. (3) Bank owners express outrage if they are investigated by the Central Bank, and expect bad and fraudulent loans to be overlooked. (4) The Central Bank threatens, but fails, to prosecute bank owners for violation of its regulations. (5) The Central Bank claims to be impartial in its supervisory efforts, despite the clear centrality of political factors in determining the treatment of any given bank. (6) Courts declare the Central Bank to be arbitrary in its treatment of a given bank, and castigate it for not offering sufficient assistance to ensure a bank's survival (even errant banks are not to be liquidated, because such a process would undermine the confidence in the banking system that the Central Bank is duty-bound to preserve). (7) In later years, those who nonetheless lose their banks commonly point to appreciation of their assets (especially real estate holdings) to argue that their banks are no longer insolvent and should be reopened. Al-

[37] Interviews, Ramos, February 24 and March 17, 1990; *Supreme Court Reports Annotated*, vol. 41, October 4, 1971, 592, 595, 586, 592, 573, 590–91, 595, 601, 595–96. The vote was 6–2 in Ramos's favor, with three justices declining to take part in the case.

[38] Interview, former ranking Central Bank official, 1990; *Manila Times*, June 25, 1972. At this point, Licaros estimated loans to directors, officers, stockholders, and related interests at P72 million—more than double the Central Bank's 1968 estimate.

though new elements of the story get added in subsequent episodes, as we shall see, the basic failure of the Central Bank to effectively regulate the banking system endures. In the next section, I examine a bank organized to overcome ineffective Central Bank regulation by enforcing an effective system of regulation within.

Self-Regulation: Far East Bank and Trust Company

The story of Far East Bank and Trust Company begins with the story of its founder, Jose B. "Jobo" Fernandez Jr., who in the course of his career was to become the most prominent individual in the postwar banking sector. After completing his degree at Harvard Business School, Fernandez took up a position as assistant to the president of the Philippine Bank of Commerce (PBC) in 1949. It is hard to imagine a better place to begin a banking career or to develop close associations with the leading lights of the Philippine banking sector. Miguel Cuaderno, who had been president of PBC since it opened (as the first Filipino bank) in 1938, had just resigned to become the first governor of the Central Bank. Fernandez's boss, the new president of PBC, was Don Jose "Pepe" Cojuangco Sr., head of a prominent clan (and father of future president Corazon Cojuangco Aquino). Don Pepe had been a congressman and close associate of President Quezon in the 1930s; according to a nephew, the political ties that he forged in those years were later central to his "mastery of the art of lending."

Fernandez spent ten years with PBC, and eventually became the bank's vice president. Don Pepe, as he recalls, "gave me my first meaningful insights into the workings of Philippine business. I sat with him everyday [*sic*] and discussed [bank affairs] as well as . . . the political situation, the general economic situation. . . . If you are a banker, you must understand business—who's who, what's what, whatsoever they're doing, who's making money, how strong is his business, how weak is his business, who wields political patronage, who does not. All that. How a business survives. Don Pepe had always been in business all his life [and] he had been a politician all his life."[39]

But the lessons learned by young Fernandez were not entirely positive; in fact, perhaps the deepest imprint was made by lessons of a negative example: the deeply divisive interfamily and intrafamily feuds that rent Philippine Bank of Commerce in the years after the war. PBC was established in 1938 by three families: the Cojuangcos (with a 40 percent share),

---

[39] Licuanan, 134–39 (at 136, 138–39); Far East Bank and Trust Company, *A Vault of Memories: Far East Bank's Thirty-year Chronicle* (Manila, 1990), 24.

the Jacintos (40 percent), and the Rufinos (20 percent). The bank was one of the few to remain open during the war, but by 1945 its assets were nearly worthless. After the war, the bank got back on its feet with government assistance (from the Rehabilitation Finance Corporation) and a major equity contribution from the Cojuangco family, which had sold enough rum during and after the war (to both Japanese and American soldiers) to maintain the family fortune.

The Jacintos and Rufinos, on the other hand, were hard-hit by the devastation of the war, and were unable to keep up with the Cojuangcos. This led to major resentment, with the Jacintos and Rufinos wanting prewar arrangements respected and the Cojuangcos insisting on management power commensurate to their postwar contribution. By 1951, the Jacintos and Rufinos pulled out of PBC and started their own bank, Security Bank and Trust Company.

On the surface, it would seem that PBC now had everything going for it: a wealthy and prominent family was at the helm, and a former employee—Miguel Cuaderno—headed the agency that allocated all-important exchange licenses (while another, Nicanor Tomas, became superintendent of banks). By the late 1950s, however, the interfamily feuds of earlier years had been replaced by intrafamily feuds among the four Cojuangco brothers (Jose, Antonio, Juan, and Eduardo) who ran the bank. "It was like *Dallas*," explained one banker, as conflicts developed over the allocation of loans and other issues.[40]

Fernandez got out before the open split came in 1963 (when Don Pepe's branch of the family broke off to establish First United Bank). But the disputes seem to have had a great impact upon him. Years later, he spoke of it as a possible "indictment of Filipino business psychology," and lamented how the fierce infighting did not create an atmosphere able to nurture "true professionalization." Much of the fighting, he said, originated from "really extraneous matters that happened within the family [and were then] taken into the boardroom." When he left PBC in 1959, Fernandez set out to start a new bank "with a different capitalization and a different orientation." The key, he thought, was to bring together carefully chosen investors from many backgrounds and hope for "dynamic tension" among them. Fernandez knew that where one or a few families dominated a bank, it was easy to extract loans for family enterprises—regardless of what laws might be on the books. "That's why I wanted eleven directors . . . of different interests. I think that gave me the protection I needed from a greedy stockholder." Fernandez had no problems with situations in which one of the directors had a project for which he wanted a loan and the rest of the board approved it. But he did want to guard against rampant milk-

[40] Licuanan, 133–34, 138; Anonymous interview, former bank president, 1989.

ing of the loan portfolio, and quite self-consciously organized Far East Bank and Trust Company in such a way as to curb the tendencies of owners to milk their banks. In sum, Fernandez seems to have concluded that since external regulators didn't do a comprehensive job of bank supervision, he had to devise a system of self-regulation instead. To a greater extent than any other, Far East Bank avoided captivity to particular family interests by balancing its ownership among a relatively large number of family conglomerates.

While the bank was not among the most prominent in its early years, it soon became clear that by building a broader ownership base Fernandez had created an institution that ran far more smoothly than the feud-ridden Cojuangco bank he left behind.[41] Fernandez retained strong and enduring personal influence within the new bank—far exceeding his one-eleventh share of total start-up equity. At least one of his original investors seems to have been thoroughly converted to Fernandez's vision: "It is about time," he remarked, "that we have a bank that is professionally run . . . [and] not family-oriented."[42] But because there was only one Far East Bank—and instability from the likes of Republic Bank and Overseas Bank continued to rock the system—the Central Bank was forced to continue its efforts to strengthen the regulation of the system as a whole.

New Attempts at Regulation

In the wake of the problems caused by Republic Bank in 1964, Central Bank Governor Castillo lectured the bankers on their "responsibility to maintain and keep the public trust." He continued, "We must realize while so much interest in banking has been generated . . . the actuations [sic] of banks and bankers come under more searching public scrutiny. . . . [T]he furor sometime this year over alleged anomalies by the former management of one of our commercial banks. . . . incited a run on the bank . . . and threatened the stability of the more conservatively managed banks. The costly lessons learned from the operations of the "progressive bankers" . . . should not be forgotten so soon if this country is to develop under conditions of stability."   One of the most important of the "costly lessons" of Republic Bank, however, was that the system of bank regulation had serious deficiencies. New banks were sprouting at an unprecedented

[41] Interview, Fernandez, April 6, 1990. Throughout the period discussed in this chapter, Far East's position relative to other banks changed little: it was the sixteenth-largest bank at year-end 1960, and the thirteenth-largest bank at year-end 1972. The bank enjoyed quite favorable allocations of government deposits in its first full year of existence (1961), but seems not to have relied heavily on this source of funds in later years. SGV, *A Study of Commercial Banks in the Philippines,* various years.

[42] Licuanan, 137; *A Vault of Memories,* 26 (quoting Ramon del Rosario Jr.).

rate, thanks to Castillo's liberal policy of handing out bank licenses, and the Central Bank was becoming increasingly ill-equipped to supervise them. As Castillo himself admitted, the Central Bank's Department of Supervision and Examination "has not been able to expand in step with the tremendous growth of the banking system," as large numbers of its most experienced bank examiners were "pirated" by the commercial banks.

With such a weak bureaucratic apparatus to call upon, Castillo had little choice but to make an appeal to a sense of professional responsibility. "Rules and regulations can only go so far," he wrote, "and considerable areas of discretion lie within the scope of authority of the individual bankers themselves. . . . *Whether . . . Central Bank rules will be followed to the letter, or whether they will be bent, twisted or even broken for the sake of quick profits remains largely an individual management decision.* . . . A real banker would never evade his responsibility to maintain and keep inviolate the public trust, which is the very essence of his profession, and to cooperate with the monetary authorities in maintaining stability within which economic activity may proceed on an orderly and rational basis." Even in the best of circumstances, it is difficult to imagine an entire group of bankers responding to such an appeal, and foregoing profits merely for sake of professional responsibility. The particularly low degree of professionalization in the banking sector in the early 1960s made Castillo's appeal ring especially hollow (indeed, in his own estimation new banks lacked "efficient management personnel").[43]

Bankers, it is clear, had (and continue to have) little respect for those charged with the task of bank supervision. As one veteran banker quipped, bank supervisors "usually work with their adding machines more than anything else," while the Central Bank lawyers "are only good for notarization. They've never won cases." A former governor of the DBP labeled the bank supervisors "weak and unintelligent and sometimes downright stupid," and complained at how poorly they had investigated the credit records of bank founders.[44] It is little surprise, then, that those bankers determined to milk their own banks continued to do so. For many bankers, perhaps, the lessons of the bank failures of the 1960s were simple (in case they didn't know them already): enormous profits can be made from favorable access to the political machinery, and there is a good likelihood that obstacles presented by bank supervisors can eventually be overcome by favorable decisions from the courts.

Despite their inherent weakness, however, the Central Bank authorities

[43] Castillo, "Bankers and Their Responsibilities," 141–42 (emphasis added).
[44] Interview, Babst, May 3, 1990; Interview, Castro, February 14, 1990. See also Bernardino P. Ronquillo, "The Outlook for Credit and Banking in the Philippines," *The Fookien Times Yearbook 1968*, 96, 335.

were forced by the Republic Bank debacle to devote greater attention to major problems in the banking sector. "By the mid-1960s," note Patrick and Moreno, "the monetary authorities were concerned about the small size of banks, mismanagement, and the possibility (and actuality) of bank runs and financial crisis."[45] First, regulations on government deposits were gradually imposed, reducing one of the key government incentives that had helped lure new families into the banking system in the early 1960s. In 1964, after much equivocation, the Central Bank put limits on holdings of government deposits, and required a "liquidity floor" to support their receipt.[46] Simultaneously, maturing government deposits began to be withdrawn from private banks, and by 1966 private banks were no longer entitled to accept government funds. In the analysis of one banker, the system had spawned excessive inflation, and the allocation of deposits "had become scandalous."[47] The withdrawal of funds brought serious difficulties to many banks and contributed, by 1965, to "the worst bank liquidity crisis which the Philippines had ever seen."[48]

Second, the problem of weak capitalization was a growing concern to Central Bank authorities, who had long given out bank licenses without requiring high levels of minimum capitalization. In 1966, banks were given four years to increase their minimum capitalization to P20 million, but regulatory officials acknowledged that there was little difficulty meeting this new requirement.[49] In short, the new regulations were too weak to have much impact. As the next chapter explains, it was not until the declaration of martial law in 1972 that the regulatory authorities could even begin to contemplate seriously addressing the problem of low capitalization.

Third, after the Republic Bank scandal the Central Bank attempted to provide stronger sanctions against DOSRI loans—loans to directors, of-

[45] Patrick and Moreno, 326. These concerns, they noted in the early 1980s, are "continuing to this day."

[46] The effective date of the regulation was repeatedly delayed, and even after it took effect the Central Bank reported widespread deficiencies in the "liquidity floor" requirement. Central Bank Circulars No. 163 (February 7, 1964), 166 (March 20, 1964), 175 (June 3, 1964), 179 (July 8, 1964), and 180 (August 1964); Central Bank Memorandum to All Commercial Banks, June 18, 1964; Central Bank, *Annual Report, 1964,* 8.

[47] Castillo, "Bankers and Their Responsibilities," 178; Interview, Babst, May 3, 1990.

[48] Andres K. Roxas, "The Commercial Banking System: Past and Future," in "Top 100 Corporations" (a *Manila Chronicle* special report), September 22, 1969, 20–21 (at 20); Central Bank Circulars 200 (June 14, 1965) and 220 (April 15, 1966); Emmanuel Tiu Santos, "The Banking System: Its Structure, Functions and Performance," in *The Fookien Times Yearbook 1967,* 144, 146–48. Early in 1964, the Central Bank was forced to make special advances to banks especially hard-hit by the withdrawal of government deposits. Central Bank, *Annual Report, 1964,* 9.

[49] Central Bank, Memorandum to Authorized Agent Banks, August 22, 1966; Interview, Valenzuela, March 22, 1990.

ficers, stockholders, and related interests.[50] DOSRI regulations in the General Banking Act of 1948 were both weak and weakly enforced; late in 1964, the Central Bank issued a circular that specified its requirements more clearly. In 1965, anti-DOSRI provisions were applied to loans extended to the corporations in which bank directors, officers, and stockholders held equity.[51] But as subsequent cases were to reveal, the Central Bank was far from capable of enforcing its own rules. Fourth and most important, the Central Bank "quietly imposed" a "moratorium on the licensing of new commercial banks" at some point in late 1965.[52] After the rapid proliferation of bank licenses since 1961, the Central Bank seems to have finally decided to shift its attention from expanding the number of banks to addressing the growing problems of those banks already in the system.

The even greater instability caused by the Overseas Bank failure brought further pressures for reform. In addition to rocking the system as a whole, the Overseas Bank affair left behind two major sets of losers: first, the smaller depositors (who probably did not enjoy under-the-table kickbacks when they first placed their money in the bank), and taxpayers (whose funds were squandered with impunity). The Central Bank responded to the problems of Overseas Bank by pushing for the establishment of the Philippine Deposit Insurance Corporation, in 1969.[53] The PDIC, however, was merely a mild (and ultimately rather ineffectual) palliative, and one veteran banker responded to the Overseas Bank case with demands for far more fundamental reform of the banking sector. In early 1969, former Finance Secretary Pio Pedrosa organized the National Association of Bank Depositors, which called for (1) improving the Central Bank's staff of bank examiners, so that examinations could take place at least twice a year; (2) providing greater punitive powers to the superintendent of banks; and (3) implementing more effective curbs on DOSRI abuses. "Unless these corrective measures are . . . immediately implemented," Pedrosa warned,

[50] Central Bank Circular 183, September 4, 1964; and Central Bank Circular 199, May 27, 1965.

[51] Republic Act 337 ("The General Banking Act"), Section 83; Central Bank Circulars No. 183 (September 4, 1964) and 199 (May 27, 1965).

[52] Roxas, 20. So quiet was this moratorium, in fact, that it is difficult to find any reference to it in 1965 Central Bank documents. In August 1966, however, the Monetary Board issued a memorandum stating that no new commercial banks will be allowed in the Greater Manila area "until the end of 1967." If this prohibition was extended in later years, there seems to be no formal record of it. Memorandum to Authorized Agent Banks, August 22, 1966.

[53] Although legislation for the PDIC had first been passed in 1963, "it was never really implemented, since the entity was set up with a skeleton staff, without the resources to come to the aid of troubled banks." Governor Calalang was successful in persuading President Marcos and the Congress to provide resources to the PDIC, and it began to insure small deposits up to P10,000. *Central Bank of the Philippines: January 3, 1949—January 3, 1974* (Manila: Central Bank of the Philippines, 1974), 231.

"the irregularities that rocked . . . the foundation of the local banking system in recent months would persist and generate greater confusion in the national economy."[54] As we shall see in subsequent chapters, "greater confusion" was indeed yet to come.

Conclusion

Implicit in Pedrosa's list of corrective measures was an awareness of two major problems. First, many family conglomerates were milking the loan portfolios of their own banks. In the course of the 1960s it became ever more apparent that the roots of bank instability were to be found, first of all, in the purposes for which banks were initially formed. As Central Bank Governor Licaros was later to explain, "the average Filipino banker is in banking not for banking profits; he uses his bank for allied businesses."[55] Loyalty was rarely to banking per se, but rather to the family conglomerate that the bank was meant to serve. The most abused banks soon encountered serious liquidity problems. Second, the Central Bank lacked the strength and capacity to regulate the banks effectively and curb behavior that was creating instability for the banking system as a whole. As the episodes in this chapter reveal, the mushrooming of family-owned banks in the early 1960s was accompanied—and followed—by a high degree of bank instability. Indeed, by the end of the decade one scholar observed that the Philippines "has probably had more financial scandals or financial institutions in distress than any other Southeast Asian country."[56] Like the American bank robber Willie Sutton, many families had gone into banking "because that's where the money is." The regulations of an ineffectual bureaucratic apparatus were not going to deter them from using their banks as a source of funds for related family enterprises, and the problem of bank instability endured.

In the course of only half a decade, there had been major changes in the structure of the financial system, as a host of new entrants—representative of powerful social forces—had flocked to the banking industry. Private domestic commercial banks were increasing their dominance within the system as a whole, although PNB and the four foreign banks remained very influential actors. In the midst of this rapid change, regulatory capacity

[54] *Daily Mirror*, January 4, 1969 (the exact wording of the quote is from the *Daily Mirror*, not from Pedrosa). Pedrosa was at the time president of Prudential Bank and Trust Company, one of the most conservative and stable of the family-owned banks. He had been finance secretary between 1949 and 1951 (during the Quirino administration).

[55] *FEER*, April 7, 1978, 80 (the exact wording of the quote is from *FEER*, not Licaros).

[56] Robert F. Emery, *The Financial Institutions of Southeast Asia: A Country-by-Country Study*, (New York: Praeger Publishers, 1970), 482.

seems to have actually weakened; to the extent that regulation existed, it had to be provided internally.

Ultimately, the problems that emerged from the banking sector in the 1960s were merely symptomatic of fundamental characteristics of the larger Philippine political economy; as this book argues, it is especially important to understand the predatory strength of the oligarchy and the patrimonial nature of the state. First, the "open sesame" of new bank licensing was determined more by the needs of the diversified conglomerates of major oligarchic families than by the imperatives of national development. In historical context, the expansion of the banking sector was merely one more source of booty for an oligarchy that had long preyed on the state in order to promote its own capital accumulation. Second, the favor and disfavor of those currently holding official position was clearly a central determinant of a bank's success or failure. When state agencies such as the Central Bank or the executive branch did flex their muscles, the exercise of this power was highly uneven—more often determined by personalistic factors than by institutional interest. In short, the "open sesame" and financial instability that surfaced in the 1960s can be traced to deeply entrenched relations of power and characteristics of the state; until these obstacles are challenged effectively, even the most sincere and well-designed attempts at "corrective measures" are unlikely to enjoy sustained success.

CHAPTER SIX

Bank Reform and Crony Abuses:
The Martial Law Regime Deals
with the Banking Sector, 1972–1980

In the course of the 1960s, the Central Bank presided over the creation of a family-based banking system prone to high levels of instability. As demonstrated above, it was unable to resolve the many problems that this system spawned. Given the profound weakness of regulators vis-à-vis the regulated, one might surmise that the only period in the postwar Philippines when the state might have been able to effect serious reforms in the banking industry was after the declaration of martial law by President Marcos in September 1972. A Joint IMF-CBP Banking Survey Commission had just completed the first comprehensive effort to address the problems of weak family-owned banks, and with few modifications its recommendations were promulgated, by decree, in November. Marcos gave public support to the financial reform measures and later included them among the major achievements of his "New Society."[1] Banking patterns of the "old society," he declared, frequently meant that a small group of officers and stockholders "pre-empted limited credit facilities to the detriment of more productive but perhaps less opportunely-situated users of credit. This situation has contributed considerably to lopsided incomes and to widen the already huge gap between the rich and the poor. . . . [F]unds are borrowed ostensibly to engage in priority projects but in reality are spent not for investment but for consumption goods such as mansions, so-called high living and travel abroad. This is not only irresponsible but downright criminal under certain circumstances. . . . [T]hese

---

[1] "After we instituted martial law on September 21st, 1972 to stave off our most serious social and political crisis in post-war years," declared Marcos in a January 1974 speech, "I vigorously pushed long delayed economic reforms. Government was overhauled. Inefficient and corrupt officials were weeded out. Tax and tariff codes were made more progressive. Banking laws were revised. Agrarian reform was implemented. Peace and order were restored." *CB News Digest,* January 3, 1974, 3.

borrowers are often welchers and remain delinquent without any qualms at all."

Yet as the history of his now legendary system of crony capitalism reveals, President Marcos's personal interests took clear precedence over the rationalization of the Philippine political economy; in fact, by the end of his term he and his wife had an almost unparalleled worldwide reputation as profligate borrowers, wild spendthrifts, and brazen "welchers." Martial law created many new opportunities for reform, but at the same time facilitated the capture of the state by new—and more centralized—regime interests. As Marcos's chief ideologue remarked, Marcos "believed he could have a vision for society . . . and still loot it."[2] In the end, the Marcos regime's love of looting swamped all serious efforts at reform, and the problems of bank instability endured.

This chapter begins with analysis of the larger political economy both prior to and after the declaration of martial law in 1972. The second section details the major components of the banking reforms of the early 1970s, the most important of which were efforts to address the problems of weak family-owned banks. In the third section, I discuss the recurring episodes of bank instability, especially those that rocked the financial system in the mid-1970s. The chapter concludes with an examination of the rise of cronyism, as the favoritism already prevalent in the 1950s and 1960s blossomed into unprecedented levels of rapaciousness among those enjoying closest access to the political machinery.

Martial Law and the Centralization of Patrimonial Plunder

Thus far, we have seen that the process of decontrol in the early 1960s preserved a stagnant program of import-substitution industrialization—now moving beyond its "easy phase"—without laying new foundations for export-oriented growth. Exports were buoyed in the short term by natural resource exploitation (in mining and logging), but by 1967 exports became sluggish once again. At decade's end, yet another balance-of-payments crisis sent the economy reeling. The crisis was triggered by one politician's particularly shameless efforts to maintain a grasp over the reins of the political machinery. To ensure his reelection in 1969, President Marcos raided the public treasury and thereby hastened the arrival of the young republic's third major balance-of-payments crisis. As his defeated opponent grumbled, "[We were] out-gooned, out-gunned and out-gold."[3]

[2] *CB News Digest,* March 27, 1973, 3–4; Interview, Adrian Cristobal, June 19, 1989.
[3] John H. Power and Gerardo P. Sicat, *The Philippines: Industrialization and Trade Policies* (New York: Oxford University Press, 1971), 50; Emmanuel S. de Dios, "A Political Economy of Philippine Policy-Making," *Economic Policy-Making in the Asia-Pacific Region,* ed. John W.

The economy simply could not support the political system; enormous resources were invested in appropriating wealth that had already been produced, and insufficient resources were left over for investment in production itself. Consistent with James Scott's model of "patron-client democracy," the state had a weak revenue base but was nonetheless faced with "intense distributive pressures . . . especially in election years." In 1969, all candidates (led by Marcos) reportedly spent the equivalent of nearly one-fourth of the national budget. While the economy stagnated, demand for patronage resources was probably heightened by a proliferation in the number of local candidates.[4]

The post-election balance-of-payments crisis was followed by a devaluation, which fueled inflation. This, in turn, heightened mass demands for change.[5] In a period of constricted opportunity, the oligarchs became especially vicious in clawing for the booty of state. Marcos, in particular, was determined to extend his tenure beyond the two-term limit prescribed by the 1935 constitution. "American-era inhibitions slackened," notes Anderson, and "it was only a matter of time before someone would break the rules and try to set himself up as Supreme Cacique for Life."

In the short term, martial law resolved the overload on the state's "distributive capacity": expensive intra-elite electoral competition was eliminated, and mass demands immediately restricted. At the same time, Marcos worked on the supply side problems of the system's overload, and for a full decade very adroitly managed to extract enormous quantities of

---

Langford and K. Lorne Brownsey (Halifax, Nova Scotia: The Institute for Research on Public Policy, 1990), 111–12; and Jose Veloso Abueva, "The Philippines: Tradition and Change," *Asian Survey* (1970), 56–64, at 62. On economic performance in this period, see Romeo M. Bautista, John H. Power, and Associates, eds., *Industrial Promotion Policies in the Philippines* (Metro Manila: Philippine Institute for Development Studies, 1979), 5–9; and Manuel F. Montes, "Financing Development: The 'Democratic' versus the 'Corporatist' Approach in the Philippines," *The Political Economy of Fiscal Policy,* ed. Miguel Urrutia, Shinichi Ichimura, and Setsuko Yukawa (Tokyo: The United Nations University, 1989), 88–89.

[4] James C. Scott, "Patron-Client Politics and Political Change in Southeast Asia," in *Friends, Followers, and Factions,* ed. Steffen W. Schmidt et al. (Berkeley: University of California Press, 1977), 143; David Wurfel, *Filipino Politics: Development and Decay* (Ithaca, N.Y.: Cornell University Press, 1988), 100; Thomas C. Nowak and Kay A. Snyder, "Clientelist Politics in the Philippines: Integration or Instability," *American Political Science Review* 68 (1974), 1147–1170, at 1151–54. The revenue problems are systemic: "A regime that is dependent on its particularistic distributive capacity . . . [will] have a most difficult time raising revenue from internal taxation. A rise in direct taxation would threaten their base of support, and in fact, they are notorious for the undercollection of revenues due them, since favors to their clients often take the form of either leaving them off local tax rolls or ignoring debts they owe the government. . . . a stagnating economy or declining world prices [threatens] the entire structure" (Scott, 143).

[5] These demands related both to domestic politics and to ongoing neocolonial ties to the United States. A major focus of both contention and uncertainty was the status of U.S. investments in the country, since "parity rights" granted in 1946 were due to expire in 1974. See Stephen Rosskamm Shalom, *The United States and the Philippines: A Study of Neocolonialism* (Philadelphia: Institute for the Study of Human Issues, 1981), 165–67.

funds from the IMF and World Bank, bilateral donors, and commercial banks. He began martial law with the good fortune of high international commodity prices, which "generated windfall profits for the Philippine economic elite, dispelling whatever doubts it still had about the Marcos dictatorship."[6] Later in the decade, the regime took full advantage of the availability of cheap petrodollars, at negative real rates of interest.

But good fortune alone cannot explain the regime's success. Two generations of Filipino oligarchs had tapped American patronage to boost their personal positions domestically, but among postwar leaders Marcos displayed particularly keen insights into the nature of the neocolonial bond—and knew that U.S. strategic needs presented ample opportunity for private gain.[7] Especially at a time when the military bases were offering such important support to U.S. forces in Vietnam, Marcos could approach Washington aid-givers from a strong position. Indeed, the United States rewarded martial law with very large increases in grants and loans.[8]

At the same time, close relations with the United States assisted Marcos's efforts to cultivate close relations with the IMF and the World Bank. He brought a corps of technocrats into his government and promulgated a series of reform agendas that ensured the steady flow of multilateral and commercial bank loans. Marcos technocrats were "intensely admired figures" within these institutions, one banker reports, but over time it became increasingly evident that "the agenda was ultimately set by business and political interests closer to the Palace."[9] As economist Raul Fabella ex-

[6] Benedict Anderson, "Cacique Democracy and the Philippines: Origins and Dreams," *New Left Review* no. 169 (May/June 1988), 3–33, at 18; Nowak and Snyder, 1170; Rigoberto Tiglao, "The Consolidation of the Dictatorship," in *Dictatorship and Revolution: Roots of People's Power*, ed. Aurora Javate-de Dios, Petronilo Bn. Daroy, and Lorna Kalaw-Tirol (Metro Manila: Conspectus Foundation Incorporated, 1988), 26–69, at 38.

[7] On the historical process of tapping American patronage, see Ruby R. Paredes, ed., *Philippine Colonial Democracy*, Yale University Southeast Asia Studies Monograph No. 32 (New Haven, 1989). Shalom documents neocolonial ties, while Raymond Bonner highlights the Marcoses' skill in playing to the Washington crowd. See his *Waltzing with a Dictator: The Marcoses and the Making of American Policy* (New York: Times Books, 1987).

[8] Anderson, 21; Wurfel, 191. Although the primary means by which Marcos ingratiated himself to the United States was by providing unhampered access to the military bases, he also resolved important issues related to the status of U.S. assets in the Philippines in favor of U.S. investors. See Charles W. Lindsey, "The Philippine State and Transnational Investment," *Bulletin of Concerned Asian Scholars* 19, no. 2 (1987): 24–41, at 27; and Shalom, 169–170, 176–77.

[9] Stephan Haggard, "The Political Economy of the Philippine Debt Crisis," in *Economic Crisis and Policy Choice: The Politics of Adjustment in the Third World*, ed. Joan Nelson (Princeton: Princeton University Press, 1990), 215–55, at 219; William H. Overholt, "Pressures and Policies: Prospects for Cory Aquino's Philippines," in *Rebuilding a Nation: Philippine Challenges and American Policy*, ed. Carl H. Landé (Washington, D.C.: The Washington Institute Press, 1987), 89–110, at 98; and de Dios, "Policy Making," 115. On the consistent circumvention of IMF advice, see Mark Thompson and Gregory Slayton, "An Essay on Credit Arrangements Between the IMF and the Republic of the Philippines: 1970–1983," *Philippine Review of Economics and Business* 22 (1985), 59–81. The rise of the technocrats in the previous decade

plains, technocrats provided the public rhetoric to keep the loans flowing in, but regime interests "then allowed the *unconstrained introduction of exceptions* that made complete mockery of the spirit and letter of the plans."[10]

While the World Bank and the IMF were more comfortable with the technocrats, they ended up providing enormous support to the crony system.[11] On the whole, Marcos was usually able to take the money and run. Certain elements of the externally induced reform agendas were initiated in the early 1980s, when the scarcity of funds on international capital markets increased the leverage of multilateral institutions. But Marcos did not bring any fundamental shift in development policy—there was continued promotion of exports, but at the same time continued protection of ISI firms. Manufactured exports did, indeed, post major gains in the late 1970s and 1980s, but the major supporters, the technocrats and the multilateral agencies, were unable to do much more than create one more avenue of diversification for the major family conglomerates to pursue. The nontraditional exports were not only dominated by the already established family conglomerates; they were also so highly import dependent that their existence did not create a clear new constituency demanding an end to the longstanding overvaluation of the peso.[12] As long as external funds were readily available, it was most expedient simply to adopt the strategy of "debt-driven growth." Throughout the Marcos years, de Dios concludes, "the issue of the development strategy could be essentially avoided."[13]

The logic of the Marcos regime, like the logic of the earlier Philippine political economy, is much better understood in terms of strategies of accumulation by diversified family conglomerates than in terms of battles among coherent economic strategies or sectors. Marcos and his cronies used access to the political machinery to accumulate wealth, and—like the major families of the pre–martial law years—had little loyalty to any particular sector. The cronyism of the Marcos regime is more obvious than

is chronicled in Amando Doronila, *The State, Economic Transformation, and Political Change in the Philippines, 1946–1972* (Singapore: Oxford University Press, 1992), 133–138.

[10] Raul V. Fabella, "Trade and Industry Reforms in the Philippines: Process and Performance," in *Philippine Macroeconomic Perspective: Developments and Policies,* ed. Manuel F. Montes and Hideyoshi Sakai (Tokyo: Institute of Developing Economies, 1989) 183–214, at 197 (emphasis added).

[11] As de Dios writes: "There were many instances when the more 'irrational', 'inefficient', at times blatantly corrupt, aspects of the dictatorship were countenanced or accommodated by these institutions, particularly its net lending operations and crony bail-outs." Emmanuel S. de Dios, "The Erosion of the Dictatorship," in Javate-de Dios et al., 122.

[12] See Manuel F. Montes, "Philippine Structural Adjustments, 1970–1987," in Montes and Sakai, 45–90, at 71–73; World Bank, "Philippines Staff Appraisal Report on the Industrial Finance Project," Report No. 3331-PH (Washington, 1981), 1; and de Dios, "Erosion," 119–120.

[13] The term "debt-driven growth" comes from Montes, "Financing Development," 90; de Dios, "Philippine Policy-Making," 116.

cronyism of either the pre-1972 period or post-1986 years, since the regime had more centralized control over the state apparatus and enjoyed much longer tenure in office. But amid important change in the political economy was a remarkable continuity in the nature of business-government relations; as de Dios explains, "the crony phenomenon was no more than a logical extension and culmination of the premartial law process of using the political machinery to accumulate wealth."[14]

In declaring martial law, Marcos promised to respond to the widespread disillusionment with the political system and the major families that had presided over it. He pledged reforms that would usher in equality of opportunity and save the country from "an oligarchy that appropriated for itself all power and bounty."[15] But while Marcos did, indeed, tame selected oligarchs most threatening to his regime, a new oligarchy (of Marcos and his relatives and cronies) achieved dominance within many economic sectors. In exchange for the dismantling of democratic institutions, the Filipino people enjoyed only fleeting economic gain. While foreign loans sustained growth in the 1970s, crony abuses brought economic disaster in the early 1980s. Most fundamentally, martial law perpetuated important shortcomings of Philippine capitalism, because Marcos was merely expanding on earlier patterns of patrimonial plunder. Particularistic demands continued to prevail, with the difference that one ruler was now appropriating a much larger proportion of the state apparatus toward the service of his own private ends. The failure of reforms and the triumph of a more centralized form of patrimonial plunder becomes especially evident in surveying the evolution of the Philippine banking sector in these early years of the martial law regime.

The Reforms of the Early 1970s

The Joint IMF-CBP Banking Commission was first convened in December 1971, and submitted its ninety-nine recommendations to President Marcos in August 1972—only four weeks before the declaration of martial law. The commission was made up of three representatives from the IMF as well as Armand V. Fabella (co-chairman), Jose B. Fernandez (president of the Bankers Association of the Philippines), and a Central Bank representative. The commission's recommendations—almost all of which were

[14] De Dios, "Philippine Policy-Making," 114. *Crony* is used to describe those whose positions are particularly favored by the current regime, regardless of their origins. An *oligarch* may not be a current crony but in either case has already established his or her fortune in earlier dispensations. Under the Marcos regime, both "old oligarchs" and "new men" gained crony status, and they were referred to collectively as the *new oligarchy*.

[15] Ferdinand E. Marcos, *The Democratic Revolution in the Philippines* (Englewood Cliffs, N.J.: Prentice-Hall International, 1979 [originally printed 1974]), 6.

later promulgated by presidential decree—included three particularly important elements.

First, they led to changes in the composition of the Monetary Board, the governing body of the Central Bank. The governor of the Central Bank replaced the secretary of finance as the board's chairman, a seemingly uncontroversial change (even in the Finance Department) that merely affirmed the governor's longstanding dominance of the Board and the relatively weaker institutional base of the Finance Department.[16] In addition, it was decided that neither the president of the PNB nor the chairman of the DBP should remain on the Monetary Board, because their membership "puts them in the improper situation of performing the role of supervisor and supervised."[17] Despite this change, the Central Bank—as "supervisor"—seems to have provided little obstacle to the regime's blatant abuse of these state banks.

Second, the supervisory reach of the Central Bank was extended to include the money market. The money market was an important element of the Philippine financial system that had been developed by so-called investment houses since the 1960s. The money market was an unregulated arena of financial intermediation involving short-term instruments, and its creation was in direct response to interest rate ceilings imposed by usury laws (which, with climbing interest rates, became effective in the mid-1960s). By providing large investors with an easy means of evading the ceilings, it led to the growth of a two-tiered system: large investors could obtain market rates in the money market, but the smaller savings deposits of the general public remained at controlled, below-market rates.[18] The earnings

---

[16] Cesar Virata, the finance secretary at the time, actually claims that he was the one to suggest this change. Ever since the time of Cuaderno, he explained, the Central Bank governor had monopolized the right to determine the agenda of the Monetary Board meetings so as to ensure that the finance secretary would not be able to dominate him. Interview, Cesar Virata, former prime minister and finance minister, May 24, 1991. The Finance Department does not have a strong institutional base, and important bureaus (internal revenue and customs) that nominally fall under its jurisdiction are actually controlled by the Office of the President. Heads of Finance "spend most of their time at the Central Bank," and very little time at their offices in the antiquated Department of Finance building. Anonymous interview, Finance Department official, 1989.

[17] Joint IMF-CBP Banking Survey Commission, *Recommendations of the Joint IMF-CBP Banking Survey Commission on the Philippine Financial System* (Manila: Central Bank of the Philippines, 1972), 63. The new Monetary Board was composed of the Central Bank governor, the secretary (later minister) of finance, the head of the National Economic Development Authority (NEDA), the chair of the Board of Investments (BOI), and "three part-time members from the private sector." The president retained the power to replace the heads of NEDA and the BOI with other officials as he "may determine." Presidential Decree No. 72, November 29, 1972.

[18] See Jaime C. Laya, "Floating Interest Rates in the Eighties: A New Dimension in the Philippine Financial System," *Fookien Times Philippines Yearbook 1981–82*, 147; Edita A. Tan, "Philippine Monetary Policy and Aspects of the Financial Market: A Review of the Literature," in *PIDS Survey of Development Research I* (Metro Manila: Philippine Institute for Development

of investment houses generally depended overwhelmingly on the money market (and, given the weakness of the stock markets, very little on traditional merchant bank dealings in securities and equities).

Because investment houses were able to skirt ceilings and offer higher interest rates, investors flocked to their doors and observers marveled at their sophistication. The money market is estimated to have grown 34 percent per year between 1966 and 1973—providing the first serious competition to the deposit-generating capacity of the commercial banks.[19] By the early 1970s, explains Fabella, "the banks were up in arms at the incursions of the investment houses," and pressed for a "rationalization" of the system so they "would have a decent chance at survival." They resented the fact that an unregulated and growing segment of the financial system was able to outbid them for deposits, and able to charge higher rates of interest for loans.[20] When investment houses began to be regulated by the Central Bank in 1972 and the instruments of the money market were officially recognized as "deposit substitutes," many commercial banks proceeded to get a piece of the action by either setting up their own investment houses or developing close ties with existing houses. Between roughly 1972 and 1974, some twelve new investment houses were formed, many of which had close ties to commercial banks.[21]

As part of this process, commercial banks came to rely to a greater extent on money market instruments as both a source of funds and as a more lucrative investment outlet. There was rapid growth in deposit substitutes, and by 1974 they were equivalent to 80 percent of the total of time and savings deposits. One 1975 report describes the money market as "the vigorous tail which wags a rather sickly dog. [It] has grown in strength and importance because of the sheer inadequacy of other mechanisms . . . [as

---

Studies, 1980), 177. The money market helped to bridge the gap between the formal and informal credit markets, and seems to have played an especially important role in mobilizing and allocating funds among Chinese-Filipino entrepreneurs. See Manuel F. Montes and Johnny Noe E. Ravalo, "The Philippines," in *Financial Systems and Economic Policy in Developing Countries,* ed. Stephan Haggard and Chung H. Lee (Ithaca, N.Y.: Cornell University Press, 1995), 164–65.

[19] Victoria S. Licuanan, *An Analysis of the Institutional Framework of the Philippine Short-term Financial Markets* (Manila: Philippine Institute for Development Studies, 1986), 6, 18; *Asian Finance,* December 15, 1977–January 14, 1978, 75; *Euromoney,* August 1976, xxxi; *FEER,* September 13, 1974, 45; Hugh Patrick and Honorata A. Moreno, "Philippine Private Domestic Commercial Banking, 1946–80, in the Light of Japanese Experience," in *Japan and the Developing Countries: A Comparative Analysis,* ed. Kazushi Ohkawa and Gustav Ranis (New York: Basil Blackwell, 1985), 323, and *FEER,* August 8, 1975, 49.

[20] The investment houses, it must be noted, were not alone in getting around the usury laws. Statutory ceilings were evaded not only through the use of unregulated money market instruments, but also through service fees and other charges that commercial banks required of their lenders. See National Economic Council et al., *Report of the Inter-Agency Committee on the Study of Interest Rates* (Manila: National Economic Council, 1971), 2, 56–62.

[21] Interview, Armand Fabella, June 8, 1990; *FEER,* September 13, 1974, 63.

evidenced by] antiquated banking laws; weak, family-oriented banks; [and] a low level of personal savings. . . . [S]ome commercial banks fund themselves as much through the money market . . . as through more normal avenues as deposits from the public."[22]

The reforms served to legitimize a very unstable form of financial intermediation. Before 1972, unregulated transactions in the money market had been dominated by the investment houses; after 1972, nominally regulated transactions in the money market permeated the entire financial system—and especially the commercial banks that dominated that system. By 1974, Governor Licaros was voicing concern over the "anomaly" in which "millions of pesos are placed by one financial institution with another [in the money market] on the strength of a mere telephone call, but a personal loan of P1,000 [from a bank] has to be fully documented."[23] The combination of enduring DOSRI abuses and increasing reliance on money market funds created major problems of bank instability by mid-decade.

Third, and of greatest significance, the commission proposed a major reform agenda to address weaknesses in the banking sector that had caused major problems of instability in the 1960s. Their goal was to encourage banks to improve themselves, and also to strengthen the capacity of the Central Bank to regulate the banks. According to co-chairman Fabella, the reformers first divided all private domestic banks into three categories: "brown" (Filipino), "yellow" (Filipino of Chinese descent), and "white" (Filipino of Spanish or American descent). "We were concerned that [the brown banks] were being used as part of a conglomerate, and used to support the projects the family were involved in. . . . We wanted to give them a fighting chance [to improve], but not let them preserve their fiefdom. . . . The family banks just wanted to be a big frog in a small pond—they didn't want to be disturbed."[24]

There were four major ways in which the final reform package sought to force these banks to improve themselves: (1) increased minimum capitalization requirements (to P100 million, both to strengthen the banks and to encourage mergers and foreign equity infusions); (2) infusion of foreign equity (foreign banks were allowed to invest in the domestic banking

[22] Licuanan, 8, 18, 37; World Bank–International Monetary Fund, *The Philippines: Aspects of the Financial Sector* (Washington, D.C.: The World Bank, 1980), 26, 61; *FEER*, August 8, 1975, 50.

[23] *CB Review*, August 13, 1974, 7; see also *FEER*, August 16, 1974, 37.

[24] Interview, Fabella, June 8, 1990. There were, of course, many yellow banks that were family-owned—and supporting family projects—but improving them seems not to have been nearly as important a goal of the reformers. The Chinese-Filipino banks were not, however, bereft of support; as we shall see, Governor Licaros provided many of them with very favorable access to Central Bank resources through the course of the decade. Fabella also noted that there was one Filipino bank, Far East Bank and Trust Company, with fairly broad ownership.

industry up to 30 percent of total equity—or 40 percent with special permission from the President—thus overturning the 1957 regulation requiring 100 percent Filipino ownership of all new banks); (3) mergers; and (4) diffusion of ownership within banks. The first two elements were added by Governor Licaros to Marcos's November 1972 presidential decrees, but the latter two were part of the commission's original recommendations. According to Fabella, the commission had upheld the 1957 prohibition on new foreign equity; Licaros, however, wanted foreign banks in the system because he felt that they "will not go in for the shenanigans [and] . . . will be a stabilizing influence." Licaros also worried that the family banks were too small, and would "go under with the first big wave."[25] In addition to these reforms, the Central Bank declared that no new bank licenses were to be allocated, thus formalizing the informal cap on new banks imposed in 1965.[26]

After the reforms were promulgated, Fabella headed the Central Bank Advisory Group, which oversaw banking reform efforts throughout the 1970s. The 1973 increase in minimum capitalization requirements was an important impetus for foreign investment, and within three years thirteen foreign banks infused equity into ten local banks. Unfortunately, however, the opening to foreign equity was not entirely successful in achieving Licaros's aim of stabilizing the banking system. In general, amicable ties developed only among banks that were already more broadly held and more professionally managed (in these instances, the foreign banks commonly played a minor role in bank management while enjoying all the advantages of being on the inside of a highly lucrative protected market). In banks that were full of "shenanigans," on the other hand, major disputes commonly arose over the composition of loan portfolios.

Among many of the family-controlled banks, it seems, a major motivation for inviting in foreign partners was to avoid sharing the loan portfolio with other local families. Before long, however, families and foreign investors often fought over the allocation of loans—and the ultimate problem of weak, family-controlled banks remained unresolved. Licaros observed in 1976 that there was often a fundamental incompatibility between local bankers and their foreign partners; in his view, the foreign investor was more likely to observe objective, impersonal rules in making decisions about loans, while the Filipino banker was more likely to be influenced by

[25] Interview, Fabella, June 8, 1990; Presidential Decree No. 71, November 29, 1972. In Fabella's account, therefore, it was not the IMF that *forced* the entry of foreign banks; rather, it was Licaros who *invited* them in.

[26] Despite this general policy, however, Licaros granted a license to the Co family (from the Marikina shoe industry) for Producers Bank in 1971. This, along with other special favors granted to other banks later in the decade, contributed to widespread gossip regarding Licaros's relationship to certain Chinese-Filipino families. Anonymous interview, former ranking Central Bank official, 1990.

personal factors. Subsequent disputes over loan portfolios have often ended in the exit of the foreign investor: of the eighteen equity infusions in the two decades after 1973 (the bulk of which were in 1973 through 1975), a full one-third ended in divestment. As Fabella concludes, "there's not a single case of divorce that didn't result from [disputes over] lending policies."[27]

In short, the presence of foreign investors did little to reduce the milking of the loan portfolios of many family-controlled banks. There was, however, one side benefit of the policy that helped support the debt-driven growth of the 1970s: for every dollar that a foreign bank invested in the Philippine banking industry, it was required to provide its domestic partner with $10 worth of loans, half on commercial terms and half on concessional terms. Indeed, Licaros was a master at bringing in the foreign loans that both sustained the entire system of crony privilege and fed the growth of the local banking system; in the course of his tenure, from 1970 to 1981, foreign loans ballooned from $200 million to $12.3 billion. (Licaros also permitted foreign banks to establish offshore banking units, or OBUs—the major purpose of which was to facilitate the country's large-scale borrowing in Eurocurrency markets. Because OBUs were restricted from carrying out onshore peso lending and deposit taking, they did not pose a threat to local banks.)[28]

The encouragement of mergers seems to have achieved even less success than foreign equity infusion in resolving the problems of weak banks. In 1973, when the minimum capitalization levels were raised to P100 million, some confidently predicted that the majority of commercial banks would go out of business.[29] In fact, the reduction in numbers was far more modest: by year-end 1977, mergers had reduced the number of private domestic banks from thirty-three to twenty-six. Fabella explains that the

[27] *FEER*, August 17, 1976, 76; Interview, Fabella, June 8, 1990. In one instance, hoodlums were used by majority interests in a Chinese-Filipino bank to intimidate the officials of an American partner bank that was felt to be exercising an excessive degree of control within the bank. Soon thereafter, the American bank sold out its interests to a close associate of President Marcos. According to this source, the American bank became a laughingstock and was considered weakhearted. Anonymous interview, former bank president, 1990.

[28] *FEER*, July 15, 1974, 50 and April 25, 1975, 57; CB Memorandum to All Commercial Banks, August 6, 1973. In 1974, one of the earliest years of extensive borrowings, two-thirds of the growth in resources of the commercial banks came from external loans. *Asian Wall Street Journal* (hereafter *AWSJ*), January 15, 1981; *FEER*, April 25, 1975, 56. See also James K. Boyce, *The Political Economy of External Indebtedness: A Case Study of the Philippines* (Manila: Philippine Institute for Development Studies, 1990). On OBUs, see *FEER*, October 15, 1976, 57–61, April 1, 1977, 30–31 and April 7, 1978, 95; and *The Banker*, December 1978, 61–65.

[29] A *FEER* correspondent said, "the number of commercial banks is certain to drop from 39 [that is, 33 private domestic banks, 2 public banks, and 4 foreign banks] . . . to about one-third of this number." *FEER*, April 9, 1973, 86. In 1974, the Monetary Board stated that it planned to reduce the number of commercial banks to "around eighteen." *FEER*, May 27, 1974, 45.

initiative for mergers came from the banks themselves; his Advisory Group acted more as an "officiating priest" than as a "marriage broker." The stronger banks had little incentive to absorb the weaker banks— particularly those whose assets included large quantities of bad (often DOSRI) loans. "I guess the owners of the banks were not willing to give up control," notes one senior bank supervisor, "and you cannot force them to sell out." Where mergers did occur, they often merely united weak entities—and the surviving entity in many cases ended up facing serious difficulties in later years. Some of these mergers were last-minute "shotgun marriages" to meet the September 1975 deadline by which all banks were to have increased their paid-up capital to P100 million.[30] Many, however, failed to meet the capitalization requirement until the end of the decade—and even then relied on infusions from government banks.[31]

Finally, new regulations seeking to restrict the holdings of a particular family within a bank were especially ineffective. Bank owners could easily ignore or circumvent the rules requiring that no stockholder own more than 20 percent of outstanding shares; as a 1979 internal Central Bank memorandum acknowledged, "it is common knowledge" that some of the stockholders officially listed are "dummies . . . of the controlling stock-holders." According to Fabella—the primary overseer of the reform effort—"no family in its right mind would diffuse ownership. . . . There was no incentive." Some of the technical people wanted to force diffusion, he recalled, but "anyone with any political savvy . . . said that's not going to fly." Central Bank officials were afraid to enforce the rules, Fabella ex-plained, because of concerns over economic destabilization. If families thought they were going to lose control of their banks, they would siphon off funds and perhaps trigger a bank run—the fear of which, he said, "has always been paramount" within the Central Bank. "We didn't want to rock the boat," Fabella acknowledged, especially given ongoing problems of bank instability.[32]

[30] Interview, Fabella, June 12, 1990; Interview, Feliciano L. Miranda Jr., managing director of the Central Bank's Supervision and Examination Sector, May 17, 1990. Five of the six mergers faced difficulties in subsequent years: three (Associated-Citizens, Filipinas Manufac-turers, and PCIB) required large quantities of assistance from state institutions in the early 1980s, one (Pacific) closed down in 1985, and one (IBAA) was itself absorbed by a larger bank in 1985. Despite its years of trouble, PCIB received large equity infusions from the government in the late 1970s and emerged as one of the strongest banks by the late 1980s. It was, in fact, the bank that absorbed IBAA in 1985. See Appendix 2.

[31] Republic Bank and Producers Bank were among the banks having difficulties meeting the requirement, and reportedly accepted equity from DBP to reach the P100 million level. As late as 1978, four banks had yet to reach the goal; the last to succeed was Filman Bank, assisted by an equity infusion from PNB in March 1980. *FEER*, September 26, 1975, 62; October 24, 1975, 63; August 12, 1977, 81; April 7, 1978, 79; and April 4, 1980, 93.

[32] Interview, Fabella, June 12, 1990; Memorandum of Arnulfo B. Aurellano, special assis-tant to Governor Licaros, discussing the Joint IMF–World Bank Mission, October 8, 1979, 6. Related restrictions on interlocking directorates, imposed throughout the 1960s and 1970s,

As noted earlier, the reforms of the early 1970s aimed not only to encourage banks to improve themselves; they also sought to increase the regulatory powers of the Central Bank and finally enable it to curb the worst tendencies of the family-dominated banking system. The Overseas Bank of Manila debacle laid bare the regulatory deficiencies of the Central Bank, and even before the Joint Commission convened there had been halting attempts to try (once again) to curb continuing DOSRI abuses.[33] The commission made several recommendations intended to strengthen the powers of bank supervisors, including the ability to impose administrative penalties and sanctions without going through the court system and to disqualify directors and officers guilty of bank fraud. The subsequent presidential decree put the bulk of these powers in the hands of the governor himself.[34]

From the standpoint of top bank supervisors, however, the impact of these measures was less than satisfactory. The effectiveness of bank supervision became dependent to a greater extent than ever on the governor—for whom supervision was only one of many responsibilities.[35] Most of all, bank supervisors resented instances in which bankers (especially commercial bankers) could use their connections to lobby the governor and his aides and ensure that regulations were thoroughly diluted and bank supervisors were "sobered up" (that is, their vigilance was curbed). In their view, provisions for disqualifying bank officers had little practical value in disciplining the banks because their recommendations were often ignored by an influential upper-level official who had "many friends [from the banking sector] all around." In one instance, a lower-level bank examiner's recommmendation for disqualification of an errant banker was reportedly referred up to this executive, who called up the bank examiner and told him to quit harassing the banker. Later, the banker informed the bank examiner that he was actually present in the official's office when the call was

tried to restrict familial ties among different banks, between banks and allied enterprises, and between banks and investment houses. The use of dummies, however, seems to have made these regulations just as ineffective as the regulations on diffusion of ownership. CB Memoranda, December 6, 1960, January 6, 1961, July 24, 1962; and July 2, 1965; CB Circular No. 378 (August 15, 1973); and *FEER,* April 7, 1978, 78.

[33] Early in 1971, the Central Bank decreased the permissible level of DOSRI loans and strengthened the penalties against violations of DOSRI rules—and then relaxed the regulations a mere three months later. Queried about the episode, Fabella explained that "if you see a diminution of [Central Bank] powers, or backtracking . . . you can bet that somebody screamed." Central Bank Circular 318 (January 13, 1971); Central Bank Circular 318 (revised) (April 30, 1971); Interview, Fabella, June 12, 1990.

[34] IMF-CBP, 54–60; Presidential Decree (P.D.) 71, especially sections 20–21, 25 and 48; and P.D. 72, section 28.

[35] Interviews, Carlota P. Valenzuela, former deputy governor, Supervision and Examination Sector, March 22 and April 25, 1990. Feliciano L. Miranda Jr., who later headed SES, agrees that the new powers of the governor "definitely weakened the supervisor" and represented "a reduction in status." Interview, May 17, 1990.

made. In such an environment, explains the senior official who related this story, even the most vigilant bank examiners soon stopped recommending that erring bankers be disciplined. "What kind of discipline can you have in an office like that? . . . [Eventually] the examiner says, 'What's the use? I get paid just the same whether anyone [is] disqualified or not!' "[36]

One particularly troublesome obstacle to the work of bank supervisors was the "Law on Secrecy of Bank Deposits," originally passed in 1955 to prevent the Bureau of Internal Revenue (BIR) from investigating bank deposits—and thus encourage greater mobilization of savings. From the outset, the law prevented bank supervisors, as well, from gaining access to information about individual bank deposits; as a former top supervisor explains, "this made us very ineffective in catching the rascals in the banking system." Implicit in the law, of course, is the idea that the overall financial system is better served by mobilizing—rather than turning away—the savings held by tax-evaders, "rascal" bankers, and other law-breaking elements of the asset-holding population. Funds from such sources, one major financial executive explains, are "not an unimportant business line of the banks."[37]

The bank run that accompanied the declaration of martial law put this notion to an immediate test. As the Central Bank history explains, a bank run in late September and early October led to net withdrawals totaling P344 million. "But because of the President's assurance that the secrecy of bank deposits would be respected," and because of the Central Bank's granting of emergency advances and loans, "public confidence was restored and normalcy returned after three weeks." Fabella explains that the president was "worried sick that all the banks were going to be used by the BIR to go after tax evaders," and that people were taking their money out of the banks. There was particular concern not to lift the provisions of the deposit secrecy law applying to foreign currency deposits, out of fear that foreign currency depositors might withdraw their savings. In later months, Marcos strengthened the provisions of the deposit secrecy law by decreeing that anyone accused of violating its provisions would be tried by military tribunal. It is not known whether these tribunals were ever used to enforce the law, but the threat implied by Marcos's general order seems to have helped quell any lingering anxiety over the security of bank deposits

---

[36] Anonymous interview, 1990.

[37] Valenzuela, March 22, 1990. Back-to-back transactions provided hefty profits to the banks and great advantage to the customer. Typically, these transactions work as follows: a customer comes into a bank with an unexplainable source of funds, opens a deposit account, takes out a loan on the deposit, and walks out of the bank with an explainable source of funds. Interview, Sixto K. Roxas, founder and former president of Bancom Development Corporation, March 8, 1990. In a 1977 speech, Marcos discussed how the "Secrecy Act in Banking" enabled individuals to conceal their income and evade taxes. "A Stronger Partnership," *CB Review,* August 9, 1977, 4.

in the New Society. Bank supervisors were more hobbled than ever in tracking down "rascal" bankers, but others in the Central Bank justify the actions in no uncertain terms. "I'd rather have difficulty proving DOSRI abuses," said Fabella, "than have a loss of faith in the banking industry."[38]

In larger perspective, the deposit secrecy law highlights an important aspect of the relationship between state and oligarchy in the Philippines. Said by the World Bank to accord an unusual degree of protection to depositors, its major function is to ensure that private sector secrets are not revealed to public sector officials. If Philippine bureaucrats were to become privy to the contents of bank deposits, it is feared that their knowledge would leak outside the bureaucracy. As Fabella explains, "nobody believes you can obtain this information and it will remain confidential." It is striking that even under martial law, there were no comparable sanctions to protect the secrets of the bureaucracy itself. In a modern bureaucracy, Weber argues, the "office secret" is "the specific invention of bureaucracy," and defended with a fanaticism that "cannot be justified with purely functional arguments." In the Philippines, however, legal sanctions do far more to protect the secrets of the oligarchy than the secrets of the bureaucracy.[39]

In the end, martial law did little to promote the effectiveness of bank supervisors. On one hand, there was a certain strengthening of the powers of the regulators relative to the regulated, as many banks were forced to do certain things (such as increase their capitalization) that they might not have otherwise done. At the same time, technical aspects of the bank supervisor's job were promoted in the early 1970s by the first deputy governor for supervision, Jaime C. Laya (who codified regulations, computerized operations, and rationalized reporting requirements) and later in the decade by the Central Bank Institute, which provided more systemic training of technical personnel. On the other hand, however, there were clear limits to which the powers of martial law would be used to ensure more effective banking supervision. Laya, a close associate of the Marcoses and the head of the Central Bank's supervisory apparatus between 1974 and 1978, seems to have had little desire to apply the powers of martial law toward the task of bank supervision. Unlike Fabella or Licaros, who clearly exerted major effort envisaging the future shape of the banking sector as a whole, Laya occupied himself with far more menial tasks. "It's not as if . . .

[38] Republic Act No. 1405, September 9, 1955; Interview, Valenzuela, March 22, 1990; *Central Bank of the Philippines*, 123; Interview, Fabella, June 12, 1990; General Order 26, March 31, 1973; Interview, Miranda, May 17, 1990.
[39] World Bank, *Philippine Financial Sector Study,* Report No. 7177-PH (Washington, D.C., 1988), xii; Interview, Fabella, June 12, 1990; Max Weber, *Economy and Society* (Berkeley: University of California Press, 1978), II: 992.

we were ready to go to war," responded Laya when asked about new opportunities for tougher supervision presented by the reforms.[40]

Within about five years after their promulgation in 1972, the banking reforms began to lose steam. As problems of instability endured and even deepened, it seems that Licaros himself lost faith in the central elements of his reform package, including the mandated increases in minimum capitalization. In 1977, he concluded that "compelling banks to increase paid-up capital would not necessarily eliminate or even lessen the risks" of bank failure; the troubled banks, he felt, had suffered more from poor internal policies than from inadequate capitalization. Although the governor lamented that "caution and conservatism are now the exception among many bankers," he seems to have found himself with little ability to instill such qualities in the banks he was supervising. Like Castillo before him, he found that the absence of regulatory capacity forced him to fall back on lofty appeals for professional responsibility. "Licaros has been going from one public forum to another," reported one observer in 1977, "preaching the virtues of prudence and warning of the dangers of over-exposures, over-expansion and over-diversification financed by costly credit."[41] But his sermons seem to have produced little effect. Moreover, as the decade progressed it became more apparent than ever that the preacher (and his boss at the Palace) were hardly practicing the virtues that they preached. As a result of the many limitations of the reform efforts of the 1970s, the problems of weak family-controlled banks ended up outliving the reforms that had targeted their demise.

Bank Instability: The Problems Deepen

As the previous chapter's discussion of the cases of Republic Bank and Overseas Bank of Manila makes clear, bank instability was already a major ailment of the financial system in the 1960s. In the 1970s, however, long-standing problems of DOSRI abuse combined with increasing commercial bank involvement in the relatively new money market, and the postwar financial system experienced its worst shocks yet. Two cases were particularly disruptive: the dramatic failure of Continental Bank in 1974 and the closure of General Bank and Trust Company in 1976. In each case, the banks were not only weakened by DOSRI abuse but had also become overextended in the poorly collateralized and unstable money market. Both banks had affiliated investment houses, and long-term investments were being financed with short-term instruments.[42]

---

[40] Interview, Jaime C. Laya, May 21, 1990.
[41] *FEER*, March 11, 1977, 52.
[42] See Tan, "Philippine Monetary Policy," 199; Patrick and Moreno, 327.

The Continental case became public in June 1974, when Chinese-Filipino businessman Vicente Tan was arrested and stripped of his assets by agents of General Fabian Ver, Marcos's intelligence chief and head of the praetorian Presidential Security Command. Tan's arrest triggered the worst bank run yet to hit the Philippine banking system, and initiated a complex set of legal actions involving Tan, the Palace, the Central Bank, and the Manila Archdiocese. In the course of this byzantine story, Tan emerged from obscurity to gain control of two commercial banks—Continental and Philippine Trust Co. (Philtrust)—and later sank back into obscurity without a bank to his name.

Tan began with diversified operations in insurance and real estate, and acquired an increasing stake in Continental Bank beginning in the mid-1960s. After a power struggle with a co-owner who was also milking the bank for related enterprises, Tan assumed 85 percent control of the bank in late 1972.[43] At the same time, Tan was cutting a deal with his friend, Rufino Cardinal Santos, Archbishop of Manila, to acquire majority interest in the Archdiocese's bank, Philtrust. In exchange for generous loans to the Archdiocese, Tan was chosen as buyer of 60 percent of the bank's shares. In May, 1973, Tan and Cardinal Santos went to Rome to finalize arrangements for the sale, and by early 1974 the final documents were signed. The Cardinal had died in the interim, but the Archdiocese nonetheless proceeded with the arrangements for the sale. Tan assumed control of the bank in February 1974, and by early 1975 (after the final payment) was to have become official owner of his 60 percent share. As of early 1974, then, Tan controlled two banks; in line with Central Bank policies at the time, Tan announced plans to merge the two entities.[44]

The relationship between Tan and the Archdiocese, however, went sour—quite probably because Tan reportedly helped himself to unsecured loans from Philtrust (still partly owned by the Archdiocese), invested P1 million Philtrust money in his own investment house, Victan and Co.; and planned to merge the bank with Continental. It also seems that the new Archbishop, Jaime Cardinal Sin, was unhappy with his pre-

[43] Interview, Vicente T. Tan, former majority owner of Continental Bank, May 15, 1990; Vicente T. Tan, "The Uneven Hand: The Exercise of Central Bank Powers to Close Banking Institutions." Ph.D. diss., University of Santo Tomas, 1982, 150, 218, 169, 189–90. The DOSRI abuse by both Tan and the co-owner (Valeriano Bueno, a Mindanao logger close to Marcos) was confirmed in an anonymous 1990 interview with a former "bad loans" officer of the bank.

[44] *FEER*, August 4, 1978, 32–33; Tan, "The Uneven Hand," 247–48; "Facts and Events Behind the Closure of Continental Bank," a pamphlet printed by Tan in 1987, p. 1; Interview, Vicente Tan, May 15, 1990; *FEER*, May 7, 1973, 30. The loans were used, quite appropriately, to help construct the Cardinal Santos Memorial Hospital in Manila. One factor behind the Church's decision to sell the bank was the Central Bank's requirement that banks increase their capitalization to P100 million. Philtrust's capital amounted to a mere P25 million. *FEER*, August 4, 1978, 32.

decessor's decision to sell majority interest in the bank, a major source of funds for the Archdiocese.[45]

According to one former bank president, Tan had too many powerful persons lined up against him, and the milking of his banks provided these persons with a chance to move against him. Considered a maverick within the Chinese-Filipino community, Tan was outside the Chinese-Filipino protection racket that collected so-called donations for the Marcos regime. Another former bank president close to the Chinese-Filipino community considered Tan's origins "hazy," and said no one understood where he had gotten the money to buy into the two banks.[46] While not without allies (the board of Victan and Co. was chaired by Miguel Cuaderno and included both Marcos's tourism minister and influential corporate lawyer Edgardo Angara), Tan had a series of powerful enemies: he'd antagonized the very powerful Cardinal Sin, probably because of the deal he'd struck with the late Cardinal Santos, and later managed to alienate Marcos's chief bodyguard, General Ver. According to Tan himself, he'd supported Marcos's opponent in the presidential election of 1965, and had been active in the Philippine Constitutional Association that opposed Marcos in the early 1970s. Moreover, he said, Marcos "was not happy because I didn't allow his people to take part in our business."[47] For many reasons, then, Tan was a vulnerable target: he was clearly on the outs, and the powers of martial law enabled the regime quite readily to arrest and expropriate the assets of those in its disfavor.

Soon after his arrest on the morning of June 15, 1974, Tan experienced the full weight of the martial law regime's discretionary power: solitary confinement at a military camp, and the subsequent arrest of key officers of the bank, Central Bank examiners who had apparently been too friendly to Tan (their examinee), and eventually even his wife.[48] Continental, already weakened by both the plunder of its loan portfolio and its heavy reliance on the poorly collateralized and unstable money market, was seemingly devastated by the resulting bank run.

At first glance, one might view Tan's imprisonment as the action of a government finally determined to prosecute errant bankers for violations of banking regulations. Closer examination, however, reveals that the

[45] *FEER*, August 4, 1978, 32–34, quote from 32; "Facts and Events Behind the Closure of Continental Bank," p. 2.

[46] Anonymous interviews, 1989 and 1990.

[47] Tan, "The Uneven Hand," 285; *FEER*, August 4, 1978, 32–33; Interview, Vicente Tan, May 15, 1990.

[48] *FEER*, August 4, 1978, 33; Interview, Vicente Tan, May 15, 1990; Tan, "The Uneven Hand," 129–130; "Facts and Events Behind the Closure of Continental Bank," 2–3. One of the regime-controlled newspapers claimed that Tan was about to fly out of the country with a suitcase full of dollars; *FEER* reported in 1978 that he had been arrested "while attempting to leave Manila airport for an overseas trip . . . and detained for misappropriation of deposits and other financial irregularities."

stated procedures for dealing with a failed bank, recently revamped in the 1972 reforms, were almost entirely circumvented—and the Central Bank let Ver's Presidential Security Command take charge of its own, extralegal, punishment of Tan. The Monetary Board ordered the closure of the bank on June 24, but—contrary to the provisions of the law—did not even examine the bank's condition until after it was closed down.[49] Meanwhile, Marcos signed letters of instruction for Ver to seize Tan's assets and to turn them over to the Central Bank. But according to a senior Central Bank official involved in examining Tan's assets, they never heard from—and never challenged—Ver's intelligence agency if Ver got to an asset first.[50] Tan was initially charged by the military with violating "anti-graft" statutes, and the Central Bank's own charge sheet against Tan never prospered.[51]

If the regime were sending a message to bankers, the Central Bank's charges could have been most prominently and forcefully pressed. But as a former president of the Bankers Association of the Philippines speculated, Tan was arrested "not in connection with his shenanigans in the banking industry, but to teach him to be more pliable."[52] Indeed, there was nothing unusual about his shenanigans: many commercial banks were heavily reliant on the volatile money market, and many bankers were plundering their own banks for loans to related family enterprises. His crime, if one can call it that, was the crime of poor connections—of lacking the sine qua

[49] The examination (which found a condition of insolvency) was not completed until August—weeks after the bank's closure. Ramon Orosa, the banker who in later years acquired the banks from Tan, maintains that the Central Bank undervalued the bank's assets in the examination. Moreover, he said it was conducted specifically to "justify the closure," and was initiated after the Central Bank received "a call from the Palace." Tan, "The Uneven Hand," 206; Interview, Ramon Orosa, former president of Philippine Commercial and Industrial Bank and former chairman of International Corporate Bank, May 4, 1991.

[50] Letter of Instruction No. 199, from President Ferdinand E. Marcos to the Secretary of National Defense and General Fabian Ver, National Intelligence Security Agency (NISA), June 29, 1974. According to the Central Bank official, Tan's properties were very valuable; he used the money that he acquired (often fraudulently) from his banks and his investment house to invest in "good property." Anonymous interview, mid-1990. Tan provided (under duress, one might guess) powers of attorney for the NISA colonel in charge of his investigation and interrogation, thus facilitating the "legal" expropriation of his assets; in 1976, this colonel told Tan's lawyer in a courtroom that Ver would "account" for Tan's "securities, moneys, collectibles, and dividends . . . in due time." *Quisumbing, Caparas, Ilagan, Alcantara & Mosqueda* v. *Vicente T. Tan [and corporations]*, Civil Case No. Q-25330, Court of First Instance of Rizal, Quezon City Branch, May 30, 1978, 22.

[51] According to the Central Bank official, there was essentially no interagency cooperation and Tan was never formally prosecuted. Ver's NISA looked to the Central Bank to build the legal case, but many in the Central Bank felt that the National Bureau of Investigation should handle the case since many of the allegations against Tan dealt with "violations of non-banking laws." In any case, this official admitted, the Central Bank lacked lawyers "competent . . . to build the case." Anonymous interview, 1990. Tan finds it "lamentable" that the Central Bank "did not even lift a finger to prevent a palpable travesty upon its own powers." Tan, "The Uneven Hand," 196, 246.

[52] Anonymous interview, former president of a Chinese-Filipino bank, 1990.

non of big-time success in Philippine business. In the future, other busi-
nesspeople (especially those in the more vulnerable Chinese-Filipino community) no doubt thought twice before refusing to cooperate with the
Marcos regime. For Tan, the only Philippine banker to endure such severe
punishment for his crimes, the major question was "Why me, and not
them?" In his Ph.D. thesis on the topic, Tan wrote: "Why the Continental
Bank appeared to have been especially singled out to suffer a dismal fate
from among *so many other banks where the closure order would probably be more
justified,* seemed inexplicably beyond comprehension."[53] He was correct:
as far as the rule of law was concerned, many other banks would probably
deserve to be shut down, as well. As far as political connections were
concerned, however, it was hardly a matter "inexplicably beyond comprehension."

For the next three years after the bank closing, complicated legal cases
ensued, involving Cardinal Sin, General Ver, Governor Licaros, and others.
The case did not move forward until 1977, when, in exchange for his
release after three years in the stockade, Tan signed over all of his remaining assets and liabilities (including Victan and Co. and his claim to the two
banks) to Ramon Orosa, a close associate of crony Herminio Disini. For
Tan, the offer was a "passport to freedom."[54] Orosa, meanwhile, worked
out a clear division of the booty with his associate, Disini, who had long
"been wanting a bank." In the words of Orosa, they agreed that "I'll
take the dead one [Continental] and you [Disini] take the living one
[Philtrust]."[55]

The Cardinal, however, thought he was going to get the losing end of
the deal, because Tan's agreement with Orosa neglected to recognize
Philtrust's P1 million investment in Victan and Co. In any case, the Archdiocese no longer showed any desire to give up its bank. The Cardinal
wrote a stinging letter to President Marcos, lambasting "all these uses of

[53] Tan, "The Uneven Hand," 203 (emphasis added). Tan's dissertation was completed
four years after he was released from prison, and criticized the Central Bank's handling of the
Republic Bank, Overseas Bank, and Continental Bank cases. Quite incredibly, the committee
that supervised this thesis lambasting the Central Bank included not only an ex-bank examiner (Jose P. Sevilla, formerly on the board of Victan and Co.) but also Andres V. Castillo, the
former governor.

[54] *FEER,* August 4, 1978, 34; Tan, "The Uneven Hand," 218. See also *"Quisumbing [et al.] v.
Vicente T. Tan [and corporations],"* May 30, 1978, 38–49, and "Facts and Events Behind the
Closure of Continental Bank," p. 5.

[55] Interview, Orosa, April 30, 1991. In late 1977, Orosa reopened Continental Bank as
International Commercial Bank, or Interbank. Several observers of the banking industry
explained that Philtrust had a far healthier loan portfolio than Continental's, because the
Roman Catholic Archdiocese of Manila had long practiced a very conservative loan policy.

The Investment and Underwriting Corporation, an investment house jointly owned by the
Orosa family and the Herdis (Herminio Disini) Group, had been hard-hit by the closure of
Continental Bank, since they had a gross exposure of P22.5 million in the failed institution.
FEER, August 4, 1978, 34.

governmental power in order to favor [the Disini] group of businesses." Cardinal Sin was now attacking the regime that had earlier, in 1974, done him a good turn by going after Vicente Tan. Whereas in 1974 Sin had expressed pleasure with the fact that Licaros and Ver had taken control of Tan's assets, in 1978—now in the midst of a heated dispute with Disini— he said that Philtrust had "suffered more than enough from the persistent efforts of the Herdis group to gain control of the bank, by means that do not sit well with the lofty ideals and moral principles of the New Society." Licaros, who had been engaged in an increasingly bitter and complex dispute with Sin over the disposition of Philtrust, seemingly sided with Disini and used the powers of the Central Bank to harass the Archdiocese and Philtrust.[56]

Later in 1978—probably in exasperation—the Archdiocese sold its still-undisputed 33 percent share of Philtrust to a businessman by the name of Emilio Yap, an associate of the family of First Lady Imelda Romualdez Marcos. This shifted the dispute from Church versus Disini to Imelda versus Disini—in effect, it was now a dispute *within* the Palace. Imelda pressured Disini (the husband of her cousin) to sell his share in Philtrust to Yap, and in the end Disini's people kept one bank (Continental), while Imelda's people got the other (Philtrust). In this way, two factions of the Palace got in on the booty.[57]

[56] It seems that Sin wanted the bank back, and Licaros wanted the final payment of the original sale to be completed (using funds presumably obtained from the seizure of Tan's assets). In August 1976, General Ver had arbitrated an agreement between Sin and Licaros in which the Archdiocese would retain a majority holding in the bank yet return a P30 million loan that Tan had earlier granted. Marcos approved the agreement five months later, but then did a quick about-face; as the *FEER* reported, "the suspicion was that Herdis had lobbied against the [Sin-Licaros] agreement" so that he and Orosa would obtain controlling interests in the two banks.

In 1977 (apparently in support of Disini), Licaros resurrected the issue of Philtrust's 1974 investment in Victan and Co., and demanded that Philtrust withdraw the investment. The Archdiocese, which had earlier disapproved of the investment, was now reluctant to withdraw it because through its "continuing stake in Victan . . . the bank retains a legal standing to question the transfers made by Tan of his assets to the Herdis group." As punishment for not divesting, the Central Bank cut off Philtrust's rediscounting facilities and branching facilities in late 1977—the first time in six years that such a penalty had been levied against a commercial bank. The Church seems to have been greatly agitated at the severity of this treatment, and soon thereafter gave up its fight to retain Philtrust. *FEER*, August 4, 1978, 32–35.

[57] *FEER*, September 29, 1978, 65; August 4, 1978, 35; Anonymous interview, former bank president. Meanwhile, Orosa was eased out of the deal altogether. Although he had been the one to reopen Continental as International Corporate Bank (or Interbank) in September 1977, he had to sell the bank to Disini in 1980. Knowledgeable observers describe it as a "friendly deal," but it was not a deal that Orosa chose to make. As Orosa explained, "nobody came and threatened me," but there was "a 'suggestion' from the Palace" that he sell. Interview, Orosa, May 4, 1991.

After the fall of President Marcos in 1986, Vicente Tan continued to press lawsuit after lawsuit for the return of the bank to what he considered "its rightful owner"—himself. But he seemed to lack any effective inside connections to the Aquino Palace; since he was a nobody,

The case of Continental Bank highlights the continuing fragility of the Philippine financial system, even in the midst of the first major reform effort of the postwar years. Licaros dubbed himself a "frustrated administrator," and found it "unfortunate that time was against us in the case of Continental Bank." Quite clearly, the entire system of bank supervision was at fault for not detecting and curbing the rampant abuse of Continental Bank at any earlier date; the Central Bank's failure to adequately supervise the banking system led to the worst bank run yet to hit the postwar financial system. In broader terms, the case displays the heightened arbitrariness of state power at a time when the powers of the state were greatly augmented by martial law. Shenanigans notwithstanding, the prosecution of Tan was a blatant abuse of state power by a regime intent on harassing political opponents and seizing their assets. The powers of martial law did little to strengthen the Central Bank as an institution; rather, it was enlisted as a junior partner in pursuing the aggrandizing goals of the Marcos regime.[58]

The instability of Continental Bank's closure was followed two years later by a run on the Yujuico family's General Bank and Trust Company, or Genbank. In 1974, the bank had been among those that experienced a run on its resources in the wake of Continental Bank's troubles, but neither equity infusion from DBP nor partnership with a foreign bank had been successful in restoring it to good health.[59] Crisis struck once again in late 1976, when problems at the Yujuico-owned investment house provoked a second run on the bank. The Central Bank arranged for emergency loans from state-owned Land Bank, but unlike the 1974 bailout, this time the government took over Genbank management. As we shall see, in a matter of months the bank was sold—at very favorable terms—to a group of investors led by a rising Marcos crony.

Given the severity of the abuses that were publicized in later years, it is hard to imagine that the Central Bank had no early warning signals about problems within Genbank. After closing the bank in 1976, the Central Bank disclosed details of heavy DOSRI abuse—and by 1978 considered

he got nowhere with his claims. In the late 1980s, his business empire was so diminished as to be based in a small apartment fronting Manila Bay (on the wall of the apartment, it is interesting to note, hung a life-size oil portrait of his old friend, Cardinal Santos). Interview, Vicente Tan, May 15, 1990.

[58] *CB Review*, August 13, 1974, 7. A fuller account of the Continental Bank episode can be found in Hutchcroft, "Power and Politics in the Philippine Banking Industry: An Analysis of State-Oligarchy Relations," in *Patterns of Power and Politics in the Philippines: Implications for Development*, ed. James F. Eder and Robert L. Youngblood (Tempe: Arizona State University Program for Southeast Asian Studies, 1994).

[59] *FEER*, August 2, 1974, 30, August 27, 1976, 75, January 14, 1977, 56, March 3, 1978, 53, and August 18, 1978, 53; SGV, *Directory of Key Officers and Board Members of Commercial Banks in the Philippines*, various issues.

filing criminal charges against the Yujuicos in connection with these loans. In the end, the family lost its bank but managed to escape further punishment for its misdeeds; to be sure, they could be thankful for treatment far more lenient than that earlier accorded Vicente Tan.[60]

The bank runs of the mid-1970s, especially the Continental Bank debacle, forced the Central Bank to respond. As we have seen, the financial difficulties of 1974 and 1976 can be traced to inadequacies of the regulatory apparatus, continuing DOSRI abuse, and the instability of the money market. The first two problems were of course central targets of the reforms of 1972, but within five years even Licaros seemed to be pessimistic that they would be resolved any time soon. The third problem, however, could be more effectively addressed. Licaros blamed the Continental Bank mess on inadequate supervision of the money market and the investment houses, and eventually (in early 1976) the Central Bank adopted a series of measures that greatly reduced both the attractiveness and the role of money market instruments.

The impact on investment houses was most severe, since the central element of their business was now greatly curtailed. The commercial banks, however, had little to lose: their substantial business in deposit substitutes was replaced by increases in savings and time deposits (for which they faced no competition from investment houses). In the early 1970s, many banks had rushed to develop ties with or establish investment houses; by the late 1970s, however, the rapid growth of the investment houses and the money market had been arrested by Central Bank regulations that clearly favored the banks and their more standard financial instruments.[61] Just as the Central Bank was proving incapable of effective reform of the banking sector, it nonetheless displayed the capacity to rechannel financial intermediation away from the investment houses and

---

[60] In 1974, Licaros tried to explain away the difference between the treatment of Genbank and Continental Bank by saying that Genbank qualified for government equity assistance by virtue of its solvency and the absence of "large-scale frauds by officers or principal stockholders that would impair the viability of the bank itself." Such arguments became increasingly problematic in later years, when it was revealed that Genbank's DOSRI loans totaled P172 million, 29 percent of the bank's total loan portfolio. Of the DOSRI loans, 56 percent were unsecured. "Speech Delivered by Central Bank Governor G.S. Licaros During the 58th Anniversary of the Philippine National Bank, Manila, July 22, 1974," *CB Review*, August 13, 1974, 6–7, at 7; *FEER*, March 3, 1978, 145.

[61] The Central Bank increased taxes and reserve requirements on money market instruments, introduced an interest rate ceiling on short-term deposit substitutes, and raised the minimum size of money market placements. At the same time, it raised interest rate ceilings on savings and time deposits. Licaros speech to PNB, *CB Review*, August 13, 1974, 7; Licuanan, 38; World Bank–IMF, 26–27, 61–63; *FEER*, September 21, 1979, 77. Licuanan reports that deposit substitutes registered 50 percent annual growth in the two years prior to the 1976 regulations, and 5 percent annual growth a year afterward. According to World Bank–IMF data, deposit substitutes declined from 80 percent of the total of time and savings deposits in 1974 to 43 percent in 1978.

toward the commercial banks. A major reason for the success of the 1976 measures, one might surmise, is that they provided little challenge to the powerful social forces found within the banking system.

The Rise of the Cronies

The preceding discussion highlights how obstacles to bank reform and problems of financial instability were far from resolved by martial law; above all, however, this period is best remembered as one in which crony capitalism, as it came to be known, brought unprecedented changes to the ownership structure of the banking system. We have already noted the enormous degree of favoritism in the state apparatus in the pre–martial law years; under Marcos-style authoritarianism, however, the ruler's favor or disfavor achieved more importance than ever. Vicente Tan experienced the ruler's disfavor in an especially dramatic way, and later complained bitterly of what the "uneven hand" of bank supervision did to him under the martial law regime. The favor of the regime, however, produced some equally dramatic success stories, as those with the best access to the political machinery reaped unprecedented gains. PNB and DBP loan portfolios were now monopolized by a much smaller segment of the elite—and, as we shall see, the shameless plunder by Marcos and his cronies in the 1970s continues to be a drag on public finances in the 1990s. A dozen banks— the vast bulk of which were in a weak position—ended up in the hands of Marcos and his associates. Moreover, certain banks were highly favored by the Central Bank and the Palace in the granting of selective credit and special privileges.

The case of Allied Bank is particularly illustrative of the success that can come from favorable access to the political machinery. The bank's founder, Lucio Tan, was probably a Marcos associate even before 1972, when he owned a small cigarette factory in Ilocos (the home region of the president). But it was only with the declaration of martial law in that year that his meteoric ascent began. By 1980, thanks to extensive support from the Palace in gaining tax, customs, financing, and regulatory favors, his Fortune Tobacco Co. had become by far the country's largest maker of cigarettes. In return, Lucio Tan is said to have provided large contributions to Marcos and his New Society Movement, and cut the president into a large equity stake in his firms. Marcos also signed into law a cigarette tax code that had actually been written by Fortune Tobacco, and—as if writing the tax laws wasn't enough—Tan allegedly printed, with impunity, his own internal revenue stamps for use on cigarette packs.[62]

[62] By the end of the Marcos years, Tan had diversified his interests into chemical manufac-

Lucio Tan's entry into the banking sector came in 1977, with the failure of Genbank. As noted, Genbank experienced a second major bank run in December 1976, after which the Central Bank arranged for it to be rescued—and taken over—by Land Bank of the Philippines. According to press reports at the time, Licaros indicated that Genbank "is likely to be a State bank for a long time, if not permanently"; in early 1977, "high Central Bank officials" were assigned to "sensitive posts" within the bank. Land Bank held 60 percent of the bank's shares, and a number of parties expressed interest in the 40 percent share of the Yujuicos. The *CB Review* reprinted a local press story explaining that this minority interest was to sell for roughly P200 million; after payment, the Yujuicos were to forward the money to the Central Bank to cover the roughly P200 million in advances that had already been given to the troubled bank.[63]

In late March, however, there seems to have been an abrupt change in the government's plans for Genbank. The Central Bank declared the bank insolvent, and warned that its continuation in business would entail "a loss to depositors and creditors." Interested parties were given only three days to submit bids, and in a rush sale Lucio Tan and his associate, textile industrialist Willy Co, won out over other bidders. According to charges made in a 1990 court case, Tan allegedly conspired with Licaros to purchase the bank at the rock-bottom price of P500,000—a mere fraction of the P200 million price tag reported only weeks before. Land Bank faded out of the picture altogether, and it is not clear what price it received (if any) for its 60 percent share. Despite the official ban on new bank licenses, Genbank's license was discontinued and Allied Bank began as an entirely new legal entity. The exact reasons for this are not known, but it probably released Allied from assuming some of the bad loans of its predecessor.[64]

---

turing, hog farming, textiles, distilling, brewing, trading, real estate, hotels, and banking. See *FEER*, December 15, 1988, 112–16. Background on Lucio Tan also comes from Yoshihara Kunio, *The Rise of Ersatz Capitalism in South-East Asia* (Quezon City: Ateneo de Manila Press, 1988), 71, 188–89.

[63] *FEER*, January 14, 1977, 55 and February 11, 1977, 104; *Philippines Daily Express*, February 26, 1977, reprinted in *CB Review*, March 1, 1977, 6. The Yujuicos were forced to sell out; all the prospective buyers were Chinese-Filipino. Because no new bank licenses were to be granted, purchasing a defunct institution such as Genbank was the best way to get into the banking business.

[64] *FEER*, April 8, 1977, 145, and December 15, 1988, 113; *Newsday*, August 28, 1990. Graft charges were filed on August 27, 1990 against Tan and others by the Aquino government's Philippine Commission on Good Government (PCGG). The charges were based on testimony from former Governor Laya and a senior deputy governor. Two former senior Central Bank officials confirmed that the sale took place under highly questionable circumstances. Anonymous interviews, 1990. The PCGG charged that Tan purchased the bank for only P500,000, when its actual value was P688 million (that is, the bank was purchased for less than 1 percent of its actual value). While the PCGG's valuation was probably high, the final price was nonetheless widely considered an extraordinary bargain—especially given the prevailing restrictions on bank licenses. See *FEER*, April 8, 1977, 145, and August 24, 1989;

Finally, there are charges that even before the bank reopened its doors the Central Bank provided it with an "emergency loan" of P350 million.[65]

According to SEC records, there were seven investors, including Tan, each holding 10 percent to 15 percent of bank shares. By 1978, a business correspondent reported that the bank "serves as model for other similarly-afflicted banks, and its transformation is being cited by the Government as an argument for broadening ownership and professionalizing management of banking institutions and also for breaking up capital links between bank and non-bank undertakings."[66] But the ownership picture is seemingly far more complicated than SEC data would lead us to believe. In later years, there were allegations that Marcos himself acquired 60 percent of the bank; indeed, many of the investors were charged with fronting for the Palace. Although there is seemingly no firm evidence available on Marcos's precise share of the bank, it is clear that what was to remain a "State bank" quite quickly became a "regime bank" instead. Far from being a model for "broadening ownership," Allied was rather an exemplar of crony-capitalist acquisition.[67]

Regardless of the precise extent of Marcos family ownership, it is clear that Tan and Vice-Chairman Willy Co enjoyed stellar political connections. Co's excellent access to the Central Bank (he was a frequent visitor to the governor's office, one veteran journalist recalls) seems to have been espe-

---

and *Newsday*, August 28, 1990 and September 1, 1990. The PCGG seems to have derived its valuation from a late 1980s lawsuit brought by the Yujuicos, who charged that Tan "arbitrarily and fraudulently" took over the bank with the support of Licaros. *FEER*, December 15, 1988, 112.

[65] *Manila Chronicle*, February 18, 1989. The valuation of Genbank's debt to the Central Bank increased from roughly P200 million to over P300 million, and Allied reportedly began to repay this debt in July 1977. *Asian Finance*, May 15, 1976, 73.

[66] Data of the Securities and Exchange Commission on corporate organization and ownership (hereafter "SEC data"); *FEER*, March 3, 1978, 52.

[67] These charges were made by the PCGG, which claimed that equity shares were provided to Marcos in exchange for "presidential favors and other concessions." *Manila Chronicle*, July 28, 1989, and *Newsday*, January 22, 1991. It is not known when and to what extent Marcos acquired a stake in the bank, but according to Rolando Gapud, Marcos's financial adviser, Marcos had by 1985 "formalized" a 60 percent equity stake in Shareholdings, Inc., a holding company that, in turn, owned shares in many Tan enterprises (including Allied Bank). Rolando Gapud, "Sworn Statement," Hong Kong, January 14, 1987. Tan himself acknowledges that Marcos took a stake in his firms. In response to charges that he was a Marcos crony, Tan "insisted that he was not a crony and was in fact a victim of the former president *who took over huge shares in his businesses*." *Manila Chronicle*, November 9, 1989 (emphasis added).

One possibility is that Marcos simply assumed the (60 percent) Land Bank share of Allied, and Tan and his associates purchased what was formerly the (40 percent) Yujuico family interest. While it is not possible to identify the dummies that Marcos may have used, it is worth noting that one stockholder was formerly head of Metrocom, Marcos's "special paramilitary and police unit" and another the husband of the president's private secretary. *Newsday*, January 22, 1991; Ricardo Manapat, *Some Are Smarter Than Others: The History of Marcos' Crony Capitalism* (New York: Aletheia Publications, 1991), 347; *Philippines Daily Globe*, October 23, 1990.

cially beneficial: Allied was among the most favored commercial banks in
selective credit allocation between 1977 and 1980, with over 36 percent of
its assets financed by two key sources of largesse.[68] Moreover, Allied had
the most favored access to both government-guaranteed foreign loans and
the "jumbo loans" of the "Consolidated Foreign Borrowing Program" (a
source of riches, between 1978 and 1983, in which the Central Bank
contracted large amounts of foreign debt, assumed the currency risk, and
disbursed the loans to favored banks). In effect, Allied was able to bypass
the painstaking process of building up a large deposit base, financing its
assets instead through booty readily grabbed from the Central Bank. The
bank enjoyed swift growth in total assets, and went from thirteenth-to
third-largest bank between year-end 1977 and year-end 1979 (exceeded in
size only by PNB and Citibank).[69]

Allied Bank, of course, is only one of many examples of banks that
ended up in crony hands and received special favors from the Central
Bank and the Palace. Because Marcos had more power and longer tenure
than any other Philippine president, he and his associates had unprecedented opportunities to reap patrimonial largesse—an important part of
which was the acquisition of a major chunk of the private banking system.
These acquisitions, however, were not part of a general policy of expropri-
ating the assets of the banking community as a whole. As the regime's chief
ideologue explains, the impulse toward crony capitalism was present from
the start, but Marcos often had to take "measured steps" and wait for
opportunities to present themselves. The fact that oligarchs controlled
crucial independent resources meant that he could not afford to antago-
nize them as a group; in a world of mobile capital, Marcos knew that he
would undermine overall business confidence if he acted too generally
and too rashly against his rivals. Those who "stay[ed] in the middle of the
stream" faced no clear threat of losing their banks to regime forces. The
regime's acquisitions seemed to follow a "kick 'em when they're down"
approach: as opportunities presented themselves, the regime did not hesitate to move against selected targets—most of all bankers swimming

[68] Interview, Leo Gonzaga, former business correspondent of the *FEER*, February 6, 1990.
The two selective credit programs—rediscounting and swaps—are discussed further later in
this chapter. Former senior Central Bank officials have confirmed that the Licaros–Willy Co
relationship was central to these favored allocations—particularly swaps. Anonymous interviews, 1990.

[69] Allied tops all other private commercial banks in the amount of medium-and long-term
foreign direct borrowings: $68 million, or 18 percent of all direct borrowings in which private
commercial banks are listed as original obligor. The loan guarantor was the national government. Central Bank of the Philippines, *Total Foreign Exchange Liabilities as of December 31, 1986*,
vol. IV (Manila: Central Bank of the Philippines, n.d. [1987?]). The vast bulk of "jumbo
loans" went to PNB, DBP, and the national government, but the Central Bank acknowledged
the unique role of Allied in the program. *CB Review*, August/September 1982, p. 23; see also
Central Bank, *Statistical Bulletin*, various issues. See Appendix 2 for a ranking of banks by size.

against the prevailing political currents, or bankers whose banks had hit the rocks.[70]

Some twelve banks—almost all of which were in a weak position—ended up in the hands of Marcos and his cronies during this period: Continental Bank was reopened as *International Corporate Bank* under the control of crony Herminio Disini. *Pilipinas Bank* of crony Ricardo Silverio (the successor to a bank formed from a 1976 merger) was kept alive with generous equity assistance from state banks. Jose Cojuangco's First United Bank was purchased by his nephew, Eduardo "Danding" Cojuangco, on behalf of the Philippine Coconut Authority and with funds provided by the coconut levy, renamed *United Coconut Planters Bank,* and controlled by a small group centered on Cojuangco. Genbank became *Allied Bank,* under a group of investors led by Lucio Tan. Emerito Ramos eventually sold Overseas Bank of Manila to a group close to Herminio Disini, which renamed the bank *Commercial Bank of Manila.* The *Philippine Bank of Communications* was steadily acquired by a group of investors led by Ralph Nubla, the main liaison between Marcos and the Chinese-Filipino business community. Controlling interest in the *Philippine Commercial and Industrial Bank* of the powerful pre–martial law clan of Eugenio Lopez was assumed by regime interests led by Benjamin "Kokoy" Romualdez (the brother of First Lady Imelda Marcos). *Philippine Trust Company* ended up in the hands of Emilio Yap, a friend of the First Lady's family. *Philippine Veterans Bank,* a bank nominally owned by World War II veterans and almost entirely beholden to the government for support, had most of its shares "held in trust" by the veteran with all the bogus medals, Ferdinand Marcos. Republic Bank, after the death of Pablo Roman in 1978, was transferred to Roberto S. Benedicto, a fraternity brother of Marcos who was head of the Philippine Sugar Commission, and renamed *Republic Planters Bank.* Traders Commercial Bank also went to Benedicto, was renamed *Traders Royal Bank,* and used to handle financial transactions for the regime. Finally, *Security Bank* reportedly came to be controlled (through front companies) by Marcos himself, and took major responsibility for the president's personal financial transactions.

Each case, of course, is a story unto itself; together, they reveal how Marcos and his cronies were quick to seize the many opportunities that

[70] Interview, Cristobal, June 19, 1989; Interview, Chester Babst, former president, Pacific Banking Corp., April 27, 1990. Babst's swimming metaphor was advice he gave to his former boss, the Chinese-Filipino founder and chairman of Pacific Banking Corporation, Antonio Roxas-Chua. After the declaration of martial law, Roxas-Chua was detained for about a week (apparently on charges of "economic sabotage"). He had supported Macapagal in the election of 1965, and gotten on the wrong side of the regime. After Babst helped him get out of jail, he listened to the advice and subsequently supported Marcos—"at great cost." The benefits, however, seem to have exceeded the costs: with Babst's help, Roxas-Chua never again tangled with the Marcos regime.

5. The Central Bank of the Philippines headquarters, an imposing structure on the shore of Manila Bay, constructed during the term of Governor Gregorio S. Licaros (1970–1981). Photo credit: From the *Business World* collection.

presented themselves. After acquiring their banks, Marcos and his cronies used them in much the same manner as the earlier bank owners had: to support diversified family conglomerates and to extract as much booty as possible from state agencies. (A crony conglomerate, observes Fabella, is merely a family conglomerate "with additional clout thrown in.")[71] The major difference is that martial law provided particularly sustained and unhampered access to patrimonial largesse.

This "additional clout" enabled them to grab large quantities of selective credit and other benefits. The most important privileges to be gained from the Central Bank, aside from the bank license itself, were rediscounts, foreign exchange swaps, foreign loans, government deposits, and branch licenses—all of which were disbursed with a great deal of favoritism. Moreover, troubled banks with good connections enjoyed emergency loans and generous equity infusions from state banks—while other unfortunates in similarly dire straits were taken over. Examples include the receipt of bank licenses by Allied and Producers, contrary to general policy; Allied's very favorable allocations of foreign loans, rediscounts, and swaps; equity infusions for Pilipinas Bank and Republic Bank; and UCPB's

[71] Interview, Fabella, June 12, 1990.

6. First Lady Imelda R. Marcos, President Ferdinand E. Marcos, Finance Secretary Cesar Virata, and Central Bank Governor Gregorio S. Licaros (1970–1981) at the blessing of the Central Bank mint in Quezon City, September 1978. Photo credit: From the *Business World* collection.

interest-free deposit of the coconut levy. Metrobank, furthermore, was given a highly disproportionate number of branch licenses between 1974 and 1977; other Chinese-Filipino banks also did very well for themselves during the Licaros years.

Rediscounting, the most important source of selective credit over time, became important to private banks in the 1960s. As in earlier years, however, lists of priorities remained nearly all-encompassing—and the selection of recipients had little to do with any objective development criteria.[72] There was particularly clear-cut favoritism in the allocation of Central Bank rediscounts during the Marcos years. Crony banks such as Allied Bank, Interbank, and Republic Planters Bank were at times able to finance one-quarter to one-half of their assets from subsidized credit—a level that far exceeded the average of all private domestic commercial banks.

The disbursement of foreign exchange swaps was especially important in the late 1970s and early 1980s—and in early 1981 became a major

---

[72] Anonymous interview, former bank president, mid-1990. The list is discussed and reprinted in Winifrida V. Mejia, "Financial Policies and Industrial Promotion," in *Industrial Promotion Policies in the Philippines,* ed. Romeo M. Bautista, John H. Power, and Associates (Manila: Philippine Institute for Development Studies, 1979), 409–28, at 416–17, 421–28.

factor in Licaros's resignation. Swaps occur when "a commercial bank obtains a foreign currency loan or deposit, converts the currency (typically dollars) into pesos, and purchases forward dollars at a favorable rate from the Central Bank"—effectively shifting currency risk from the private sector to the public sector. This privilege accorded high profits to beneficiaries, and was disbursed on a highly discretionary basis. Patrick and Moreno reported that "control over large amounts of rediscounts and even modest amounts of swaps has been centralized at the highest levels," and that Licaros seemed to have "personally approved every swap transaction over $1 million. . . . Favoritism, rather than equal opportunity to Central Bank credit by objective criteria, seems important." Again, among the largest recipients were crony banks (PCIB, Allied, and Security). Other beneficiaries reportedly paid kickbacks for favorable allocations.

There is strong evidence that controversy over the allocation of swaps forced Licaros to resign his post in early 1981. Licaros's successor, Jaime C. Laya, acknowledged soon after taking office in 1981 that there was a "house-cleaning" effort within the Central Bank in the wake of alleged irregularities in allocations of "jumbo loans" and swaps. One ranking Central Bank official explained that Licaros's son was involved in the allocation of swaps. ("It was understandable if you go to someone in the Central Bank [to arrange swaps]," he said, "but to go to the son?") Another senior official freely discusses how Licaros "got caught with his hand in the till."[73]

Conclusion

If there was one period in the postwar Philippines when the state might have been able to effect serious reforms in the banking industry, it was after the declaration of martial law in 1972. The powers of state regulators were heightened relative to the longstanding power of the social forces in the Philippine banking industry, and it might have been possible to begin to resolve some of problems created by a banking system so thoroughly dominated by the particularistic interests of oligarchic families. Moreover, by the late 1970s the Central Bank was handing out particularly large quantities of foreign loans and other instruments of selective credit, and one

[73] Patrick and Moreno, 322; Laya, "A Period of Adjustment," *Fookien Times Philippines Yearbook 1983–84*, 161; *Fortune*, July 27, 1981, 34; Anonymous interviews, 1990. Moreover, *Fortune* explicitly connects corruption over foreign exchange deals with the quiet resignation of a senior Central Bank official who was never punished, and Virata—who, as we shall see, played a major role in Licaros's resignation—admits they had disagreements over swaps. Interview, Virata, May 24, 1991. Data on selective credit allocation come from SGV, CB, and PNB sources, and are found in tabular form in Hutchcroft, "Predatory Oligarchy, Patrimonial State: The Politics of Private Domestic Commercial Banking in the Philippines" (Ph.D. dissertation, Yale University, 1993).

might initially presume that the distribution of such largesse would be an opportunity to increase institutional leverage in such areas as bank reform and bank supervision.

The power to dispense privilege, however, was squandered for particularistic gain, and the Central Bank failed to acquire such leverage. Although Marcos professed the need to curb the powers of "an oligarchy that appropriated for itself all power and bounty," his dominant goal was merely to reappropriate the power and bounty into the hands of a new oligarchy based within his own regime. The bank reforms were ultimately unsuccessful, and the problems of bank instability deepened. Just as Marcos's modest land reform program was counteracted by the regime's rampant land grabbing, so were Marcos's modest bank reforms counteracted by the bank grabbing of Marcos and his cronies.[74]

As contradictory as his actions may appear to be, however, Marcos probably saw a real complementarity between reform and plunder; indeed, he seems—quite rationally—to have viewed reform merely as a means of expanding opportunities for capturing whatever booty the system had to offer. It is as if Marcos grabbed power with a long-term vision of plunder, and knew that the more he built up the system the more booty there would be for him and his associates to enjoy. In the same way that Weber allows for a "bureaucratic rationalization of patrimonial rulership" that does not undermine the essential nature of that rule, one can say that Marcos's efforts at reform were intended to streamline the plunder of the state.[75]

An important consideration, it seems, is a regime's security of tenure. If there is a feeling that the regime will endure into the long term, there is no necessity to maximize gains in the short term. After the declaration of martial law, Marcos seems to have felt secure enough to know that he, personally, would be able to reap the benefits of a better-run state apparatus. He and Licaros wanted enough reform to help curb the crippling problem of bank instability and to improve the functioning of the banking system as a whole—but at the same time wanted to ensure their ability to milk the system selectively for their own benefit. Both of them began their careers of booty-gathering with close involvement in the Central Bank's allocation of foreign exchange licenses in the 1950s, and both had an intimate knowledge of the enormous opportunities and fundamental weaknesses of the Philippine financial system. The more the weaknesses could be cured, they understood, the more secure their opportunities for

[74] Marcos, *The Democratic Revolution*, 6. Similarly, Doner found that major participants in the Progressive Car Manufacturing Program "felt that the impact of martial law was largely to disrupt routine procedures and institutions." Particularly disruptive to the overall effort was the relationship between Marcos and his favored crony in the auto industry, Ricardo Silverio. Richard F. Doner, *Driving a Bargain: Automobile Industrialization and Japanese Firms in Southeast Asia* (Berkeley: University of California Press, 1991), 171.

[75] Weber, *Economy and Society*, II: 1098 (see also 1028).

plunder would ultimately become. In short, it was entirely logical both to *deal with* problems in the banking sector and to *make deals within* the banking sector.

If we treat reform and plunder as complementary goals, we can better understand how even in the midst of clear attempts at increased regulatory capacity one finds the endurance of a high degree of arbitrariness in the operation of the state apparatus. In an era of tightening regulations, those with Palace connections could easily evade them; similarly, the targets of reform could be chosen quite selectively, depending on their relationship to the regime. As the powers of the Central Bank increased, little heed was paid to the nondiscrimination clause found in the recommendations of the 1972 IMF-CBP Commission, meant to "assure equitable treatment" in all aspects of bank regulation. Indeed, one former Central Bank official regarded it as nothing more than a "motherhood statement," contradicted by "so many exceptions" made on the basis of "instructions from above." She concludes that—despite all the reform efforts—bank supervision actually "deteriorated under martial law."[76]

In summary, not only did the reforms of 1972 fall short of the mark but the rise of the cronies bred even greater havoc for the system as a whole. Under martial law, there were unprecedented changes to the ownership structure of the banking system and unprecedented advantages to those closest to the political apparatus. Indeed, as noted earlier, it was controversy over the allocation of selective credit that led to the resignation of Governor Licaros in early 1981. The technocrats and the multilateral institutions—increasingly at odds with Licaros—probably expected that under his successor, Jaime Laya, the environment would become more hospitable to thoroughgoing reform. As we shall see, however, the logic of booty capitalism continued to overwhelm the need for reform.

[76] IMF-CBP, 60; Interviews, Valenzuela, April 25 and May 9, 1990.

CHAPTER SEVEN

Further Reform, Further Failure: Technocrats, Cronies, and Crises, 1980–1983

In the morass of crony abuse afflicting the Central Bank, a textbook-style liberalizing reform effort intended to promote competition, longer-term credit, and greater mobilization of savings was undertaken between 1979 and 1981 by the World Bank, the IMF, and Finance Minister Cesar Virata. By neglecting to pay adequate attention to the political realities around them, however, these would-be reformers created a package incapable of addressing the major problems of the Philippine banking system. Their efforts were almost immediately overtaken by the financial crisis of 1981, triggered by the flight of a Chinese-Filipino businessman who left behind nearly $85 million in debt. An even larger political and economic crisis came in the wake of the assassination of former Senator Benigno Aquino in August 1983. In the end, such problems as cronyism and instability not only undermined the financial reforms; they also proved far more important than the reforms themselves in determining the nature of change within the financial sector.

This chapter begins by discussing the composition of the reform package and the politics of its promulgation. In the second section, I examine the politics of the financial crisis, and the massive bailout operation that fueled increasing business resentment against crony capitalism. The third section analyzes the overall impact of reform and crisis on the financial sector, and the conclusion examines the political and economic upheaval that began to shake the foundations of the Marcos regime in late 1983. By the end of this short period, it became increasingly obvious—even to the somewhat slow-witted multilateral institutions—that the endurance of longstanding political problems placed enormous constraints on the cause of financial and economic reform.

The Financial Reforms of 1980 and 1981

The 1980–1981 reforms consisted of three major elements, the first of which was introduction of universal banks, able to underwrite securities and take equity positions in manufacturing, agricultural, and other enterprises. The goal was to encourage banks to make equity investments, as well as to promote longer-term lending and to inject competition into the financial system. Second, the reforms sought to liberalize interest rates and thus promote competition and savings mobilization. Third, selective credit allocation was to be restructured with the goals of giving increasing weight to economic criteria and promoting longer-term planning. Virata, who claims parentage over the package as a whole, explains that its various components were motivated by concern that the bulk of long-term finance came from foreign rather than domestic sources.

Overall, Virata's reform package seems not to have conformed to Central Bank thinking. The 1972 reforms, of course, were crafted by Licaros and attempted to address increasing Central Bank concern over the stability of the banking sector. The new reforms, on the other hand, devoted surprisingly little attention to issues of bank supervision or bank instability, despite the overarching centrality of these issues in previous years (and quite unlike either the recommendations of the 1972 Joint Commission or the later 1988 World Bank report, both of which were heavily influenced by Central Bank anxieties). The first key element of the reforms, the creation of universal banks, was a source of particular dispute. As Fabella explains, "Licaros was *not* in favor of unibanking, Virata was— and Virata prevailed."[1]

To be sure, Virata and Licaros had very different approaches to the problems of the financial sector. The latter, as we have seen, was a career Central Bank official who possessed an intimate understanding of how the banking system actually worked—and at the same time ensured that a portion of the system's benefits would land on his own plate. Like Marcos, Licaros could simultaneously pursue the goals of reform and plunder. Virata, on the other hand, led the "technocrats," a group of well-trained officials looked upon kindly by foreign bankers and multilateral institutions. He was far more comfortable addressing technical issues and macroeconomic goals than the power dynamics of the banking industry—and widely perceived to be above the fray of cronyism and corruption that surrounded him.

New conditions provided Virata and his allies in the World Bank and IMF with the leverage to push through their own brand of reforms. Up until about 1978, recalls Virata, it was "relatively easy" to obtain international loans; by 1980, however, the business press reported that "bank-

[1] Interviews, Cesar Virata, May 24, 1991, and Armand Fabella, June 8, 1990.

ers were hardening their lending rates (and attitudes) to the Philippines." The imprimatur of the multilateral institutions became ever more important for ensuring continuing access to international loans. Marcos understood the game all too well, and readily elevated the public stature of his technocrats and their reform agenda. As he proclaimed to *Fortune* in mid-1981, "I'm going to sit back and let the technocrats run things."[2]

When Virata, the IMF, and the World Bank proposed major reforms of the financial sector and the tariff structure between 1979 and 1981, Marcos—and all those with an interest in continued access to foreign finance—could ill afford to ignore them. Even those in the Central Bank who initially opposed the reforms later went along with them because they understood the stakes involved. "You have to see this in proper perspective," one official explained, noting that Philippine "involvement with the World Bank. . . . is a good relationship, with lots of loans." Licaros, meanwhile, was resigned to being a "guinea pig."[3]

The reform effort began with a joint World Bank–IMF study of the financial sector in early 1979. The mission's main criticism of the financial system was its failure "to provide adequate long-term finance," and the report argued that breaking down the functional separation between the activities of commercial banks and other financial institutions (particularly investment houses) would generate longer-term lending (as well as "term transformation," whereby banks utilize short-term deposits in making longer-term loans). In addition, they hoped to promote the development of the country's weak capital markets, and encourage competition and efficiency within "a [banking] community which does not, by tradition, welcome competition."

In response, Licaros in August 1979 created the Financial Reforms Committee—headed by long-time adviser Armand Fabella—which voiced major objections to the World Bank–IMF plan.[4] The 1976 regulations discouraging investment in money market instruments, argued one top Licaros adviser, were already moving the system toward longer-term lending. In a report that probably expressed Licaros's views, he notes "strong reservations" against allowing banks greater freedom to invest directly in nonfinancial enterprises, in part out of fears that it would risk excessive concentration of economic power. Most important—given a history in which bank managements commonly lacked objectivity in "processing

---

[2] *Central Bank Review,* January 23, 1979, 7; Interview, Virata, May 24, 1991; *The Banker,* April/May 1980, 137; *Fortune,* July 27, 1981, 37; see also Robin Broad, *Unequal Alliance, 1979–86: The World Bank, the International Monetary Fund, and the Philippines* (Berkeley: University of California Press, 1988), 177.

[3] Broad, 147 (quoting Benito Legarda Jr., former Central Bank deputy governor).

[4] World Bank–IMF, *The Philippines: Aspects of the Financial Sector* (Washington, D.C.: The World Bank, 1980), ii, vii, 71, 76 (quote from vii); *CB Review,* September 4, 1979, 6; August 19, 1980, 12.

loan applications of firms with special relationships with the bank" and most bank failures could be traced to excessive DOSRI loans—the report warned of increased "probability of abuse in the extension of credit." There were already problems controlling insider loans, noted the adviser; "to allow banks to acquire equities of private corporations would give rise to *similar or perhaps more difficult problems.*"[5]

While Fabella's committee was unwilling to break down all functional differentiation between banks and investment houses, it did propose that a new category of larger, better capitalized banks (officially known as expanded commercial banks, or ECBs, but popularly known as universal banks, or unibanks) be enabled to move into investment banking functions. In Fabella's view, it was dangerous to adopt the German pattern of enabling all commercial banks to become universal banks (as the multilateral institutions were proposing) because it ignored the fact that while German banks "are professionally controlled by managers," Philippine banks "are almost entirely family-controlled" and sometimes "made to bleed to support other family problems." Given such realities, Licaros and his advisers urged that only the larger banks be eligible for universal bank licenses. While the World Bank subsequently expressed disappointment at the Central Bank's "cautious approach," it seems to have eventually resigned itself to the modification of its recommendations. The Central Bank, in the process, began to give strong public support to the implementation of the financial reform package.[6]

The issue of universal banking was widely discussed and debated in business and political circles. The Bankers Association of the Philippines gave its broad support to the new entities in a November 1979 memorandum to the Central Bank. While noting concern—likely among the smaller banks—that banking would become an "Exclusive 'Big Boy's Game,'" the BAP probably viewed the reforms as a way of finally squashing what was left of the challenge from investment houses. Fabella notes that although there were divisions within the BAP along the lines of big banks, small banks, and foreign banks, "they were monolithic as far as threats" from investment houses were concerned. The bankers showed little enthusiasm for the goal of promoting longer-term lending, merely noting that

[5] Internal Central Bank Memorandum of Arnulfo B. Aurellano, special assistant to Licaros, on "Report of the Joint IMF–World Bank Mission on aspects of the financial sector in the Philippines," October 8, 1979, 1–2, 6 (emphasis added). Thanks to Robin Broad for sharing this and other documents from the period.

[6] *Business Day,* August 28, 1980; Central Bank of the Philippines, "The Financial Reforms of 1980," *CB Review,* September 16, 1980, 4; World Bank, *Philippines Staff Appraisal Report on the Industrial Finance Project* (Washington: World Bank, 1981), 21–22. See also Fabella's remarks in Broad, 146, on how the World Bank–IMF recommendations were "toned down." By November 1979, Licaros had already begun to shift toward public support of the "multipurpose banking" proposals. *CB Review,* November 27, 1979, 4.

they already provided such finance through the common practice of rolling over short-term loans.[7]

The Investment Houses Association of the Philippines, on the other hand, viewed the reforms as unfair. Unibanks would retain their cheaper sources of funds (regular deposits) and gain the right to expand into investment houses' turf, while investment houses would enjoy no expansion in their scope of activity. To be sure, the influence of this sector had rapidly declined over the past decade; from their freewheeling, unregulated origins in the late 1960s, they were increasingly squeezed out by Central Bank regulations (especially the 1976 curbs on the money market) and overshadowed by the commercial banks. Sensing that the reforms would give commercial banks the opportunity to come in for the kill, perhaps, their major argument against unibanking was that it would bring a "politically dangerous concentration of economic power." Others—including elements of the Left, the elite opposition to Marcos, and the Philippine Chamber of Commerce and Industry—voiced similar fears.

Investment houses also challenged World Bank–IMF claims that unibanking would promote competition between commercial banks and investment houses[8]—a problematic claim indeed for a plan that actually encouraged commercial banks to absorb, not compete against, the investment houses.[9] While the investment houses had basis for complaint, however, they had little power to stop the reforms. In any case, those owned by families that also owned commercial banks had little cause to worry: the net impact on the family conglomerate was likely to be slight.

In April 1980, legislation drafted by the Fabella committee sailed through the rubber-stamp parliament—after Marcos threatened to pass the seven laws by presidential decree in the event that the lawmakers would not act favorably on them. In their final form, the reforms allowed

[7] Bankers Association of the Philippines, "Statement of Views Re: Proposal to Permit/ Encourage the Development of Multi-Purpose Financial Institutions," November 20, 1979; Interview, Fabella, June 8, 1990.

[8] Investment House Association of the Philippines, "IHAP Position on Universal Banking," unpublished manuscript, n.d.; Sixto K. Roxas, "The Philippines' Third Wave?" *Fookien Times Philippines Yearbook 1981–82*, 164, 170, at 164; *FEER*, September 21, 1979, 78. On other groups' opposition to the reforms, see Diwa Guinigundo, "What Is Unibanking?" *Diliman Review* 28, no. 3 (May-June 1980), 3–6; *The Philippine Financial System: A Primer* (Manila: Ibon Databank Phil., Inc., 1983), 97–102; Broad, 142–48, 162–77; and *Philippine Daily Express*, February 8, 1980, reprinted in *CB Review*, February 12, 1980, 5.

[9] After proclaiming that the reforms would bring "direct competition" between commercial banks and investment houses, the World Bank–IMF mission quickly noted that "this is perhaps less a conflict than it appears, as it is recalled that the present investment houses have close links with the banks and are also actively involved in the money markets." World Bank–IMF, 80. The claim was made even more problematic since the reforms were to have led to the creation of fewer (but bigger and more efficient) financial institutions—hardly a sure means of injecting competition into an already uncompetitive environment.

banks with P500 million capitalization (then equal to $68 million) to apply for an expanded commercial bank license. Unibanks were allowed to own up to 35 percent equity in so-called nonallied enterprises (that is, firms engaged in a range of nonfinancial activities), and—to encourage diffusion of bank ownership—required to publicly list 10 percent of their required minimum capital. Consolidation was to be promoted with tax breaks to institutions that merged to qualify for a unibanking license.[10]

While Licaros ended up playing a major role in promoting the reforms that Virata initiated (albeit in modified form), the two men continued to disagree over other issues, the most important being the allocation of foreign exchange swaps. In early 1981, Virata seemingly played a major role in forcing Licaros's resignation from the post of Central Bank governor.[11] The new governor, Jaime Laya, was a close associate of Virata, with strikingly similar background and perspectives: both had formerly taught business administration at the University of the Philippines and been a part of the country's premier accounting firm, Sycip, Gorres & Velayo.[12] While both clearly preferred to dwell in the realm of the "should be" rather than the "what is," Virata was particularly renowned for his lack of political savvy. It was this ability to ignore larger issues of power and privilege, perhaps, that enabled them to serve the Marcos regime faithfully to the end, even as other technocrats resigned out of frustration over repeated defeats and "constraints on their powers."[13]

Virata was able to hand-pick not only Laya but also a number of other key economic policymakers, and was himself elevated to the post of prime minister later in the year. These changes reinforced perceptions that the

[10] Broad, 148; *CB Review,* August 26, 1980, 5; September 16, 1980, 4; September 9, 1980, 5; and August 16, 1980, 4; *Business Day,* August 25, 1980, reprinted in *CB Review,* August 26, 1980, 7; and "The Financial Reforms of 1980," a Central Bank document reprinted in the *CB Review* between August 19 and September 16, 1980. The 35 percent level was meant to guard against excessive dominance of banks in industry; there was also a prohibition on ECBs investing more than 50 percent of their own total net worth in nonallied enterprises.

[11] Licaros resigned one year before completing his second six-year term as governor; according to *FEER,* some "bankers and politicians" suggested that "Virata, in a private confrontation with Marcos, was prevailed upon to remain in the cabinet if Licaros were to resign." Virata, in fact, felt confident enough in his power to boast that "[if] I [had] wanted [the Central Bank governorship], I would have got it and there's no doubt about that." Ten years later, when asked about his relationship with Licaros, Virata remarked that he had a "difficult period" with Licaros in 1979 and 1980, when "we had differences of opinions about swaps"—reportedly the issue over which Licaros was forced to resign. *FEER,* January 23, 1981, 38; Interview, Virata, May 24, 1991.

[12] As noted, Laya was Central Bank deputy governor for supervision between 1974 and 1978; in addition, from 1975 to 1978, he concurrently held the post of budget minister. In 1978, after he was elected to the rubber-stamp parliament (the Interim Batasang Pambansa), he remained budget minister but had to resign his Central Bank post.

[13] *FEER,* January 23, 1981, 39; Broad, 90; *AWSJ,* August 15, 1981, October 22, 1981, May 27, 1983. Virata is entirely at ease when discussing issues of macroeconomic policy, but visibly stiffens when asked about the corruption of those for whom he formerly worked. When asked about such matters, he gives the distinct impression that he does not even consider them worthy of academic study. Interview, Virata, May 24, 1991.

technocrats were in the ascendent. Soon after taking office, Laya—in cooperation with Virata—complemented the introduction of unibanking with the two other elements of reform: interest rate liberalization and changes in the allocation of selective credit. With such a major reform agenda in place, there were widespread expectations of a major transformation of the Philippine financial system. One bank's 1981 annual report proclaimed "a new era" of efficiency, productivity, and prudence in which "banks no longer enjoy the protective benefits of the past." The Central Bank expected that expanded functions for banks would result in economies of scale, and larger financial institutions would both "provide services more efficiently" and "compete more effectively" in the international sphere.[14] In the end, however, the technocratic effort at financial reform was drowned by larger economic and political crises afflicting the martial law regime. Before analyzing the failure in greater detail, it is necessary to examine the first torpedo to smash the reform armada: the financial crisis of early 1981.

The Dewey Dee Caper: "These Things Happen"

As discussed earlier, the financial reform package gave little attention to a history of weak bank supervision and major bank instability. Within the Central Bank, memories of the mid-1970s bank travails remained vivid. According to Fabella, fear of bank runs was "always . . . paramount" among Central Bank officials, and the Continental Bank affair was treated as a "watershed development" punctuating the system's deep-seated instability. Virata, on the other hand, seems to have been scarcely impressed by the bank runs of 1974 and 1976, and little interested in issues of bank supervision (which he considered "an internal matter of the Central Bank.") He and his allies from the multilateral institutions confidently pushed their macroeconomic goals with little regard for the historical and political context in which the goals were to be accomplished. The World Bank–IMF report reveals particularly appalling ignorance of the history and politics of the Philippine banking system in casually noting that while "all-purpose banking" would "make bank supervision more difficult," such "problems will arise only if the degree of sophistication of bank supervisors does not keep step with that of bank managers." At another point, they even stated that "prudent expansion of term transformation does not need to be limited by *the remote possibility of a general panic.*"[15]

[14] Insular Bank of Asia and America, *1981 Annual Report,* 3; Central Bank, "The Financial Reforms of 1980."

[15] Interviews, Fabella, June 8 and 12, 1990; Interview, Jaime Laya, May 21, 1990; Interview, Virata, May 24, 1991; World Bank–IMF, iv, 78 (emphasis added). As we have seen, bank supervisors had long been unable to keep step with bank managers. Virata and Laya both

In fact, the possibility was far from remote, and it was not long before just such a panic hit the financial system. On January 9, 1981—less than two years after the reforms were initiated, and in the very midst of their promulgation—Filipino-Chinese textile manufacturer and banker Dewey Dee fled the country, leaving behind nearly $85 million in debt. The result was a widespread bank run that eventually led to the closing of two prominent investment houses and to changes of ownership of several banks. The financial crisis ended up overshadowing and derailing the reform package, and produced changes in the financial system that were of far more lasting significance than the financial reforms themselves. As Laya was later to explain, after the Dewey Dee caper "there were just so many fires to put out it distracted us from [the financial reforms]. . . . Long-term objectives had no place in the problems of the moment."[16]

Dee was among a group of Chinese-Filipino businessmen (known as the "Four Horsemen of the Apocalypse") that owned an interest in Interbank in the late 1970s before buying into Security Bank in 1980. He and certain friends were suspected of involvement in such illegal activities as "black-market foreign exchange operations, smuggling, and even arson," and were thought to have used government connections (presumably with high Central Bank officials) to obtain a range of cheap credit: rediscounts, foreign loans, and swaps. Dee also had a reputation as a "big-time gambler . . . very popular in Las Vegas and Macao" who also dealt heavily on the commodities markets; prior to his departure, he was said to have lost large sums trading in sugar and gold. He and other textile manufacturers had recently been hard-hit, as well, by recession, cheaper imports, and smuggling.[17]

Regardless of the precise details, Dee was in desperate financial straits. When he fled the country, he left behind debts to sixteen commercial banks, twelve investment houses, and seventeen other financial institutions—as well as some $4 million in postdated checks that were floating around the informal financial markets of Binondo, Manila's Chinatown. The money market was especially hard hit by Dee's departure, as fund placers demanded early termination of their holdings of commercial pa-

---

claimed in interviews that they did not remember any of the details from the Continental Bank case, despite the fact that they occupied key positions either during or in the immediate wake of Vicente Tan's arrest (Virata was finance minister, while Laya assumed the post of deputy governor for bank supervision in late 1974).

[16] Interview, Laya, May 21, 1990.

[17] Bank of the Philippine Islands document on the Chinese-Filipino community. Dee quickly sold out of Security Bank, in December 1980. Manapat provides additional information on Dee, but it is difficult to believe his assertion that Dee was a Marcos crony—and preposterous to suppose that Dee's departure was part of a Marcos effort to move money out of the country. See Ricardo Manapat, *Some are Smarter than Others: The History of Marcos' Crony Capitalism* (New York: Aletheia Publications, 1991), 428–31.

per. Rumors circulated that other highly indebted Chinese-Filipino businesspersons were also skipping town. "For a time," reported the *Far Eastern Economic Review*, "the air was so thick with speculative talk that one businessman found it necessary to surrender his passport just to show he had no intention of leaving the country. And when, one payroll day, some construction workers queued before the teller's window of a Filipino-Chinese-owned bank, word went around that there was a run." Another recent bank run, as well as fears that many others in similarly dire financial straits might follow Dee's example, created an atmosphere in which "every bank and every banker was virtually suspect."[18]

Dee's swindle came only five days before Laya's January 14 assumption of the governorship, although it was seemingly not until late January that creditors learned they had been swindled and panic spread throughout the financial community. In an effort to calm nerves, Laya's first reaction was to downplay the incident. "Some banks run away with money," he said, "some banks get held up. Some banks get flooded out. These things happen." Marcos insisted that the banking system remained sound despite "defalcations by some individual bankers." Before long, however, the authorities were forced to initiate a massive effort to try to restore the confidence of a badly shaken financial sector.

As Laya faced the herculean task of cleaning up a mess whose origins long preceded his ascent to the governorship, he was forced to acknowledge that the financial crisis exposed "fundamental weaknesses" that "were easy to disregard, to conceal and overlook, in times of easy credit, high growth and rapid inflation. . . . Forgotten were the fiascos of old, Victan and Continental Bank." Because of the underlying fragility of the system as a whole, he concluded, "Dewey Dee's flight had a far greater impact than might have been expected with the amount of money that he took with him." Unfortunately, however, the reform agenda of the day was not designed to deal with the type of "fundamental weaknesses" that Dewey Dee's swindle exposed—precisely because its major proponents had, indeed, forgotten the quite recent lessons of Continental Bank and earlier bouts of bank instability. For Central Bank officials long worried about the system's fundamental instability, on the other hand, Dewey Dee's flight merely "clinched the problem."[19]

[18] *FEER*, February 13, 1981, 64 and March 27, 1981, 86; *AWSJ*, January 30, 1981; Anonymous interview, 1990. There had been a short bank run on Consolidated Bank earlier in January—and the previous month an officer of Pacific Banking Corporation fled the country, seemingly with $4 million in taxes that the bank had collected for the government. See *AWSJ*, January 30, 1981; *FEER*, January 23, 1981, 39; February 13, 1981, 64; March 27, 1981, 86; and May 5, 1983, 97.

[19] *AWSJ*, January 30, 1981; *FEER*, February 6, 1981, 87; Jaime C. Laya, "End of the Crisis of Confidence," speech delivered at a dialogue on the Philippine financial situation, Central Bank of the Philippines, August 18, 1981, published in *CB Review*, September 1981, 1, 11–

Dewey Dee's flight contributed to a hasty, piecemeal attempt at a more relevant type of bank reform, one that would increase the powers of the Central Bank to regulate the banking sector. At some point in late January or February, as the extent of the crisis became ever more apparent, Laya obtained a presidential decree that would grant greater powers to bank supervisors; of particular significance was the relaxation of the "secrecy of deposits" law so that bank supervisors could more readily examine bank deposits and discover bank fraud. In addition, the Central Bank tightened restrictions on DOSRI credit.[20]

The most urgent task was to assess the damage done to particular institutions and to decide how to respond to what he termed a "crisis of confidence." Not surprisingly, institutions with which Dee had earlier been affiliated (including Interbank and Security Bank) turned out to be among his biggest creditors. But it eventually became clear that Dee's firms were by no means the only large casualties of the financial crisis, and four leading economic empires were in deep trouble: Herminio Disini's Herdis group of companies, Bancom Development Corporation and its related enterprises, Ricardo Silverio's group of automobile and financial firms, and Rodolfo Cuenca's construction-based group. With the exception of Bancom, all these empires were controlled by Marcos cronies whose success had depended critically upon their access to the Palace. For many years, their political connections had been readily translated into easy access to money market borrowing, and in the process their financial position became highly leveraged and very precarious. The Dee crisis threatened to bring them down in one fell swoop.[21]

19, at 11; Interview, Fabella, June 8, 1990. As chief of bank supervision in the 1970s, it will be recalled, Laya seemingly spent more time worrying about the internal efficiency of his department than the overall effectiveness of bank supervision.

[20] The decree (P.D. 1792) was promulgated in mid-February but antedated to mid-January in order to be given a date *prior* to the January 17 "lifting" of martial law. Although Marcos formally lifted martial law (first imposed in September 1972) to give the appearance of political liberalization, he retained most of the emergency powers of martial law in practice. Despite earlier statements to the contrary (*AWSJ*, February 17, 1981), Laya confirmed that the decree was antedated (Interview, May 21, 1990). Foreign currency deposits were excluded from the decree. *FEER*, March 27, 1981, 89; *AWSJ*, February 13 and 17, 1981; *CB Review*, January 1982, 12, and January 1984, 7; Jean-Claude Nascimento, "Crisis in the Financial Sector and the Authorities' Reaction: The Philippines," in *Banking Crises: Cases and Issues* ed. V. Sundararajan and Tomás J. T. Baliño (Washington, D.C.: International Monetary Fund, 1991), 202–3.

[21] *FEER*, January 30, 1981, 63; February 13, 1981, 64; and June 12, 1981, 81. Bancom had independent standing in the financial community, and cannot be considered a crony firm. But its close ties to the Palace must not be overlooked: one of Bancom's top executives, Rolando Gapud, was Marcos's personal financial adviser, and its founder, Sixto K. Roxas, was said to be "very close" to President and Mrs. Marcos. Mahal Kong Pilipinas, Inc., *VIPs of Philippine Business* (Metro Manila: Mahal Kong Pilipinas, Inc., 1988), 281. Other major Dee creditors included Atrium Capital (Disini's investment house, formerly controlled by the Orosa family in the mid-1970s with Dee as a minority stockholder), DBP, Citibank, and several Chinese-Filipino banks.

Laya put in place an elaborate rescue operation, with the goal of re-habilitating the distressed financial institutions and industrial firms. As Laya said at the outset, "we want (the financial institutions) to survive, but a little bruised."[22] In the end, the banks did indeed survive but each of the four major empires hit by the crisis had been greatly transformed. One major impact of the rescue operation was to increase the government's direct involvement in the banking sector. Government agencies and banks assumed a majority stake in four banks (Interbank, Combank, Union Bank, and Pilipinas Bank); a fifth bank (Leonardo Ty's Associated Bank, seemingly unaffected by the Dewey Dee crisis) also had the good fortune of government rescue.[23] Although the banks were still officially classified as private entities, "[c]ritics screamed that government was taking advantage of the recession [and using public funds] to expand its private sector control and to enrich itself."[24]

Even more vociferous criticism came from the fact that the biggest beneficiaries of the bailout had been crony-owned firms. Jaime Ongpin, president of a major mining firm (and—quite interestingly—the brother of Industry Minister Roberto Ongpin, who headed one of the rescuing agencies, the National Development Corporation), led the charge in accusing the government of "throwing good money after bad." In his view, the incompetent firms had little going for them aside from their political connections, and pumping more money into them would "merely prolong their agony." Ongpin called the bailout "the most obscene, brazen and disgraceful misallocation of taxpayers' money in the history of the Philippines." At a time when many businesspersons considered high interest rates a major problem, they resented the fact that relatively cheap funds were going to the president's friends and felt that the money could be better spent on supporting healthy firms.[25] Anger over the bailout became

22 The overall design of the plan is described in Laya, "End of the Crisis," 12–15; *FEER*, June 12, 1981, 80–81; and *AWSJ*, August 18, 1981. Laya is quoted in *AWSJ*, February 13, 1981.

23 The DBP provided equity in and took control of Associated in late 1981. Once DOSRI loans were written off, Ty was left with a mere 2.5 percent share of the bank—but nonetheless, in early 1982, given "right of first refusal" to reclaim the institution he had plundered. Ty, a monosodium glutamate tycoon, held the influential position of chair of the Federation of Filipino-Chinese Chambers of Commerce and Industry between 1976 and 1981. *FEER*, December 4, 1981; Yoshihara Kunio, *The Rise of Ersatz Capitalism in South-East Asia* (Quezon City: Ateneo de Manila Press, 1988), 188; *Business World*, March 1, 1988; *Philippine Daily Inquirer*, December 12, 1995.

24 *FEER*, March 19, 1982, 74; March 26, 1982, 88. Another private bank, Republic Planters Bank, came under the joint ownership of DBP and the Philippine Sugar Commission in the late 1970s. The U.S. Embassy was later, in April 1983, to publish a confidential study entitled "Creeping State Capitalism in the Philippines." *AWSJ*, November 8, 1983.

25 *FEER*, July 10, 1981, 60; *AWSJ*, November 8, 1983, August 20, 1981, and August 18, 1981. As president of the Benguet Corporation, Ongpin was by no means a disinterested party in making these criticisms. On the one hand, he was a victim of cronyism: Cuenca's construction firm, CDCP, was the major competitor of Benguet's subsidiary company, Engineering Equipment and had long been favored in the granting of government contracts. On

one of the major issues to energize business opposition to the Marcos regime; in late 1981, the Makati Business Club (named after the premier center of finance and business) was formed to give vent to growing concerns about cronyism and the overall ill health of the economy.

Jaime Ongpin argued that Laya would have been wiser to "place the companies in receivership and wind down their affairs in orderly fashion."[26] Similarly, some note that Laya could have adopted a strategy of liquidating distressed financial institutions and providing funds for those who wished to withdraw their money from them; in this way, the distressed financial institutions could have been liquidated while investors' nerves were calmed at the same time.[27] In the end, however, Laya adopted a bailout strategy that rescued most crony enterprises and at the same time resulted in the marked decline of the three crony empires. The best way to understand the eventual configuration of the bailout, it seems, is to view it from the perspective of Marcos. In the wake of the crisis, it was in Marcos's interest to restore business confidence, retain the diversified holdings he had so studiously built up with the help of his cronies, and give international observers the impression that the technocrats had the upper hand over the cronies. Laya, widely known for his close ties to the regime, crafted a strategy that achieved each of these goals.[28]

First, it addressed the crisis of confidence that could have threatened Marcos's entire political and economic realm. Laya explained that neither the public nor "better managed" enterprises could withstand "such a string of failures" among financial institutions and corporate borrowers. The crony firms had to be "serviced" first, he said, because it was their borrowing that put the greatest strain on the investment houses and the financial system in general.[29] Second, by rescuing rather than liquidating the crony enterprises and facilitating their transfer from the hands of declining crony empires to regime-controlled government entities, Laya

---

the other hand, the firms that Ongpin managed were not themselves bereft of crony influence: after 1986, it was learned that Benguet had been secretly controlled by Benjamin Romualdez (a brother of the First Lady) from 1974 to 1985. One might suppose that the Romualdez link was not an entirely useless asset in the day-to-day operations of either Benguet or Engineering Equipment. *FEER*, July 31, 1981, 79; *AWSJ*, April 4, 1986.

[26] *FEER*, September 24, 1982, 107–9; *AWSJ*, August 20, 1981. Other major grievances were the coconut levy and the generally depressed outlook for the economy as a whole.

[27] One of Laya's former colleagues at the Central Bank notes that because there was a policy not to close banks, the weak institutions just continued to endure on borrowed funds. The institutions survived, but the overall system emerged no stronger. *AWSJ*, December 14, 1981; Anonymous interview, former senior Central Bank official, 1990.

[28] On Laya's close relationship to the First Couple, see, for example, *AWSJ*, January 15 and December 14, 1981. One former colleague remarked that "Laya had always to think what the powers-that-be would want." Anonymous interview, former Central Bank official, 1990.

[29] Laya, "End of the Crisis," 15, 19, 16; *FEER*, June 12, 1981, 80; *AWSJ*, August 18, 1981.

helped the regime retain a strong grip on the enterprises it had so assidu-
ously acquired through the years; the premier crony empire, the Marcos
empire, was very much intact. At the same time, it should be recalled, the
still-healthy crony empires of Benedicto, Cojuangco, Tan, and others continued to enrich the regime as a whole.

Third, the eventual course of Laya's bailout strategy gave him a good
defense against charges of favoring the three cronies. He claimed that "all
of those cronies were really wiped out . . . [and] not rehabilitated." On
closer examination of each bailout, it seems that the decline of crony
empires was accomplished with considerable ambivalence, and decided
on an ad hoc, case-by-case basis. Disini, for example, was at first allowed to
retain a share in Interbank and his businesses, but later forced to sell off
nearly everything (even his second bank, Combank, which was not directly
affected by the Dewey Dee crisis) to pay off his debts. For reasons that are
not entirely clear, Disini was in the end given worse treatment than non-
relative Alejandro Ty; after their firms were rescued by government entities, Disini was forced to sign a no-buy-back agreement while Ty was given
the right of first refusal to reclaim what he had lost. Disini was much
aggrieved, and Laya even claims (apparently in an effort to dispute frequent observations that he was close to the Palace) that "I got scolded by
Mr. and Mrs. Marcos, particularly over [my treatment of] Disini."[30] Silverio's empire was undermined with much less hesitation, no doubt in part
because he lost favor with the Palace. Once again, government entities
acquired its major elements.[31] Overall, while there seems to have been an

[30] *AWSJ,* April 22 and July 23, 1981; *FEER,* July 13, 1981, 78 and May 14, 1982, 86–87;
Victoria S. Licuanan, *An Analysis of the Institutional Framework of the Philippine Short-term Financial Markets* (Manila: Philippine Institute for Development Studies, 1986), 24; Laya, "End of
the Crisis," 15–16; Interview, Laya, May 21, 1990. Disini was forced to provide assurances that
he would never "buy back any of the [transferred] firms . . . and that he could not expand
into businesses which would compete with any of the companies just absorbed by the government." In a setting where failed bank owners are commonly given a second chance to
mismanage their institutions, this was unusual indeed. Although Laya had earlier provided
assurances that the former owners would be given a "right of first refusal" to purchase back
those assets taken over by the government and stated that government banks "stand ready to
dispose of their investment to private interests," he was now sealing the fate of a crony empire
and protecting the investments of government corporations. It is not known who extracted
the assurance from Disini, but the former president of Combank noted that "Laya wanted
Disini out of the financial system." Interview, Antonio P. Gatmaitan, September 18, 1989.

[31] His troubles were reportedly compounded by large debts to Mrs. Marcos's Ministry of
Human Settlements (MHS) and by the displeasure of the Marcoses over the course of a
romance between Silverio's son and their daughter, Imee. In mid-1981, Marcos ordered Laya
to "throw the book" at the Silverio group for alleged violations of banking regulations, and
on an official visit to Washington in late 1982, Marcos (trying to deny charges of cronyism)
called Silverio a "nobody." *FEER,* July 10, 1981, 60; September 4, 1981, 79; April 16, 1982,
60, 62–63; May 14, 1982, 87–88; October 1, 1982, 94; January 6, 1983, 61; and March 8,
1984, 105; Richard F. Doner, *Driving a Bargain: Automobile Industrialization and Japanese Firms
in Southeast Asia* (Berkeley: University of California Press, 1991), 182; *AWSJ,* April 22, 1981.
The personal factors that soured the Marcos-Silverio relationship were confirmed by two

initial effort to preserve as much as possible of the crony empires of Disini, Silverio, and Cuenca, they were in the end forced into major decline.

The weakening of the three empires was later highlighted by the regime to show that the cronies were being tamed by the technocrats. Marcos, clearly sensitive to the way mounting criticism of the cronies could undermine his "developmentalist" reputation among foreign aid agencies and international creditors, wanted to send a clear message that crony capitalism was being tamed by such technocrats as Virata, Laya, and Roberto Ongpin. By curbing—but not destroying—the empires of his three worst-performing cronies, Marcos made it appear that the allies of his foreign creditors were in the ascendent. Disini, in fact, complained that he was "being made an example to prove the fiction of cronyism and to prove that technocrats . . . are firmly in charge." Marcos must have been especially pleased when, over a year after the bailout began, the *Asian Wall Street Journal* reported a widespread perception that "the technocrats are riding high," and asserting their control over the cronies.[32] While there is no question that the technocrats did, indeed, have heightened influence over policymaking during this period, it became increasingly apparent that Marcos was placing clear limits on the extent of their new powers. The goals of the technocratic-sponsored reforms were soon to be swept aside not only by all the uncertainties generated by Dewey Dee's flight, but also by the endurance of a cronyism that was still—despite occasional appearances to the contrary—"firmly in charge."

Assessing the Impact: Reforms, Crisis, and Cronyism

Judged by its various goals, the reform package introduced in 1980 and 1981 was largely unsuccessful; in the end, one can say that a combination of crisis and cronyism proved far more important in determining the shape of the financial system. It is instructive to analyze each of the components in turn.

The universal banking experiment was not successful in changing bank behavior. Fabella, who modified the original proposal to account for the strongly familial basis of the banking system, later readily acknowledged that the reforms failed to promote equity investment precisely because of the endurance of this central characteristic of Philippine banks. In effect, the

former senior Central Bank officials in anonymous 1990 interviews.

[32] *FEER,* May 14, 1982, 87; *AWSJ,* August 27, 1982. As early as 1978, Marcos displayed great sensitivity to reports of cronyism that began to appear in the Western press. See *FEER,* January 27, 1978, 49–50, for an account of Marcos's response to stories about the multi-million dollar commission that Disini allegedly received for brokering the Westinghouse nuclear reactor deal.

unibanks were being asked "to lose their shirts in equity positions" of
family enterprises that they didn't control. If they invested in companies
that they already controlled, on the other hand, this was merely a formalization (and legitimation) of existing DOSRI abuses. Especially given the
uncertain economic outlook, bankers were understandably cautious about
taking equity investments in enterprises over which they would have little
control. Enrique Zobel, president of the Bank of the Philippine Islands
(then the largest private bank) voiced this hesitation as early as 1980: "Do
banks really want to go into this? There is no assurance you can get your
money back. . . . this is an investment and not a loan and therefore, there
are no collaterals [*sic*] to fall back on. . . . [W]hen you are not sure, wait."
The wait-and-see attitude of the banking community endured throughout
the decade, encouraged further by the paucity of opportunities for investment in publicly held companies. Contrary to the confident expectations
of the 1979 World Bank–IMF mission, universal banks scarcely availed
themselves of the powers that were granted them to make new types of
equity investments.[33]

As expected, unibanks did take the opportunity to formally acquire the
investment banks with which they had so often had close ties since the
early 1970s, and through which they often became heavily reliant on the
money market. To provide just one example, the Ayala-controlled Bank of
the Philippine Islands became a unibank after it formally acquired (from
the Ayala Corporation) the Ayala Investment and Development Corporation—the investment house with which it had long worked very closely.
But as Zobel's remarks make clear, the mere possession of a unibanking
license did not make banks anxious to rush into new lines of business
(either underwriting or the acquisition of equity investments).[34]

Second, the unibanking reforms did not reorient banks toward either
long-term lending or term transformation. Ten years later, Fabella readily
acknowledged that commercial banks are "basically short-term fund pro-
viders." Bankers lacked the capacity for project analysis that was necessary
for monitoring long-term loans, and had long relied instead on high levels

[33] Interviews, Fabella, June 8 and 12, 1990; *Business Day*, August 28, 1980; World Bank–
IMF, 75–76. Between 1982 and 1988, equity investments totaled only 17.4 percent of unibanks' average net worth, far below the 50 percent that was permitted. Of these investments,
84.7 percent were *already* permissible before 1980, and only 15.3 percent were in the "nonallied undertakings" made permissible by the 1980 reforms. *Philippine Daily Globe*, January 30,
1990. Unlike Fabella, Virata puts the locus of the blame on economic instability. Interview,
Virata, May 24, 1991.
[34] *AWSJ*, August 6, 1980; Interview, Gatmaitan, January 31, 1990; Colayco, 186, 189; *CB
Review*, September 9, 1980, 5. In 1980, of the top four investment houses (which together
made up 70 percent of the industry's total resources), three had close ties to commercial
banks: Atrium Capital (with Interbank), Ayala Investment and Development Corp. (with
BPI), and Bancom (with Far East Bank). Licuanan, 43.

of collateral on most (non-DOSRI and nonprime) lending. Term transformation was approached with particular skepticism. Although the Central Bank publicly assured bankers that "there exists a continuing substantial permanent core of even short-term deposits that can safely be used for long-term finance," it seems that many within the Central Bank were actually quite cynical about the entire concept and were only responding to the "current fads" within the World Bank and IMF. Fortunately, most bankers apparently ignored the advice they were given;[35] later in the decade, as we shall see, the World Bank found banks quite rational in their rejection of term transformation and their inability to make any major shift toward longer-term lending.

Especially amid the traumas of the Dewey Dee crisis, banks withdrew into an extremely cautious stance; they not only shied away from equity investment, longer-term lending, and term transformation, but even minimized their normal short-term lending activities. "In the early 1980s," explains Fabella, "no banker in his right mind would think towards expanding. . . . They were consolidating, in a conservative way." Laya urged banks not to be excessively cautious in their lending, but to no avail: even prime borrowers were having a hard time securing or renewing their credit lines.[36] Ironically, reforms that set out to encourage longer-term thinking were overwhelmed by crises that ensured the continuing dominance of short-term perspectives.

Third—and not surprisingly—the absorption of investment houses by universal banks did not serve the goal of promoting competition. In fact, a major legacy of the Dewey Dee scandal was the decimation of the investment house industry and the dramatic shrinking of the money market. In effect, the financial crisis was the conclusion of a long-term process by which the commercial banks defeated and coopted a force that had, especially in the late 1960s and early 1970s, posed a major competitive challenge to their interests. By the early 1980s, the commercial bankers faced no serious competition in the arena of financial intermediation. Contrary to the stated aims of the reforms, the long-uncompetitive commercial

---

[35] *CB Review,* September 9, 1980, 6; World Bank–IMF, 14, 16; *AWSJ,* November 9, 1981. In 1972, Fabella recalls, the IMF mission favored matching the maturity of deposits and loans, but the 1979 World Bank–IMF mission had a new line. The Central Bank advisers seemed to think that they could wait out the latest round of advice. As Fabella explained: "You shouldn't think of the World Bank and the IMF as monolithic, abstract giants. They have constant bureaucratic infighting. You had to keep an ear to the ground, and determine which were the current fads. . . . We said, 'We'll consider it, but we're not going to force it.'" Interviews, Fabella, June 8 and 12, 1990. Banks using short-term deposits for long-term loans will lose, said former Central Bank Governor Andres Castillo, president of Metropolitan Bank. In his view, the World Bank simply didn't understand local conditions. *AWSJ,* November 9, 1981.

[36] *FEER,* March 26, 1982, 89, March 13, 1981, 74, and April 3, 1981, 43; Interview, Fabella, June 8, 1990. Edward S. Go, "Philippine Banking in Transition," *Fookien Times Philippines Yearbook 1981–82,* 160–63, 170, at 160.

banking sector could now enjoy an even less competitive environment.[37] (Moreover, as we shall see, a key hindrance to competition—continuing restrictions on the issuance of new bank licenses—was not lifted in any systematic way until the mid-1990s.)

The major impact of the introduction of universal banks was to differentiate more clearly the larger banks from the smaller banks. Because unibanks had to achieve a higher minimum capitalization than other commercial banks, they merely became a club within a club. The first universal bank was the PNB, followed by the crony-owned United Coconut Planters Bank. By year-end 1983, ten out of thirty-four commercial banks had received universal bank licenses.[38] The formation of such a club was enhanced not only by the reforms but also by the "flight to quality" during the financial crisis. Depositors shifted their savings from investment houses to commercial banks, and from the weaker banks (as well as banks unjustly damaged by rumors) to the larger and stronger banks. In an effort to bolster the overall system, the stronger banks recycled many of these funds back to the weaker banks from whence they had come—but the shift of funds nonetheless resulted in a greater concentration in assets among the stronger banks.[39]

In the end, the unibanking reform not only proved to be far less important than its proponents had proclaimed it would be; it also proved to be far less dangerous than its opponents had feared it might be. While there has indeed been greater concentration within the banking sector, this has largely come about (as we shall see) for reasons that have little to do with the aims of the reforms. The shift of funds toward the stabler banks, to note just one factor, continued into subsequent years of uncertainty and crisis as well.

The result of the unibanking reforms and the financial crisis was the worst of two worlds: the continued fragmentation of a poorly regulated banking sector along familial lines and the creation of a club of big banks at the top that could more easily collude on behalf of the banking community as a whole. Certain banks got bigger, but their growth did not lessen the degree to which they remained under the control of family

---

[37] Licuanan, 43, 9; *AWSJ*, April 22, 1981; *FEER*, September 24, 1982, 96. See also *AWSJ*, August 18, 1981. Ten years later, Sixto K. Roxas argued the importance of "a separate merchant banking community that would keep the commercial banks on their toes," especially "once banking spreads go too high." Interview, March 8, 1990.

[38] Broad, 165 (December 1980 interview with Armand Fabella); Interview, Fabella, June 12, 1990; Central Bank, *Factbook: Philippine Financial System, 1983* (Manila: Central Bank of the Philippines, n.d.), 74. The unibanks were PNB, UCPB, Allied Bank, Bank of the Philippine Islands, Family Bank, Far East Bank, Manilabank, Metrobank, Philippine Commercial and International Bank, and Citytrust; the government's Land Bank of the Philippines also became a unibank, but is not classified as a commercial bank.

[39] Laya, "End of the Crisis," 13; *FEER*, February 6, 1981, 87; *AWSJ*, August 18, 1981; Nascimento, 207.

conglomerates, and did not automatically encourage tendencies toward either longer-term lending or heightened efficiency. Moreover, the reforms themselves did not bring about a flood of bank mergers, as many supporters and opponents predicted they would; in fact, many of the stronger banks had little interest in acquiring weak banks full of bad loans to family enterprises.[40]

In conclusion, it is interesting to note that both the World Bank and IMF and their strongest critics had one thing in common: they did not fully appreciate the deeply familial basis of the political economy, and as a result their analysis went astray. The World Bank and IMF underestimated the degree to which the strength of family conglomerates explain the large number of banks in the system, and their critics underestimated the degree to which the strength of family conglomerates puts a structural brake on the process of excessive concentration. While there is no arguing with the fact that wealth and economic power in Philippine society is very much concentrated at the top, it is also true that—within the oligarchy at the apex of this social pyramid—the strength of familial units perpetuates a relative fractionalization of big capital. It is this familial structure that undermined the intent of the reforms, and ensured that banks neither took full advantage of their new powers nor merged in any systematic way.

Interest rate liberalization did not promote competition or savings mobilization. A 1974 International Labour Office study had termed the existing system of interest rate ceilings a "regulated monopoly," with high spreads "producing windfall profits for the banking system."[41] As noted in Chapter Five, such ceilings first became effective in the 1960s, as credit demand increased. Although interest rate ceilings began to be adjusted upward after 1973 (to better reflect market conditions), effective loan interest rates usually exceeded formal ceilings because of an array of fees and service charges commonly charged by lenders. Since loan rates were already higher than the ceilings, their liberalization was, to a certain extent, merely a formalization of longstanding informal practices. Credit continued to go toward large, established, heavily collateralized borrowers.[42]

---

[40] Mergers were widely predicted (see *Business Day*, August 28, 1980; Broad, 146–47, 167; Guinigundo, 6) and clearly favored by the World Bank–IMF mission (v, 81). The only bank merger during this period, however, was BPI's acquisition of Commercial Bank and Trust Co. in early 1981, bringing BPI's capitalization above the P500 million level. Nonetheless, BPI waited a year before acquiring the Ayala investment house and obtaining an expanded commercial banking license. See Maria Teresa Colayco, *A Tradition of Leadership: Bank of the Philippine Islands* (Manila: Bank of the Philippine Islands, 1984), 186, 189.

[41] International Labour Office, *Sharing in Development: A Programme of Employment, Equity and Growth for the Philippines,* (Geneva: International Labour Office, 1974), 240, 242; further condemnation of the system is found in Hugh Patrick and Honorata A. Moreno, "Philippine Private Domestic Commercial Banking, 1946–80, in the Light of Japanese Experience," in *Japan and the Developing Countries: A Comparative Analysis,* ed. Kazushi Ohkawa and Gustav Ranis (New York: Basil Blackwell, 1985), 351.

[42] Or, as the World Bank later put it, the change from "circumvented" ceilings to a formal

On the deposit side, however, the liberalization of interest rates held much greater promise, since interest rates quite clearly remained well below market-determined levels. If the Central Bank had in fact actively supported competition in the industry, the goal of increasing savings mobilization might have been achieved. Instead, however, the monetary authorities were determined not to let market forces take control, and allowed the banks to cooperate quite openly in setting unofficial ceilings on deposit interest rate ceilings. As a result, one economist laments, "the move towards a fully flexible interest rate regime did not increase at all the flow of loanable funds."[43]

As the date of liberalization approached and banks were "worried because they may have to settle for narrower spreads," the BAP decided to help guide the determination of interest rates. Laya, meanwhile, called for an "orderly transition" and actually offered to use "moral suasion" to prevent an interest rate war.[44] In effect, the banks were simply provided an opportunity to establish deposit rate ceilings by other means. With such public support from the monetary authorities, the BAP president felt no need to conceal arrangements "to allow more orderly adjustment in interest rates." Small savers were to receive a fixed rate of 9 percent, while large savers enjoyed floating interest rates.

Just as in the 1970s, a two-tiered market endured: lower rates for small savers (formerly officially controlled, now unofficially controlled) and higher, market-determined rates for large savers. The keenest competition would continue to be found in servicing the needs of larger savers, with the major difference that in the 1980s banks no longer faced any serious competition from investment houses. While this state of affairs was clearly advantageous to the banks, the near-absence of competition among banks at the lower end of the savings deposit market greatly inhibited the goal of increased savings mobilization. Real interest rates for small savers remained negative through most of the 1980s, just as they generally had in the 1970s.[45]

---

lifting of the ceilings "brought greater transparency to the system." World Bank, *Philippine Financial Sector Study*, Report No. 7177-PH (Washington, D.C.: World Bank, 1988), 13. Lending rates in the 1970s had soared above 30 percent, roughly twice the officially permissible rate. World Bank–IMF, ii; Patrick and Moreno, 351, 353; *FEER*, June 12, 1981, 81.

43 Gerardo P. Sicat, "Towards a Flexible Interest Rate Policy or Losing Interest in the Usury Law," in *Report of the Inter-Agency Committee on the Study of Interest Rates*, ed. National Economic Council et al. (Manila: National Economic Council, 1971), 69–78, at 73–75; Laya, "Floating Interest Rates," 146; Mario B. Lamberte, "Financial Liberalization: What Have We Learnt?" *Journal of Philippine Development* 12 (1985): 274–89, at 286.

44 *FEER*, July 3, 1981, 56; *AWSJ*, June 30, 1981; *FEER*, March 19, 1982, 74–75.

45 Go, "Philippine Banking," 162; Lamberte and Remolona also note "the oligopoly power exercised by commercial banks over the market for [small] deposits." Eli M. Remolona and Mario B. Lamberte, "Financial Reforms and the Balance-of-Payments Crisis: The Case of the Philippines, 1980–83," *Philippine Review of Economics and Business* 23 (1986): 101–41, at 137. Between 1959 and 1987, excluding 1979 and 1981 (for which data are not available),

The agreement to freeze interest rates probably accorded especially well with the current needs of the larger and more stable banks, which had been flooded with the deposits of nervous customers in the early 1980s and therefore felt little need to campaign for depositors by offering higher rates of interest. Laya may have become particularly anxious, in the wake of Dewey Dee's departure, to ensure that the interest rate reforms would not put additional pressure on financial institutions already teetering on the brink of disaster. The Central Bank governor expressed confidence that banks would put the maintenance of "good banking relationships" above the temptation to outbid each other. When the Philippine National Bank began to offer lower fees and slightly higher deposit rates to customers (10 percent rather than 9 percent, reportedly because its president was angry over his failure to assume the BAP presidency), Laya stepped in with the warning that he did not want rates to "run out of control."[46]

By his own actions, therefore, Laya stood in the way of his earlier predictions that the removal of interest ceilings would bring a "freer play of supply and demand forces in credit allocation" and discourage "the oligopolistic power of financial institutions." Indeed, both Virata and Fabella stated in 1980 that a key test of the success of the entire reform package would be the narrowing of interest rate spreads.[47] With the active assistance of Laya's Central Bank, however, market forces were squelched—and oligopolistic power was refined, fortified, and extended

---

real rates of return on savings deposits were negative every year *except* 1959 (3.9 percent), 1961 (1.4 percent), 1965 (1.4 percent), 1966 (0.4 percent), 1968 (3.4 percent), 1969 (4.0 percent), 1976 (0.9 percent) and 1985 (9.0 percent). The high real rates in 1985 must be seen in the context of a deep recession, which brought the inflation rate down to 1.8 percent. Real rates of return on time deposits, however, had been positive since 1975 and remained so through the 1980s (with the exception of 1983, when the inflation rate hit 49.8 percent). World Bank–IMF, 60; World Bank, *Philippine Financial Sector* (1988), Annex 3, 3.

[46] Go, 162; *FEER*, July 3, 1981, 56–57; Interview, Virata, May 24, 1991; *AWSJ*, June 30, 1981; *FEER*, March 19, 1982, 75–76; Anonymous interview, former bank president, 1990. In promoting competition (albeit with little success), PNB was playing the role it was often envisaged to play. As Fabella explained, PNB was meant to be "a source of countervailing pressure" on such matters as increasing the savings rate. Fabella, June 8, 1990. Domingo claimed sound motives for his behavior, but (as *AWSJ* reported) other bankers "privately suggested that PNB's policy of setting interest rates itself is 'Panfilo's revenge' for not being elected president of the Bankers Association this year."

[47] Fabella told the press that "if the interest spreads remain wide over the next few years, then we can say we failed. Because this proves that banks have grown so big that they can dominate the market and dictate the interest rates." A major Central Bank document on the financial reforms of 1980 highlighted the importance of discouraging "collusive arrangements among banks and other forms of oligopolies," and Fabella declared that the Central Bank was closely monitoring the five largest banks. "The Financial Reforms of 1980," *CB Review*, August 26, 1980, 4; *Business Day*, August 28, 1980. Virata, as well, recognized "the influence of oligopolistic elements" in financial markets, and treated the narrowing of spreads as an important objective of the reforms. Letter of Cesar E. A. Virata to Robert McNamara, president of the World Bank, 7–8; *Business Day*, August 28, 1980.

to new fields of banking activity.[48] Whereas the Central Bank had earlier promised to monitor the banks to discourage anticompetitive arrangements, it eventually did so to ensure their successful maintenance. Ironically, one can say that as collusion replaced formal ceilings, "liberalization" enabled the banks' oligopolistic power to come to full fruition.

Unfortunately for the overall health of the Philippine financial system, other factors besides oligopolistic power hindered savings mobilization during this period. First, liberal rediscounting policies encouraged banks to rely heavily on Central Bank borrowing to the detriment of their role as savings mobilizers. Second, the inflationary conditions of this period (to which the liberal rediscounting policy contributed) also made it more unlikely that positive real savings rates would be achieved. Third, the financial crisis and bank instability of the early 1980s undermined confidence in the banking system.[49]

Initiatives to restructure the allocation of selective credit became mired in cronyism and crisis, and failed dramatically. Under this aspect of the reforms, preferential credit was to be disbursed to fewer and better defined targets on the basis of "rigorous economic analysis." In addition, a "lender-of-last-resort" rediscounting facility was established to give the banks greater confidence in providing longer-term loans.

Reform of the system of selective credit was initiated, in large part, in response to corruption within Licaros's Central Bank. As Laya assessed his achievements, he assumed the governorship amid rumors about "irregularities . . . in the management of the international reserve, approvals of Jumbo Loan applications and foreign exchange swaps, and the issuance of banking licenses"—but responded with "quiet housecleaning and gradual reorganization" that "has, to all indications, been successful."[50] In fact, however, the problems that Laya said he had addressed only became more apparent.

In the allocation of foreign exchange swaps, cronyism remained the

[48] Laya, "End of the Crisis," 17, and "Floating Interest Rates in the Eighties: A New Dimension in the Philippine Financial System," *Fookien Times Philippines Yearbook 1981–82*, 146–59, at 159.

[49] Remolona and Lamberte, 113; Lamberte, "Financial Liberalization," 286–89. Further critique of rediscounting policies of the period is found in Nascimento, 196. The subsequent post-1983 balance-of-payments crisis made the goals of increased savings mobilization all the more elusive. See Manuel F. Montes and Johnny Noe E. Ravalo, "The Philippines," in *Financial Systems and Economic Policy in Developing Countries,* ed. Stephan Haggard and Chung H. Lee (Ithaca, N.Y.: Cornell University Press, 1995), 156–57, 161.

[50] Laya, "End of the Crisis," 17–18; Laya, "The Years of Adjustment," *CB Review,* January 1984: 4–8, 21, at 8. Upon assuming office in 1981, Laya implicitly acknowledged past problems but quickly tried to refute "an impression that wholesale investigations are being conducted and that anomaly after anomaly is about to be unearthed." Probably in an effort to calm nerves, he was forced to specifically deny that the Central Bank had deposits in a "'post office bank' in the New Hebrides and "non–interest bearing deposits with a named Swiss bank." "End of the Crisis," 19.

dominant theme: Marcos's newly acquired "personal plaything," Security Bank, enjoyed unprecedented access to this lucrative source of booty, as swaps accounted for 115 percent of the bank's total assets in 1982 and an astounding 185 percent in 1983. The average private bank, meanwhile, financed no more than one-fifth of its assets from this lucrative source. Security's heavy involvement in foreign exchange transactions is consistent with subsequent testimony that Marcos used the bank for stashing funds overseas (including the purchase of Manhattan real estate). Other banks, such as Traders Royal Bank (controlled by Benedicto, the sugar industry crony) also did very well in the allocation of swap privileges. While there are absolutely no indications that Laya personally benefitted from these transactions—as Licaros allegedly did—this was indeed a strange variety of housecleaning. Promises of reduction and rigor quite clearly fell by the wayside, as aggregate quantities of swap transactions almost tripled between 1980 and 1984. In subsequent years, as we shall see, the foreign currency risk that the Central Bank so kindly assumed on behalf of these borrowers saddled it with enormous debts.[51]

In rediscounting, as well, cronyism and expansion swamped the key goals promulgated by Virata, Laya, and their international allies: to cut down the number of areas in which preferential rates were available, base allocation on "rigorous economic analysis," and reduce banks' dependence on "cheap Central Bank funds" by ensuring that rediscounting facilities would no longer serve as the first refuge of banks in need of funds.[52] An examination of the rediscounting data reveals outcomes quite the opposite. Rather than a consolidation of priority areas, one finds instead a mushrooming of new rediscounting windows from 1981 through 1983, covering everything from tobacco trading to the trading of blue-chip stocks to coconut milling. The generosity of the Central Bank can, in part, be explained as a countercyclical response to the 1980–1982 world recession. But as in the past, "virtually all economic activities can qualify for rediscounting." Moreover, "instead of being the 'lender of last resort' . . . the Central Bank . . . continued to be the 'lender of first resort.' "[53]

---

[51] *FEER*, May 23, 1991; Rolando Gapud, president of Security during these years, made these revelations in the 1990 New York trial of Imelda Marcos. *Philippine Daily Globe,* July 2, 1990. Allocations of swaps grew from roughly P21 billion in 1980 to P54 billion in 1983 and P70 billion in 1984. Tabular data on swaps and rediscounts are found in Hutchcroft, "Predatory Oligarchy, Patrimonial State: The Politics of Private Domestic Commercial Banking in the Philippines," (Ph.D. dissertation, Yale University, 1993), and derived from SGV, Central Bank, and PNB data.

[52] World Bank–IMF, viii, 57–58; World Bank, *Philippines Staff Appraisal Report on the Industrial Finance Project,* Report No. 3331-PH (Washington: World Bank, 1981), 19–20, 24 (emphasis added); Laya, "Floating Interest Rates," 149; Virata, letter to McNamara, March 13, 1981, 4.

[53] Remolona and Lamberte, 113–116 (quote at 113); see also Armida S. San Jose,

An IMF study notes that banks could obtain rediscounting privileges "at their own initiative." Clearly, however, some had better success in obtaining these subsidized funds than others, and cronyism continued to dominate the process of allocation: Republic Planters Bank, controlled by Benedicto, financed nearly one-half of its assets with Central Bank credit in the years between 1979 and 1984—two and one-half times the industry average. The dominance of cronyism endured, as well, in the allocation of "jumbo loans" (although this source of funds began to taper off by 1983) and in the disposition of the coconut levy (still the key to success for United Coconut Planters Bank).[54]

The ultimate disposition of the new "lender-of-last-resort" facility itself is one more indication of reform gone awry. The rediscounting program was meant to help banks resolve temporary liquidity shortages and broaden their planning horizons, but in the midst of the Dewey Dee crisis it was quickly transformed into a tool to bolster short-term confidence in the basic viability of the financial system. Total availments exceeded the facility's P1.5 billion ($189 million) in resources, and two institutions monopolized the funds: P1 billion went to the Herdis Group's financial institutions and P400 million to Bancom.[55]

Piecemeal measures to improve bank supervision, added to the reform package after the Dewey Dee scandal, proved ineffectual. The loosening of restrictions on the secrecy of deposits was intended to make it easier for bank supervisors to examine deposits and thus to discover bank fraud; as Laya recalled, with a tone of indifference, the change "added more comfort to the lives of

---

"Central Bank Rediscounting Operations," *CB Review,* September 1983, 12–28. Laya defends the expansion of rediscounting as a policy "imposed on the Central Bank" in which the major beneficiaries were "exports and food." Virata points out that certain groups, including the World Bank and AID, pressed for increased rediscounting privileges. Interviews, Laya, May 21, 1990, and Virata, May 24, 1991. Indeed, the World Bank at certain times favored "nonallocative" rediscounting and at times favored the creation of special rediscounting windows intended to benefit export-oriented industrialization. Contrast, for example, World Bank–IMF, 57–58; and World Bank, *Philippines Staff Appraisal Report* (1981), 7.

54 Nascimento, 196; Jaime C. Laya, "Strengthening Philippine Financial Foundations," *CB Review,* November 1983, 5–10, at 7. As de Dios discusses, the sugar industry's heavy use of the rediscounting window was an important issue in the mounting tensions between cronies and technocrats in 1982. See Emmanuel S. de Dios, "The Erosion of the Dictatorship," in *Dictatorship and Revolution: Roots of People's Power,* ed. Aurora Javate-de Dios, Petronilo Bn. Daroy, and Lorna Kalaw-Tirol (Metro Manila: Conspectus Foundation Incorporated, 1988), 107–8. In early 1983, Republic Planters Bank faced large fines for reserve deficiencies, but the prospective Central Bank penalties were overturned by Marcos via a "Letter of Instruction." As one anonymous official complained, "It's favoritism. It's demoralizing. . . . And it isn't the way to run a Central Bank." *AWSJ,* November 8, 1983.

55 *AWSJ,* August 6 and September 10, 1980, and August 18, 1981; Laya, "End of the Crisis," 13; *FEER,* August 14, 1981. Similarly, the World Bank–sponsored Apex Development Finance Unit, created in 1980 as an autonomous unit within the Central Bank to promote industrial exports, was later enlisted in the post–Dewey Dee effort to rescue crony firms. Memorandum from ADFU head E. M. Villanueva to Governor Laya, April 14, 1981; see also World Bank, *Philippine Financial Sector Study* (1988), 128–29.

bank examiners." But the top bank examiner at the time, Carlota P. Valenzuela, reports that there was no positive impact. Central Bank legal officials required them to request Monetary Board authorization to examine specific bank accounts, and by the time they got to the account the funds had commonly already been transferred. "You can't go fishing," they were told, and the result was little practical relaxation in the law.[56] Unfortunately, greater attention to the deficiencies of supervision had to wait until after the next round of bank instability in the mid-1980s.

Conclusion: The Crisis Intensifies

Broadly speaking, the 1980–1981 reform package was scuttled both by inattention to questions of political power and by imbalances in the distribution of political power between regulators and regulated. The unibanking reforms ignored the reality of familial power within the Philippine political economy, the interest rate reforms were gutted by the oligopolistic power of the banking sector, and the selective credit reforms were overwhelmed by the power of cronyism. None of the three major elements of the original reform package paid sufficient attention to longstanding problems of bank instability—a problem which was, in itself, largely traceable to the weak degree of political power enjoyed by the regulatory authorities.

The belated bank supervision reforms of early 1981 were arguably more attuned to questions of political power (by seeking to strengthen the power of regulators vis-à-vis the social forces concentrated in the banking sector) but in the end the Central Bank—seemingly fearful of lawsuits against it—balked. Ten years later, an IMF study strongly criticized the failure of the reforms to "tighten bank supervision" and concluded that resulting "weaknesses of the regulatory framework and loose banking practices triggered and exacerbated the crisis." In short, "factors within the financial system" are to blame.[57]

Just as important, the reformers—most notably Virata and his multilateral allies—displayed little conception of the limitations of their own power in the crony-infested environment in which they operated. By at least 1983, observers became increasingly aware that—promotion of technocrats and their high-minded reform agendas notwithstanding—the resilience of "crony capitalism" was not to be underestimated. Just as he used

---

[56] World Bank–IMF, 78; Interviews, Laya, May 21, 1990, and Carlota Valenzuela, May 9, 1990.

[57] Nascimento, 227 and 177; see also 204–5. As Montes and Ravalo point out, one cannot blame the liberalization program itself for the crises that followed (p. 154). One can, however, fault the reforms for ignoring longstanding problems that were revealed—once again—in the midst of crisis.

the 1981 "face-lifting" of martial law to try to obscure the underlying endurance of authoritarian rule, Marcos used the agenda of reform to try to conceal the underlying endurance of cronyism. Virata and his technocrats accomplished little beyond providing technical expertise to economic policymaking agencies and supplying the Marcos regime with the developmentalist rhetoric and liberalizing agenda that brought in the international resources necessary for perpetuating the system as a whole.[58]

The resilience of cronyism became especially apparent when an April 1983 caucus of Marcos's political party, the Kilusang Bagong Lipunan (KBL), turned into a concerted attack on Prime Minister Virata and his policies. Here, Marcos sat back and let the cronies run things: a number of his close associates, including crony Roberto Benedicto, assailed Virata's policies and his alleged subservience to the World Bank and the IMF. Observers recalled that Marcos never set a fixed term for Virata's tenure as prime minister, and had earlier discussed regularly rotating the post; many thought he might be on his way out. Foreign observers were reportedly "extremely nervous" at the KBL spectacle, and it was no exaggeration for observers to say that Virata's departure from the government "could easily send international lenders scurrying."[59]

Virata stayed on, but by that time it was obvious that he faced major constraints in translating foreign respect into domestic influence. Marcos needed Virata to take care of economic matters on the international front, but kept him on a short leash at home; as a result, Virata's battles against crony excesses met with little success. He successfully won repeal of the coconut levy in September 1981, only to have it reinstated as soon as he was out of the country. Similarly, even some of the cronies who were supposed to have been smashed in the wake of the Dewey Dee crisis began to enjoy renewed access to the trough of power in later years. Disini, for example, who after the crisis had been used as an example of a crony reined in, was the recipient of special privileges in a 1983 presidential decree lowering import duties on a raw material for cigarette filters, a market over which he enjoyed 75 percent control. Benedicto and Cojuangco were also the beneficiaries of other Marcos directives issued at the time.[60] Quite clearly, arbitrariness in the political sphere continued to be a major determinant of economic outcomes.

At no time did the detrimental impact of this rampant arbitrariness

[58] Even after being overwhelmed by crises and cronyism, Virata and Laya blame the failure of the financial reforms on such external shocks as increased oil prices and the decreased availability of international credit. Given such circumstances, Virata argues, "I don't see how the banks could change." Interviews, Virata, May 24, 1991, and Laya, May 21, 1990.

[59] *FEER*, May 5, 1983, 44; *AWSJ* May 27, 1983.

[60] *AWSJ*, October 22, 1981 and May 27, 1983; *FEER*, June 30, 1983, 50–51.

become more obvious than with the August 1983 assassination of former Senator Benigno Aquino, Marcos's most prominent political opponent. Extrajudicial executions had become a regular feature of the Philippine political scene, but with this assassination it became clear that targets could include even major political figures with prominent family names. A sense of panic once again swept through the streets of the financial district, but this time it was accompanied by widespread demonstrations attracting some of the country's leading bankers and businesspersons (many of whom had been organizing since 1981 out of anger at the excesses of crony capitalism).

As capital flight mounted, the country was soon faced with another major balance-of-payments crisis. A moratorium was declared on repayments of principal due on the country's external debt, making the Philippines Asia's first major problem debtor. International bankers were nervous, and demanded that Virata and Laya remain in their posts; the removal of either, explained a U.S. banker, "would be the final blow to the government's international credibility." That final blow, however, came from within the Central Bank itself: in December it was discovered that Laya's personnel had been overstating foreign reserves by $600 million throughout much of the year—in a desperate effort to reassure foreign lenders and investors. This revelation "infuriated" foreign bankers, who began to question "the competence of the once widely respected technocrats." "Jimmy messed it up," said one leading banker, while another said Laya's "credibility is very, very low." A month later, Marcos demoted Laya to the post of education minister and named veteran banker Jose Fernandez the new Central Bank governor. Contrary to Laya's claims that he succeeded in his housecleaning at the Central Bank, the institution's reputation plunged to an all-time low under his stewardship.[61]

As the crisis intensified, the IMF transformed itself from "doting parent" to "vengeful god." Meanwhile, the last four months of 1983 brought "a massive wave of deposit withdrawals," and the banking system was once again facing enormous instability.[62] The multilateral institutions, which in the 1980–1981 reforms had paid little attention to such matters as cronyism, bank instability, and weak regulation of financial institutions, finally

[61] *AWSJ,* October 17, 1983, December 14 and 19, 1983; January 12, 1984; and *Wall Street Journal,* October 17, 1983. Only a few months earlier, the *Asian Wall Street Journal* had reported that foreign bankers, diplomats, and IMF officials speak of Laya "in near-reverential tones. They say his continuing struggle for honest government is one of the few hopeful signs they see in the Philippines" (May 27, 1983). In a sign of their continued support for Laya, Marcos and Virata actually described the new job at the Education Ministry as a promotion. *Asiaweek,* January 27, 1984, 47.

[62] Manuel F. Montes, cited in Emmanuel S. de Dios, "A Political Economy of Philippine Policy-Making," *Economic Policy-Making in the Asia-Pacific Region,* ed. John W. Langford and K. Lorne Brownsey (Halifax, Nova Scotia: The Institute for Research on Public Policy, 1990), 121; *FEER,* April 26, 1984, 113, and May 5, 1983, 96–97.

began to see that these matters would need to be attacked head on; the short time horizons of bankers noted in 1979 had grown yet shorter, and could no longer be blamed merely on incorrect financial sector policies. Whether or not Virata and Laya were willing to acknowledge it, even many erstwhile Marcos supporters now understood that cronyism ultimately determined the agenda of economic policymaking, and the economy's greatest problems lay in the political sphere. Governor Fernandez faced a financial system under mounting stress, as even the government institutions commonly used to rescue distressed banks, PNB and DBP, were so decimated by crony abuse that they were soon to require a major rescue operation on their own behalf. The 1980–1981 financial reforms had low priority in the midst of such upheaval; instead, Fernandez was forced to concentrate on the far more pressing—and relevant—problems of bank instability and deficiencies of bank supervision.

CHAPTER EIGHT

Cleaning Up:
The Fernandez Years, 1984–1990

Veteran banker Jose B. "Jobo" Fernandez became governor of a
tarnished Central Bank just as the economy was going into free fall and the
Marcos regime was facing unprecedented popular opposition. Under
these conditions, crisis management supplanted the 1980–1981 reform
agenda, and the Central Bank's work became "basically a fire-engine job."[1]
The two most important fires to douse were the balance-of-payments
crisis—the worst of the entire postwar era—and the mounting danger of a
yet another round of extensive bank failures. Fernandez proved more than
ready to confront the economic crisis with draconian stabilization measures, and he at the same time set out to "purify" the banking system. In
the end, as we shall see, efforts to address these problems gave the largest
of the commercial banks spectacular new opportunities for profit and
advantage. Indeed, one can say that Fernandez was not only attempting to
clean up the system; he was, at the same time, giving the big banks a
chance to clean up.

This chapter begins by examining the first two years of Fernandez's
"crusade" to reform the banking sector, coinciding with the final two years
of the Marcos regime. In the second section, I discuss Fernandez's survival
through the February 1986 "people-power revolution" and analyze his
continuing "crusade" under the administration of Corazon Aquino. The
conclusion summarizes Fernandez's overall record: while continuing
weaknesses of bank supervision plagued efforts to deal with the problem of
weak banks, there was enormous success in consolidating the position of
the largest and strongest banks. As financial burdens were shifted to the
increasingly overwhelmed coffers of the Central Bank and the Treasury,

---

[1] Interview, Armand Fabella, June 8, 1990.

the overall banking system was far healthier by decade's end. Despite the enormous expense to the public, however, the system continued to do far more to obstruct than to promote national developmental objectives.

The Fernandez Crusade, Part I: Riding into Marcos's Sunset

In the wake of Jaime Laya's forced resignation from the Central Bank governorship, Ferdinand Marcos was in a tight spot. Laya and Virata had come to supply the bulk of the regime's credibility abroad, and now they were themselves tainted by the overstatement of international reserves. Marcos not only lost the services of a trusted associate at the Central Bank; of far more consequence was the fact that his regime was rapidly losing legitimacy at home and abroad. International supporters were at last forced to confront the primacy of crony capitalism and the hollowness of Marcos's proclaimed developmental objectives. The strategic importance of U.S. military bases assured Marcos of continued external support, but the granting of support came in an atmosphere of mounting distrust and suspicion. Laya's replacement would need to be someone who could win back the confidence of international creditors and donors.

Jobo Fernandez fit the bill. Within the banking community, few could match his prominence: he was founder and chairman of Far East Bank and Trust Company, and former president of the Bankers Association of the Philippines. He had represented the banking community in the Joint IMF-CBP Banking Survey Commission in the early 1970s, and enjoyed close ties with two major international banks (Chemical Bank and Mitsui Bank) through joint ownership of Far East Bank. During the Marcos years, Fernandez's bank had continued its steady ascent to the upper rungs of the banking system (climbing from thirteenth-largest bank at year-end 1972 to eighth-largest bank at year-end 1983). But Fernandez's initial rise to prominence predated both martial law and the rise of the Marcos-era technocrats; while Fernandez quite surely knew how to play ball with Marcos, he was by no means tainted with the label of either technocrat or crony.

According to one report, when Marcos first offered him the post of Central Bank governor, Fernandez "tried to beg off, saying that, without him, Far East Bank might collapse." Marcos responded by focusing attention on the object of Fernandez's greatest loyalty, a tactic that was apparently persuasive. "Your bank will collapse anyway," said Marcos, "if our (external debt) problem is not solved and the entire (financial) system goes down." Even after he took over the "papacy of the local banking world," Fernandez seems not to have left behind an overarching concern for his own beloved archbishopric, Far East Bank—which did especially well during the years when its founder took over at the helm at the Central Bank.[2]

At a much earlier point in his career, it is worthwhile noting, Fernandez had planned to go to work for the Central Bank. Soon after returning from Harvard Business School in 1949, the young Fernandez wanted to enter the newly formed institution—but was advised not to by the man who was soon to be his boss, Don Pepe Cojuangco of the Philippine Bank of Commerce. Don Pepe told Fernandez that he was "'too young and too poor to be in government service' and should join it only when he was 'old and rich.'" In fact, he was being advised of the wisest path to power within a patrimonial oligarchic state: join the bureaucracy after developing a strong independent base outside the state apparatus. By 1984, the sixty-year-old Fernandez could take the helm of the Central Bank from a position of wealth and stature.

When Fernandez became governor in January 1984, the economic crisis was mounting in severity. "Gentlemen," he announced in his first briefing to cabinet ministers and businessmen, "I feel that all of us are just shuffling deck chairs on the *Titanic*."[3] The major means by which Fernandez's Central Bank sought to respond to the balance-of-payments crisis was through the floating of high-interest bills—popularly dubbed "Jobo bills"—beginning in March 1984. With this one financial instrument, Fernandez simultaneously provided short-term solutions to a number of pressing problems: he reduced excess liquidity in the system, stabilized the currency, curbed capital flight, and provided a beleaguered banking sector (along with other large asset-holders) with high-interest, low-risk investments. As the *Asian Wall Street Journal* reported, "Local banks snapped up the profitable bills, and their customers went without credit."

Even by the standards of the IMF—the world's foremost bearer of contractionary policies—the Jobo bills were later judged a "dramatic" means of monetary tightening; similarly, a leading economist explains that they brought "the decimation of industry as firms stopped operation due to [the] very high cost of money."[4] One might expect that such an outcome

[2] "Industry Report," a supplement to the *Business Journal* (a publication of the American Chamber of Commerce of the Philippines), June 1984, S-3 (parentheses in original). See also *Asiaweek*, January 27, 1984, 48.

[3] Virginia Benitez Licuanan, *Money in the Bank: The Story of Money and Banking in the Philippines and the PCIBank Story* (Manila: PCIBank Human Resources Development Foundation, 1985), 138–39; *Asian Wall Street Journal Weekly*, January 23, 1984, 2; *AWSJ*, June 13, 1986. The origins of the balance-of-payments crisis are examined in Emmanuel S. de Dios, ed., *An Analysis of the Philippine Economic Crisis: A Workshop Report* (Quezon City: University of the Philippines Press, 1984).

[4] *AWSJ*, June 13, 1986; Jean-Claude Nascimento, "Crisis in the Financial Sector and the Authorities' Reaction: The Philippines," in *Banking Crises: Cases and Issues*, ed. V. Sundararajan and Tomás J. T. Baliño (Washington, D.C.: International Monetary Fund, 1991), 195; Raul V. Fabella, "Trade and Industry Reforms in the Philippines: Process and Performance,"

would elicit the strongest of reactions from the powerful oligarchic forces that were mobilizing in opposition to the Marcos regime. But it did not: although anti-Marcos businesspersons readily blamed the regime for creating the crisis, they generally did not begrudge Fernandez for the measures he adopted.

The explanation, it seems, lies in the continuing diversification of family conglomerates. Even at the height of the crisis, it is important to note, there was no sign of any clear division between financiers and manufacturers—precisely because the major families incorporated both segments of capital under one roof.[5] From the perspective of diversified family conglomerates, therefore, the Jobo bills were by no means unwelcome. They addressed pressing economic problems, offered hope that the country's credibility with international creditors might be restored, and—last but by no means least—provided the major families with a ready means of weathering the crisis. While the manufacturing firms of the major conglomerates foundered, their banks were enjoying windfall profits in low-risk investments; while the national economy was forced to its knees, the major families were given a new means of enriching themselves at the public trough. In the end, the balance-of-payments crisis only reinforced the oligarchic domination of the economy, as many small-and medium-scale enterprises went bust. During the crisis, there might have been an opportunity to attempt a genuine restructuring of an inefficient, privilege-ridden economy; instead, policy measures merely ensured that the country's major diversified family conglomerates had the opportunity to ride out the crisis. The larger political economy remained thoroughly unreconstructed, and Central Bank coffers increasingly strained.

From the start, the floating of Jobo bills took into account the special desires of the banking community. At the suggestion of the Bankers Association of the Philippines, the minimum lot available to savers was set at a high level, "so that the traditional market segment of banks, which consists

---

in *Philippine Macroeconomic Perspective: Developments and Policies,* ed. Manuel F. Montes and Hideyoshi Sakai (Tokyo: Institute of Developing Economies, 1989), 191. Nascimento, author of the IMF study, reports that between 1983 and September 1986, "real credit to the private sector fell a staggering 53 percent, and cumulative output fell by 9 percent." Nascimento, 217.

5 In the mid-1950s, it will be recalled, there was a clear debate over the direction of macroeconomic policy, with two definable camps of oligarchic families pitted against each other; in the mid-1980s, there was no basis for such an intersectoral debate. As de Dios explains, elite interests are "not sufficiently differentiated to represent fixed economic interests, even between landowners and capitalists. . . . In whichever sector large property is found, it is distinguished by its reproduction through exclusion and monopoly. . . . [A]ccess to the state machinery will always command a premium and struggles are bound to develop to obtain that access." Emmanuel S. de Dios, "A Political Economy of Philippine Policy-Making," *Economic Policy-Making in the Asia-Pacific Region,* ed. John W. Langford and K. Lorne Brownsey (Halifax, Nova Scotia: The Institute for Research on Public Policy, 1990), 140.

of small-and medium-sized investors, can be retained by them." At the same time, the BAP sought to "[i]ncrease the differential between the rates paid on CB/Treasury Bills sold to banks and those sold to individuals. . . . [to] somewhat shield the banking system from a massive shift of deposits into CB/Treasury Bills." The Central Bank was remarkably forthright in explaining that their bills were "aimed at the upper bracket of the market," and that the minimum placement excluded "most savers or the general public which the banks depend upon for much of their business." This merely served to reinforce the longstanding two-tier market, in which small savers were locked into low-paying bank deposits (generally at negative real interest rates), while large savers could avail themselves of attractive positive real rates of interest.[6] The most liquid banks (those who paid least heed to earlier World Bank–IMF–Virata efforts to promote longer-term lending) were best poised to shift assets toward the highly lucrative bills.

As helpful as the Jobo bills were to banks, they were not enough to rescue all banks from crisis. When Fernandez assumed office, there was a clear sense of panic in the banking community. Deposits were being taken out of banks perceived as weak, and ending up both underneath mattresses and in the larger and stronger banks (including the four foreign banks). In the face of economic travails, many loans could not be collected; as international reserves plummeted and lines of international credit dried up, the banks' lucrative business of financing trade was sharply curtailed. Banks with large quantities of foreign exchange had enjoyed windfall profits from the 1983 devaluations of the peso, but as of late 1983 all banks were forced to turn their foreign exchange over to the Central Bank. In the midst of this jittery environment, there were widespread expectations of a major shakeout in the banking sector as a whole.

In response to the banking crisis, Fernandez declared a three-part "crusade" in August 1984. First, he promised to get tough in dealing with the problem of the weak banks, and prosecute those responsible for fraud, mismanagement, and DOSRI abuses. Second, Fernandez sought to consolidate the position of the stronger and more conservatively managed banks by improving their public image. In particular, he hoped to bring hoarded funds back into the banking system. Third, the Central Bank was both to suggest and arrange options for mergers and acquisitions.

After a decade of Marcos-style authoritarian rule, political arbitrariness was a major issue of the day. In addition, it had become obvious that the response to the previous financial crisis—the Dewey Dee affair—had

---

[6] *Times Journal,* October 16, 1984, quoting a BAP document; *CB Review,* June 1984, 23. On the two-tier market in the 1980s, see Edita A. Tan, "Bank Concentration and the Structure of Interest," University of the Philippines School of Economics, Discussion Paper 8915 (Quezon City, 1989), 21–22.

done little to resolve longstanding problems within the banking sector. In the analysis of one observer, post-1981 actions had "merely papered over the problems" through Central Bank emergency loans and rescue by public sector banks, and "many feared the current crusade will be diverted in similar fashion." The observer went on to comment, "Political considerations cannot be underestimated [as a factor guiding the response to the last crisis] . . . many of the worst offenders with regard to prudent banking and investment had government backing, [some as] . . . direct paybacks for political loyalty. . . . the central bank must . . . convince the public (and foreign creditors) it is more than 'just another government ministry.' " Fernandez addressed both issues head-on. "Uniform application of [banking] law is of primary importance," he said. "Don't think we announce a crusade and not do anything." In addition, he rejected the post–Dewey Dee strategy of "shoring up the weaker members of the system. . . . at a net cost of several billion pesos," and displayed a readiness to let certain banks fail.[7]

Indeed, in this latest round of bank instability, the Central Bank did not coordinate a rescue of all failing banks by government agencies and banks. Between 1984 and 1986, one large savings bank (Banco Filipino) and two commercial banks (Pacific Bank and Philippine Veterans Bank) were closed down. In 1987 one more commercial bank (Manilabank) was forced to shut its doors. In each case of bank closure, DOSRI abuses were cited as a major cause of failure. The crusade notwithstanding, the former bank owners had far more success in prosecuting the Central Bank for closing their banks than the Central Bank had in prosecuting errant bankers for fraud and DOSRI abuses. And, as the following analyses of the closures reveals, the issue of political arbitrariness only became more acute: Fernandez's many critics accused him of using personalistic criteria in deciding which banks to close and which banks to support, and the bank closings generated great controversy and innumerable lawsuits.

Banco Filipino, a savings bank founded by the Aguirre family in 1964, had long cultivated the business of even the smallest of depositors.[8] By late

[7] *FEER*, September 13, 1984, 56; Jose B. Fernandez, "The Momentum of Economic Recovery," a speech delivered to the Management Association of the Philippines, Metro Manila, June 29, 1987.

[8] Although a savings bank and thus technically outside the focus of this study, Banco Filipino warrants careful examination both because of its size and because of the magnitude of the shockwaves generated by its closure. Overall, this category of financial institution held only 1.3 percent of the total assets of the financial system at year-end 1983, but Banco Filipino was the largest of all savings banks (in terms of total assets), and actually exceeded the size of all but ten private domestic commercial banks. In the 1980s, savings banks had all the powers of commercial banks except those that permit international transactions. World Bank, *Philippine Financial Sector Study*, Report No. 7177-PH (Washington, D.C.: World Bank, 1988), Annex 5; *Business Day Corporate Profiles 1984* (Metro Manila: Business Day), 57; and SGV, *A Study of Commercial Banks in the Philippines* (Metro Manila: SGV, 1984).

1983, many of its some three million customers responded to the jittery economic environment by pulling their money out the bank. The situation stabilized by early 1984, but by June and July (after the May parliamentary elections) the bank runs had become more intense than ever. It is not entirely clear what initially spurred the runs, but there were reports of anonymous leaflets being circulated on July 13, urging depositors to withdraw their money from banks before they closed down. Most banks contained the problem, but Banco Filipino withdrawals were especially great because of reports—emanating from the Central Bank—that "a big savings bank was under surveillance." In addition, Fernandez had just announced that the Central Bank was no longer going to come to the assistance of banks that were mismanaged. Fernandez also appeared on television, and advised the public "to be choosy" as to where they deposited funds. On the same public affairs program, Fernandez accused Banco Filipino's owners of diverting (partly to related enterprises) about one-third of the roughly P1 billion in emergency funds they had received from the Central Bank.[9]

On July 23, the bank closed its doors, and blamed the Central Bank for causing its difficulties through "arbitrary actions." Bank officials maintained that the institution was solvent, and claimed that if only the Central Bank would provide "unlimited and unrestricted financial support" their institution could regain the confidence of its depositors. Their lawyer lambasted the Central Bank for its "insinuation" about the diversion of funds, and an Aguirre family member told Marcos that his intercession would likely be necessary given the "arrogant attitude and endless scheming" of Jobo.[10]

In addition, the Aguirre family charged that Fernandez had demanded they turn over 51 percent of bank shares "for sale to an unnamed buyer at an unnamed price." According to the *Asian Wall Street Journal,* these shares were actually pledged to Fernandez in late July. Rumors circulated that the 51 percent shares were going to be assigned to Eduardo "Danding" Cojuanco (the Marcos crony active in the coconut monopoly) or to other Palace interests, but by late August it was reported that Fernandez was planning to sell the shares to the Ayala's Bank of the Philippine Islands. Either way, Fernandez seemed to be assuming an unprecedented role in trying to force the sale of the bank, and the Aguirres charged him with "unethical conduct." The Central Bank had withheld aid, they said, to

[9] *Business Day Corporate Profiles 1983* (Metro Manila: Business Day), 70; *Business Day Corporate Profiles 1984,* 57; *AWSJ,* July 23, 1984; *FEER,* August 2, 1984, 78, and August 30, 1984, 48; Letter of Norberto J. Quisumbing (Banco Filipino's lawyer) to Central Bank Deputy Governor Gabriel Singson, July 26, 1984, 2. There were also bank runs and heavy withdrawals at three other savings banks. *AWSJ,* July 24, 1984.

[10] *FEER,* August 2, 1984, 78; Quisumbing letter, 1; *AWSJ,* July 23, 1984; Letter of Tomas B. Aguirre, chairman of the board of BF Homes, Inc., July 26, 1984.

allow Fernandez to force the sale. In the end, however, BPI backed out of
the deal because of the way Banco Filipino had been hurt by bank runs and
bad publicity.[11]

While the bank was closed, "the Aguirres and Fernandez were not only
hotly debating in public the issue of when the central bank should come to
the aid of a troubled institution, and to what degree, they also were threatening each other with suits and countersuits." In the midst of this un-
seemly "press relations battle" (as the Aguirres later called it), President
Marcos interceded on behalf of the bank, and on August 1 the bank
reopened its doors under Central Bank conservatorship. Unfortunately for
the Central Bank, however, the first conservator (the president of Land
Bank) seems to have taken the side of the Aguirre family, and was replaced
after only a week on the job by another conservator (the head of the Social
Security System). On orders of the Palace, the Central Bank provided an
additional P3 billion ($167 million) in assistance.[12] Within a week, the
Aguirre family sued Fernandez and the Monetary Board for "wilful [sic]
infliction of injury" on the bank. Later, they sought an injunction prohibit-
ing Fernandez from issuing "provocative statements which would violate
the CB charter." "It came as no surprise to the business community,"
reports *FEER*, "that the rescuer was being brought to court by the bank, or
that a supposedly independent central banking authority was being told by
the president what to do about an institution under its direct supervision."

The Central Bank, meanwhile, maintained its earlier position that the
Aguirres needed to sell out to a new group. It also revealed that Banco
Filipino had many bad loans in Aguirre family property development and
hotel projects (the value of which was surely depreciating in the midst of
the deep recession of the mid-1980s); when asked if the owners had "plundered" their bank, Fernandez gave an affirmative reply.[13]

[11] *AWSJ*, July 23, 1984; *FEER*, August 2, 1984, 78–79, and August 30, 1984, 49. According
to one former bank president, Fernandez wanted to obtain the 51 percent shares so he could
have leverage over the family and they wouldn't be able to tie him up in court. Another
former bank president contends that Fernandez acquired the shares on behalf of President
Marcos's daughter Imee. The Aguirres themselves at first suspected that Fernandez wanted
the shares for Far East Bank. Anonymous interviews, 1990 and 1991; Interview, Anthony C.
Aguirre and Teodoro O. Arcenas Jr., chairman of the board and president (respectively),
Banco Filipino, April 27, 1993.

[12] *FEER*, August 9, 1984, 62–63, and August 30, 1984, 48–49 (quote at 48); Interview,
Banco Filipino officials, April 27, 1993. The first conservator later said that the management
of Banco Filipino "was okay, was competent." Banco Filipino lawyers maintain that Fernandez
covered up a report from the first conservator that urged the "normalization of BF's operations." *Business World*, May 24, 1991; *Malaya*, November 5, 1987. The second conservator had
a more contentious relationship with management, the upshot of which was an Aguirre
lawsuit (against the Monetary Board) for his "illegal and clandestine investigations of the
bank's transactions." *Business Day*, January 17, 1985.

[13] *FEER*, August 30, 1984, 48–49; *Metro Manila Times*, August 31, 1984; *Business World*,
May 20, 1991.

The reasons why Marcos temporarily sided with the Aguirre family against the Central Bank are difficult to determine, but it seems likely that in the midst of an already highly unstable political and economic situation he was trying to avoid further political fallout from disgruntled depositors.[14] In a few months, however, the tide turned against the Aguirre family. The IMF—whose relationship to the Philippines was now that of a "vengeful god"—was not at all pleased at how emergency loans to Banco Filipino and other banks were making it impossible for the country to meet the money supply targets of the stabilization program. As early as February 1984, Central Bank aid to several other troubled financial institutions had reached P6 billion. In April, the Central Bank gave P4.9 billion in cash advances, which were thought to have been used by the Marcos regime in the May 1984 elections. When an additional P3 billion in emergency loans were granted to Banco Filipino in late 1984, the targeted liquidity reductions went further amok—and likely forced the floating of even larger quantities of Jobo bills. Despite Banco Filipino's casual request for "unrestricted financial support," there were indeed limits to how much the system could bear. In any case, one can imagine that Fernandez was seeking any excuse to reverse Marcos's August decision and get on with the job of closing down Banco Filipino.

The conservator made his report in mid-January 1985, and the Monetary Board subsequently ordered Banco Filipino to be placed under receivership. As hundreds of soldiers and policemen were dispatched to Banco Filipino branches, the bank charged the Central Bank with "Gestapo" techniques. In late March, the bank was liquidated. The Central Bank reported that 60 percent of the loan portfolio went to the Aguirre family and its companies, and that these insider loans added up to an amount that was eight times greater than the bank's paid-up capital.[15]

It is not entirely clear why the Aguirres felt the wrath of Jobo more intensely than most other errant bank owners. On the one hand, there was ample evidence that the family was milking its bank. Viewed from this perspective alone, it is easy to applaud Fernandez's resolve—and argue that the Aguirres got what they deserved. On the other hand, it seems that Fernandez had particular antipathy toward the Aguirre clan. Many banks were guilty of DOSRI abuse, but the Central Bank and Fernandez singled out Banco Filipino for a powerful barrage of bad publicity in July 1984,

[14] *FEER*, August 30, 1984, 48–49, and December 26, 1991, 68–69.

[15] *Business Day*, May 4, 1984; *FEER*, August 30, 1984, 48–49 (quote at 48), and April 4, 1985, 65; *Malaya*, January 29, 1985. A detailed analysis of the abuse of the loan portfolio can be found in *Business World*, May 20, 1991. During the 1983–1985 crisis, among the banks that received emergency advances were the following: Pacific Bank (which received P2 billion), Allied Bank (P3 billion), Manilabank (P3 billion), Producers Bank (P2 billion), Philippine Veterans Bank (P60 million), and Banco Filipino (in excess of P3 billion). *FEER*, May 7, 1987, 82.

pulling nervous depositors out of the woodwork and pushing the bank over the brink. According to charges later brought by government prosecutors, there was bad blood between Fernandez and the Aguirre family going back nearly a decade, related to how the Aguirres reportedly spurned a 1976 Far East Bank attempt to purchase Banco Filipino. Regardless of the precise history of the feud, it endured for years. The Aguirre family's lawsuits against Fernandez and the Central Bank continued into the early 1990s.[16]

The second bank to shut its doors during this period was *Philippine Veterans Bank*, more than half of whose shares were personally held by Ferdinand Marcos (albeit technically owned by the veterans of World War II). In this closure, explains Armand Fabella, there was no "triggering development" of a bank run (since its major depositors were government agencies); rather, the bank was simply "closed because it was falling apart." Its major ill was insider abuse, as the original P100 million in capitalization dwindled to P28 million. Looking at his flunkies in Philippine Veterans Bank, who were feuding among themselves and ripping the institution to pieces, Marcos seems to have concluded that there was little point throwing good money after bad—especially at a time when external auditors (the IMF) were carefully watching the money supply. In any case, by 1985 Marcos's strategies of plunder had a far more cosmopolitan aspect: he was more concerned with funneling money overseas (much of it through one of his other banks, Security Bank) than with rescuing a minor institution like Veterans Bank.

When Veterans Bank was shut down, the press revealed a litany of bank abuses (secret accounts, uncollateralized loans, assets and land titles faked to serve as collateral, and flagrant window-dressing of bank accounts) as well as rampant patronage in the hiring of the bank's workforce. As a headline in the opposition paper *Malaya* explained, the "cronyism" and "politics" behind the collapse provided a clear example of "how not to run a bank." But angry bank employees picketed near the Palace, complaining bitterly about the mismanagement of the bank and the inadequacy of Central Bank assistance (in particular, at how their bank had received far less in emergency advances than other troubled banks had). Together with the veterans, they approached the Supreme Court to request assistance. Such grievances eventually led to the reopening of the bank in the early

[16] Fernandez also faced charges from the antigraft prosecutor, the Tanodbayan; one justice said he acted in an "arbitrary and capricious" manner, "giving rise to a conclusion that ulterior motives were behind the liquidation of BF." *Philippines Free Press*, September 5, 1987, 16, 26; the 1976 proposal to purchase BF was confirmed in an April 27, 1993 interview with BF officials. The Aguirres, as relative parvenus, also expressed resentment over dominance of the Monetary Board by an established "crowd" from prestigious firms who "[stick] together like plaster."

1990s. In the meantime, schools and local governments were forced to absorb the loss of deposits in the bank.[17]

The third and final bank closed down during this period was *Pacific Banking Corporation,* founded by Chinese-Filipino sugar trader Antonio Roxas Chua in 1955. According to a longtime president of the bank, serious plunder of the bank's loan portfolio did not begin until after Chua's death in the late 1970s, after which it was taken over by Chua's children. Although the bank is said to have suffered heavy losses in the wake of the 1981 Dewey Dee caper, it was not until 1985 that its poor condition began to be discussed with some regularity in the business pages. After a major run on the bank early in the year, the Chua family entertained offers from investors able to bail them out.[18]

Governor Fernandez's approach to the problems within Pacific Bank were a marked contrast to his earlier methods of dealing with Banco Filipino. The Aguirre family was treated in a punitive manner, as Fernandez trumpeted their misdeeds on television and tried to force them to sell majority control in the bank; in the Pacific case, on the other hand, the Chua family received kid-glove treatment while Fernandez devoted enormous energies to finding a buyer for the bank. Between early 1985 and early 1986, a number of parties expressed serious interest in acquiring some part of the bank, but prospective investors seem to have feared its acquisition (and its lopsided balance sheet) might turn out to be more of a curse than a blessing. One backed out after learning that Pacific Bank's net worth was "at best zero" (because of what were estimated at nearly P1 billion in bad loans); others were deterred after failing to convince the Central Bank to lower the interest rate on its outstanding loans. The Central Bank was keen on finding a buyer, however, both because of its desire to avoid a messy bank collapse and because it had lent the bank some P2 billion in emergency funds. Important concessions were eventually granted to a partnership of the Bank of Hawaii and sugar trader Antonio Chan in July 1985, but negotiations to sell the bank for P200 million nonetheless fell through.[19]

In November, the Central Bank changed tack again, and—at short

[17] Francisco B. Quesada, "Vet Bank," *Fookien Times Philippines Yearbook 1975* 177, 183; Anonymous interview, former board member, Philippine Veterans Bank, 1991; *FEER,* April 11, 1985, 92–93, and April 25, 1985, 149; SGV, *Key Officers and Board Members: Commercial Banks, Investment Houses, Offshore Banks (Philippines)* (Metro Manila: SGV), various issues; *CB Review,* March 1984, 2; *Business Day,* April 11, 1985, June 7 and 18, and July 2, 1985, and January 6, 10, and 24, 1986; *Malaya,* May 5, June 13, October 3, and December 15, 1985; *AWSJ,* April 11, 1985; Interview, Fabella, June 12, 1990.

[18] Interview, Chester Babst, former president of Pacific Bank, May 3, 1990; *Business Day Corporate Profiles 1985* (Metro Manila: Business Day), 257. Babst says he "could not get along with the young Chuas," and retired from the bank in 1980.

[19] *Business Day,* February 26, March 18, June 14, June 21, June 26, July 8, July 10, July 15, August 9, and November 14, 1985; Interview, Babst, May 3, 1990; *Bulletin Today,* September 27, 1985; and *Business Day Corporate Profiles 1985,* 257.

notice—put Pacific Bank on the auction block. Far East Bank, Metropolitan Bank, and Rizal Commercial Banking Corporation all made bids, and Fernandez assured observers that the highest bidder would obtain the bank. According to press reports, Far East Bank offered P200 million for the right to buy just the branches of Pacific Bank; because the opening of new branches was greatly restricted by the Central Bank, the extensive branch network of Pacific was the most prized asset of the failed bank. The Far East bid was the same price that the Bank of Hawaii and Antonio Chan had earlier offered to pay for the entire bank, *including* its bad loans and its debts to the Central Bank. Bankers were quoted as saying that the Far East bid was "too cheap," and there was also concern that the bidding might be perceived as "rigged" on behalf of Fernandez's former bank. But "some bankers," reported the government's news agency, "feel that Fernandez is not afraid that a controversy may arise if Far East wins the auction."

As it happens, the Far East bid was judged most acceptable—but for at least three months (in what turned out to be the final days of the Marcos regime), Fernandez provided mixed signals as to whether the final disposition of the bank was to be decided by bidding, liquidation proceedings, or further negotiations with prospective buyers. In May 1986, Far East Bank concluded a deal with the Central Bank in which—according to Babst—it assumed all the deposit liabilities (an estimated P590 million) in exchange for all the good assets (the branch network, some of the good loan accounts, and so on). If this is an accurate summation of the deal, Far East ended up paying a higher price than it had initially bid—but succeeded in acquiring all the good assets without assuming the two major burdens that had scared off earlier prospective investors: P1 billion in bad loans and P2 billion in debt to the Central Bank.

Fernandez's spokesperson vigorously defended the propriety of the bidding process, but suspicions linger to this day. There was considerable lag time between the auction and the sale, and indications are that the terms were worked out more through negotiation than through impartial bidding. Many bankers were reportedly quite bitter over the deal, but others seemed to treat it as part of the normal process of booty collection accompanying entrance into government service. When it later brought formal charges against Fernandez for "schem[ing] to enable Far East to eventually acquire Pacific," the union of Pacific Bank workers was supported by the prosecutors from the government's Tanodbayan (an antigraft unit). Among the most damning allegations was that the Central Bank consultant in charge of the Pacific Bank negotiations was a Far East Bank vice president—who, after completing the deal, returned to Far East Bank and was promoted to senior vice president.[20]

[20] *Business Day,* November 14, 1985, January 6, 10, 14, 15, and 22, 1986; *Malaya,* January 26 and 27 and May 30, 1986; *Manila Bulletin,* February 25 and May 10 and 11, 1986, and

The Central Bank was much reviled for the closures of these three banks, often by the same forces opposed to the Marcos regime. Three opposition members of parliament urged the rehabilitation of the banks, arguing, "If the government can pump huge amounts [of money] to re-habilitate distressed industries, many owned by cronies of the President who are guilty of mismanagement, why cannot the CB rehabilitate a distressed bank in order to restore public confidence in the banking sys-tem and prevent . . . [bank] employees from being thrown to the streets? . . . Why should the bank employees be penalized for the failure of the CB to monitor and supervise banking operations?" Within the banking com-munity, there was anger over the Central Bank's "bad taste" in giving out awards to outstanding banks at a time when so many banks were going under. One banker compared the Central Bank to "a father who, after beating the wife and kids, takes them out to the carnival and pampers them with cotton candy, pop corn and balloons."[21]

In responding to widespread criticism of the closure of Banco Filipino, Philippine Veterans Bank, and Pacific Bank, Central Bank Senior Deputy Governor Gabriel Singson explained that "the Central Bank Act prescribes medicine for certain specific illnesses which may afflict banks and the CB merely administers the medicine prescribed by law." As has been demons-trated, however, the legal process and the regulatory machinery was any-thing but impersonal and automatic, as the Central Bank doctored its prescriptions in accordance with a range of personalistic factors. Fer-nandez's crusade had many worthy goals, but it quickly lost credibility and faltered in its execution because the state machinery was so thoroughly incapable of impersonal application of the law. His initial promises not-withstanding, it was impossible to expect "uniform application" of the laws. As discussed in the opening chapters of this work, the Philippine state is a particularly long distance from the ideal-typical bureaucratic state, which is capable of "adjudicating and administering according to rationally established law and regulation . . . just like the expected perfor-mance of a machine." In the Philippine context, it is generally foolhardy to even attempt to discuss larger legal or policy measures without careful attention to the byzantine personalistic factors that complicate their implementation.[22]

January 27, 1989; *Manila Chronicle,* January 21, 1990; Anonymous interview, former bank president, 1989. It is worth noting that the branches were themselves booty—the harvest of Pacific Bank's good relations with Governor Licaros in the late 1970s. "The Central Bank became more lenient" toward Chinese-Filipino banks, explains Babst, "I took advantage of it by filing applications right and left." Interview, Babst, May 3, 1990.

[21] *Malaya,* November 2 and June 19, 1985.

[22] *Bulletin Today,* November 25, 1985 (quote is a paraphrase of Singson's explanation); Max Weber, *Economy and Society* (Berkeley and Los Angeles: University of California Press, 1978), II: 1394.

By objective standards, it is difficult to discern why some weak banks were closed down, yet others were permitted to survive. DOSRI abuses and mismanagement were by no means confined to the three banks that Fernandez closed, and these three banks were by no means the only ones teetering on the brink. Producers Bank, Republic Planters Bank, and Manilabank were also known to be in a sorry state, but it was widely suspected that their connections to the Palace or the Central Bank were helping keep them afloat. The issue of bank closures remained highly contentious in the years to come. Moreover, the rehabilitation of government financial institutions hopelessly plundered during the Marcos regime demanded early attention by the following administration.

In addition to dealing with the problems of the weak banks, there were two other elements to the crusade that Fernandez announced in August 1984. One was his determination to bolster the position of the stronger banks (including, as was to become obvious, his own Far East Bank and Trust Company). According to one Central Bank insider, Fernandez thought that the system needed "a few large banks, able to withstand any crisis."[23] During this period, the strong got stronger through the windfall profits provided by Jobo bills and through the transferral of deposits from weaker banks to stronger banks. Fernandez did not take a laissez-faire approach to deposit transfers—as discussed earlier, he actively encouraged people to be "choosy" in their selection of deposit-taking institutions. In addition, three major banks—including Far East Bank—were enlarged by the promotion of mergers, the final element of the Fernandez crusade.[24]

Ancillary to Fernandez's crusade in the banking sector was a major revamping of the system of selective credit. In particular, rediscounting and swaps became far less important in financing the assets of the commercial banking sector as a whole, and far less important a source of booty for individual members of the banking system. The proportion of total commercial bank assets financed by Central Bank loans and rediscounts dropped from 20.3 percent in 1984 to 6.5 percent in 1985—and became even less important through the rest of the decade. Among the major recipients in 1984 and 1985, however, were three of the troubled banks that Fernandez had not closed down: Republic Planters Bank, Manilabank, and Producers Bank.[25]

---

[23] Interview, Fabella, June 12, 1990. Fabella remained a ranking CB consultant until 1989.

[24] After BPI gave up on the possibility of acquiring Banco Filipino, it instead took over the Gotianun family's Family Bank in late 1984. Philippine Commercial and International Bank benefitted from a longstanding internal legal squabble within the International Bank of Asia and America (between the Gotianun family and the Kalaw-Ilusorio group), and absorbed IBAA in late 1985. The third, a quasi-merger, was Far East Bank's highly profitable absorption of the prized assets of Pacific Bank.

[25] Central Bank, *Fact Book*, various annual issues. Central Bank loans and rediscounts financed roughly 10–16 percent of commercial bank assets between 1975 and 1979, and

There were also major changes in the allocation of foreign exchange swaps, the Central Bank program that very generously transferred currency risk from the private to public sector. Total swaps increased between 1983 and 1984 (both in absolute terms and as a proportion of total commercial bank assets), and 1984 devaluations resulted in Central Bank losses estimated at over $500 million. From 1985 on, however, swaps became an increasingly less important source of funds for the commercial banks. In terms of allocation to particular parties, Fernandez was just as generous to the Palace as had been his predecessors, Laya and Licaros. Two banks especially important to Marcos's personal finances continued to enjoy enormously favorable allocations of swaps: in 1984, Security Bank financed 196 percent of assets through this source of booty, and Traders Royal Bank 104 percent. Whether coincidental or not, it is also worth noting that—throughout these years of decline in the aggregate levels of swaps—Far East Bank also fared quite well comparatively in swap allocations (averaging nearly 30 percent of assets in 1984 and 1985).[26]

As the result of these changes in selective credit programs, Governor Fernandez was later to declare—with some exaggeration—that the Central Bank's "developmental function" was "a thing of the past."[27] Yet while programs proclaiming benefits for economic development were being reduced in scale, developmental efforts on behalf of the large banks were to become more plentiful than ever. Despite important changes in selective credit programs, there was no end to banks' longstanding practice of raiding the booty of state; the search for booty was merely redirected toward new pots of gold. Jobo bills already provided new sources of windfall gain to banks and major asset-holders; as the economic situation began to stabilize later in the decade, other novel forms of giveaways became available for banks—especially those that were most favored.

The Fernandez Crusade, Part II: The Aquino Dawn and Beyond

For many members of the coalition that supported Corazon Cojuangco Aquino before, during, and after the "people power" revolution of Febru-

roughly 18–22 percent between 1980 and 1983. As part of the revamping of the system of selective credit, the Central Bank also reduced the subsidy element of its rediscounting program in November 1985. World Bank, *Philippine Financial Sector* (1988), 133, 143; *CB Review*, November 1985, 1; Purita F. Neri, "Current Policy Considerations on Credit Allocation," *CB Review*, March 1985, 9.

[26] *Business Day*, June 19 and 21, 1984. This form of selective credit financed roughly 7–15 percent of commercial bank assets in the period 1975–1980, 18–23 percent of assets in the years 1981–1984, and 9–11 percent of assets in 1985–87. Tabular data on swaps and rediscounts are found in Hutchcroft, "Predatory Oligarchy, Patrimonial State: The Politics of Private Domestic Commercial Banking in the Philippines," (Ph.D. dissertation, Yale University, 1993), and derived from SGV, Central Bank, and PNB data.

[27] *Business World*, November 16, 1987.

ary 1986, deposing Jobo Fernandez from the Central Bank was part and parcel of deposing Ferdinand Marcos from Malacañang Palace.[28] The string of bank closures had of course won him many enemies, and he was widely accused of accommodating Marcos's monetary needs during the May 1984 and February 1986 elections. Moreover, his economic policies were broadly unpopular both for conforming to IMF–World Bank guidelines and for bringing stringent stabilization measures, high interest rates, and economic dislocation upon the general public. Many considered Fernandez's heavy-handed use of political power to be a clear vestige of the dictatorship they had just overthrown.

More influential within the new administration, however, were the fervent supporters of Fernandez. Among them were Jaime Ongpin, a dominant figure in the ad hoc coalition of business interests formed in opposition to the excesses of Marcos cronyism (held to be responsible for constricted economic opportunities and loss of credibility with international creditors) and galvanized in anger over the 1983 assassination of Benigno Aquino. After voicing a strong critique of the post–Dewey Dee bailout, Ongpin went on to play a major role in the Makati Business Club, anti-Marcos activities, and the Aquino presidential campaign. When Aquino asked him to become finance minister, his acceptance was contingent on an agreement that Fernandez stay at the Central Bank. Ongpin acknowledged the unpopularity of Fernandez's unusually "hard-nosed" approach, but insisted that the governor "consistently behaved in a professional manner." More important, he knew that Fernandez had enormous support among foreign bankers, and felt that he would provide continuity to ongoing negotiations with external creditors. "If Fernandez is fired because of these attacks on him in the irresponsible local press," exclaimed one American banker, "I can assure you that it will have major international repercussions for the Philippines."

In any case, Fernandez enjoyed close ties to the president's family, and these ties were probably quite important in providing job security. He first learned the techniques and politics of banking as an assistant to Aquino's father, Don Pepe Cojuangco, and was related by affinity to the president. Years of experience in Philippine banking, moreover, provided valuable expertise in adapting to shifts of power, and Fernandez seems to have had little difficulty changing allegiance from the dying dictatorship to the fledgling democracy. In the 1986 presidential campaign, Fernandez sported a button in support of Marcos; weeks later, his column in the *CB Review* registered admiration for "the people's revolution" and exclaimed at how "we are now filled with hope for the future of ourselves and our children."

---

[28] On the fall of Marcos, see Mark R. Thompson, *The Anti-Marcos Struggle: Personalistic Rule and Democratic Transition in the Philippines* (New Haven: Yale University Press, 1995), 114–61.

The fact that Aquino decided to keep Fernandez on the job, however, did not make him a well-liked man. Aside from the real issues that fueled his unpopularity, Fernandez also projected an image of haughtiness and arrogance that did little to endear him to the average person on the street. He rarely spoke Tagalog, and his English carried an affected Harvard accent derived from two years of study in Cambridge, Massachusetts, several decades earlier. Fernandez's upturned eyebrows contributed further to an overall demeanor of pomposity. The *Asian Wall Street Journal* described his profile as something that "would seem more appropriate on a Roman coin than on a Philippine bank note," and even President Aquino jested that the "misperception" that Fernandez is "indifferent to the common man . . . has more to do with his disdainful eyebrows than with the substance of his prudent policies." Early in the Aquino administration, a major newspaper called Fernandez "the most discredited Central Bank governor since the founding of the bank" ("a bold charge," adds the *AWSJ*, "considering some of Mr. Fernandez's predecessors"); the head of the Anti-Graft League described him as "very wrong, very wicked, vicious, pernicious and heartless"; and a dismissed bank employee vowed to fast until Aquino fired her Central Bank governor. A disgruntled Central Bank employee sent out an anonymous open letter to Fernandez in 1987, criticizing him for using the Central Bank both to benefit Far East Bank and to attack his rivals, and alleging numerous improper perks enjoyed by the governor and his associates; the letter closes by urging Fernandez to "Go Back to [Far East Bank]. You own it."

So widespread were the charges against Fernandez that he felt the need to respond to them all, point by point. A letter from his spokesperson to the newspapers in May 1986 explained that Fernandez was "a true professional," had never been a "Marcos man," and had never issued currency for the benefit of the Marcos family, the Romualdez family, or Marcos's political party. The spokesperson also explained that Fernandez and President Aquino were related only by affinity, and therefore not subject to laws on nepotism. Furthermore, he had only closed insolvent banks, and had never given Far East Bank special privileges. Finally, the letter explained that Fernandez had earlier been "threatened with bodily harm" and was therefore entitled to "reasonable security measures."[29]

Despite the charges against him, Fernandez carried his crusade for the banking system into the new administration with characteristic aplomb. Between 1984 and 1986, he had been far more successful at bolstering the position of the strong banks than at dealing with the problems of the weak banks. Fernandez's closure of three banks generated great controversy,

[29] *AWSJ*, June 13, 1986; *Manila Chronicle*, November 10, 1987 and March 13, 1990; *CB Review*, January-February, 1986, 1; Anonymous ["A Very Concerned CB Employee"], "An Open Letter to Governor Jose B. Fernandez Jr.," February 27, 1987; *Malaya*, May 30, 1986.

but produced little real effect in terms of strengthening the day-to-day task of bank supervision. If anything, it had merely exposed Central Bank weaknesses. Deputy Governor Singson acknowledged in late 1985 that there were enormous deficiencies in the capacity of the Central Bank to supervise the banking sector. Speaking on a televised public affairs program, Singson said that monetary officials were hard-pressed to monitor developments within troubled financial institutions because bank examiners could only go through bank records once a year, and admitted that this "makes it difficult for the CB . . . to detect and avert possible looting and other abuses by bank officials such as diversion of funds for their personal interests." At a bankers' forum, also in late 1985, some bankers concluded that self-regulation by industry organization had been unsuccessful in curbing the "looting" of banks by some owners and officers, and called for tighter government regulation of their industry. Fernandez himself readily acknowledged the enduring problem of weak banks; as he said in mid-1986, "I spend an inordinate amount of time looking at reports on individual [banking] institutions. The system has got to be purified."[30] Much of Fernandez's attention, quite probably, was drawn to the rapid increase in the proportion of overdue loans to total loans: from 11.5 percent in 1980 to 13.2 percent in 1981 and 19.3 percent in 1986. Supervisory capacity, strained even in the best of times, was now further tied down by the closure of dozens of small thrift and rural banks (in addition to the three major banks discussed earlier) since 1981.[31]

The banking crisis of the mid-1980s was not limited to private banks. Unlike any previous postwar bout of bank instability, this crisis affected even those public banks that had been, in earlier years, called in repeatedly to rescue the ailing private institutions. More clearly than ever, the rotten foundations of the two major government financial institutions—the Philippine National Bank and the Development Bank of the Philippines—were exposed to view. PNB had long been known as an institution where it is "difficult to borrow . . . unless you have phone calls" from influential persons; similarly, DBP was said to have "the easiest touch in town. People with good political connections could get loans with only a few questions asked." As discussed in Chapter Four, the loan portfolios of both institutions had been raided from the time of their inception. "Money from PNB has always been a subsidy," reflected Fernandez, and

[30] *Malaya*, September 9 and November 9, 1985; *AWSJ*, June 13, 1986. Singson's remarks, interestingly, came only two months before his confident assurance (quoted earlier) that the Central Bank merely administered the prescriptions required by law.

[31] Nascimento, 209. Since 1981, Nascimento explained, the Monetary Board had chosen not to force banks to provision for bad debt in order to "give troubled banks time to overcome their financial difficulties." This choice "accelerated the deterioration of bank finances" (p. 206).

the bank itself "was some kind of a milking cow . . . with low interest rates and low credit standards."[32]

Even given this history, however, it can be said that Marcos managed an attack of unprecedented proportions: by the end of the Marcos regime, it was estimated that the two banks had bad loans totaling P119 billion ($5.9 billion). "Both banks became insolvent," the World Bank notes dryly, "largely due to problem loans granted on political rather than economic grounds." *Behest loans* (loans made at the behest of the Palace) bloated the size of the banks' nonperforming assets to such an extent that when rehabilitation did take place, in 1986, it involved the reduction of DBP assets by 86 percent, and of PNB assets by 67 percent! (PNB remained the largest bank in the system, but its proportion of total commercial banking assets declined from 26.7 percent in 1985 to 14.3 percent in 1986). The rehabilitation, not surprisingly, was conducted at the expense of the public weal: P55 billion (over $2 billion) in PNB liabilities were transferred to the central government, and P47 billion in assets were transferred to the Asset Privatization Trust. A similar process occurred at DBP.[33] After dumping their entrails on other government entities (and proceeding to invest in high-yielding government securities!) both institutions were on the road to better health.

A broad campaign against Marcos-era cronyism was a high priority of the incoming Aquino administration, and grew out of extensive boycotts of crony banks and firms in the weeks immediately prior to the February 1986 revolution.[34] Aquino's first executive order as president created the Philippine Commission on Good Government, directed to recover "ill-gotten wealth" acquired by the previous regime. In dealing with crony banks, the PCGG sequestered a controlling interest in United Coconut Planters Bank and Traders Royal Bank; shares of Allied Bank, Philippine Commercial International Bank, and Republic Planters Bank; and documents pertaining to Security Bank. But there was enormous divergence in the treatment of the various banks. UCPB (whose leading light, Aquino's first cousin and long-time political rival Danding Cojuangco, fled the country with Marcos) was thoroughly sequestered and brought under a new management team, while Lucio Tan's Allied Bank evaded PCGG's grasp with the help of clever political maneuvers. (Tan very wisely spread lots of money around in the 1987 congressional elections, and developed

[32] Interview, Fabella, June 8, 1990; *AWSJ*, March 26, 1982; Interview, Jose B. Fernandez Jr., April 6, 1990.

[33] *FEER*, May 8, 1986, 86; World Bank, *Philippine Financial Sector* (1988), 16.

[34] Aquino urged depositors to pull their money out of banks known to have particularly close ties to the Marcos family and its associates. Large withdrawals were reported from Security Bank, United Coconut Planters Bank, Republic Planters Bank, Traders Royal Bank, Union Bank, and Commercial Bank of Manila. P1 billion was withdrawn from Security, bringing it close to collapse. *Malaya*, February 6 and 20, 1986; *FEER*, July 10, 1986, 79, and May 23, 1991, 65.

close relations with Aquino's executive secretary and uncle as well as a former business associate of her family's sugar plantation.)[35] In Security Bank, the PCGG was reportedly outflanked by other forces within the administration, as Marcos's holding companies were quickly and quietly sold to investors said to be close to members of Aquino's family.[36]

Overall, there were many reports of shady practices at the "good government" agency, including the selling off of documents to those seeking to protect themselves from investigation—or to those accumulating damaging information useful for attacking their enemies. In 1988, Aquino's own solicitor general (who handled legal cases on behalf of the PCGG) accused it of "ineptness, incompetence, and corruption." While the agency's actions affected the ownership structure of certain banks, bankers as a group—after some initial anxieties—seem to have been little threatened (knowing, as one explained, that just because "the next guy gets it doesn't mean I'm next").[37]

Meanwhile, Fernandez's own crusade resumed in earnest with the closing of one more private commercial bank in 1987. The case of *Manila Banking Corporation, or Manilabank* was as steeped in the rough-and-tumble of power politics as were the three earlier bank closures; moreover, it demonstrated important continuities—from Marcos to Aquino—both in the relationship between the Palace and the Central Bank and in the personalistic manner in which the power of the state was manifested.

Licensed in 1961, Manilabank was controlled from the start by the family of Gonzalo Puyat, who began with a furniture business at the turn of the century and later diversified into logging and construction materials. His eldest son, Gil, became a prominent senator (at one point president of the Senate), while another son, Eugenio, took over the management of the family conglomerate. The family bank registered relatively steady growth through the 1960s and 1970s, and was generally among the fifteen largest banks throughout the 1970s and early 1980s. Gil's son Vicente "Teng" Puyat rose in the ranks to the post of president, while a cousin, Maria Consuelo "Baby" Puyat-Reyes became executive vice-president and treasurer. In 1982, it became the eighth bank to be awarded a unibanking license, and even opened a subsidiary foreign branch in Los Angeles.[38]

35 *FEER*, December 15, 1988, 112–116, and August 24, 1989, 66; *Manila Chronicle*, May 19, 1989 and December 11, 1989; and *Philippines Daily Globe*, May 18, 1990.

36 *FEER*, September 17, 1987, 25, and May 23, 1991, 64–65.

37 To address the problem of missing documents, the new agency transferred many files to the safest place in town: the Central Bank vaults. Anonymous interview, business journalist, 1990; *AWSJ*, August 19–20, 1988; *FEER*, February 8, 1990, 8, and December 27, 1990, and September 17, 1987, 22–27; anonymous interview, former bank president, 1990. On bankers' initial anxieties, see *Business Day*, April 17 and May 11, 1986; and *AWSJ*, August 13, 1986.

38 Yoshihara Kunio, *The Rise of Ersatz Capitalism in South-East Asia* (Quezon City: Ateneo de Manila Press, 1988), 160–61; *The VIPs of Philippine Business 1988*, (Manila: Mahal Kong Pilipinas, Inc.), 268–69; *Manila Chronicle* special report on Manila Banking Corporation, n.d.

By 1983, however, the bank began to experience serious difficulties. Whether consciously or not, it seems that Teng Puyat followed the much-distrusted 1979 World Bank–IMF recommendation of "term transformation": he was using the short-term deposit base of the bank to invest in long-term projects. Throughout the early 1980s, Puyat gave loans to himself, which were then invested in a number of agricultural ventures; as one banker was later to observe, Teng Puyat "was a great visionary who went to big projects and forgot all along that Manilabank had short-term funds not suited for development projects such as agricultural ventures."[39] When interest rates rose sharply in 1983 and 1984, the bank was squeezed in two ways: first, many lending assets were in jeopardy, since Puyat's projects depended on low interest rates, and second, the bank did not have the liquidity to take advantage of the high-interest Jobo bills that began to be floated in early 1984. For those banks that were liquid, of course, the Jobo bills provided an opportunity to reap windfall profits in low-risk investments. But Puyat made the mistake of investing in long-term productive enterprises, and the bank's health was quickly imperiled.

Puyat and Fernandez reportedly had longstanding ill feelings toward each other, so there was little hope of ready assistance from the Central Bank. Indeed, Fernandez obstructed Manilabank's efforts to obtain funds from the interbank loan market in May 1984, contending that the bank was already too heavily overdrawn. Puyat, on the other hand, accused Fernandez of purposefully instigating a run on the bank. Three weeks later, the Monetary Board placed Manilabank under comptrollership and forbade it from extending any new loans.[40]

The Puyat family, however, had decades of experience in adroit manipulation of the political machinery, and they quickly cultivated their ties with those who could save them. In a move widely perceived as an effort "to assure that the bank received all the CB support it needed," Puyat made Marcos's son-in-law vice chairman of the bank at some point in 1984. After the entrance of Gregorio "Greggy" Araneta III (husband of Irene Marcos and scion of a prominent clan) Manilabank was once again in the money. There was complete reversal in its relationship with the Central Bank—and the proportion of bank assets financed by the monetary authority

[1972?]; *Manila Times,* November 24, 1961; *FEER,* June 11, 1987, 109; *Business Day Corporate Profiles 1983,* 250.

39 *Manila Chronicle,* May 27, 1987. As discussed in Chapter Seven, many in the Central Bank privately considered the technocrats' and multilaterals' advice foolish, but publicly embraced the reform package as a way to ensure an unimpeded flow of external credit. The next major World Bank study of the banking sector, in 1988, dismissed the possibilities of promoting "term transformation" in a setting with such a recent history of liquidity crises. See World Bank, *Philippine Financial Sector,* xviii, 17–18.

40 *FEER,* June 11, 1987, 109; Anonymous interview, 1990; *Philippines Daily Globe,* March 23, 1990; *Asiaweek,* June 14, 1987, 48; *Manila Chronicle,* June 6, 1987.

increased from 13.4 percent in 1983 to 36.8 percent in 1984 and 37.9 percent in 1985. So generous was the support for Manilabank that when Banco Filipino's lawyer sought Central Bank assistance in July 1984, he requested "what is now popularly called 'the Manila Bank solution', *that is, unlimited and unrestricted financial support*."[41]

Teng Puyat, however, did not restrict his political activities to one side of the fence. At the same time he cultivated beneficial ties with Marcos's son-in-law, he was also among the members of the business community actively involved in the mounting protests against Marcos. After the Aquino assassination, it was later recalled, Puyat had become close to the former senator's family and was even a founding trustee of the Benigno Aquino Foundation. Once Corazon Aquino came to power, however, Puyat had a falling out with the new administration. He was reportedly very disturbed at the retention of Fernandez, and became a vocal critic of the governor's economic policies—especially his highly accommodating stance toward external creditors. Reportedly because of his critical stance, Puyat was not included in the president's slate of candidates in the May 1987 congressional election. Thus excluded from the group of *Coryistas*, Puyat switched over to the opposition ticket (the Grand Alliance for Democracy, dominated by a number of former *Marcosistas*) but lost his bid to follow his father's footsteps into the halls of the Philippine Senate.[42]

Once Puyat was clearly on the outs politically, Fernandez could move against Puyat with the blessing of the Palace. In April, the Central Bank called forth its powers to disqualify bank officers and directors—powers very rarely employed against commercial bank personnel—and removed Teng Puyat from the board of Manilabank. The board of directors quite wisely replaced Teng with someone on the correct side of the political fence: his cousin, Baby Puyat, who was at that time President Aquino's hand-picked candidate for the congressional seat from Makati (the premier center of finance and business).

On May 26, 1987, two weeks after the elections, the Monetary Board declared Manilabank insolvent and placed it under receivership. By that point, monetary authorities were anxious to point out, all means of rehabilitation had been exhausted and the bank's debts to the Central Bank

[41] *Manila Chronicle*, May 27 and June 9, 1987; *Asiaweek*, June 14, 1987, 48; Central Bank data on bank ownership; *FEER*, August 30, 1984, 49; Quisumbing letter to Singson, 1 (emphasis added). Central Bank officials later acknowledged that Araneta "helped ward off official pressure" on Manilabank. *FEER*, June 11, 1987, 109. Another well-connected member of the board of directors was Edgardo Angara, a law partner of Defense Secretary Juan Ponce Enrile, and the Marcos-appointed president of the University of the Philippines. SGV, *Directory of Key Officers and Board Members of Selected Financial Institutions of the Philippine Financial Sector* (Metro Manila: SGV, 1984).

[42] Puyat's exclusion from the ticket was reported by Rene Saguisag, former Aquino adviser and later senator. *Manila Chronicle*, March 21, 1990; *Philippines Daily Globe*, March 23, 1990; and *FEER*, June 11, 1987, 109. See also *FEER*, August 30, 1984, 49.

amounted to P6.1 billion (almost $300 million). But since roughly half this debt had been overdrafts incurred since year-end 1986, there were questions as to how the Central Bank—which had its own comptroller within the bank—let things run out of control so quickly. Indications are that interference from the Palace was again a major factor. Aquino's spokesperson denied that the closure had any political motivations, but acknowledged that the Palace had asked the Central Bank to defer action until after the elections in order "to avoid such accusations." Starting in late April or early May, he said, the bank had been receiving particularly large infusions of Central Bank assistance. "If the bank had been closed earlier," one banker speculated, "Puyat would have emerged a martyr and won handsomely."[43] If these accounts are accurate, the Central Bank seems to have squandered a large sum simply to ensure that the administration would not be embarrassed by a bank closure prior to the elections.

In the wake of the closure, Baby Puyat, now a congresswoman and no longer president of the bank, thought that Manilabank should get the same sort of bailout as PNB and DBP had, and proposed that the bank's debts to the Central Bank be set aside as "non-performing accounts." Teng Puyat accused the Central Bank of "a classic act of political vendetta," sued Fernandez for damages, and filed a charge against Fernandez in antigraft courts. (In refusing an emergency loan in 1984, Puyat complained, the Central Bank neglected its "mandated duty.") By July, a lower court ruled that the Central Bank's closure of Manilabank was "arbitrary, whimsical, capricious and made in bad faith," and concurred with Puyat's charge that the bank run of 1984 had been instigated by Fernandez. While the litigation continued, the Central Bank went ahead with the liquidation of Manilabank in November 1987. An early 1988 Supreme Court ruling supported the Central Bank's actions, but the following year the high court did a major flip-flop and accused the Monetary Board of denying due process to the closed bank—even as Manilabank's lawyers acknowledged the institution's insolvency.[44]

---

[43] The spokesperson is also reported to have said that the government "did not want to be accused of political persecution and that was why the bank had lived as long as it did." Although the bank had been in trouble for months, it wasn't closed down because the government "was seriously studying its political implications." *Manila Chronicle*, April 4, 1987 and June 9, 1987; *Malaya*, June 1, 1987; *FEER*, June 11, 1987, 109; *Asiaweek*, June 14, 1987, 48.

[44] Manilabank's lawyers quite audaciously suggested to the Supreme Court that the bank could return to solvency if it sold all seventy-two of its branches, collected old loans, and foreclosed on properties—and thus "start all over again even with only its main branch operating without danger to the investments made by the depositors." *FEER*, June 11, 1987, 109, and May 5, 1988, 91; *Asiaweek*, June 14, 1987, 48; *Business World*, December 26, 1988; *AWSJ*, March 11, 1988; *Manila Bulletin*, January 11, 1989.

The problems of Manilabank and other banks prompted Fernandez to try to effect important changes in laws related to bank supervision and closure. In June 1987, at the peak of the Manilabank controversy and only a few weeks before the new Congress would be seated, Fernandez asked the Aquino administration to use its soon-to-expire emergency powers (assumed after the 1986 uprising against Marcos) to decree major reforms in the supervisory structure of the banking system. Among the nineteen suggested amendments to the banking laws were proposals to facilitate bank closures and curb subsequent legal action against the Central Bank, give the Monetary Board more power to curb DOSRI loans, increase penalties for banking law violations, and grant "cease and desist" powers to the Central Bank.

It is indeed ironic that after an authoritarian regime had fallen, the Central Bank now pressed a democratic administration to implement new laws by decree. As discussed earlier, however, strengthening bank supervision was never a major part of Marcos's agenda. Unfortunately for the Central Bank, such reforms were not a high priority for the Aquino administration, either. Only two of the amendments were acted upon (tightening the definition of insolvency and expediting procedures for putting a bank under receivership or liquidation), and the task of changing banking laws was left to the new Congress.[45]

While Fernandez's efforts to strengthen bank supervision were stalled, government provision of profitable opportunities to banks—and particularly profitable opportunities to big banks—continued unabated. In the Aquino era, the major source of largesse shifted from Central Bank–issued Jobo bills to government-issued treasury bills—important not only as an element of monetary policy but also as a means of financing a ballooning government deficit. Either way, however, banks enjoyed high-interest yields without the inconvenience or risk of making commercial loans. In larger perspective, their heavy reliance on government securities beginning in the mid-1980s represented a monumental switch in the direction of lending between banks and the government. With the declining importance of rediscounting and other sources of selective credit, as discussed earlier, commercial banks had less opportunity to borrow from the government; through their purchases of government securities, they instead be-

---

[45] *Malaya*, July 2, 1987; Mario Lamberte and Julius P. Relampagos, "An Assessment of Policies Affecting the Financial Sector, 1986–1988," Philippine Institute for Development Studies, Working Paper Series No. 90–05 (Metro Manila, 1990), 15; *Philippine Star*, July 31, 1987; *Business Star*, August 4, 1987; *Business World*, August 5, 1987; and *CB Review*, June 1987, 1. It is not clear why President Aquino did not act upon more of the proposals, but one can note a general reluctance on her part to employ the emergency powers and usurp the role of Congress. It is also possible that distrust of the Central Bank—and of Fernandez in particular—made many in the diverse Aquino administration loath to increase the powers of bank supervisors.

came major lenders to the government. In effect, the loss of subsidized credit was compensated by the gain of profits from another source, government securities.

Between 1986 and 1990, the government's domestic debt expanded over threefold, from P88.4 billion to P291.3 billion; by 1990, the value of outstanding government securities actually exceeded the value of all bank deposits (P256 billion, or $9.9 billion, versus P220 billion), and a full 30 percent of the government's budget was consumed by interest payments on these debts. While such borrow-and-spend policies were a vicious cycle for the nation as a whole, they were an exceptionally virtuous cycle for the banks. "It would be an achievement if the government had used the T-bill proceeds productively," noted *FEER*, "but it has not done so." As long as the banks "can earn a steady income from the T-bills, why should they bother to lend to risky (i.e. any) commercial borrowers? . . . The last people to complain about this state of affairs are commercial bankers."[46] While productive ventures were deprived of credit, the general public was prevented from enjoying the high rates of interest offered by the treasury bills: as with Jobo bills, high minimum trading lots excluded small investors and thus shielded banks from losing the depositors who provided ready quantities of cheap funds.

Two other sources of easy gain in the Aquino years were of particular benefit to a few chosen banks. Beginning in late 1986, a network of dealers—comprising eighteen financial institutions, fourteen of which were commercial banks—was chosen to auction off government securities. This restricted dealership "disallowed fair auction or competitive bidding," explains Edita Tan, and provided dealers with "a degree of monopoly power." The chosen few thus enjoyed enormous profits not only from the instruments themselves, but also from the role of dealers within a protected market (according to one conservative calculation, banks' earnings from trading government securities totaled at least P2.8 billion in 1990 alone). The privileged eighteen included both Far East Bank and its

[46] A. M. Mendoza Jr., "The Record of a Non-Confrontational Debt Management Approach" (Quezon City: UP Center for Integrative and Development Studies, 1992), 9; *FEER*, November 8, 1990, 48, and July 16, 1992, 58. Analysis of the high domestic public debt is beyond the scope of this work, but three factors are worth mentioning: (1) the low revenue capacity of the Philippine government; (2) spillover from foreign debt (Mendoza reports 58 percent "of the growth in public local liabilities was due to . . . foreign debt operations," including "interest payments of foreign loans assumed by the national government" and Central Bank debt-to-equity conversions); and (3) bailouts and giveaway programs, most dramatically the 1986 bailout of government financial institutions. Between 1987 and 1989, the World Bank explains, "the perverse relationship that leads from domestic debt accumulation to high interest rate and appreciated exchange rate, to worsening fiscal balances, and back to domestic debt accumulation, had turned into a vicious circle." World Bank, "The Philippines: An Opening for Sustained Growth," Report No. 11061-PH (Washington, D.C.: World Bank, 1993), 66.

subsidiary investment house, FEB Investment. Far East Bank became the biggest dealer of all.[47]

The second major new source of booty began in 1987, when the government transferred large quantities of government deposits from government institutions to the five largest private domestic banks (including Far East Bank). Initially, the banks were not required to pay any interest at all on these deposits, but in 1988 the government asked for 5 percent interest on its money. Using these low-cost or no-cost funds, the banks could turn around and invest in government securities yielding 20 percent interest and more. In other words, funds borrowed from the government were re-lent to the government at much higher rates! The program was terminated in 1989 (and government banks once again became the sole repository for government funds), seemingly both to control excess liquidity and to ease the resentment and clamor of other banks.[48] As long as it lasted, however, this arrangement gave a fat advantage to the five banks, and was a significant factor in the increasingly dominant position they enjoyed by decade's end.

The extraordinary success of the largest banks, however, did nothing to solve the enduring problems of weak banks, ineffectual bank supervision, and DOSRI abuse. To bolster his position in dealing with these issues, it seems, Fernandez invited a World Bank mission to examine problems in the banking sector in late 1987. Their 1988 report took an entirely different approach than that of the 1979 World Bank–IMF study: instead of beginning with textbook presumptions about how a financial system might optimally be organized, they began their study with a certain basic concern for how the Philippine financial system really worked. Not surprisingly, this produced more attention to problems of bank supervision and bank instability than any other previous analysis by the multilateral institutions.

The 1988 report focused significant attention on three issues of particular relevance to the analysis in this book. The first was the frequent lawsuits against Central Bank personnel and the weak laws and regulations dealing

[47] Edita Tan, "How to Bring Down the Interest Rate on Loans," *Issues and Letters* 1, vol. 10 (n.d.) [1991?], 3–4; *FEER,* January 24, 1991, 48, and July 16, 1992, 58; E. Ealdama Jr., "The First Full-Year Cycle of Treasury Bills Under the New Auction System," *CB Review,* October 1987, 25–34; Isagani L. Landicho, "The 1988 Dealer Network for Government Securities," *CB Review,* November 1988, 17–22.

[48] In addition to Far East, the other beneficiaries were Bank of the Philippine Islands, Metropolitan Bank, United Coconut Planters Bank, and Philippine Commercial International Bank. The ostensible purpose of the program, called the "new disbursement scheme," was to facilitate the disbursement of government funds. In addition, both Fernandez and the budget minister reportedly agreed "that government banks should not be given the edge over commercial banks as depository banks." *Manila Chronicle,* June 10 and August 5 and 22, 1988, June 2, August 3, and December 27, 1989, and January 5, 15, and 22, 1990; *Business Star,* September 13 and November 24, 1988; Interview, Babst, May 3, 1990.

with bank supervision, for which the report urged a major strengthening of the regulators vis-à-vis the regulated. The second issue was the presence of too many small, weak banks, for which the report proposed consolidation of the banking sector. The third was the high profit rates for the large banks, for which the report recommended increased levels of competition through the licensing of new banks and other means.

The report was especially frank in discussing the Central Bank's weakness in dealing with the powerful interests that controlled the country's private commercial banks. It explained, for example, that as a result of the many lawsuits against Central Bank personnel in the wake of the bank failures of the mid-1980s, the "CBP staff . . . feel personally vulnerable to suits brought against them for their official acts, and this is now affecting their performance." In effect, the report acknowledged that in the Philippines, CB officials were more likely *to be intimidated* than *to intimidate.* "In the future," it suggested, "the CBP should consider adopting a firmer approach in dealing with banks which violate its rules and regulations." After a "rash of recent bank failures" and "ensuing litigation," explained the report, it was necessary to reexamine the "inadequate legal framework and insufficiency of available instruments" related not only to these issues but also to the problem of insider abuse.

An entire volume of the study, in fact, was devoted to addressing the legal and regulatory deficiencies responsible for the past "image of indecisiveness/weakness." Procedures for dealing with failing banks and "fraudulent or unsound" banking procedures, the report concluded, were "cumbersome and antiquated." The law did not provide "objective criteria" for making decisions as to how to deal with failing banks, and the Central Bank was frequently hobbled by lawsuits and charges of conflict of interest. The Philippine Deposit Insurance Corporation, the report noted, was heavily indebted to the Central Bank and did little to fulfill its task of promoting confidence in the banking system. Moreover, bank supervisors were "severely hampered in their power to anticipate insider abuse" by the law on the secrecy of bank deposits (first discussed in Chapter Six). Finally, "procedures governing CBP emergency advances to banks in difficulty appear to be ad hoc in nature and lacking in consistent application."[49]

Second, following up on longstanding concerns and repeating earlier recommendations, the report suggested that the Central Bank work toward strengthening the banking industry through mergers and acquisitions, and "not sustain all weak and marginal banks indefinitely." The third element of the report (quite likely the one for which Fernandez had the

[49] Interview, Carlota Valenzuela, May 9, 1990; World Bank, *Philippine Financial Sector* (1988), viii, x, 159, 157, and vol. II, 1–3.

least enthusiasm) discussed the extraordinary profitability of the Philippine banking sector, especially for the stronger banks. While the report recognized that high intermediation costs explained part of the high spread between cost of funds and loan rates, the data also showed pretax profit margins in the Philippines to be 271 percent higher than the average of such margins in eight other countries. If only "strong domestic banks" were considered, the profit margin in the Philippines was 343 percent higher than in the other sample countries. The analysis concentrated on the distinction that must be made between the profit structures of the stronger and the weaker banks in the Philippine banking system: "The high profit margin in the Philippines [as compared to the other sample countries] was the result of continued tolerance of small and weak banks with high operating costs in the system; the more efficient banks priced their products and services with reference to the cost structure of the smaller banks, a practice which effectively enabled them to capture higher profits." In response to these profit margins, the report suggested that the Central Bank "should be particularly concerned with impediments to competition," and urged that the Central Bank consider opening the system to new banks (including new foreign banks) and liberalizing policies on the establishment of new branches.[50]

The mere availability of relevant analysis and recommendations from the World Bank, however, did not mean that fundamental change was on the horizon. World Bank conditionality notwithstanding, Congress displayed little enthusiasm for strengthening the hand of the Central Bank. While there were many obstacles to pushing a reform package through Congress, one particular hindrance was the unpopularity of Fernandez himself. At roughly the same time the World Bank mission was in Manila, the governor was called before a special Senate subcommittee created specifically to investigate charges that Fernandez's 1984 divestment of shares from Far East Bank had been simulated, and to examine the rapid growth of the bank since Fernandez took office (from year-end 1983 to year-end 1988, it climbed from eighth-largest to third-largest commercial bank in terms of total assets, making it the premier private domestic commercial bank). The "pressing, pulsating and pertinent" question, declared Senator Aquilino Pimentel, is "why did Far East Bank do well, very well indeed, after Mr. Fernandez left it to become Central Bank governor?" He demanded that Fernandez resign, charging that his continuance in office hindered "the even-handed application of our laws." Fernandez challenged Pimentel to substantiate any connection between his own position

---

[50] World Bank, *Philippine Financial Sector* (1988), ii, iii, vi, 73, 157 (quotes from ii, iii, and vi, emphasis in original).

7. Central Bank Governor Jose Fernandez Jr. (1984–1990) testifies before a congressional committee. Photo credit: From the *Business World* collection.

and the bank's success, but admitted that the firm established to buy his
Far East shares was owned by business associates and family members.[51]

Many legislators set their sights not only upon Fernandez, but upon the
very perpetuation of the Central Bank itself. As part of a reaction against
the Marcos-era fiscal excesses and the overstatement of international reserves under Laya's governorship, there was strong sentiment within Congress to dismantle the Central Bank altogether and replace it with a central
monetary authority (CMA) that would exercise greater independence
from the executive branch. The 1986 constitution had called for the creation of an independent CMA, and many in both the House and Senate
were determined to follow through. Since the legislators mandated that
the new entity's budget would be subject to congressional approval, however, it would have done little to provide the CMA with any degree of

[51] *Manila Chronicle*, November 10 and 26, 1987; *Malaya*, December 3, 1987; and *The
Financial Post*, March 18, 1988. Just before his retirement, once again defending himself
against these charges, Fernandez said the bank "seems to have moved from strength to
strength without me." Speech to Management Association of the Philippines, Metro Manila,
February 1, 1990. As of 1979, Fernandez's JBF Investments owned an 8.6 percent share of the
bank.

8. Central Bank Governor Jose Fernandez Jr. (1984–1990) greets Jaime Cardinal Sin, Archbishop of Manila, at a 1989 awards ceremony honoring Fernandez for assisting in the stabilization of the economy and the banking sector. Photo credit: From the *Business World* collection.

independence from those social forces that the Central Bank had had such difficulty regulating since 1949. Deputy Governor Singson called the proposal "destabilizing," and contended that the constitutional provisions could be satisfied by amending the Central Bank charter. While these particular proposals eventually lost steam, they did demonstrate that the Central Bank would have to exert enormous effort simply to defend past powers—and would need to give up on any hope of acquiring new ones. By the time the World Bank report came out in 1988, Fernandez must have known there was little chance to break through mounting distrust and persuade Congress to reform banking laws and strengthen the powers of the Central Bank.[52]

Congress did come forth with its own proposals to strengthen laws against DOSRI abuses (including one bill that would have introduced an outright ban on the practice!), but officials from the Central Bank, PNB, and BAP quickly counseled the lawmakers that DOSRI problems were caused not so much by deficiencies in the laws as by deficiencies in the system of regulation. As Senior Deputy Governor Singson told a House

[52] *Business World,* October 30, 1987 and February 11 and September 5, 1988; *Philippines Daily Globe,* January 5 and 17, and June 5, 1988.

committee, "We have good, beautiful rules and yet fail." The BAP similarly maintained that while the Central Bank had enough regulations on the books, it did not implement them effectively.[53]

Given congressional reluctance to deal with broader issues of bank supervision—either the amendments first proposed to the Palace in July 1987 or those that came out of the World Bank study—the Central Bank moved on its own to convince the World Bank of the government's commitment to reform. In a major statement of policy change in March 1989, the Monetary Board declared that although branch licensing was to remain "discretionary," bank licensing would be fully liberalized. Moreover, weak banks were no longer to be sustained, and would instead be encouraged to merge or consolidate with healthier institutions. Broader ownership of banks would also be encouraged to help resolve problems of insider abuse. Finally (perhaps to allay the fears of those who had observed patterns to the contrary), the monetary authority vowed to "continue [sic] to apply its rules and regulations uniformly and without discrimination upon all commercial banks."[54]

Despite the rhetoric of 1989, as we shall see in the next chapter, there was in fact little progress toward addressing the problems of limited competition, weak banks, and weak supervisory capacity. Very few new bank licenses were granted until liberalization was pressed more forcefully in the mid-1990s, and mergers and consolidations were even more rare. Not only were existing weak banks sustained, but formerly closed banks actually came back from the dead. Meanwhile, the Central Bank continued to be charged with uneven application of its rules, and to be hobbled by a host of lawsuits.

World Bank pressure also encouraged continuing attention to the task of privatizing the six banks acquired by various government agencies earlier in the decade: Associated Bank, Commercial Bank of Manila, International Corporate Bank, Pilipinas Bank, Republic Planters Bank, and Union Bank. Although a $300 million economic recovery loan was made conditional on their privatization by late 1988, only two banks (Combank and Pilipinas) were in majority private hands by 1990. Government agencies pumped equity into these banks precisely because they were in trouble, and their loan portfolios generally continued to be of poor quality. Sale of the banks was further complicated by charges of favoritism in bidding

---

[53] *Business Star,* September 17, 1987 and November 11, 1988; *Business World,* August 25, 1988. The BAP also made the important point that "Dosri loans are not good or bad per se. A loan, whether Dosri or not, becomes good or bad depending primarily on the viability of the project or the business that it is going to finance." DOSRI loans become "undesirable only when they are granted in violation of safe and sound banking practice." Officials acknowledged, however, that DOSRI loans had figured prominently in past bank failures. *Manila Chronicle,* July 1, 1988.

[54] Central Bank Circular 1200, May 16, 1989.

processes and a range of legal battles (including those waged by Emerito Ramos and Vicente Tan, each seeking to regain control over banks they had earlier lost).[55] The World Bank was seemingly overtaken by a measure of dogmatism in its push for privatization, unwilling to distinguish essentially sound state-owned banks (such as Union Bank) from those considered hopelessly flawed (such as Republic Planters Bank).

In larger perspective, it is important to note the particular character of privatization in settings where patrimonial features are strong—and thus not pin unrealistic hopes on the exercise. In the Philippines, such programs are commonly doing little more than making private sector assets out of public sector assets that are, in essence, already privatized. There are indeed valid arguments for selective dismantling of the state, but in doing so it is essential not to ignore a more fundamental developmental task: constructing a state apparatus in which the distinction between public and private is more clearly delineated, and thereby promoting the political and procedural predictability necessary for more advanced forms of capitalist accumulation.

Private Gain, Public Drain: Winners and Losers in Fernandez's Crusade

Upon his resignation as governor in February 1990, Fernandez described his term as "six years of permanent siege." Not only was he attacked in the press, the Congress, and the courts, Fernandez also faced a serious assassination attempt in 1989, thought to be connected to his closure of one of the commercial banks. Indeed, the man who set out to strengthen the hand of the Central Bank in dealing with the many problems and great instability of the banking sector left behind an institution that remained ineffectual in regulating the powerful social forces concentrated in the banks. Despite all the talk of increasing the Central Bank's powers, the institution ended the decade with a growing internal financial crisis and a host of lawsuits against it and its increasingly demoralized personnel.[56]

[55] One other successful privatization was DBP's 1987 sale of its one-quarter share in a seventh bank, Philippine Commercial and International Bank, to a consortium of the Lopez and Gokongwei families. In addition, privatization of PNB began in 1989 but (as discussed in Chapter Nine) was not completed until late 1995.

[56] *Manila Chronicle,* April 21 and 28, 1989 and February 2, 1990. Upon receiving a Management Association of the Philippines award in February 1990, Fernandez jested that he did not know "what I had done to earn it. . . . surely, it could not have been from managing the Central Bank where the visible results of my efforts have been scores of lawsuits." Even as many in the business community lauded his success in stabilizing the economy (and saving their hides) amid the crisis of the mid-1980s, Fernandez remained widely unpopular in other circles. He was "a man people (read: politicians, kibitzers and owners of foreclosed financial institutions) love to hate." *Manila Chronicle,* January 21, 1990.

The direction of legal actions was essentially one-way: extensive and protracted litigation by aggrieved bank owners, without successful prosecution by the Central Bank of the owners of failed commercial banks for fraud or mismanagement (indeed, commercial bankers generally considered it an outrage even to be investigated by the Central Bank). Cases related to Banco Filipino, Veterans Bank, and Manilabank endured in the courts at decade's end, and two of the banks were successfully reopened by 1994. The Pacific Bank litigation was transformed into charges brought against Fernandez before a special court that tries graft cases against government officials. After entering a plea of "not guilty" on charges of "simulated divestment" of his Far East Bank shares in 1984, Fernandez encountered a small group of demonstrators with placards labeling him a "bank killer" and a "power grabber."[57]

In the end, it was the errant bankers who got tough with Fernandez and used a porous administrative and legal system to strike back at any who dared challenge the way they mismanaged their banks. Lawsuits, explains one former bank president, are a way "of preventing officials from implementing the regulations. You intimidate the bureaucracy." Bank regulators were defended by a Central Bank legal staff widely ridiculed for its mediocrity, while the bankers were able to go on the attack with the country's best legal talent. Soon after his retirement, Fernandez acknowledged that lawsuits and low pay made it difficult to recruit the kind of "shrewd, capable" persons needed for bank supervision. Because of pending lawsuits, he explained, some supervisors without any other livelihood were unable to obtain their retirement pay. "I feel very sorry for them." As one pensionless former official complained, the standard concerns of other central banks (such as credit and foreign exchange risk) "pale in comparison to the risks we have in the Philippines, where supervisors are sued by the supervised."[58]

Demoralization in the ranks was heightened in 1989, when the Central Bank lost control over setting salary rates for its own employees—a privilege it had enjoyed since its founding in 1949. Whereas they were formerly able to attract better talent than the rest of the bureaucracy (but

[57] According to prosecutors, Fernandez's sale of his bank shares had an unusually long payment period of fourteen years (without interest), and a clause that makes a "single default enough reason for the seller to reclaim the shares." Moreover, as noted earlier, the shell company to which the shares were sold included many relatives and business associates of Fernandez. *Manila Chronicle,* April 18 and 20, 1990; *Philippines Daily Globe,* April 18, 25, and 27, 1990.

[58] Interviews, Antonio P. Gatmaitan, September 18, 1989; Fernandez, April 6, 1990; and Ramon Tiaoqui, former managing director, Supervision and Examination Sector, April 26, 1993. Fernandez had begun to use private lawyers to defend the Central Bank, but the government's Commission on Audit forbade the practice in 1988. An exception was made for the Banco Filipino case, since a private law firm had been contracted as early as 1985. *FEER,* July 18, 1991, 55.

generally far lesser talent than the private banks), they were now forced to pay salaries commensurate to the low levels generally found throughout the Philippine bureaucracy. As Deputy Governor Singson complained, "it's increasingly difficult to get competent people." This surely did little to curb the longstanding tendency of the regulated to outwit the regulators.[59]

Meanwhile, the problems that motivated the crusade six years earlier—weak banks and the dangers of renewed bank instability—remained unresolved. The system as a whole was far healthier at decade's end than it had been in 1981 or 1985, thanks to the many sources of booty (swaps, rediscounts, equity infusions, bailouts, Central Bank bills, and T-bills) that Fernandez and others made available to the banks; as an IMF study of the banking crises of the 1980s later concluded, "interventions by the authorities prevented the banking sector from collapsing, but at a high financial cost to taxpayers." Until underlying weaknesses of bank supervision could be addressed, the danger of further crises quite clearly endured. Even after Fernandez's crusade, regulators remained hamstrung in dealing with such root causes as insider abuse; as Fernandez himself admitted in 1990, the Central Bank's ability to prevent such abuses was "still not adequate."

The Fernandez crusade was undermined not only by weakness in the courtroom and deficiencies of supervision, of course, but also by widespread perceptions that the power of the state was being used to punish and favor particular individuals and banks (despite earlier promises of "uniform application" of the law). It was one thing for Fernandez to try to get tough, and quite another for a large measure of that toughness to be used for the particular benefit of Palace and Central Bank favorites and the particular detriment of Palace and Central Bank enemies. Precisely because of the lack of uniformity in the application of legal sanctions and the allocation of privilege (both during its "authoritarian" and its "democratic" phases), the credibility of Fernandez's crusade was quickly undermined. The persistence of this underlying arbitrariness cast doubt on the World Bank's confident prediction that with an "improved legal framework and additional regulatory instruments," the "CBP should in the future act firmly and quickly."[60]

The other major element of Fernandez's crusade—bolstering the position of the stronger banks—was a resounding success. Here, indeed, are the winners of the crusade: in the course of the decade, the five largest private domestic banks increased their share of total systemwide assets

[59] *FEER*, September 24, 1992, 70, and July 18, 1991, 54–55; Interview, Iñigo Regalado, former deputy governor and general counsel of the Central Bank, April 23, 1993.

[60] Nascimento, 177 (see also 195); Interview, Fernandez, April 6, 1990; World Bank, *Philippine Financial Sector* (1988), 157.

from 22.1 percent in 1980 to 26.4 percent in 1985 and 38.0 percent in 1990.[61] We have seen that the 1980 introduction of universal banking set the stage for increasing differentiation between larger and smaller banks; in the crisis of the mid-1980s, depositors shifted funds toward the more stable banks—in part because they were being encouraged to do so by the Central Bank governor himself. At various points during the Fernandez years (even as earlier forms of booty, such as swaps and rediscounts, were being scaled back), larger banks benefitted by availing themselves of high-yielding Jobo bills and treasury bills (to the detriment of lending for productive uses), trading in government securities, absorbing smaller banks, and—for the lucky five between 1987 and 1989—turning government deposits into investments in government securities.

Meanwhile, Fernandez did nothing to stand in the way of collusive practices among the banks—despite World Bank concerns over how the more efficient banks enjoyed high profits by setting prices in accordance with the cost structure of the less efficient banks. In a 1990 interview, the executive officer of the BAP admitted that the association's Operations Committee set minimum spreads on letters of credit and on foreign exchange transactions, both major sources of profits. "More or less, it's a cartel," he remarked. According to other reliable sources, the largest banks maintained a "gentlemen's agreement" on minimum spreads between the cost of funds and loan rates. Fabella explained that because there is "not ease of entry" into the industry, it is "easy for the large banks to fall into collusive arrangements." Former Governor Laya said that the Central Bank has "never challenged" the BAP on interest rate determination, "neither then, or now." While he doesn't perceive a "strict oligopoly situation," he presumes that the big banks "probably talk among themselves."[62]

The general public, meanwhile, emerged as the biggest loser. At the end of Fernandez's term, the banking system had become an enormous drain on public resources yet still did little to promote forms of financial intermediation beneficial to the vast majority of the Filipino people. Valid arguments can be advanced for public rescue of private institutions, as long as certain benefits from that rescue are eventually realized by those who shoulder the burdens. But at the end of the decade, the Philippine people still had little to show for all the public money that had coursed into the country's banks. As the deficits of the Treasury and the Central

[61] If PNB is included among the five largest banks, there is actually a decline in the concentration ratios because of its shrunken role after 1986. The largest private domestic banks, however, enjoyed an increasingly prominent role (see Appendix 3).

[62] Interview, Edgardo J. Carvajal, executive officer, Bankers Association of the Philippines, May 14, 1990; Anonymous interview, international economist, May 1990; Interview, Fabella, June 8, 1990; Interview, Jaime C. Laya, May 21, 1990.

Bank weighed ever more heavily on both taxpayers and consumers of essential public services, small savers were lucky to get positive rates of interest on their deposits and small borrowers were rarely served by the banking sector at all. Meanwhile, high minimum trading lots prevented the general public from obtaining the handsome returns offered by the government on instruments of public debt. As we shall see, even greater burdens were yet to come: the clearly beleaguered bankers' bank, its stature sapped rather than enhanced after years of dispensing privilege and riches, would itself soon require a massive public bailout.

CHAPTER NINE

Death, Resurrection, and Renovation:
The Philippine Banking Sector in the 1990s

The new decade initially brought little change in the overall configuration of the Philippine banking sector. The liberalization of bank licenses proclaimed in 1989 had almost no impact, and key trends of the late 1980s persisted. The oligopolistic dominance of the top banks was unchallenged, weak banks endured without major event, the system as a whole persisted in feeding off lucrative instruments of public debt, and the Central Bank continued to face internal problems and external challenges. Stark contrasts among winners and losers endured—in the years 1990 through 1993, the national economy stagnated (with annual growth of gross domestic product averaging only 1 percent) while commercial banks averaged 17.9 percent annual growth in total assets and nearly 20 percent return on equity.[1]

Beginning in 1993, however, the new administration of President Fidel V. Ramos pushed two major changes in the banking system. First, the death of the Central Bank of the Philippines was followed by its resurrection as the debt-free *Bangko Sentral ng Pilipinas* (and P331 billion, or $12 billion, of debt was dumped onto a national treasury already overburdened by earlier bailouts of PNB, DBP, and other state agencies in the 1980s). The following year, a substantial liberalization of bank licensing opened the door to more new entrants than at any point since the early 1960s, amid promises that the industry would at last become more competitive and thus more responsive to developmental needs. It remains doubtful, however, whether the problems of the past can be resolved by

---

[1] Carlos C. Bautista, Roy C. Ybañez, and Gerardo Agulto Jr., "The Behavior and Performance of the Philippine Commercial Banking Industry, 1980–1994," in *The Philippine Financial Services Industry: Prospects and Challenges in the Next Decade*, ed. Rafael A. Rodriguez (Quezon City: University of the Philippines Press, 1995); SGV, *A Study of Commercial Banks in the Philippines* (Metro Manila: SGV), various issues.

these attempts at renovation: the supervisory structure remains weak in the face of powerful social forces concentrated in the banking sector, and the bulk of the market is relatively untouched by new competitive pressures. While the reforms raise expectations of improvement, banks have yet to prove that they can at last begin to deliver the goods and be a positive force in promoting national development.

The first section of this chapter analyzes how the Central Bank died, and the measures taken both to bury its body and to resurrect a new monetary authority under a new name (with many of the same personnel and same problems). The second section analyzes the key motivations behind the liberalization program and its likely impact in future years, and the third discusses ongoing weaknesses in supervisory capacity and problems of bank instability. The conclusion examines the banking sector at mid-decade, and the limits to liberalization in a setting where there has been little corresponding strengthening of the state regulatory apparatus.

The Death and Resurrection of the Monetary Authority

The Central Bank's dire financial condition, increasingly evident in the late 1980s, demanded priority attention by the early 1990s. The *Far Eastern Economic Review* observed in 1992 that the "lender of last resort is bleeding red ink," and the World Bank judged the financial crisis of the country's leading economic policymaking agency to be one of the country's two largest economic problems (along with "external debt overhang"). Central Bank losses were fifteen times greater than its net worth; they averaged more than 2.5 percent of GDP from 1983 into the early 1990s and came to constitute a full 55 percent of the consolidated public sector deficit. The financial rot can be traced to three major types of giveaway programs: the assumption of some $3 billion in foreign debt (in the process of rescheduling external obligations, some of which were originally part of the "jumbo loan" program); losses arising from swaps and forward exchange cover programs, both of which transferred foreign exchange risk from the private sector to the public sector; and the floating of high-interest, low-risk Central Bank bills—particularly the Jobo bills of the mid-1980s.

As interest on past obligations accumulated, the World Bank declared in 1993 that Central Bank losses "are of serious concern" not only because of damage done to public finances but also because the basic task of monetary control was greatly hampered. Open market operations were severely restricted by losses from Central Bank bills, so the monetary authorities had to rely heavily on reserve requirements. The extraordinary level of these reserves—a full 25 percent throughout 1991 and 1992, by far the highest in the region—was determined not by the imperatives of "monetary control or developmental objectives" but rather by the cash flow needs of the Central Bank. Overall responsibility for mopping up excess liquidity came to be shared with the national government: treasury bills were issued in greater quantities than were needed to finance government deficits and the proceeds deposited with the Central Bank (interest-free since 1990, thus subsidizing the monetary authority). While affirming that such measures generally "[precluded] the monetization of central bank deficits" (unlike the experience "in most other heavily indebted countries"), the World Bank nonetheless gave clear priority to the goal of "[r]estoring the central bank to a position of dominance in monetary policy implementation."

The deficits had other deleterious consequences as well. First, explained the World Bank, domestic borrowing undertaken to finance interest payments on foreign debt "raised interest rates, crowded out private credit, and appreciated the exchange rate." Second, the financial crisis indirectly hindered the promotion of exports: because the bulk of the debt was in foreign currency (including both losses from foreign exchange operations and the foreign debt assumed from other agencies), the Central Bank was loath to let the peso depreciate lest it heighten its own fiscal problems.[2]

The 1986 constitution, as noted earlier, called for the creation of an independent central monetary authority (CMA). In the early Aquino years, Central Bank authorities were very resistant to congressional initiatives to fulfill the provisions of the constitution, since the overall intent was generally to curb the powers of an often highly unpopular institution. By the early 1990s, however, the Central Bank embraced the constitutional provisions as a convenient way of addressing three increasingly grave challenges: mounting deficits, ongoing lawsuits and overall weakness of bank supervision, and low salaries. In creating a new CMA, officials hoped to clean up their balance sheet, enhance legal safeguards for a supervisory staff long under siege, and break loose from the salary standardization measures that had reduced compensation to highly unattractive levels. The World Bank provided a carrot to the Philippine Congress by making the creation of a new CMA a condition for a $450 million financial sector adjustment loan, and the Ramos administration provided further grease through its skillful disbursement of discretionary funds to legislators.[3]

[2] *FEER,* June 14, 1990, 44–45, October 17, 1991, 72, and July 23, 1992, 44–45 (quote at 44); World Bank, *The Philippines: An Opening for Sustained Growth,* Report No. 11061-PH (Washington, D.C.: World Bank, 1993), 9–10, 24, 69, 78–80, 105–6 (quotes from 9–10, 79); BSP, "Primer on NG Deposits with BSP and Old CB," reprinted in *Manila Bulletin,* April 8, 1994; M. B. Suleik, "The Central Bank Suspense Accounts," *CB Review,* January, February, and March, 1993; *Business World,* July 19, 1994; Jannalenna B. Sheng, "Central Bank Losses and the Conduct of Monetary Policy in the Philippines" (Graduate research paper, M.A. Program in Development Economics, Williams College, 1994); *Philippine Star,* January 5, 1994.

[3] *Philippine Times-Journal,* June 14, 1993. The first half of the $900 million loan was

The creation of the new institution, however, generated considerable controversy. In December 1992, the House of Representatives deleted provisions for transferring the P308 billion in liabilities to the national government, merely creating a commission to study the matter. Later versions of the bill provided only partial transfer of the liabilities, and some legislators demanded an investigation into $1 billion of Central Bank funds allegedly "spent by former First Lady Imelda Marcos for her shopping binges abroad and on real estate purchases." But Central Bank Governor Jose Cuisia (Fernandez's successor since 1990) urged legislators not to "get distracted"; with the support of the Ramos administration, the World Bank, and the BAP he pushed for a bill as advantageous as possible to the new CMA. A conference committee finally produced a bill in June 1993 (just before the World Bank's June 30 deadline) creating the Bangko Sentral ng Pilipinas (BSP)—and leaving it up to a special committee to decide, as one newspaper reported, "which of the old CB's losses would be transferred to the BSP and which shall fall under a category meant for creative financing options."[4]

The BSP emerged with a clean balance sheet, but promises of creativity seem to have been ignored. By the end of 1993, the former liquidator of banks was itself turned over to the Central Bank–Board of Liquidators, which assumed a phenomenal P331.2 billion in liabilities from the dead institution—even more than initially proposed to Congress in 1992! With a tone of generosity, however, the BSP later explained that the liquidators would hand over the liabilities to the national government "gradually up to a period of 25 years" rather than "in one fell swoop." The corresponding amount of assumed assets consisted overwhelmingly of so-called suspense accounts that the BSP admitted "are in reality expenses already disbursed years earlier but kept on the books as assets . . . [with] no real value." Analysis of the three "worthless asset accounts" reveals little suspense: as noted above, they are quite easily traceable to such earlier sources of oligarchic gain (and Central Bank losses) as assumed foreign debt, swaps, and Jobo bills.

---

released in 1989. Ramos's skill in managing ties with Congress in the early years of his administration is further analyzed in Hutchcroft, "Unraveling the Past in the Philippines," *Current History*, December 1995, 430–34.

[4] U.S. Embassy cable (unclassified), February 9, 1993; *Philippine Star*, March 8, 1993; *Manila Chronicle*, March 23, 1994; *Business World*, March 25 and 29, and June 10, 1993; *Philippine Daily Inquirer*, May 20 and June 10, 1993; *Philippine Times-Journal*, June 14, 1993 (quotes from *PDI* May 20, *BW* March 25, and *PTJ*.) The committee making these decisions included the BSP governor, two other members of the new Monetary Board, the secretary of finance, the secretary of management and budget, and the chairs of the House and Senate committees on banks. Gabriel C. Singson, "Maintaining Price Stability," *Fookien Times Philippines Yearbook 1994*, 176–77. Contrasting versions of the CMA bills are analyzed in Teresa V. Taningco, "A Primer on the Financial Restructuring of the Central Bank," Center for Research and Communication, Economic Policy Papers No. 4 (Metro Manila, 1993).

The national government's overall assistance included not only the bailout of the old monetary authority, but also P10 billion in initial capitalization for the new BSP and P220 billion of treasury bills to reinvigorate open-market operations. The new institution was soon proudly proclaiming its profitability, and issuing dividends—as provided by law—to offset damage done by its predecessor. New profits, however, were dwarfed by old losses. In the first year, 1994, the net cost of restructuring (P24.3 billion in liabilities passed on by the Board of Liquidators minus P5.3 billion in profits passed on by the BSP) added P19 billion in burdens to the national budget—equal to $730 million, or roughly $11 for each Filipino citizen. The net cost in 1995 was P16.4 billion, and that of first semester 1996 over P7 billion; the total government outlay for health in each year, by comparison, was less than P12 billion.[5]

While, technically, the bailout of the monetary authorities merely shifted liabilities from one branch of the government to another, the overall effort exposed more clearly than ever how much distress the immense financial mess at the Central Bank would end up causing both taxpayers and consumers of public services. The major business daily paper predicted the restructuring will "haunt taxpayers," and (according to Finance Secretary Roberto F. de Ocampo) contribute to "drastic cuts in capital outlays" for infrastructural programs. While extraordinary national government proceeds from privatization masked fiscal woes in the short term, the Central Bank bailout can be singled out as a leading contributor to a very troublesome longer-term scenario. Ongoing efforts to contain the overall deficit, predicted political economist Amado Mendoza, "will force government to continue curtailing vital expenditures or imposing easily-collectible regressive taxes."[6]

The reminting of the Central Bank as the Bangko Sentral was most successful in dumping old debts on the treasury and enabling the new BSP to begin life (on July 3, 1993) free of debt. At the same time, other reforms attempted to redress past problems. Salaries could once again be set at levels higher than the rest of the bureaucracy, although compensation remained far inferior to that available in the private sector. The new gover-

---

[5] BSP, "Primer," *Manila Bulletin*, April 8, 1994; Singson, 176; *Business World*, July 14, 1995; Filomeno Sta. Ana, "Budget Call," *Politik*, November 1995, 34. The data on net costs of restructuring come from the Bureau of Treasury; another source estimates the total cost of restructuring in 1994 to be much higher: P55.8 billion rather than P24.3 billion. See *Business World*, July 19, 1994 (citing figures of former budget official Benjamin E. Diokno).

[6] *Business World*, June 29, 1994; World Bank, *An Opening for Sustained Growth* (1993), 24; A. M. Mendoza Jr., "The Record of a Non-Confrontational Debt Management Approach" (Quezon City: UP Center for Integrative and Development Studies, 1992), 26. For an analysis of longer-term fiscal problems, see Emmanuel S. de Dios, "The Philippine Economy: What's Right, What's Wrong," *Issues and Letters* 4, no. 4–5 (April-May 1995): 1–10, at 2–3. In 1994 and 1995, privatization contributed to the first national budget surpluses in twenty years; if Central Bank liabilities are included, however, the overall budget remained in deficit.

nor, Gabriel Singson, was paid over seven times the paltry remuneration of P20,000/month ($800) endured by Cuisia, and the Monetary Board began to enjoy attractive levels of compensation as well. The number of personnel, meanwhile, was reduced almost 20 percent from 5,724 to 4,630, and several departments were abolished. After over a decade in which "no one has taken care of the Central Bank internally," the new law encouraged technical training of BSP personnel.[7]

The restructuring, however, did little to resolve the continuing weakness of supervisory capacity. There was "no hope," reported the top supervisor in 1993, that Congress might actually proscribe lawsuits against individuals within the BSP, and in the new law supervisors do indeed remain open to "suits arising from the normal performance of duties"—that is, personally vulnerable for acts undertaken in an official capacity. Nonetheless, Singson argues that officers and examiners are given "greater protection" since their legal defense against lawsuits is assumed by the Monetary Board. Unfortunately, this provision is unlikely to provide much solace to the vulnerable employees of a besieged state: in the event that they are found guilty of negligence or misconduct (in courtrooms where their banker adversaries likely have much higher-priced lawyers), BSP personnel must repay all legal expenses earlier advanced!

Another longstanding cause of weak supervisory capacity, as discussed earlier, was a bank secrecy law that—from a comparative standpoint—placed unusual restrictions on the examination of deposit transactions by supervisors seeking to curb fraudulent activities of bankers. The provisions of the 1993 law actually made such examination even more difficult. Singson later referred to it as a "deliberate" effort "to control the powers of the central bank," and a former BSP lawyer suggested that the Philippines may now have the "strictest" secrecy law in the world—surpassing even that of Switzerland. The following year, as we shall see, this provision was among the factors hobbling efforts to deal with a major scam involving treasury bills.[8]

Despite all the efforts at renovation, many perceive little change in the overall character of the monetary authority. "What is worrisome," complained economist Benjamin Diokno, formerly a budget adviser to President Aquino, "is that [after] huge outlays of public funds . . . [t]ired, old, ineffective policies are being pursued by the same old CB officials." The new Monetary Board is dominated by the private sector to promote greater

[7] *FEER*, December 3, 1992, 60; Singson, 176; *Business World*, August 26 and September 8, 1994 and July 13, 1995; *Philippine Daily Inquirer*, May 20, 1993; Interview, Vitaliano N. Nañagas II, president, PDIC, April 23, 1993; Republic Act 7653.

[8] Interview, Feliciano L. Miranda Jr., managing director, Supervision and Examination Sector, April 28, 1993; Singson, 177; Republic Act 7653; World Bank, *Philippine Financial Sector* (1988), xii; *Business World*, May 19 and August 25, 1995.

9. Lucio Tan, tobacco magnate and founder of Allied Bank, chats with Bangko Sentral ng Pilipinas Governor Gabriel Singson before teeing off at the Manila Golf Club, February 1995. Photo credit: Jose Reinares Jr.

independence from the executive branch, but most members are none-theless said to be Singson's own nominees. More important, the choice of Singson as first governor did little to signal a striking new degree of inde-pendence from either the executive branch or banking interests. His ap-pointment was reportedly assisted by his cultivation of Chinese-Filipino business support for Ramos in the 1992 elections, but more longstanding ties were probably most important: the two men came from the same barrio (in Pangisinan province), went to school together, and regularly played golf together. His career with the Central Bank went back to 1955, and by the 1970s he headed up the legal office widely known for its poor record of litigation. As rumors of close ties with prominent Chinese-Filipinos endured, it was only fitting that Singson declared former Gover-nor Licaros to be his "role model."[9]

Liberalization: Promise and Prospects

In addition to creating a new monetary authority, the Ramos administra-tion also pushed for a substantial program of banking liberalization. Pres-

[9] *Business World,* July 19, 1994, and May 1, June 14, July 13 and 14, 1995 and September 5, 1996; *FEER,* May 20, 1993.

sures for opening up the industry can be traced to the 1988 World Bank report, which argued that "the strong domestic banks should not feel forever insulated from competition." But initial response was essentially limited to the Central Bank's March 1989 declaration that purported to remove restrictions on new commercial bank licenses and reorient other key aspects of supervisory policy. This display of reformist zeal, however, was probably meant to have more impact on the release of the first tranche of the World Bank's financial sector adjustment loan than on the financial sector itself. No licenses were granted until Cuisia's term began in 1990—and then only to two savings banks, which were allowed to upgrade themselves to commercial banks. In fact, no genuinely new players were allowed into the system until 1994. Under Cuisia, the only real progress toward liberalization was the loosening of previously tight restrictions on the opening of new branches.[10] The broader reform initiative of the late Aquino years was the "New Economic Program" launched by Finance Secretary Jesus Estanislao in 1990. While it included a denunciation of "the banks whose profits are bulging from cartel-type practices," however, no serious challenge to the banking sector was actually attempted. Even the central element of the program, tariff reform, was generally thwarted by ISI interests.[11]

By 1992, a combination of international and domestic factors promoted much greater momentum toward a wide-reaching program of economic liberalization. The Ramos administration displayed new perceptions of the Philippines' place in the world, and a clear sense of the country's weakness in competing effectively in the international and regional economies. This new momentum (the origins of which are analyzed further in Chapter Ten) was manifested by a significant degree of liberalization of foreign exchange, foreign investment, and trade, as well as a major challenge to cartels and monopolies in the telecommunications and shipping industries. In time, Ramos's advisers and other advocates of liberalization trained their sights on the country's most heavily fortified bastion of privilege and profits, the banking sector.

Liberalization efforts were assisted by earlier disruption in the cordial relations that had long existed within the banking industry; in particular, the introduction of automatic teller machines in the late 1980s encour-

---

[10] World Bank, *Philippine Financial System* (1988), vi. In 1991, Cuisia began to provide many more branch licenses through an auction process (a key motivation for which was to provide revenue to an impoverished Central Bank). An even more permissive policy was instituted in 1993, when branch licenses became available to any bank satisfying certain minimum capital requirements. *Business World*, December 14, 1994; World Bank 1993, 80; *Philippine Daily Inquirer,* April 26, 1993.

[11] Estanislao declared—with great fanfare—that he was going to "radically [rewrite] the rules of doing business in the Philippines." *Manila Chronicle,* June 2 and 3, 1990. Manuel F. Montes, "The Politics of Liberalization: The Aquino Government's 1990 Tariff Reform Initiative," in *The Politics of Economic Reform in Southeast Asia,* ed. David G. Timberman (Metro Manila: Asian Institute of Management, 1992), 91–115.

aged growing tensions between the stronger domestic banks and the foreign banks. While the former were rapidly expanding their share of the lower end of the deposit market (where funds could be obtained at generally negative real rates of interest), the latter were restricted to three branches and forced to raise funds at the upper end of the deposit market (at much higher, positive real rates of interest). In response to these limitations, perhaps, Citibank went public in 1991 with a careful analysis of the large intermediation spreads earned by Philippine-based banks. While high reserve requirements and other regulatory factors partially accounted for the big spread, the Citibank economists asserted, "oligopolistic market power" was also very much to blame. They further declared that banks with greatest access to regular deposits (that is, the largest domestic banks) were enjoying "excessive profit margins," and should begin paying savers positive real rates of return (with "a risk premium for keeping their savings in the Philippines"). Their analysis concluded by urging that the overall system be "gradually deregulated" and opened to new entrants. In a letter of response, the president of the BAP made clear that Citibank's public break with the ranks was not appreciated.[12]

As momentum for liberalization gathered steam over the next two years, the BAP eventually adopted the approach of supporting reform in general terms—but curbing it as much as possible in its specifics. This became most apparent in 1993, when the Ramos administration proposed its major initiative toward liberalization of the banking sector: allowing more foreign banks to establish wholly owned operations in the Philippines. The number of banks enjoying such privileges was restricted to four in the late 1940s, at a time when, as noted in Chapter Four, many felt that the "foreign banks were not using their resources, derived in large measure from local deposits, to promote the growth of the national economy." Forty-five years later, many felt that the banks—foreign and domestic banks alike— were still not using their resources to promote national economic growth. Particularly offensive was the fact that the banks' resources were now derived not just from "local deposits" but also from massive plunder of public resources (the painful details of which were being highlighted, at this time, by the ongoing bailout of the Central Bank).

As debate over the entry of more foreign banks shaped up in late 1993 and early 1994, the key question was not whether the reform would take place but how. On one side of the debate were those favoring more liberal terms of entry: Ramos and his key advisers (particularly the powerful national security adviser, Jose Almonte, a vocal critic of "cartels and monopo-

---

[12] Citibank study, "Bank Intermediation Spreads," unpublished manuscript, n.d. [1991?]; Letter from Xavier P. Loinaz, president of the BAP (and the Bank of the Philippine Islands), to William Ferguson, vice-president, Citibank, N.A., February 1, 1991; *FEER*, December 9, 1993, 73 (see also *FEER*, March 28, 1991, 62–63).

lies" and oligarchic privilege), the House of Representatives (in general very supportive of Ramos's economic liberalization program), the four foreign banks, multilateral institutions, and the U.S. government. "*Even* the Central Bank [*sic*]," explained a BSP spokesperson with perhaps unintended candor, "has taken the position that it is amenable to some degree of liberalization." The side seeking to restrict the terms of entry was led by the BAP, which relied in turn on vital assistance from key allies in the Senate.

Major issues in the debate included how many foreign banks would be allowed to enter, how much capitalization would be required of the new entrants, and how many branches each would be entitled to open up. The bill enacted by the Senate in April 1994 was far more restrictive than that earlier passed by the House: it permitted only six to eight new entrants (rather than leaving the matter up to the Monetary Board, as did the House bill), required $16 million in capitalization (rather than the roughly $5 million required by the House), and sanctioned only six branches (rather than giving the foreign banks the same privileges as the domestic banks). Uniting the two sides were promises that liberalization would both promote competition and encourage foreign investment.[13]

The major argument of the BAP was that, to ensure a "level playing field," foreign and domestic banks should have the same minimum capitalization requirements ($27 million for non-unibanks). On the question of branches, however, they desired a field most unlevel: retention of the three-branch limit for foreign banks, thus ensuring that the vast bulk of depositors would remain outside the reach of external competition. As the debate heated up, the BAP "[waged] a media campaign to weaken" the extent of actual liberalization and support the more restrictive Senate version of the legislation. Ramos aide Jose Almonte later recalled that "the bankers . . . really put up a fight," and even warned that liberalization could bring bank runs and the possible collapse of the financial system. Ramon del Rosario, a banker who had earlier served as Ramos's finance secretary, countered BAP proposals by commenting that "it would be very comical, if not pathetic, if we liberalise in name but no bank actually came in because the entry requirements were stringent. It would be like throwing a party and having no one come."

The foreign banks already in the system—in particular Citibank, by far the largest and most influential of the four—actively supported the less

[13] *FEER*, December 9, 1993, 73; Joint Philippine-American Finance Commission, 55; *Business World*, August 26, 1993 (emphasis added), April 15, 1994, December 2, 1993. The U.S. government position was made known in a November 1993 joint letter from the treasury secretary and trade representative to the acting secretary of finance, emphasizing that "the U.S. objective is substantial liberalization and we do not consider [satisfactory] a standstill that locks in present levels of discrimination and insufficient access." *Malaya*, December 8, 1993.

restrictive terms of entry. In a joint statement, they claimed that while they would be "most directly impacted competitively by new entrants," they nonetheless supported liberalization out of a "conviction that . . . [it] brings economic dynamism and growth." A strong desire for more branches, one might guess, also stimulated their enthusiasm.[14]

As the conference committee convened to reconcile the differences between the two bills, tensions escalated between House and Senate, foreign and domestic banks, avid and reluctant reformers. After deadlocks, "frayed nerves," and "acrimonious debates" among key sponsors, the House and Senate forged a May 1994 compromise allowing a total of ten foreign banks to begin operations in the Philippines, and—most important—sticking with the Senate's earlier six-branch restriction on the scope of their operations. Minimum capitalization of roughly $9 million bought the rights to three branches, and $13.5 billion the rights to six. The new law also provided a second mode of entry for those banks not among the ten granted rights to wholly owned operations: up to 60 percent ownership of a domestically incorporated bank (as compared to the 30 percent to 40 percent permissible since the early 1970s). Chief House sponsor Margarito Teves said negotiations for the bill were more strenuous than those for the previous year's creation of a new central monetary authority, and lamented the Senate's rejection of more liberal provisions. A top BSP official acknowledged that the Senate version had prevailed, and the BAP made no effort to hide its pleasure over a compromise package that turned out to be very favorable to the interests of domestic bankers: the final law, explained the association's president, "met [our] standard in terms of balancing the national interest with the country's need for globalization without making too many unnecessary concessions."[15]

Twenty-one banks applied for entry, and in early 1995 the "magic ten" were selected. A year later, all had opened shop—and by the way they did so it was quickly evident that their direct impact on competition within the banking sector would likely be confined to the very top end of the market. In general, they established offices on the upper floors of Makati skyscrapers, and did not bother with the expense of lobbies or tellers. As Far East Bank (and past BAP) president Octavio Espiritu explains, "The new

[14] *FEER*, December 9, 1993, 73, and November 2, 1995, 28; Interview, Jose Almonte, June 6, 1996. The BAP's 1994 position paper on the issue does not take a stand on how many foreign banks should be allowed to enter, although in 1991 the BAP responded to Cuisia's initial talk of new foreign banks by suggesting that the number of entrants be limited to three, with each required to lend out $100 million to the country on concessional terms. See Philippine Exporters Confederation, ed., "On the Liberalization of the Entry of Foreign Banks: To Be or Not to Be" (Manila: Philexport, 1994), 3–16; *Manila Chronicle*, October 22, 1990 and January 17, 1991.

[15] *Malaya*, May 7, 1994; Republic Act 7721; *Business World*, May 12, 1994; Rafael B. Buenaventura, "At the Forefront of Change," *Fookien Times Philippines Yearbook 1994*, 180.

foreign banks can only make a dent in corporate banking and trade financing, *where there's already been keen competition.*"[16] With such institutional infrastructure as large branch networks already in place, the domestic banks would have no problem retaining their dominance in other (by clear implication, far less competitive!) segments of the banking market.

The only foreign bank that even began to have the institutional strength to tap a larger segment of the market and offer new competitive pressures was long-established Citibank, whose total assets in 1994 were nearly twice those of the other three existing foreign banks combined. With the new law in place, the U.S. bank expressed plans to put up new branches. Even with such horizontal expansion, however, Citibank seemed likely to stay away from lower segments of the market; indeed, the bank continued to require minimum deposits of $10,000 and P300,000 (for dollar and peso accounts paying 2 percent and 3 percent per annum, respectively) and was noted for its "arrogance and discriminatory attitude." Citibank's top officer acknowledged that while retail operations would be expanded there would be no effort to operate on "the same scale as local banks."[17]

With few exceptions, leading bankers have expressed little concern over the new entrants. Ramon del Rosario, president of a small bank targeting corporate accounts, predicted that "we will be forced to be on our toes a little bit more." But the president of PNB, the largest bank, said there will be "no threat to us [because] most of them will concentrate on wholesale banking, except maybe Citibank." Rafael Buenaventura of PCIB explained that the new banks "will be cherry picking," concentrating on multinational corporations and wealthy individuals and bringing no direct benefits to small-and medium-scale enterprises. The entry of foreign banks has created "false hopes," he continued, and should not be treated as "the panacea to all our problems." Noting the foreign banks' past preference for the top end of the market, he declared it "highly unprobable that they will change their ways." Similarly, the officer of one of the British banks complained of "so many false expectations on the entry of foreign banks," and suggested that lending rates might be unaffected. The most hopeful predictions of change came from those who speculated that new foreign banks, by heightening competition at the top end of the market, would at last force domestic banks to provide sound financial services to small-and medium-scale enterprises. Echoing Buenaventura, however, one may reasonably question whether domestic bankers will so easily change their ways.

[16] *FEER*, November 9, 1995, 65 (emphasis added). In addition to the areas mentioned by Espiritu, new entrants may also become active in the financing of infrastructure, as well as in particular niches in which they have special expertise.

[17] *Business World*, December 2, 1993; *Manila Chronicle*, November 18, 1993.

If the new foreign banks were unlikely to have a major impact on competition, the other promise of liberalization—promotion of foreign investments—had far more hope of success. After all the talk of enhanced competition, in fact, the first BSP circular on the entry of foreign banks listed greater foreign investment, not enhanced competition, as the first objective of the measure. Indeed, the "magic ten" were strategically selected from countries thought most likely to bring in new investment (Japan, Taiwan, South Korea, Thailand, Singapore, Germany, the Netherlands, Australia, and the United States). Facilitating such investment would be the "biggest impact of bank liberalisation," predicted a top finance department official in 1993, because potential investors would "feel more comfortable" dealing with compatriot banks operating in the Philippines.[18]

The entry of foreign banks was accompanied by a quieter process of liberalization in the dispensing of domestic commercial banking licenses—the most significant expansion in three decades. In 1994, two so-called Chinese-Filipino *taipans* were beneficiaries: Henry Sy's Banco de Oro was elevated to the status of commercial bank, and Andrew Gotianun (who had sold out of two banks in the 1980s) reentered the industry by opening East-West Bank. In 1995 and early 1996, two additional licenses were granted to domestic investors, and there were three new banks 60 percent owned by foreign banks (one each from Taiwan, Hong Kong, and Spain). Meanwhile, further sale of government shares in PNB turned it into a majority private-owned bank in late 1995. Including the ten new foreign banks, the number of commercial banks expanded from thirty-two at year-end 1993 to forty-seven in early 1996.[19]

The willingness of the BSP to expand the number of domestic banks was propelled by the Ramos administration's larger momentum for liberalization, but other considerations also made the timing right. Efforts to privatize the banks acquired by the government endured—despite a 1988

[18] *Manila Times,* November 29, 1994; *Business World,* December 2, 1993; Philexport, "Liberalization," 45; *Malaya,* November 10, 1993; Enrico L. Basilio, "Banking on SMEs," Center for Research and Communication, Economic Policy Papers No. 8 (Metro Manila, 1995); *Philippine Star,* September 20, 1995; *FEER,* December 9, 1993, 73. Early in the debate, Singson publicly doubted whether more foreign banks would bring a reduction in interest rates. *Philippine Star,* January 19, 1994; Philexport, "Liberalization," 67. See Appendix 2 for a listing of the ten banks.

[19] SGV, *A Study of Commercial Banks in the Philippines,* 1995. On the rise of the *taipans,* see Temario C. Rivera and Kenji Koike, *The Chinese-Filipino Business Families Under Ramos Government,* Institute of Developing Economies, Joint Research Program Series No. 114 (Tokyo, 1995). The two other locally controlled domestic banks are International Exchange Bank and Bank of Southeast Asia; the three foreign-owned and locally incorporated banks are Chinatrust Bank, Dao Heng Bank, and Santander Bank. Mergers reduced the number of licenses by two: Union Bank absorbed Interbank in May 1994, and Metro Pacific's PDCP Development Bank (not a commercial bank) took over First Philippine International Bank (successor of the long-troubled Producers Bank) in September 1995.

World Bank deadline—into the early 1990s. Because restrictions on new bank (and branch) licenses served to increase the value of these generally weak institutions—and thus facilitate their eventual sale—there were strong vested interests helping to perpetuate the barriers to entry. These interests included not only existing banks but also government institutions trying to unload what was often damaged property and private investors who had recently bought into banks (and who knew they had paid a premium for the bank license). It is no coincidence, therefore, that new licenses were not made available until well after the bulk of the weak banks had been privatized.

While their very presence signals an important change in policy and does bring an element of new competition, it is unlikely that any of the new players—domestic or foreign—will be a significant threat to the oligopolistic structure of the banking sector. The top five banks continue to control nearly 50 percent of total assets (see Appendix 3), and their advantages in terms of capital, personnel, and technology will make it difficult for new domestic banks—all small players—to offer any significant threat in the short term. A former BAP president notes that, new entrants notwithstanding, "the gap in terms of resources between the top four or five banks and the rest is widening." While it is possible that some newcomers may someday decide not to play by the rules of the game, there is likely little incentive to risk the wrath of the major players by doing so. Although observers noted some narrowing of spreads between lending and deposit rates by 1996, Philippine banks remain notorious for the hefty margins they enjoy.

Not only have the largest banks consolidated their dominant position, but they retain the sort of cozy ties—both internally and in their relations with the BSP—that can easily perpetuate "cartel-type practices." The bankers are often reported to consider Governor Singson friendly: not only is he one "whom they can play soft music with" (in the words of the leading business daily) but he is also someone with whom they regularly play a round of golf. Moreover, while capable of confronting bankers over such issues as foreign exchange speculation, he is at the same time considered "humble enough to listen to counsel." In mid-1995, for example, Singson discussed bringing in another group of foreign banks at a time when "Palace strategists" were reportedly "mapping out a way to introduce further liberalization without unduly alarming local bankers." But the idea was quickly shot down by BAP officials who warned of "policy wavering" and "overbanking"—and Singson later said the idea would be shelved.

In any case, as the chief BAP economist pointed out at the time, adding more entrants does not necessarily bring a greater degree of competition. It is entirely possible, as pioneer investment banker Sixto K. Roxas predicted in late 1993, that the entry of foreign banks "just increases the membership of the cartel." Despite liberalization, there is little indication that cartel-type practices have faced any systematic challenge from regulatory authorities. BAP officials, for example, are not contested when they speak of overbanking—even as national levels of financial development lag far behind the rest of the region (indicating the weak capacity of the banking system to attract increased levels of savings), and the credit needs of a huge chunk of the country's businesses remain unmet. Moreover, after years of complaining that high reserve requirements contribute to high spreads between deposit and loan rates, the reduction in requirements from 25 percent in early 1993 to 17 percent in 1995 seemingly brought no pressure from the BSP to increase deposit rates offered to savers. In the midst of the more liberalized environment, there were charges in early 1996 that the bankers were initiating creative new ways of exercising oligopolistic power over loan rate determination. Although Ramos and his advisers can be credited with considerable success in confronting cartels and monopolies in other parts of the economy, they have unfortunately barely made a dent on the banking sector.[20]

Enduring Problems of Bank Supervision

In May 1994, just as President Ramos was signing the bill permitting the entry of new foreign banks, the realities of supervision intruded upon the heady promises of liberalization: A new scandal related to the trading of T-bills, the "Bancap scam," hit the banking sector. While it was—unlike the Dewey Dee caper—easily contained with little threat to the financial system as a whole, the affair nonetheless served to highlight ongoing deficiencies in the basic state role economists commonly call "prudential regulation."

It is no surprise that T-bills were at the heart of the scam. As we have seen, it is in this realm that the system derived some of its biggest profits in the late 1980s and early 1990s. Bancapital Development Corporation—a small company with considerable financial wizardry—established itself as the largest secondary dealer by promising financial institutions and several

---

[20] *FEER,* November 9, 1995, 64–65; *Business World,* May 1, and July 12, 13 and 26, 1995, January 22 and August 19, 1996; Philexport, "Liberalization," 67; *Philippine Star,* September 20, 1995; *Philippine Daily Inquirer,* November 10, 1995; *Business Daily,* July 6, 1995. In Roxas's view, universal banking's merger of investment houses and commercial banks "killed the only competition" that might force the latter to reduce spreads. *Business World,* December 1, 1993. For further data on spreads, see Joseph Y. Lim, "Financial Intermediation and Monopoly Practices in the Banking System," *Issues and Letters* 2, (November 1992): 1–11; and Carlos Bautista, Roy C. Ybañez, and Gerardo Agulto Jr., "A Study of the Philippine Financial System: Focus on the Commercial Banking System" (Quezon City, unpublished ms., 1995), 8, 47. On comparative levels of financial deepening (growth in liquid liabilities as a proportion of GDP), see Bautista et al., 4.

government agencies a higher return on T-bills. While it was not actually authorized to sell T-bills and the government agencies were supposed to course all trading through state banks, both kickbacks and kiting operations using clever new instruments seemingly maintained the scam for five or six years. When Bancap suddenly closed up shop without delivering at least P1 billion in T-bills on which it had already collected payment, its former customers were left holding the bag.

Soon thereafter, certain banks received emergency aid from the BSP and the crisis was contained. Most revealing about the scandal, however, was the subsequent failure of the regulators to prosecute any of the perpetrators. A frustrated National Bureau of Investigation official accused the BSP of being "the prosecution's biggest stumbling block," but even if Singson had wanted to sort out the mess he was greatly hobbled by the 1993 tightening of restrictions on the examination of bank deposits. Essentially, he had only two tools at his disposal: emergency loans and moral suasion. "Nothing can prevent another similar scam," declared *Business World,* "because the highest monetary policy making body of the land is a toothless tiger."[21]

Earlier in the decade, the monetary authority's weak position relative to the bankers had been made clearer than ever by continuing legal and political challenges arising from the 1985 closure of Banco Filipino (the most contentious of the banks shut down by Governor Fernandez). The House of Representatives held June 1990 hearings on the case in which the bank's chairman said Fernandez had instructed him to deliver 51 percent of the bank's shares to the Central Bank. Special prosecutors filed graft and criminal charges against Fernandez later the same year, charging not only that Fernandez had instigated the initial bank run, but also that he had violated the deposit secrecy law and "criminally become interested in acquiring directly or indirectly personal control over the bank." Fernandez refuted the charges, insisting that the shares were obtained not for personal gain but rather to encourage a strong bank to invest in Banco Filipino.

The coup de grâce, however, came with a 1991 Supreme Court decision ordering the Central Bank to reopen Banco Filipino and castigating the monetary authority for an "arbitrary" closure "committed with grave abuse of discretion." This ruling, admitted Governor Cuisia, "would have a crippling effect not only on the credibility of the Monetary Board . . . but also on the capability of the central bank to administer the banking system as a whole." The high court noted that the Central Bank had earlier given

[21] *FEER,* June 2, 1994, 58; *Business World,* May 20 and 25, 1994, and an excellent five-part investigation, "The Bancap Scam—One Year After," May 15–19, 1995. Because of restrictions on investigatory capacity, it concludes, "no one has yet come out with an accurate figure" on the magnitude of the scam.

emergency assistance to Banco Filipino, and thus in what the *Far Eastern Economic Review* described as "reverse logic . . . held that the central bank could not have regarded Banco Filipino as insolvent, because the central bank cannot legally lend to an insolvent institution." Other owners of failed banks were known to be greatly encouraged by the Aguirres' remarkable success, while continuing legal snags led one Central Bank official to predict that none of his colleagues "would now risk running after an erring bank. We're helpless now if [any crises hit the banking sector]."[22]

Despite the Supreme Court ruling, negotiation over the disposition of some P3.7 billion earlier advanced to Banco Filipino by the Central Bank and the Philippine Deposit Insurance Corporation delayed the reopening of the bank for another two and one-half years. Cuisia found Banco Filipino proposals unacceptable, but Singson—soon after taking over the new BSP—declared himself to "have an open mind" in dealing with Banco Filipino (as well as with two weak but never closed banks under close supervision, Associated Bank and Producers Bank). In late 1993, he gave permission for the bank to reopen—which it did the following year without paying a single centavo of its debt, and without restructuring either the board or management earlier charged with large-scale insider abuse. Subsequent negotiation and litigation has focused on how much debt Banco Filipino will repay (the bank itself claims only P1.2 billion in debt, and has asked to be released from the obligation of paying interest). In 1995, Cuisia and another former Central Bank official were charged with graft for allegedly delaying the reopening of the bank, and the old Central Bank was sued P18.8 billion for damages arising from its closure. Industry analysts joked about Singson's shrewdness in avoiding lawsuits himself, and the governor actually offered a public defense of Banco Filipino's newest suit, saying it was "just a consolidation" of earlier cases and "not a delaying tactic" to avoid repaying its debt. Meanwhile, the bank reported nearly P3 billion in profits from treasury bills during the period it was closed, and declared a stock dividend of 25 percent within one year after its reopening.[23]

A second institution formerly closed, Veterans Bank, was reopened in May 1992 after considerable negotiation and litigation (thus appeasing an important political constituency), and in 1995 Manilabank was involved in

---

[22] The first legal action against the Central Bank was in 1987. Soon after becoming governor in 1990, Cuisia ordered a review of the circumstances surrounding the closure, but said there was no seeming justification for reopening the bank. *Manila Chronicle,* November 5, 1987, April 4 and 20, May 31, and December 5, 1990; *Philippines Daily Globe,* February 27, June 1, and December 5, 1990; *Newsday,* December 7, 1990; *Manila Bulletin,* December 12, 1991; *FEER,* December 26, 1991, 68–69 (quote at 68), and July 18, 1991, 54–55 (quote at 54, brackets in original).

[23] *Philippine Star,* March 9, 1993; *Philippine Times-Journal,* July 15, 1993; *Business World,* February 15, 16, and 17, April 5, June 2 and 6, and November 22, 1995.

more problematic negotiations over how to repay a massive debt of P8.3 billion to the Central Bank and resume operations. The impact of these actions and negotiations on future supervisory capacity is problematic, to say the least, since in each case the banks were formerly accused of (but never prosecuted for) massive insider abuse. If the monetary authorities are unable to allow past closures to endure, there is little reason for owners of banks closed down in the future to accept their fate with any sense of finality. Owners inclined to milk their banks to death can reasonably expect their institutions either to be sustained or resurrected (despite the 1989 circular promising to "refrain from sustaining weak banks"), and can enjoy further comfort from Ramos's proclaimed policy of not allowing any bank failure during his term (a clear intrusion on the BSP's supposed independence).[24]

Moreover, as noted earlier, the charter of the new BSP did little to strengthen supervisory capacity: it provided only a thin shield of protection against lawsuits, and the ability to examine deposits in search of fraud was actually weakened. While the revamped body was given the right to pay higher salaries to its personnel, observers noted that—as of mid-1995— many positions remained unfilled. The BSP was supposed to have been able to tap "the best and brightest in the whole kingdom because they offer the best rates in government," complains economist Mario Lamberte. "We expected new blood, those with master's degrees and PhDs. But where are they?" With the entry of technologically sophisticated foreign banks, he warns, the BSP has "a lot of catching up to do." Technical capacity remains low, laments former Aquino budget aide Benjamin Diokno, yet the ones "benefiting from this present pay scale are those responsible for the excesses of the past. . . . [It's] old dogs, old tricks."[25]

In the midst of such signs of continuity, "new tricks" have nonetheless been employed in efforts to redress enduring regulatory deficiencies. Most important, the Philippine Deposit Insurance Corporation was given enhanced supervisory responsibility in 1992, and taken over by a reformer seeking to make his staff as competent as that of the banks and ensure that his agency would no longer be a mere "stepchild" of the Central Bank. Initial direction for the revamping of the agency came from the 1988 World Bank report, and late in the Aquino years it was given a new legal charter and new infusions of capital from the government. The new leadership was proud to differentiate itself from the "fogies" at the Central Bank, and expressed frustration over the failure of that institution to challenge banks to lend beyond a narrow "urban, rich" clientele. Unfortunately, however, PDIC's personnel remained vulnerable to lawsuits and

[24] *Business World,* November 7 and 9, 1994, June 1 and July 13, 1995.
[25] *Business World,* July 13 and 14, 1995.

forced to accept low salaries. Even if a distinct culture emerges internally, the strength of the newly reconstructed agency will not be tested until the country faces its next major banking crisis.

A second initiative in regulatory reform came in August 1995, when Governor Singson convened a committee to undertake a full revamping of the banking laws—the first major effort at amendment since the early 1970s. A major priority was to reverse the 1993 tightening of restrictions on examination of bank deposits. Many years earlier, it will be recalled, Singson told Congress that "We have good, beautiful rules and yet fail." Although better and more beautiful rules provide no guarantee of enhanced regulatory capacity, the effort nonetheless highlighted the need for continuing attention to longstanding problems.[26]

While efforts to improve the quality of supervision continue, the banks can boast many positive developments in their ranks. Years of government support—most recently profits from treasury bills—have bolstered the overall stability of the banking sector. As Governor Fernandez intended with the policies he promoted from the mid-1980s, this has been most evident among the largest banks. Even so, a 40 percent to 47 percent across-the-board increase in minimum capitalization requirements in late 1994 (following a 50 percent increase only two years earlier) posed few problems for the vast majority of banking institutions. There has also been a marked increase in professionalization, particularly among the top banks. The system now has far more officers in the mold of the Jobo Fernandez who started up Far East Bank in the early 1960s, that is, bankers who treat their banks as profit centers in their own right rather than as sources of cheap loans for related family enterprises. While there have always been some banks that—despite ineffectual state regulation—were not heavily plundered by their officers and shareholders, it is indeed heartening that their numbers seem to have increased in the course of the enormous prosperity of banking since the mid-1980s. Additional signs of hope are found in common reports of Filipino nationals, long regarded as "the most sophisticated and internationalised corps of bankers and financiers" in all of Southeast Asia, returning from overseas assignments to employ their skills at home. Technological advances have accompanied this process of professionalization, and contribute further to the commanding advantages of the top banks. Finally, with the rehabilitation of two banks in the doldrums since the early 1980s, Singson could proudly

[26] Interview, Nañagas, April 23, 1993; Republic Act 3591 (as amended); *Business World*, August 24 and 25, 1995. A former Central Bank official confirmed heightened tensions—and potential dangers of turf battles—in relations with a new PDIC thought to be "flexing its muscles" too much. Anonymous interview, 1993.

proclaim in late 1995 that there is "no more weakling in the banking system."[27]

Unfortunately, however, more than a few dark clouds remain on the horizon. A combination of reform (albeit limited) and globalization have created a greater likelihood of risk for particular units of the system. One major reason that barriers to entry were retained in the past was a fear that more banks would exacerbate the difficulties of regulators. Unlimited ease of entry brings the danger of unlimited entry of new family-controlled banks, precisely the type of units that have been so difficult to regulate through the years. Not surprisingly, the number of new entrants is reportedly a "very real concern" to the monetary authorities. Singson himself has noted that increased capital inflows accompanying globalization have expanded bank balance sheets; there is a danger, he warned, that both the availability of such new resources for lending and increasing competition might lead to "poorer credit choices" and eventually to a "systematic crisis." Similar fears about developing countries in general were expressed by the head of the IMF in late 1996: in the midst of recent liberalization and privatization, said Michel Camdessus, many central banks have not taken "the necessary precautions to ensure that banks and supervisors have the expertise and resources needed to cope in the new environment."[28]

Although Singson assures the public that "[a]mid the excitement of deregulation, we have not lost our focus in ensuring the basic safety and soundness of the banking system," leading figures continue to voice concern over future instability. Certain past sources of easy profit are diminishing at mid-decade: spreads between loan and deposit rates remain substantial, but interest rates for T-bills have declined, the profitability of foreign exchange operations has been reduced by the liberalization of such transactions, and a lucrative loophole exempting trust funds from reserve requirements has been closed. At the same time, the entry of foreign banks has brought widespread "pirating" of officers, and personnel costs were expected to increase 20 percent to 25 percent per year between 1995 and 1998. There is also a costly and growing problem of bank robberies since the early 1990s (in which police and military com-

[27] *Business World*, December 29, 1994; *FEER*, September 28, 1989, 105, and July 18, 1991, 54–55 (quote at 55); *Philippine Daily Inquirer*, September 25, 1995. Associated Bank, which worked out a rehabilitation plan with the PDIC and tied up with Malaysian investors, assumed new life as Westmont Bank in 1994. *Business World*, May 25, 1994. Producers Bank was taken over by PDCP Bank of the Metro Pacific Group in 1995.

[28] *Business World*, January 16, 1995 and November 25, 1994. Globalization has exposed many developing country banks to greater risks, warned Camdessus; "increased capital flows have put new strains on unsound banking systems" and it is necessary "to improve external oversight and support, especially until internal governance and market discipline become more effective." The next international economic crisis, he said, "could well begin with a banking crisis." *The Business Daily*, September 30, 1996.

plicity is widely suspected). The growth of the stock market, meanwhile, creates a new source of competition to bank lending since companies now have readier access to an alternative source of funds: stock market capitalization increased almost ninefold between 1990 and 1994, and the ratio of total commercial bank assets to stock market capitalization declined dramatically (from 3.1 to 0.7) in the same period. This poses the greatest threat to non-unibanks (which are barred from underwriting activities).

Combined with an element of new competition among banks (forthcoming both from new domestic banks and from the possibility that the foreign banks will induce a shift in the attention of domestic banks from top to middle market), some banks could face major problems of adjustment. Increased costs and competition could bring "a banking crisis maybe three, five years down the road," warned Bank of the Philippine Islands (and former BAP) president Xavier Loinaz in late 1995. "To survive some bankers may loosen up on their credit standards, and some of them could be hit." Other analysts, moreover, fear that the BSP has not given adequate attention to banks' increasing involvement in more speculative lines of business; in particular, some express concern about the potential risks accompanying growing ties between banks and the property market, as families in property development diversify into banking and many unibanks invest more heavily in real estate subsidiaries.[29]

In the midst of new pressures, old problems such as DOSRI abuse are yet to be resolved. Such abuses, of course, are historically a central cause of bank instability; as Armand Fabella explains, throughout the modern history of Philippine banking there is "not a single case where the CB moved [against a bank] where it didn't find signs of family operations involved." Although data on the problem remain closely guarded by supervisory authorities, Fernandez acknowledged continuing problems with insider loans at the end of his term, and a top supervisor says that banks can still circumvent the limits with little problem: "We only know it's DOSRI if [banks] report it as such," he said. The president of the PDIC, meanwhile, sees some decline in the relative size of the problem due to overall growth of loan portfolios—"but not too much." The banking system has had to make room for more families, and owners are now more likely to refer to "our bank" than "my bank." While families now "have to take longer to get what they want" out of their banks, he said, they remain the basic unit of

29 *Business World,* July 13 and November 6, 1995 and August 19–22, 1996; *Philippine Daily Inquirer,* September 16, 21, 23, and 29, 1995; SGV data; Eduardo de los Angeles, "The Stock Market as Financing Source," in Rodriguez, ed., 59; *FEER,* November 9, 1995, 65. Former Central Bank adviser Armand Fabella also admits to continuing worries about a "nice banking crisis." *Business World,* July 20, 1994. On trust regulation, see Bautista et al., "Philippine Financial System," 48, 88. The impact of foreign exchange liberalization on bank profits is discussed in a USAID-funded report, "Foreign Exchange Liberalization in the Philippine Economy," ed. Trent Bertrand (Arlington, Virginia: IMCC, 1992), 11.

ownership—and DOSRI loans remain a "drag on the system." Indeed, the goal of maximizing familial control of banks remains strong: despite very rapid growth in overall stock market capitalization in the early 1990s, public listing of bank shares remains notably sparse at mid-decade.[30]

While in many cases professionalization of the banking sector will provide a greater degree of internal regulation of DOSRI abuses, in other cases better trained bankers may simply become more sophisticated in the means by which they milk loan portfolios, raid state resources, and collude with each other. As Governor Licaros remarked in 1977, "many Philippine financial managers . . . fail to exercise their technical sophistication in safeguarding the soundness of their institutions," and instead apply their expertise to "uncovering loopholes in rules and regulations . . . [and] misleading their various publics through window dressing of financial statements."

The larger banks are generally viewed as the most professional, but even in their ranks the possibility of instability endures. In future years, it will be particularly important to watch trends among the unibanks, which—simultaneous to the entry of new foreign banks—were granted the right to own larger percentages of both insurance companies and other commercial banks. It will be recalled that the 1980 laws creating unibanks conferred broad powers to own so-called nonallied enterprises and diversify into investment banking. The Central Bank had earlier warned that this could merely legitimate insider abuse—but in the course of the 1980s unibanks actually took little interest in the new privileges granted them by law. In the 1990s, however, many unibanks seem to be jumping at the chance to become more truly universal in scope. Moreover, previous restrictions seeking to promote wider ownership of banks have now been junked: just as foreign banks can now own up to 60 percent of a single bank, so now may domestic corporations (some of which may be very familial in nature) own up to 60 percent of a single bank.[31] Should their investment decisions be made on wise criteria, the unibanks will only increase in strength (and perhaps, through clearer loyalty to banking as a profit center in its own right, come to be seen as a coherent "finance capital" segment of the bourgeoisie); to the extent that familial consider-

[30] Interviews, Armand Fabella, June 8, 1990; Ramon Tiaoqui, April 26, 1993; and Nañagas, April 23, 1993. Some expect that local banks will increasingly seek to expand their equity base through public offerings in the stock market; the fact that the current limited group of bank listings (usually "tightly held shareholdings," according to a leading broker) register the biggest return-on-equity among listed firms would likely contribute to such a trend. *Business World*, December 3, 1993. Even so, there continues to be only a "very limited number of stocks available to the investing public." *Philippine Daily Inquirer,* January 2, 1996.

[31] Interview, Antonio P. Gatmaitan, January 31, 1990; Licaros, *Philippine Monetary Policy-Making in the Seventies*, 312; *Philippine Daily Inquirer,* September 25 and December 13, 1995; *Business World,* January 3, 1996; Republic Act 7721.

ations cloud financial judgment, however, the potential for instability certainly increases.

In short, while the banking sector is in a relatively healthy state in the mid-1990s, there are a number of factors that could promote future instability. The liberalization of bank licenses puts greater strain on supervisory authorities who have yet to resolve old problems, and the banks themselves face higher costs, new competition (both from capital markets and from other banks), and a reduction of profits in foreign exchange transactions, T-bills, and trusts. Globalization, new privileges for unibanks, and more permissive rules on bank ownership provide both greater opportunity and heightened risks.

In the face of such changes, an optimistic scenario foresees a wave of mergers that will not only weed out the weak members of the system but also strengthen those remaining. Far East Bank (and former BAP) president Octavio Espiritu, for example, predicts "a major consolidation of the industry" in the late 1990s. Other observers, as we have seen, speak more in terms of instability and banking crises than consolidation. Many note the formidable obstacles to bringing together two distinct groups of owners and managers—especially in a family-dominated political economy—and how rare actual unions have been despite the many rumors of intended nuptials. Since the liberalization of branching, big banks themselves have generally lost any incentive to acquire small banks; indeed, the only two mergers between 1990 and 1995 involved small-and medium-sized institutions. Although earlier reforms have been accompanied by widespread predictions of mergers, it was only with clear Central Bank encouragement in the early 1970s that even a modest number of mergers were achieved. The BSP has apparently had some ambivalence as to whether to promote actively the merger of banks; this, of course, makes the ultimate goal of consolidation even more dubious.[32] It is too early to tell whether the proliferation of the mid-1990s will induce consolidation or instability by decade's end; unfortunately, however, the ongoing weakness of supervisory capacity makes an optimistic scenario far from likely.

Limits of Liberalization: The Banking Sector at Mid-Decade

Between 1993 and 1995, the Philippine banking sector experienced a degree of change rivaling that of the mushrooming of banks in the 1960s,

---

[32] *Philippine Daily Inquirer,* October 31, 1995; *Business World,* November 2, 1993, and February 15, 1995. In the months before the Congress approved the foreign bank bill, as the BSP was discussing how to bolster the overall strength of the domestic banks, BSP officials reportedly lost hope in their initial plan—to promote mergers among existing domestic banks—and decided instead to give out more domestic bank licenses. More recently, the BSP has reportedly been trying to encourage mergers. *Philippine Daily Inquirer,* November 19, 1993, and September 25, 1995; *Business World,* May 6, 1994.

the reforms of the early 1970s, and the banking crises of the 1980s. As is often observed in many realms of Philippine politics, however, there was striking continuity amid the change. First, the monetary authority itself emerged financially stronger when transformed into the Bangko Sentral, but remained weak in relation to both the private sector and the executive branch. As in the past—going all the way back to the Philippine National Bank scandal seventy years ago—the public realm is forced to shoulder the cost of private plunder. Bailing out the Central Bank (the institution long responsible for bailing out other banks) loads particular burdens on the citizenry, and will encourage both cuts in infrastructural expenditures and higher taxes well into the next century.

Second, barriers to entry were lowered, but the manner in which it was done served to highlight the substantial political power of the domestic banks; as one House leader complained, the bill permitting the entry of foreign banks "bears the fingerprints of the BAP." The scope of operations of even the most ambitious foreign banks is constrained by limits on branching privileges, and the new domestic banks begin operations with an enormous amount of catching up to do. One can hope that bolder, less risk-averse banks may emerge to offer higher deposit rates and seek out new clienteles of borrowers, but at least in the short term it will be far easier for new banks to let themselves be absorbed into the cozy clutches of the cartel. "Let's face it," explained the treasurer of a small bank of a new price-fixing strategy of the larger banks, "80 percent of the market is controlled by the major players and we in the 20 percent cannot swing the tide." The entry of new banks is unlikely to create fresh competition for the vast bulk of the market, and the oligopolistic power of the biggest banks remains very much intact. Much of their current strength, of course, derives from easy sources of profit available throughout the late 1980s and early 1990s: as one British banker complained in 1993, the local banks "get lots and lots of cheap deposits, get a big fat margin and huge sums in trust funds and Treasury bills."

Third, in the midst of major reform of both the monetary authority and the PDIC, many patterns from the past endure: the regulatory agencies and even the regulators themselves remain vulnerable to legal challenges, the greater competence of the banking community continues to facilitate the outwitting of regulators, and major legal constraints still hobble the efforts of even the most skilled and dedicated regulators to combat fraud. While it is heartening to note that many banks now enjoy increased professionalization, capitalization, and technological capacity, self-regulation alone does not offer sufficient protection against the considerable potential for future instability. Old problems such as DOSRI abuse are unresolved, even as recent moves toward liberalization and globalization present new challenges to supervisory capacity. Given the cost of past bailouts and the country's "precarious fiscal position," explains Mario Lamberte, "we cannot afford to commit more mistakes." Unfortunately, however, the Banco Filipino ruling, the weak provisions of the bill creating the central monetary authority, and the recent Bancap scam all attest to enduring regulatory deficiencies in the 1990s.[33]

This book began with an broad overview of five major areas in which the Philippine financial system fails to serve larger developmental goals. As of the mid-1990s, unfortunately, the system has yet to achieve much success in any of these areas. First, levels of financial development lag far behind the rest of the region both in absolute levels and in rates of growth. The capacity of the system to mobilize savings improved in the early 1990s (probably encouraged by the expansion of branches and automatic teller machines), but was still not significantly higher than that recorded in 1983. As through most of the 1970s and 1980s, real interest rates for small savers remain negative.[34] Second, lending continues to be restricted to a narrow clientele, biased not only toward extended family conglomerates, but also toward large, urban firms. This has hindered the growth of both agricultural and small-and medium-scale enterprises; frustrations over lack of credit are exhibited by continuing congressional initiatives to develop specialized banks to meet the needs of workers, teachers, and others.[35] Third, as discussed earlier, the financial sector as a whole continues to have a high potential for instability. Fourth, high intermediation costs notwithstanding, big spreads between deposit and loan rates are a powerful testimonial to oligopolistic power, and it is likely that the banking sector as a whole will continue to find cooperation far more lucrative than competition. Fifth, the excesses of private sector plunder continue to be a drain on public sector coffers. The public is forced to bear the enormous costs generated by a self-serving and inefficient banking sector, but gets few benefits in return.

---

[33] *Business World*, December 2, 1993; February 15 and July 13, 1995; January 22, 1996.

[34] Bautista et al. note M3/GNP ratios of 26.2 percent in 1983, dipping to a low of 19.9 percent in 1985, and then climbing to 27 percent in 1993 and 29.4 percent in 1994. See "Philippine Financial System," 33–35. (M3 is the sum of demand, savings, and time deposits.)

[35] Basilio, 1–2; Interview, Nañagas, April 23, 1993. Data on the dearth of commercial bank loans to agriculture, households, and unincorporated business is provided in Rob Vos and Josef T. Yap, *The Philippine Economy: East Asia's Stray Cat?* (New York: St. Martin's Press, 1996), 99, 112–14; in the early 1990s, agricultural loans constituted less than 10 percent of the total. Two economists' analysis of lending patterns in the 1970s remains strikingly valid: it is "biased . . . toward the most creditworthy—large firms, those with excellent collateral—and away from the more risky; toward large and against small transactions, where administrative costs are relatively higher; toward known, established borrowers and against those where costs of evaluation are greater; and toward the short term." Hugh Patrick and Honorata A. Moreno, "Philippine Private Domestic Commercial Banking, 1946–80, in the Light of Japanese Experience," in *Japan and the Developing Countries: A Comparative Analysis*, ed. Kazushi Ohkawa and Gustav Ranis (New York: Basil Blackwell, 1985), 351.

Liberalization has brought great promise of change, but its actual prospects are in fact far from rosy. Even after the reforms, complains one corporate manager, "commercial banks in this country are still one of the most protected industries from external competition." Not only was the scope of policy change constrained by the realities of bankers' political power; more fundamentally, the prospects for liberalization are limited in potential by continuing weaknesses in institutional and political foundations. If reform is not accompanied by a concerted effort to strengthen capacity, "prudential regulation" will remain weak and the likelihood of further instability will remain strong. Moreover, until the government develops both the will and the capacity to actively challenge the perpetuation of the oligopoly, it is highly doubtful that genuine competition will find its way into the Philippine banking sector. Recent price-fixing strategies were dismissed by a Treasury official as beyond the scope of government concern: "since it is private-sector driven and we're on [*sic*] an era of liberalization," she said, "we . . . tell them to go ahead."[36] As long as liberalization is defined in such narrow laissez-faire terms, its benefits to the public will remain nil. Without concerted government pressure, the developmental contributions of the financial sector as a whole will remain insufficient to the nation's needs.

In larger perspective, the most important commentary on the nature of power in the Philippine banking sector comes from the ignominious death of the Central Bank in 1993. The demise of a central bank is not an ordinary event, and its resurrection under a new name should not obscure what it says about the longstanding weakness of state institutions in the Philippines. Programs of renovation intended to strengthen the Bangko Sentral, as well as those intended to lower barriers to entry, were obstructed by the same basic imbalance of power that put the Central Bank under a state of siege in earlier times. Until basic institutional and political deficiencies are resolved, the entire program of liberalization rests on shaky foundations. More substantial reform of the banking sector, it seems, must go hand-in-hand with more fundamental change in the Philippine political economy. The final chapter explores some of the factors that may someday encourage such a transformation—away from booty capitalism and toward a political economic order more responsive to the developmental needs of the nation as a whole.

---

[36] Manuel V. Pangilinan, "A Corporate Fund User's View," in Rodriguez, ed., 9; *Business World,* January 22, 1996.

CHAPTER TEN

The Philippine Political Economy at the Crossroads

My initial motivation for this study was to explain why the tremendous developmental assets of the postwar Philippines have often failed to produce sustained developmental success. A major part of the answer can be found in the deficiencies of the Philippine political sphere; weaknesses of political development are a major obstacle to the country's long-frustrated hopes of successful economic development. This final chapter summarizes the argument and the evidence presented in the previous chapters, discusses the general lessons the Philippine case teaches us about basic political prerequisites of economic development, and concludes with a broad assessment of prospects for fundamental change. Confronting a greatly transformed external environment in the 1990s, the Philippines is quite clearly at an important crossroads.

The Theoretical Argument

There are three major aspects to the theoretical argument presented in the opening chapters of this work. First, patrimonial features hinder the development of more advanced forms of capitalist accumulation; second, it is necessary to focus attention on critical distinctions among patrimonial polities; and third, the form of patrimonialism found in the Philippines presents particularly obstinate structural barriers to the creation of a more rational-legal state (and hence to the development of more advanced forms of capitalism).

The first part of the argument derives many insights from Weber, who highlights the dependence of modern capitalism on an administrative and legal structure able to promote "political and procedural predictability." Within patrimonial polities, where bureaucratic actions are by definition highly arbitrary, it is only possible for "politically determined" forms of capitalism to thrive. While such forms of capitalism often attain "a very high level of development," according to Weber, weak degrees of calculability in the political sphere present major obstacles to the development of more advanced forms of capitalist accumulation.[1]

A great deal of additional research is necessary if we are to understand the precise composition of the political prerequisites for developmental success; such efforts are "likely to be onerous and frustrating," warns Evans, but "are crucial if we are ever to discover how Third World states might become less part of the problem and more part of the solution." There are indeed many states that should be far more selective in the tasks that they take on, but the curbing of state roles, Evans explains, needs to be accompanied by "equal attention to reforms that will help reconstruct state apparatuses themselves." Similarly, E. A. Brett asserts that it is incorrect to presume that bureaucratic failure will always lead to worse results than market failure; in many cases there is no choice but to improve "the political and administrative mechanisms which have failed." The state, he concludes, "is the only institution in society which is even potentially capable of controlling private power and ensuring that it is exercised in a manner which safeguards the integrity of the community as a whole."[2]

The Philippine experience highlights the importance of moving beyond the blind state-bashing of neoliberal ideology, toward a more sober and balanced examination of the role of the state in the process of development. Nowhere in the Third World, it can be argued, has a country received larger and more sustained doses of American antistatist ideology than the Philippines; throughout this century, to be sure, oligarchy building has very dramatically overshadowed state building. It was under American colonial rule that the oligarchy consolidated its control over a weak central state whose administrative machinery was never well developed. In the postwar era, the country's strategic importance ensured the survival of a state that had little need to guard against external threats, tame local powerholders, or develop a self-sustaining economy. In large part due to such feeble political foundations, the country has had difficulties achieving sustained developmental success.

---

[1] Max Weber, *Economy and Society* (Berkeley: University of California Press, 1978), I: 224, 240; II: 1095, 1091; and "Author's Introduction," in *The Protestant Ethic and the Spirit of Capitalism* (New York: Charles Scribner's Sons, 1958), 25.

[2] Peter B. Evans, "Predatory, Developmental, and Other Apparatuses: A Comparative Political Economy Perspective on the Third World State," *Sociological Forum* 4, no. 4 (1989): 561–587, at 566, 582–84; E. A. Brett, "States, Markets and Private Power in the Developing World: Problems and Possibilities," *IDS Bulletin* 18, no. 3 (1987): 31–37, at 35, 37. Parallel insights are found in Richard Sandbrook, *The Politics of Africa's Economic Recovery* (Cambridge: Cambridge University Press, 1993), 19–20, 59, 149.

The second part of the argument is to examine both patrimonial polities and "politically determined" forms of capitalism in comparative perspective, an exercise entirely in keeping with Weber's own complex treatment of variation among such polities and among such forms of capitalism. Because all capitalism is in some sense "politically determined," this study uses the term *rent capitalism* to describe systems in which "money is invested in arrangements for appropriating wealth which has already been produced rather than in [arrangements for actually] producing it."[3] For the purposes of analysis, I confined discussion to two broad types of patrimonial polities, and two corresponding categories of rent capitalism. In the patrimonial administrative state, the dominant social force is a bureaucratic elite, or political aristocracy, and countervailing social forces are strikingly weak. Because the major beneficiaries of rent extraction are members of a bureaucratic elite—based within the state apparatus—I have labeled its corresponding economic system *bureaucratic capitalism*. In the patrimonial oligarchic state, on the other hand, the dominant social force—an oligarchy—has an economic base quite independent of the state apparatus, but access to the state is nonetheless the major avenue to private accumulation. Both forms of patrimonial polities exhibit a weak separation between the official and the private sphere; in the patrimonial oligarchic state, however, extrabureaucratic forces overshadow the bureaucracy. The type of rent capitalism that corresponds with the patrimonial oligarchic state—*booty capitalism*—reflects the relative power of the state apparatus and business interests. The principal direction of rent extraction is the reverse of that found in bureaucratic capitalism: a powerful oligarchic business class extracts privilege from a largely incoherent bureaucracy.

The third and final aspect of my theoretical argument deals with comparative prospects for the evolution of patrimonial features. In short, I assert that over the long term, obstacles to change will tend to be far more problematic in the patrimonial oligarchic state than in the patrimonial administrative state, or bureaucratic polity. The patrimonial oligarchic state is less likely to foster new social forces able to encourage change from within; economic growth tends merely to strengthen the oligarchy that is already the major beneficiary of patrimonial largesse. As explained in Chapter Three, there has been little incentive for oligarchs to press for a more predictable political order, and no other countervailing social force has yet emerged that is able to challenge effectively either the patrimonial features of the political economy or the longstanding dominance of the oligarchy. Instead of being a "container for fundamental transformation,"

---

[3] Stanislav Andreski, ed., *Max Weber on Capitalism, Bureaucracy and Religion* (Boston: George Allen and Unwin, 1983), 9.

the patrimonial oligarchic state and its booty capitalism are a "developmental bog" in which the postwar Philippine economy—its enormous resources and talents notwithstanding—has repeatedly become mired.

The last section of this chapter continues this discussion by examining prospects for future transformation of the Philippine political economy—especially in light of recent changes in external conditions. Before doing so, however, it is important to proceed to a summary of what has been learned from the major focus of this work: the politics of the banking sector.

State and Oligarchy in the Philippine Banking Sector

Long besieged by the particularistic demands of powerful oligarchic interests, the Philippine state has rarely been able to formulate or implement a coherent policy of economic development. Only by understanding the internal logic and coherence of familial strategies of patrimonial plunder, it was argued in Chapter Two, can we comprehend the continuing incoherence of national development strategies. This combination of coherence and incoherence became readily apparent at least as early the second decade of American colonial rule, when families in agricultural export industries raided the resources of the newly established and publicly supported Philippine National Bank to such a degree that it not only threatened the existence of the bank, but drained the treasury and left the currency in a shambles. As families enjoying most favorable access to the political machinery pursued the booty of state, developmental goals were trampled underfoot.

In the midst of widespread economic, political, and social change, similar patterns of interaction between state and oligarchy have endured into subsequent decades. In the postwar era, oligarchic families began to diversify into new industrial ventures as new sources of booty became available after the 1949 imposition of import and exchange controls. Those who possessed or could purchase favorable access to the machinery of state were able to obtain import and exchange licenses that guaranteed windfall profits—whether or not productive ventures were established. In the process of creating and responding to new sources of enrichment available within the state apparatus, the economic interests of oligarchic families became widely diversified through the 1950s and 1960s.

The major focus of this book is the new source of booty that became available through the ownership of private domestic commercial banks. Although a few families went into private banking in the prewar years and many more families started banks in the 1950s, it was not until the early 1960s that commercial banking became the widely enjoyed "open sesame" unlocking countless treasures for the major oligarchic families. Just as Ali Baba and his forty companions were able to open the robbers' den, the oligarchic families and their thirty-some banks were able to open the coffers of the state and enjoy a wide range of benefits. Ownership of a bank became among the surest means of securing credit for other components of the family conglomerate, and most major families flocked to the industry.

From the start, it was clear that government regulation of the new financial institutions was woefully inadequate. The new banks pirated staff from the Central Bank's office of bank supervision, and owners could pretty much use their banks for whatever purposes best suited the family conglomerates. Within a few years, two of the new institutions faced bank runs amid scandals related both to how the banks raided the resources of state and how the families raided the resources of the bank. Despite awareness of the problems, there was little that the regulatory authorities could do; the fact that the former governor and a brother of the current bank supervisor went to work for one of the erring banks, one can also presume, did little to promote the cause of effective bank supervision.

In trying to cajole the banks into following Central Bank regulations, Governor Andres Castillo had little recourse but to appeal to a sense of "professional responsibility" among bankers, even as he himself acknowledged that such a sense of professionalism was poorly developed. Despite his impotence, however, Castillo expressed faith that somehow, someday, the banking system would advance rather than detract from developmental goals: "The unrelenting requirements of our economic development and demands upon the banking system will in time cause these family banks to come together and combine their resources in order to survive the intense competition that is developing in the field of banking. When that time comes much of the complaints about tight credit and the prevalence of pawnshop banking will have disappeared from the financial scene."[4]

Subsequent experience has belied this blind faith. Development imperatives were not enough to reform the banking sector; without effective regulation, the major families generally—and quite rationally—continued to respond instead to the unrelenting appetites of their own diversified conglomerates for cheap credit.

When martial law was declared, some expected that the chaotic free-for-all of Philippine capitalism would at last be harnessed toward sound developmental goals. Marcos sounded the alarm against the excesses of the "old oligarchy," and promised a "new society" of opportunity for all.

---

[4] Andres V. Castillo, "Bankers and Their Responsibilities," *The Fookien Times Yearbook 1964*, 141–42, 178, at 178.

Indeed, if there was ever a time in which the oligarchs and their banks might have been redirected toward greater goals, it was during the martial law years. A major bank reform was promulgated, and such longstanding objectives as increasing minimum capitalization, curbing DOSRI loans, and promoting bank mergers were given new prominence.

As we have seen, however, it soon became apparent that the primary objective of the martial law regime was not to promote more effective regulation *by the state* but rather to create and respond to new opportunities for plunder *of the state*. It is true that martial law gave the state far greater power over the citizenry: the assets of certain families could be expropriated, former senators could languish in jail, and previously contentious economic policies and reform packages could be promulgated by fiat. The exercise of these heightened state powers, however, remained highly arbitrary. First, among bankers, some errant souls got nailed to the wall, while others—guilty of precisely the same offenses—knew that the regime would place no fetters on their activities. Second, some banks were favored with enormous quantities of Central Bank credit, while others were denied assistance in the midst of crisis. Decisions had little to do with such objective criteria as the soundness of management or the developmental impact of a bank's credit allocation; rather, to paraphrase Weber, practically everything explicitly depended upon personal considerations.[5]

The contrasting cases of two Chinese-Filipino entrepreneurs illustrate how the favor and disfavor of the regime could result in greatly contrasting outcomes. Lucio Tan's rise highlights the enormous advantages that come to those who can plunder the state for particularistic advantage. Vicente Tan's decline, on the other hand, highlights both the enormous limitations of wealth accumulation in the Philippines for those lacking access to the political machinery and the harsh punitive powers that the Marcos regime was able to exact on its enemies. Despite three years in jail, Vicente Tan was never formally prosecuted for his "shenanigans" in the banking industry.

Third, the powers of martial law were translated into sweeping acquisitions of banks that were vulnerable because of poor performance or the weak political position of their owners. Between 1972 and 1980, some twelve banks were taken over by Marcos and his associates; in the early 1980s, Marcos-controlled state agencies acquired several more banks. In short, martial law did little either to promote effective state regulation or to harness the energies of the banking sector for developmental goals; the patrimonial features of the state apparatus only became more pronounced, and it became easier than ever for those close to the political machinery to reap enormous gain from unproductive endeavors. The

---

[5] Weber, *Economy and Society,* II: 1041.

patterns of plunder were familiar; as Armand Fabella explained, a crony conglomerate is nothing more than a family conglomerate "with additional clout thrown in." The magnitude of plunder, however, was unprecedented.

Martial law did permit the technocrats to enjoy a new prominence, but their roles were so carefully circumscribed by Marcos that they had little lasting impact on the shape of the economy. In the banking sector, Finance and Prime Minister Virata and other technocrats became especially prominent when Marcos most needed their help in securing foreign loans and assistance. With the 1980–1981 financial reforms, Virata and his allies in the World Bank and IMF overrode the initial objections of Central Bank Governor Licaros and brought about the promulgation of a textbook-style reform package that had little relation to the actual problems that plagued the banking sector. In the interest of obtaining international credit, even Licaros eventually supported it. But before the ink had dried on the new regulations, the reform package was undercut by precisely the problems its major backers had naively neglected: the deficiencies of bank supervision, the longstanding problems of bank instability, and the morass of cronyism in which they were promulgated. Indeed, one can argue that cronyism alone would have dragged down even the best-formulated set of reforms—which this reform package clearly was not. Eventually, it became clear that while Virata played a crucial role in pleasing the international crowd, his influence at home was compartmentalized in such a way that he would never be able to threaten the essential interests of the regime. He could, for example, get himself lauded in *Business Week* for "trying to spur greater efficiency by shaking up the family-run business groups," yet there was no chance that he would be able to raise a finger against the most important conglomerate of all: that of Ferdinand E. Marcos.[6]

In the wake of the Aquino assassination in 1983, even the multilateral institutions began to understand the calculus of power in Manila: the resilience of cronyism and the impotence of their technocratic allies. When Laya's Central Bank was caught overstating its international reserves that same year, the vaunted technocrats themselves became tainted creatures. With Jose Fernandez's ascendence to the post of Central Bank governor in early 1984, there was a clear shift in influence from scholars of business administration (Virata and Laya) to real practitioners of rough-and-tumble business. In the midst of the worst economic crisis of the postwar era, Fernandez declared a crusade against the ills of the banking system, and—unlike his predecessor—clearly understood how the system really worked.

[6] Interview, Armand Fabella, June 12, 1990; *Business Week*, May 17, 1982, 51–53 (quote at 53).

The World Bank was called in to help construct yet another reform package. Although no more successful than earlier reforms, it did at least begin to address the major problems facing the banking sector: deficiencies of supervision and dangers of instability. Concurrent with Fernandez's efforts, the incoming government of Corazon Aquino had two other crusades that affected the banking sector: a drive for privatization (to sell off the assets acquired by government agencies under Marcos) and a selective attack on Marcos cronies by the Philippine Commission on Good Government. The first of these has eventually yielded major sales of state assets (while its proponents rarely reflect on the character of privatization within a state that displays strong patrimonial features); the attack on the cronies, meanwhile, has merely proved that political arbitrariness continues to plague the Philippine state—the fall of Marcos notwithstanding.

Fernandez's declared objective of cleaning up the system was most successful in creating opportunities for the big banks to clean up. Even as the system of selective credit allocation was being narrowed in scope, new opportunities for reaping quick and unproductive gains were made available through such means as the purchase and trading of Jobo bills and the conversion of low-interest government deposits into high-interest government securities. Some of the old opportunities endured as well, in particular the acquisition of the prized assets of failed banks. By the end of Fernandez's term, the largest banks enjoyed unparalleled profits and prominence but the system as a whole remained sadly deficient in promoting larger developmental goals. The banks' gain came at the expense of a public treasury already overburdened by the costs of rehabilitating PNB and DBP in 1986.

The Fernandez crusade included the closing of three commercial banks and one major savings bank, but supporters and detractors alike could discern little objective basis for Central Bank decisions to rescue some ailing banks and let others drown. When the World Bank complained of the inconsistencies in procedures for assisting troubled banks, it was merely echoing the protests of errant banks in years gone by. For those bankers who had earlier experienced what Vicente Tan called the "uneven hand" of Central Bank regulations, the major question is, Why me, and not the other person? "That's where discretion comes in," says Emerito Ramos, "whether they throw [the book] at you or not."[7]

Finally, as analyzed in Chapter Nine, a two-pronged reform effort was initiated beginning in 1993. While the first part of the reform was forced by the death of the Central Bank, the institution that took its place was not

---

[7] As noted above, Tan entitled his doctoral dissertation "The Uneven Hand: The Exercise of Central Bank Powers to Close Banking Institutions" (University of Santo Tomas, 1982); Interviews, Antonio P. Gatmaitan, September 18, 1989, and Emerito M. Ramos, March 17, 1990.

entirely new. The public was once again forced to pay for bankers' past sins, thus ensuring that the Bangko Sentral could begin life with a sound balance sheet. But key aspects of past regulatory weakness endure, through death and resurrection, and will in all likelihood hobble the BSP's ability either to guard against or respond to future rounds of bank instability. In the more volatile and uncertain context of globalization, unfortunately, the need for effective supervision is actually heightened.

The second element of the reform was liberalization, spurred on by larger Ramos administration efforts to curb "cartels and monopolies." The process of opening up the system, however, proceeded on the terms of those already do. inating it. Foreign banks with any ambitions of expansion will be stymied by tight restrictions on branches, and the new domestic entrants lack the capital, personnel, or technology to offer any real competition to the big players. The major banks, bolstered by the very hefty profits of the past decade, have become far more professional and increasingly "universal" in the scope of their investments; indeed, the gleaming new bank headquarters towering over the skyline of Makati are sturdy testimony to their recent gains. The impact down below, however, is as yet difficult to discern, as banks continue to do a poor job of either mobilizing savings or servicing the credit needs of much of the economy. Despite new rhetorical commitments to the virtues of competition—and hopes that foreign banks' concentration on prime accounts will at last force domestic banks to pay greater heed to less affluent segments of the market—regulators still do little to confront oligopolistic privilege.

Until there is greater development of the state apparatus, the two overarching characteristics of the banking sector noted in the Introduction—rampant favoritism and the largely ineffectual nature of state regulation—will in all likelihood continue to undermine further attempts at reform. Within the banking sector these two characteristics—resulting from the patrimonial nature of the state and the weakness of the state apparatus in relation to the predatory oligarchy—have hindered developmental goals for decades, and endured despite a number of potential sources of transformation: (1) regime change (in 1972 and 1986); (2) four major banking reforms (in 1972, 1980–1981, 1988, and 1993–1994, three of which quite explicitly sought to improve the effectiveness of regulators vis-à-vis regulated); and (3) the allocation of very high levels of foreign loans and other instruments of selective credit (particularly in the heyday of debt-driven growth in the late 1970s and early 1980s), which one might expect to have given the major allocator of this largesse, the Central Bank, increased institutional leverage in implementing its stated reform agenda. While the dismantling of oligarchic control over the state and the creation of a more effective state apparatus is a critical prerequisite to the success of long-frustrated developmental goals—both for the banking sector and for the political economy as a whole—the actual construction of such a state is a task of momentous historical proportions.

Reforming the Philippine Political Economy

This analysis raises questions about a number of common prescriptions for promoting sustained economic success. At certain points in the past, many have advocated regime change as the solution to lackluster economic performance. In early 1970s, authoritarianism was declared a necessary prelude to development; in the mid-1980s, democracy was widely seen as an essential means of curbing the excesses of the rapacious leaders; and in the early 1990s there were those who once again doubted the compatibility of democracy and development. In 1992, Singaporean Senior Minister Lee Kuan Yew told the Manila business community—at that point especially frustrated over their country's laggard status—that the Philippines faced a choice between democracy and discipline. "The exuberance of democracy," he declared, "leads to undisciplined and disorderly conditions which are inimical to development."[8]

Quite conveniently, Lee neglected to note that the exuberance of the martial law regime had also failed to produce much discipline, order, or development. Unfortunately, neither Philippine-style democracy nor Philippine-style authoritarianism have strong records in terms of promoting developmental goals. There are indeed major differences in their impact: democratic regimes (elite-dominated though they may be) not only provide greater scope for expression of the popular will and a greater degree of space for political dissent but also enable a far greater number of families to claw for the booty of state. In addition, democratic procedures reorient patronage systems toward electoral competition rather than the consolidation of a dictatorial regime. But the choice between authoritarian or democratic regimes has made no dramatic difference on the country's ability to develop more advanced forms of capitalist accumulation. Lee also neglected to factor in the degree to which the Singaporean civil service has acted as a bulwark for his city-state's economic success; until a more effective bureaucratic apparatus exists in the Philippines, neither democracy nor authoritarianism is likely to produce the type of discipline that he deems essential to development.

A second common prescription for reform has been the bolstering of technocratic competence in key economic policymaking agencies. But placing more technocrats in strategic positions is not, in and of itself, likely to provide a major stimulus for change. Without their own base of power, technocrats' decisions and agendas can easily be swamped by a host of

[8] *FEER*, December 10, 1992, 29.

particularistic actions on behalf of regime interests (as occurred under Marcos). Moreover, technocrats would continue to be hobbled by the absence of support from an effective bureaucracy below them.

The third and most compelling prescription for change is liberalization and economic reform, and it is precisely this course that has been under-taken by the Ramos administration since 1992. Under the rallying cry of "Philippines 2000," Ramos and the reformers around him have sought to propel the country into the ranks of the newly industrializing countries by the end of the century. The boldest measures have been concerted attacks on the cartels and monopolies of major oligarchic family firms that have long had a stranglehold over key segments of the national economy; a wide range of measures of economic liberalization, privatization, and infrastruc-tural development, however, have also been an essential element of the larger crusade. It is important to analyze the motivations, impact, and sustainability of this far-reaching program in greater detail.

Assessing Philippines 2000

In broadest perspective, Philippines 2000 represents the first major strategic vision of Philippine political elites since the early years of Ferdi-nand Marcos's martial law regime.[9] In analyzing the origins of this reform program, the first question is how it ever came to be. Liberal ideas have been floating around in Philippine policy circles for decades—and have commonly been batted down quite decisively by those who most stand to lose from their promulgation and implementation. As discussed in Chap-ter Three, attempts at top-down reform have often been inhibited by lack of bureaucratic coherence and the concerted opposition of oligarchic interests. While such obstacles have certainly been well exhibited in the Ramos reform program, many key successes have at the same time gener-ated widespread hopes that the momentum for reform might be sus-tained. Why and how has Philippines 2000 been different?

Understanding this success requires, first of all, careful examination of the larger context in which Ramos gained power in 1992. We know in hindsight that reform of the political economy was a top priority of key elements of the incoming Ramos administration, but victory in the May 1992 campaign (with just under one-quarter of the votes) in no way rested on any clearly articulated program of reform: as in previous elections, concern over personalities and the building of pragmatic alliances with major powerholders generally crowded out careful debate of real issues among various constituencies. Many businesspersons supported Ramos, but probably more because "steady Eddie" was thought to be "predictable

[9] Joel Rocamora, *Breaking Through* (Metro Manila: Anvil Publishing, Inc., 1994), 173.

and not given to rash decisions" than because of any strong sense of what sort of economic program his administration would bring forth; another candidate, in any case, also boasted significant business backing. It is quite likely that many key business supporters would have been far more hesitant about Ramos had they known what was to come.[10]

After gaining power, some top Ramos advisers displayed little notable commitment to novel ways of doing business. Controversy over the granting of particularistic tax exemptions and import privileges to prominent business supporters rocked the administration only weeks after Ramos's inauguration, and competition among rival blocs created early turbulence in the Ramos Palace. Despite the presence of major businesspersons in the initial cabinet, however, the "unofficial power centre" was not thought to be from the corporate world: it comprised instead a group of former military officers led by Presidential Security Adviser Jose Almonte.[11]

Almonte, known as the administration's "chief ideologue," often expressed marked distrust of the Philippine business elite. The roots of rebellion in the Philippines, he proclaimed in 1993, are found not in the mountains but in the key business districts of Manila. In designing Philippines 2000, Almonte sought to promote "economic democracy," and address "overconcentration of wealth and power in a few groups of people." Such an emphasis is probably impossible to understand without examining Almonte's own background. In his own analysis, he and many military officers come from "poor beginnings," and through their experience have "the opportunity to see the real conditions in the countryside." Their training at the military academy teaches them of "duty . . . to protect the country and the people," and their awareness of how elections are conducted and how martial law had operated "made us realise that we Filipinos needed to liberate ourselves from very difficult social conditions. . . . [As] President Ramos explained [in a 1988 speech, while Aquino's Defense Secretary] . . . no government, no armed forces in the world can continue to protect the few who are very rich from the anger that arises out of the frustrations and disappointments of the many who are poor. . . . especially if the wealth of the few are acquired through means that are unacceptable to the nation as a whole." In 1993, he told

---

[10] *FEER*, April 25, 1991, 27; and March 19, 1992, 24. "Fear" of many businesspersons toward Eduardo Cojuangco, the former Marcos crony who took over San Miguel Corporation in the early 1980s, also seems to have played into Ramos's hands. *FEER*, May 28, 1992, 14–5. Ramos himself felt that "predictability" had been the decisive factor in his election, but one post-election analysis dubbed him "the most inscrutable candidate," and noted "doubts about how he would go about solving the country's problems." *FEER*, June 4, 1992, 16.

[11] *FEER*, August 27, 1992, 11, and September 3, 1992, 18 and 38; *Manila Chronicle*, July 18, 1992. The tax exemptions were eventually overturned, and a top aide resigned. A member of a major family that would allegedly benefit from the order permitting duty-free import of cement, however, remained in the cabinet.

business leaders that while reform "may hurt your small finger, it will certainly save your necks."[12]

If the reform efforts of Ramos and Almonte were inspired by past experience, they were encouraged further by at least three other factors that coincided with the beginning of the new administration. First, there was a widespread sense that new approaches were needed to reverse the country's poor economic performance. Worldwide trends of liberalization and privatization greatly influenced the choice of new strategies, particularly to the extent that they were perceived as central to the success of the country's rapidly developing neighbors. The Philippine business community was by no means demanding to be reformed, but after the laggard growth of the 1980s many felt that things were gravely wrong and somehow needed to be fixed.

In more concrete terms, the country found itself faced with decisions as to how it might participate in a series of associations that demanded greater commitment to economic openness—notably the Asia-Pacific Economic Cooperation (APEC), the General Agreement on Tariffs and Trade (GATT), and the free trade area of the Association of Southeast Asian Nations (ASEAN), known as AFTA. In each case, the Ramos reformers were eager to jump on the bandwagon—and able to garner the support of important sectors ready to try something new.

Less tangible but most important in terms of long-term national strategic perceptions was the 1992 withdrawal of the U.S. bases. To many Filipinos, the Philippine Senate's 1991 refusal to renew the bases treaty was a triumph of Philippine nationhood after nearly a century in the shadows of American power. As part of this assertion of independence, the departure of the bases left the country more exposed—and encouraged greater awareness of the country's surroundings. With the security umbrella no longer providing as extensive an overhang, one might say, there was suddenly more of a tendency to look around the neighborhood. In the process, Filipino observers commonly perceived their own house—once widely admired—to be in disrepair, and were often surprised to realize how extensive were the improvements in their neighbors' abodes. Ramos sought to compensate for the end of the "special relationship" by embarking on a series of trips to strengthen Philippine ties with its own region, and even U.S. officials—when able to go beyond feelings of resentment at being ejected from a premier global basing facility—acknowledged that the Philippines will now "have a shot at achieving independence of mind."

---

[12] *FEER*, April 8, 1993, 86; Presidential Task Force, "Philippines 2000: A Vision and Strategy of Development," (Manila: n.d.), 4; *Business Times* (Singapore), July 9–10, 1994; Speech, Jose Almonte, Asian Institute of Management, Metro Manila, April 29, 1993.

For the first time in the postwar era, Almonte similarly explains, "we must deal with [domestic and international pressures] on our own."[13]

Indeed, the new post-bases era brings unprecedented challenges to the Philippines. On the domestic front, there will no longer be an external guarantor for the continuation of the prevailing social imbalance within the Philippines. For most of this century the oligarchy's major external concern has been how to ensure continued U.S. sponsorship for its domestic hegemony; in the future, however, the oligarchy will no longer enjoy such ready foreign support. On the external front, client relations with the United States seem to have insulated Philippine elites from any real sense of intrastate competition—competition that has often been the historic starting point for serious state-building projects.[14] Until recently, the availability of external resources has greatly curbed any need for reform: the country's role as host of the U.S. military bases has helped ensure repeated rescue from the balance-of-payment crises that have plagued the postwar economy. With the withdrawal of the bases from the Philippines, the country will face increasing pressure to begin to orient its economic system toward more internationally competitive modes of operation. Moreover, the country may have increasing need to protect itself against external threats. In short, the deal cut at the turn of the century, wedding the interests of the United States to those of the major oligarchic families of the Philippines, has at last come unraveled at century's end. The country is indeed at a crossroads.

To summarize the impetus behind Philippines 2000, one can note that—although there have been efforts at reform in earlier years—it was only under Ramos that new perceptions of the Philippines' place in the world combined with new leadership to produce major goals for the wholesale transformation of the political economy. From the very beginning of his presidency, Ramos expressed a keen sense of the need for the Philippines to effect such a transformation so that the country might compete more effectively in the international economy. An early presidential order strengthening Almonte's National Security Council, it is significant to note, provided a mandate to work "towards attaining broader national goals."

[13] *FEER*, April 1, 1993, 15. Almonte, speech to the Philippine Economic Society, Metro Manila, February 9, 1996. The bases' departure was "psychological but very important," says Almonte. When under the U.S. security umbrella, "we were very complacent." Interview, Jose Almonte, June 6, 1996. On the "sour" feelings marking U.S. withdrawal, see *FEER*, April 30, 1992, 19.

[14] As Joel Migdal explains, "a prime motivation for state leaders to attempt to stretch the state's rule-making domain within its formal boundaries, even with all the risks that has entailed, has been to build sufficient clout to survive the dangers posed by those outside its boundaries, from the world of states." Joel S. Migdal, *Strong Societies and Weak States* (Princeton: Princeton University Press, 1988), 21.

The ideological influence of such a military perspective differentiates the Ramos-Almonte program from a conventional agenda of liberal reform, and makes for a sometimes peculiar combination of advocacy of a "strong state" (to combat oligarchic dominance and absorb developmental lessons from Northeast Asian newly industrializing countries) with the more conventional "minimalist state" prescriptions of U.S.-trained technocrats and multilateral institutions (to curb state regulation and promote market solutions). Behind the unusual combination of rhetoric, however, lies a fortuitous alliance of economic agenda and political savvy. While the "free market" perspective has been most important in defining the specifics of economic policy, the political strategies necessary for the implementation of new approaches were crafted primarily by Almonte and his close associate, presidential legal adviser Antonio Carpio. The technocrats' economic ideals, in other words, were backed up by very clever and well-planned maneuvers in the rough-and-tumble arena of real politics.

Political savvy aside, it would be a mistake to overemphasize the differences between Almonte and more conventional liberal reformers in the Ramos camp. First, they express a common commitment to demonstrating the mutually supportive relationship between democracy and development. In seeking to build up a "strong state," Almonte stated that his goal is a democratic entity able to "make decisions for the nation as a whole and not for the few." While "the authoritarian approach has been effective elsewhere in Asia," he said in 1994, it is not appropriate to the Philippines—which had such an opportunity under Marcos but "messed it up." As a result, Ramos has to do under democratic conditions what Marcos should have done under "constitutional authoritarianism." Second, Almonte believes that Philippine development will have to be more market-oriented and "less interventionist" than was that of the East Asian NICs, "if only because the Philippine Government's capacity to intervene is less than [that] of our neighbors." Like his more conventional allies, Almonte sees markets as a democratizing force, able to promote the "transfer of power from the few to the many."[15]

While a comprehensive analysis of the various reform efforts is beyond the scope of this work, it is important to summarize key achievements. Building on certain initiatives of the late Aquino years, the Ramos reforms began with liberalization of foreign exchange in 1992, and in subsequent years involved significant strides toward trade liberalization (long a priority of local technocrats, the IMF, and the World Bank, but now encouraged further by Philippine participation in APEC, GATT, and AFTA). Foreign

[15] *FEER*, April 8, 1993, 86; Rocamora, 183, 192; Interviews, Almonte, June 6 and 13, 1996; *Business Times*, July 9–10, 1994; and speech of Almonte to the Philippine Economic Society, Makati, February 9, 1996.

investment has also been liberalized, and a host of major firms have been at least partially privatized. By 1994, the rival stock exchanges were at last forced to unite in the midst of extraordinary growth in the long-dormant Philippine stock market. Greater political stability has emerged in the wake of major agreements with military rebels and Muslim secessionists, and the decline of the Communist Party. Finally, Ramos is credited with ending the crippling power shortages that were depriving Manila and other areas of electricity for as long as eight to twelve hours a day in 1992 and 1993—the very existence of which attests to the extraordinary neglect of the country's infrastructure in the previous decade.[16]

The freshest initiative of the new administration, led by Almonte, was its concerted attack on cartels and monopolies and the oligarchic privilege that nurtured them. The first target was the moribund and inefficient telecommunications industry, in particular the monopoly of the oft-disdained Philippine Long Distance Telephone Company—controlled by the family of Corazon Aquino's nephew, Antonio Cojuangco. While Cojuangco reportedly assisted Ramos in the 1992 elections, efforts to bring competition to the telephone industry produced a major political struggle between the two sides and their supporters. Some viewed the administration's rhetoric as "a cloak for Marcos-style corporate takeovers"; others feared "a military man's anti-business sentiment." The head of the huge Ayala conglomerate, Jaime Zobel de Ayala, spoke for many in the business community when at the height of the battle he denounced "a determined effort, on the part of some officials in sensitive places, to look upon business, particularly large and established ones, as detrimental to the national interest."[17]

Within just a few years, however, PLDT was "serving as a model for deregulation of other sectors similarly dominated by oligarchic, family-controlled firms." The former monopoly is now providing better service and quite happily making more money than ever (although many of the new competitors complain that it has often been uncooperative in facilitating interconnections for rival systems). Impressive new elements of competition are also found in other sectors, most clearly airlines and shipping.[18] While other reform efforts—such as the challenge to the banking cartel—were ultimately not very effective, the fact that they were even attempted signaled a new orientation of the political leadership. Thanks to measures liberalizing foreign exchange and foreign investment, many

[16] Moreover, the crisis highlighted the extraordinary capacity of the country's entrepreneurs to continue to function—albeit at impaired levels—amid an often highly uncertain environment.

[17] *FEER*, May 28, 1992, 14–15, and May 6, 1993, 44–45. Perceptions that certain Ramos appointments to the PLDT board were patronage-based did little to dispel doubts about administration motives. See, for example, *FEER*, October 18, 1993, 30.

[18] *FEER*, June 13, 1996, 46, 48–49 (quote at 46).

of the new competitive pressures have come from a major influx of international investment that, until recently, tended to bypass the Philippines for other locales.

By the mid-1990s, the Ramos reformers were lauded internationally for the fruits of their reform efforts. Annual GNP growth returned to respectable levels (5.1 percent in 1994 and 5.7 percent in 1995, and nearly 7 percent for 1996). Government economists now emphasize that current growth patterns—unlike those of earlier years—are driven not by external debt and aid but by foreign and domestic investment. Furthermore, the growth extends far beyond Manila to include major new regional centers, including Cebu and General Santos City in the south as well as Subic Bay and other areas near Manila. There are many fresh faces on the business scene, most notably an innovative group of exporters, as well as heightened prominence of Chinese-Filipino conglomerates (whose emergence seems to display the usual range of reliance on special privileges, but whose operations are distinguished in part by often extensive informal ties to rapidly growing neighboring economies). After years of frequently stalled reform initiatives, many observers are now confident that market-oriented, outward-looking policies have at last emerged "as the unchallenged paradigm of Philippine development."[19]

The Limits of Liberalization

These major achievements of policy reform, however, should not obscure enduring political and institutional obstacles to sustained economic growth and development. The reform measures do indeed provide a powerful stimulus to an economy long stifled by privilege for a few, but it has become increasingly apparent that even concerted efforts toward liberalization will not, in and of themselves, guarantee sustained economic growth. At one level, one must note that liberalization remains limited in scope: not surprisingly, the Ramos administration—despite a clear commitment to reform—has lacked the political strength to break all key cartels and monopolies and thus level the playing field in the economy as a whole. Alongside the successes, there have also been initiatives—such as that in the banking sector—largely stifled by those who were supposed to be reformed. As noted, the major push for change has come not from a business sector anxious to alter often unproductive modes of operation, but rather from a committed core of reformers within the Ramos administration. By exercising effective and persistent leadership at a propitious crossroads in the country's history, they have begun to effect change. But

[19] Alex Magno, "The Market Consensus," *Far Eastern Economic Review,* August 10, 1995, p. 31.

they have often encountered major resistance from segments of the business community that may voice support for liberalization in general but oppose key elements of specific liberalization measures.

At times, careful political strategies have resulted in major victories for the reformers; at other times, those who resisted reform have prevailed. Fortunately for the reformers, the business community has little experience in effective collective action on behalf of business as a whole, and has rarely defined itself or behaved in terms of any clear segments thereof. As analyzed in previous chapters, one can observe that although certain ad hoc coalitions have developed in recent years (most evident in the anti-Marcos agitation of the early and mid-1980s), businesspersons are far more accustomed to flexing their muscles for the sake of particularistic familial interests than for more broadly defined interests. When faced with a determined political leadership not averse to hurting the "small fingers" of big players, parts of the loosely organized and fractionalized Philippine business community were at times reformed against their own will. In any case, as noted, longstanding economic woes made many businesspersons open to trying new strategies for change.[20]

At another level, there is as yet little evidence of the creation of a broad social coalition able to sustain reform pressures into future years. While top-down reforms can help initiate major political economic transformation, it was argued in Chapter Three, a more comprehensive and sustained degree of transformation seems to require the emergence of concerted pressures from below. Application of Weber's "conflict theory" to the Philippines suggests a particular need to build up countervailing power able to challenge the longstanding dominance of the oligarchy. Ideally, such a challenge might arise not only from state leaders emboldened by external pressures "to stretch the state's rule-making domain within its formal boundaries" (to quote Joel Migdal), but also from groups in society with sufficient standing to "balance" and "struggle" against the power of the oligarchy (to draw on Collins' insights). Ramos himself likens the process of development to the cooking of the *bibingka*, a traditional Philippine rice cake: just as *bibingka* is cooked both from the top and from the bottom, so development must proceed from both top-down and bottom-up initiatives.[21]

[20] Unfortunately, no one has yet undertaken a comparative analysis of the politics of reform across sectors—and such a project is beyond the scope of this book. In general, however, it seems that combating monopolies (for example, in telecommunications and airlines) has been more successful than battling oligopolistic structures (for example, in banking). In the latter case, as we have seen, concerted opposition by a range of domestic banking concerns—increasingly well organized through the Bankers Association of the Philippines—proved an effective foe for the well-crafted strategies of Ramos reformers and their allies.

[21] Speech of Cielito Habito, director of the National Economic Development Authority, World Affairs Council of Northern California, San Francisco, June 28, 1995.

Throughout most of this century, the Philippine elite has displayed a remarkable degree of consensus on major issues of national policy, even as it fights with passion (and often violence) over the division of spoils. This is of course reflected in the highly nonprogrammatic, weakly institutionalized nature of Philippine political parties. As noted earlier, one of the few times this consensus was broken was with the "great monetary policy debate" of the 1950s, engendered by the tentative differentiation of agroexporter and emergent industrial interests. As more and more families diversified their conglomerates across a range of economic sectors, however, they came to share a certain homogeneity of interests on major issues of economic policy. In this process of homogenization, one dominant (albeit loosely organized) segment of capital emerged and remains dominant today: the diversified conglomerates of oligarchic families.

Might groups emerge to challenge this longstanding consensus? Thus far, Ramos's selective reforms from above show only the most tentative signs of being accompanied by the emergence of new types of entrepreneurs that might seek to sustain and deepen the reform program in future years. The occasional assertiveness of a new group of exporters—organized by the USAID-funded Philippine Exporters Confederation, or Philexport—provides a certain glimmer of hope that the diversified conglomerates of the major oligarchic families, nurtured by favorable access to the government, may at last be challenged by entrepreneurial elements whose emergence has depended far less on special privileges.[22] In the short term, however, just as the entry of new banks need not rock the banking sector, neither does the emergence of a new group of entrepreneurs necessarily do much to challenge the dominance of the diversified family conglomerates. The hegemony of the oligarchy also seems quite secure, at present, from any sustained challenge originating from elsewhere (whether the professional middle class, small-and medium-scale entrepreneurs, or popular forces).

Alternatively, might there be elements of the oligarchy itself that, in the course of liberalization, will be encouraged to eschew rent-seeking behavior in favor of more production-oriented entrepreneurship? Here the evidence is even more inconclusive, but one can observe very encouraging signs of a significant shift in the attitudes of many established Philippine businesspersons: overall, analysts note a new consensus in favor of liberalization, market discipline, and integration into the world economy. Jaime

[22] One frequent demand from this newly organized group is a devalued peso. Exporters frustrated with "the prohibitive cost of borrowing money from local banks," moreover, have made plans to set up their own bank. *Philippine Daily Inquirer,* September 26, 1995. While such initial signs of assertiveness from a newly organized section of the business class do not by themselves suggest the beginnings of the sort of "institutionalized strife" prescribed by Collins (see Chapter Two), even the most tentative signs of challenge can be taken as signs of hope.

Zobel de Ayala, for example, had by 1996 cast aside his earlier criticisms of anti–big business tendencies among top officials, and spoke with great enthusiasm of the Ramos reforms. The administration's program is clearly associated with renewed growth, and a desire to sustain the economic momentum feeds into a desire to sustain the momentum of reforms.[23] It is significant that the major concern of business leaders in preparing for the 1998 presidential and congressional elections is ensuring the continuity of the reform process into the next century. One can further hope that as more foreign investors develop a long-term stake in the Philippines, they as well may support ongoing restructuring of the political economy toward more internationally competitive modes of operation.

The creation of a broad pro-reform coalition would certainly be enhanced by ensuring that the benefits of economic expansion are felt by a larger element of the population. This task is made all the more urgent and difficult, however, by the historical absence of any thorough program of land redistribution; unlike South Korea and Taiwan at similar stages of their industrialization process, the Philippines exhibits a particularly immense gulf in levels of wealth and income between the elite and the millions of Filipino workers, urban poor, and peasants below them. Despite Ramos's strong rhetorical commitment to reducing poverty, those at the bottom of society have yet to find much reason to cheer his economic program. While attacks on cartels and monopolies and oligarchic privilege show the potential to build a populist coalition for change, the Ramos administration has not sought to do so. Other Ramos policies—particularly those that perpetuate regressive revenue structures and seek to curb civil liberties—further undercut any hope for such an "inclusionary process."[24]

One can further hope that the presence of democratic institutions might promote the creation of a broad social coalition able to sustain measures of economic reform into future administrations. From the outset, the Ramos administration has treated its economic policy reforms as an element of "people empowerment," building on the restoration of

---

[23] *Business World,* October 1, 1996; Alexander R. Magno, "The Philippines in 1995: Completing the Market Transition," in *Southeast Asian Affairs 1996* (Singapore: Institute of Southeast Asian Studies, 1996), 298–99. In praising the reform program, Ayala called it "a breathtaking ride our country has not known since . . . independence in 1946. . . . The Philippines is faring better today because we have literally changed the road map to the future."

[24] Temario C. Rivera, *Landlords and Capitalists: Class, Family, and State in Philippine Manufacturing* (Quezon City: University of the Philippines Press, 1994), 131–32. See also Rocamora, 179–80; and "Dodging the Authoritarian Temptation," *Politik,* November 1995, 40–43. De Dios discusses the government's "puzzling" tendency to reduce its tax base through a range of special exemptions at the same time it supports a new value-added tax; see Emmanuel S. de Dios, "The Philippine Economy: What's Right, What's Wrong," *Issues and Letters* 4, no. 4–5 (April-May 1995): 1–10, at 3–4.

democratic institutions since 1986. Yet while democratic institutions are indeed consolidating themselves more firmly, many sectors of Philippine society remain marginal to the overall democratic process—and decidedly undemocratic forces hold sway in many localities. Democrats the world over applaud the Ramos administration's explicit efforts to show that democracy and economic growth can go hand-in-hand, but one must recognize that Philippine-style democracy is handicapped not only by the continuing dominance of strong oligarchic forces but also by the weak institutionalization of both its party system and its bureaucracy. If Philippine democracy is indeed going to deliver the goods, economically speaking, it will probably require thoroughgoing political reform as well as the careful nurturing of institutions more conducive to the promotion of long-range developmental goals. Moreover, it is important not to forget—as do some officials and businesspersons when occasionally tempted to resort to repressive and anti-democratic measures—that Philippine-style authoritarianism proved highly inimical to the country's developmental efforts.

Sustaining the process of economic reform will require reform of a political process still dominated by traditional politicians (disparagingly referred to as *trapos*, or dishrags). In the first three years of his term, Ramos displayed considerable skill in using old-fashioned horse-trading and Philippine-style pork barrel politics to push liberalization measures through the Philippine Congress, but he subsequently faced major hurdles when a jerry-built legislative coalition (based on a loose pact among poorly institutionalized political parties) suddenly disintegrated. As Joel Rocamora observes, the administration's "continuing vulnerability to the requirements of *trapo* politics has made it difficult to clinch a thoroughgoing reform image." The price of this dependence has been remarkable: the total cost of discretionary funds granted to legislators grew to consume nearly $1 billion of the annual budget by 1996, and scandals involving persons appointed by Ramos to satisfy political debts tarnished the administration's reputation.[25]

Given the many obstacles to reform, however, it is indeed remarkable that the Ramos administration has nonetheless succeeded in pushing through such a wide array of reform measures. Contemplating the breakup of the telephone monopoly, the liberalization of foreign exchange and foreign investment and the further liberalization of trade, the uniting of the rival stock exchanges, and the restoration of electric power,

[25] Magno, "The Philippines," 291; Joel Rocamora, "The Political Requirements of Economic Reform," *Issues & Letters* 4 (October 1995), 1–4. On controversy over the discretionary "Countrywide Development Fund" and "Congressional Initiative Allocation" granted legislators, see *Philippine Daily Inquirer,* July 26 and 27, August 4 and 18, 1996. For further analysis of political trends under Ramos, see Paul D. Hutchcroft, "The Philippines at the Crossroads: Sustaining Economic and Political Reform," *Asian Update* (New York: Asia Society, 1996).

many observers—both foreign and local—were confident that the country had now resolved its economic woes. Much of this confidence was nurtured by neoliberal sorcerers who promised that the "magic of the marketplace" would pop out of the liberalization hat. Further hope of basic change emerges from a major devolution of authority from Manila to local governments since 1991, recasting major aspects of the country's governing structure (toward outcomes that are as yet unknown).

Unfortunately, a number of very fundamental political and institutional obstacles are likely to limit the impact and sustainability of even these highly impressive top-down initiatives. Just as liberalization of the banking sector by no means resolves ongoing deficiencies in regulatory capacity, neither do broader programs of economic reform obviate the need to address other political and institutional problems. The limits to liberalization are found not only in continuing difficulties in bank supervision, but also in many other arenas as well; amid the intoxication of relative success, one can note a multitude of hangovers. As efforts to address the country's notoriously poor tax collection effort remain in the balance, the future fiscal picture does not look promising. Although Ramos readily acknowledges that the bureaucracy is the weak link in national developmental efforts, little has been accomplished to improve its often lagging capacity. Stock market regulation remains weak, infrastructural improvements lag far behind the economy's needs, and 1995 rice shortages revealed longstanding neglect of agriculture. A seemingly unstoppable rash of kidnappings and bank robberies (widely thought to involve law enforcement officials) highlights the corruption and incompetence of judicial and police officials (commonly called "hoodlums in robes" and "hoodlums in uniform"). Business leaders warn of the fragility of recent gains, and demand more attention to poor infrastructure and rampant crime.[26]

On many fronts, Philippine state institutions are showing themselves to be incapable of providing the necessary political and institutional foundations required even by the laissez-faire model of development that the IMF, World Bank, and the former colonial power have long been trying to peddle to the country. While this book does not presume to provide a general agenda for political and institutional reform across these various fronts, the previous chapter has highlighted the very fundamental types of change necessary within the major focus of this work: the banking sector. Overall, it is difficult to instill long-term investor confidence when a high degree of arbitrariness reigns in the political and legal spheres; until there is greater attention to such underlying constraints, liberalization initiatives rest on less-than-secure long-term foundations. As Almonte himself has

[26] For a brief analysis of the goals and prospects of the devolution experiment, see Hutchcroft, "The Philippines at the Crossroads," 15–16. On broader concerns of political stability and regional tensions, see pp. 10–12, 17.

emphasized (in a tone seemingly at odds with the more exuberant optimism of his colleagues in the Ramos cabinet), the hardest reforms—those requiring sustained administrative capacity—are yet to come. "If our country is to organize the rational economy that will move us into the mainstream of regional development," he warned, "the State must first free itself from the influence of [the] oligarchy. . . . The paradox of market reforms is that they require capable states." Despite the clear impetus for change, he further cautioned, the "rich and powerful families" could still "prove stronger" than the forces of reform.[27]

Building Strong Political Foundations

While the renewed hopes of the mid-1990s generally ignore the limits to liberalization posed by the weak political foundations of the Philippine economy, the fact remains that few observers in 1992 would have expected Ramos and his reformers to succeed with anything near the level of liberalization that they have achieved. Much remains to be done, to be sure; merely cutting back the role of government through a conventional program of liberalization does not in and of itself ensure either an improvement in the quality of government services or a reduction in the power of the oligarchy that has long plundered that government for particularistic gain. But in pushing through a more market-oriented, outward-looking policy framework, the Ramos reformers have taken the vital first step in shaking up the old system.

In an optimistic scenario, one can hope that by reducing the sphere of rent-seeking opportunities, liberalization will disrupt old patterns of private sector plunder, nurture new patterns of entrepreneurial behavior less reliant on special privileges, and—through both the reorientation of already established business groups and the growth of new elements of the business class—create a stronger constituency in favor of developing a more capable and predictable political, administrative, and judicial apparatus. The momentum for reform has been created, and many express confidence that there is no turning back.

In a less optimistic scenario, reformers will be unable to sustain this momentum—and their past efforts will be undermined by ongoing weaknesses of political development. As this book has pointed out, there are indeed many structural obstacles to the transformation of a patrimonial oligarchic polity, and it is too early to predict whether the myriad agents of change—operating both within the government and outside it—will suc-

[27] Jose Almonte, "Building State Capacity for Reform," a speech to the Philippine Economic Society, Metro Manila, February 9, 1996. Sweeping changes in the tax and judicial systems were his top priorities for ongoing reform.

ceed in their ambitious goals. All too often in the past, ongoing deficiencies in the political sphere have hampered the country's efforts to convert
its enormous developmental assets into developmental success—and in
the process illuminated the centrality of strong political foundations to
sustained economic growth. Unlike in the past, however, this time many
key reformers have demonstrated a keen awareness of the structural obstacles that they face and the need for clear long-term strategies to overcome
them. Such awareness not only promotes effective remedies but also
discourages unnecessary demoralization.

The emergence of more advanced forms of capitalist accumulation will
likely depend on the prolonged and turbulent process of dismantling the
oligarchy's control over the state apparatus and constructing a state that is
able to provide a greater degree of calculability in its adjudication and
administration. State building arises out of a long historical process; in the
Philippines, it seems, the imperatives that force such an ambitious task are
only now beginning to have an impact on the nature of struggles in the
country's political arena.

Appendix 1. Total Assets, Philippine Commercial Banking System, 1900–1995

	Commercial Banks				
Year-End	All (mill. pesos)	Domestic (%)	Government (%)	Private Domestic (%)	Foreign (%)*
1900	40	29.4	n.a.	n.a.	70.6
1925	264	74.6	n.a.	n.a.	25.4
1950	1,079	69.7	n.a.	n.a.	30.3
1955	1,413	85.8	48.9	36.9	14.2
1960	2,337	85.1	35.8	49.3	14.9
1965	6,786	92.8	36.3	56.5	7.2
1970	13,841	91.1	34.0	57.1	8.9
1975	49,980	89.7	36.8	52.9	10.3
1980	146,026	87.2	28.4	58.8	12.8
1985	285,578	84.6	26.7	57.9	15.3
1990	497,488	87.1	13.6	73.6	12.8
1995	1,282,174	90.6	0.0**	90.6	9.3

* Totals may not add up to 100 percent due to rounding.
** As of December 1995, the Philippine National Bank became majority-owned (52.6 percent) by the private sector *(Philippine Daily Inquirer,* December 24, 1995). It should be noted, however, that public sector control endures in two "specialized government banks," neither of which is classified as a commercial bank in either this study or SGV studies: the Development Bank of the Philippines and the Land Bank of the Philippines.
Sources: Nicanor Tomas, "Banking in the Philippines from 1925–1950," *The Fookien Times Yearbook 1951,* 71, 73; Sycip, Gorres & Velayo, A Study of Commercial Banks in the Philippines, various issues; Philippine National Bank, *The Philippine Commercial Banking System,* 1990.

Appendix 2. Total Assets, Philippine Commercial Banks (by Rank and by Percentage of Total Assets of all Commercial Banks), Year-End 1955–1995

Bank	Years of Operation	1955 Rank	1955 %	1960 Rank	1960 %	1965 Rank	1965 %	1970 Rank	1970 %	1975 Rank	1975 %	1980 Rank	1980 %	1985 Rank	1985 %	1990 Rank	1990 %	1995 Rank	1995 %
Allied (formerly General, relicensed 1977)	1977–present											4	5.0	9	3.2	10	3.1	9	4.0
General	1963–1977					25	0.8	26	1.0		1.5								
Asian Bank	1990–present															30	0.4	18	1.3
Banco de Oro	1994–present																	16	1.7
Bank of Commerce (formerly Combank and Bank of Boston, renamed 1988 and 1992)	1981–present													29	0.7	26	0.7	27	0.6
Overseas	1964–1968																		
BPI	1851–present	3	5.3	4	4.4'	17	1.5	5	3.7	3	4.2	3	6.1	5	5.7	2	9.1	5	6.9
Peoples	1926–1974	8	2.7	12	2.2	5	3.3	20	1.7										
Comtrust	1954–1981	12	0.9	11	2.8	11	2.1	9	3.0	16	2.3		n.a.						
Family	1981–1985					9	2.4												
Chinabank	1920–present	2	7.8	2	7.5	4	4.2	3	4.1	7	3.1	13	2.4	19	1.6	14	2.4	11	2.7
Chinatrust	1995–present																	40	0.1
Citytrust (formerly Feati, renamed 1977)	1961–present					29	0.7	36	0.6	28	0.7	27	1.0	16	1.8	11	2.9	13	2.2
East-West Bank	1994–present																	36	0.2
Equitable	1950–present	5	3.2	3	5.7	2	4.6	4	3.9	8	2.9	17	2.0	20	1.4	9	3.3	10	3.3
FEBTC	1960–present			16	1.3	15	1.6	13	2.0	4	3.5	5	4.0	7	4.4	4	8.5	4	7.1
Pacific	1955–1985	11	1.4	13	2.1	13	1.9	10	2.8	12	2.5	15	2.3						
Progressive	1964–1975					34	0.5	38	0.4	35	0.2								

FirstBank* (formerly Producers, renamed 1993)	1971–1995									29	0.7	28	1.0	25	0.9	27	0.7	33	0.4
IBank	1995–present																	35	0.3
Manila	1961–1987					18	1.5	14	1.9	10	2.7	14	2.3	10	2.8				
Metrobank	1962–present					22	0.9	22	1.6	5	3.2	6	3.8	4	5.7	3	8.8	2	12.4
PBCommunications	1939–present	4	4.7	6	3.7	8	2.7	11	2.2	22	1.3	19	1.9	23	1.1	20	1.4	19	1.3
Philbanking	1957–present			14	1.8	14	1.7	19	1.7	15	2.3	22	1.5	24	0.9	22	1.2	24	0.8
PCIB	1960–present			9	3.0	3	4.4	6	3.6	9	2.7	8	3.3	3	5.8	6	6.7	3	7.7
PBCommerce	1938–1976	7	3.1	7	3.4	10	2.3	17	1.8	25	1.0								
Merchants	1963–1976					32	0.5	32	0.8	31	0.7								
IBAA	1974–1985									13	2.4	20	1.9						
First Insular	1961–1974					28	0.7	25	1.0										
Asia	1963–1974					27	0.8	30	0.8										
Philtrust	1916–present	6	3.1	8	3.0	16	1.5	27	1.0	30	0.7	30	0.6	28	0.8	24	1.1	23	0.9
Pilipinas (formerly Filman, renamed 1980)	1976–present											29	0.7	30	0.6	28	0.6	22	1.0
Manufacturers	1957–1976			15	1.4	19	1.3	28	0.9	34	0.3								
Filipinas	1964–1976					36	0.3	37	0.5	33	0.5								
PNB-Republic** (formerly Republic and RPB, renamed 1978 and 1992)	1961–present					6	3.2	16	1.8	32	0.6	7	3.3	12	2.1	15	1.8	34	0.4
Prudential	1952–present	9	2.4	5	4.0	7	3.1	8	3.1	14	2.4	23	1.5	17	1.7	12	2.8	17	1.5
RCBC	1963–present					26	0.8	21	1.7	6	3.1	11	2.5	13	1.9	8	4.2	6	5.5
Security	1951–present	10	2.3	10	3.0	12	2.1	12	2.1	24	1.0	21	1.8	11	2.1	19	1.6	15	2.1
Solidbank (formerly Consolidated, renamed 1988)	1963–present					20	1.2	7	3.3	11	2.5	16	2.0	15	1.9	13	2.7	13	2.4
Traders Royal (formerly Traders, renamed 1974)	1963–present					24	0.9	34	0.7	26	1.0	10	2.6	18	1.7	25	0.9	25	0.8
Union	1982–present													21	1.4	21	1.4	12	2.5
Interbank	1977–1994											24	1.1	14	1.9	17	1.8		
Continental	1963–1974					30	0.7	33	0.8										

Appendix 2. *Continued*

Bank	Years of Operation	1955		1960		1965		1970		1975		1980		1985		1990		1995	
		Rank	%	Rank	%	Rank	%	Rank	%	Rank	%	Rank	%	Rank	%	Rank	%	Rank	%
UCPB (formerly First United, renamed 1975)	1963–present					21	1.1	29	0.9	21	1.3	9	3.2	6	4.9	7	5.0	8	5.2
Urban Bank	1991–present																	31	0.5
Westmont (formerly Associated-Citizens and Associated, renamed 1981 and 1994)	1975–present									19	1.5	26	1.1	27	0.9	29	0.5	20	1.1
Citizens	1962–1975					23	0.9	23	1.1										
Associated	1965–1975					33	0.5	35	0.7										
Total, Private Domestic Commercial Banks			36.9		49.3		56.5		57.1		52.9		58.8		57.9		73.6		76.9
PNB**	1916–present	1	48.9	1	35.8	1	35.2	1	32.1	1	34.5	1	26.5	1	26.7	1	13.6	1	13.2
PNCB	1960–1972			n.a	n.a	31	0.6	39	0.2										
Veterans**	1964–85, 1992–present					35	0.5	18	1.7	17	2.2	18	1.9					30	0.5
Total, Government Commercial Banks			48.9		35.8		36.3		34.0		36.8		28.4		26.7		13.6		13.7**
ANZ Bank	1995–present																	n.a.	n.a.
Bank of America	1947–present		n.a.		n.a.		n.a.	15	1.9	18	2.1	12	2.5	8	4.0	18	1.6	26	0.7
Bangkok	1995–present																	39	0.1
Chartered	1873–present		n.a.		n.a.		n.a.	31	0.8	23	1.3	31	0.6	26	0.9	23	1.1	28	0.5
Chemical	1995–present																	43	0.0

Bank	Years															
Citibank (formerly FNCB)	1915–present	n.a.	n.a.	n.a.	n.a.	2	5.1	2	6.1	2	8.7	2	9.2	5	8.3	7	5.6
Development Bank of Singapore	1995–present															44	0.0
Deutsche	1995–present															37	0.2
Fuji	1995–present															38	0.1
ICBC	1995–present															41	0.1
ING Bank	1995–present															42	0.0
Korea Exchange Bank	1995–present															29	0.5
HSBC	1875–present			n.a.	n.a.	24	1.1	27	0.8	25	1.1	22	1.2	16	1.8	21	1.1
Tokyo	1995–present															32	0.4
Total Foreign Branches								14.2	14.9	7.2	8.9	10.3	12.8	15.3	12.8	9.3
TOTAL, ALL COMMERCIAL BANKS***								100.0	100.0	100.0	100.0	100.0	100.0	99.9	100.0	99.9

* FirstBank was taken over by PDCP Development Bank (not a commercial bank) in September 1995 (*Philippine Daily Inquirer*, September 11 and 29, 1995).

** PNB became majority-owned by the private sector in December 1995. PNB-Republic briefly became a government bank when it was taken over by PNB in 1992, and was reprivatized with its majority owner in 1995. Veterans Bank was reopened as a private bank in 1992. Therefore, while the total year-end 1995 assets for PNB and Veterans Bank equalled 13.7 percent, as shown, the actual total assets for the category "government commercial banks" became 0.0 percent. See Appendix I.

*** Total may not add up to 100 percent due to rounding.

Abbreviations: ANZ = Australia and New Zealand; BA = Bank of America; BPI = Bank of the Philippine Islands; Chartered = Standard Chartered Bank; Comtrust = Commercial Bank and Trust Co.; Combank = Commercial Bank of Manila; FEBTC = Far East Bank and Trust Co.; FirstBank = First Philippine International Bank; FNCB = First National City Bank; HSCB = Hongkong and Shanghai Banking Corp.; IBank = International Exchange Bank; IBAA = Insular Bank of Asia and America; ICBC = International Commercial Bank of China; ING = Internationale Nederlanden Groep; PBCommerce = Philippine Bank of Commerce; PBCommunications = Philippine Bank of Communications; PCIB = Philippine Commercial and Industrial Bank (after 1983, Philippine Commercial International Bank); PNB = Philippine National Bank; PNCB = Philippine National Cooperative Bank; RPB = Republic Planters Bank; RCBC = Rizal Commercial Banking Corp.; UCPB = United Coconut Planters Bank.

Sources: Sycip, Gorres & Velayo (SGV), *A Study of Commercial Banks in the Philippines*, various issues; Philippine National Bank, *The Philippine Commercial Banking System*, 1990.

N.B. Indentation of a bank's name denotes absorption by or merger into the bank listed above it. For example, First Insular and Asia merged to become IBAA in 1974; IBAA, in turn, was absorbed by PCIB in 1985.

Appendix 3. Concentration Ratios (Based on Total Assets of Largest Commercial Banks), 1960–1995

Year End	Five Largest Commercial Banks to All Commercial Banks	Five Largest Domestic Commercial Banks to All Commercial Banks	Five Largest Private Domestic Commercial Banks to All Commercial Banks	Five Largest Domestic Commercial Banks to All Domestic Commercial Banks	Five Largest Private Domestic Commercial Banks to All Private Domestic Commercial Banks
1960	n.a.	57.4	25.3	67.4	51.3
1965	n.a.	51.7	19.7	55.7	34.9
1970	49.0	47.4	18.6	52.1	32.6
1975	51.6	48.6	17.2	54.2	32.4
1980	50.1	45.2	22.1	51.9	37.6
1985	53.1	48.7	26.4	57.6	45.6
1990	48.2	46.6	38.0	53.8	52.0
1995	47.3	47.3	47.3	52.2	52.2

Sources: Data extrapolated from Sycip, Gorres & Velayo, *A Study of Commercial Banks in the Philippines,* various issues; Philippine National Bank, *The Philippine Commercial Banking System,* 1990.

List of Interviews

Unless otherwise stated, biographic details are as of last date interviewed, and interviews were conducted in Metro Manila. All interviews were conducted by the author.

Aguirre, Anthony C., and Teodoro O. Arcenas Jr. Chairman of the board and president (respectively), Banco Filipino, April 27, 1993.

Almonte, Jose T. Presidential security adviser and director-general, National Security Council. June 6, 1996, and (by telephone) June 13, 1996.

Anonymous. Business journalist. 1990.

———. Finance Department official. April 19, 1989.

———. Former director, Philippine Veterans Bank. May 31, 1991.

———. Former presidents of the Bankers Association of the Philippines. 1990.

———. Former presidents of certain commercial banks. 1989–1991.

———. Former and current officials of the Central Bank of the Philippines. 1990, 1991, and 1993.

———. International economist. Mid-1990.

———. Merchant banker. September 12, 1989.

Babst, Chester. Executive vice president, Rizal Commercial Banking Corporation; past president of the Bankers Association of the Philippines. April 27 and May 3, 1990.

Barin, Fe. Secretary to the Monetary Board, Central Bank of the Philippines. April 28, 1993.

Bautista, Germelino. Ateneo de Manila University Department of Economics. May 2 and September 22, 1989.

Briones, Leonor. University of the Philippines College of Public Administration; Freedom from Debt Coalition. March 9, 1989.

Broad, Robin, and John Cavanagh. American University and Institute for Policy Studies (respectively). February 8, 1989. Second interview with Robin Broad, August 14, 1989.

Carroll, John J., S. J. Ateneo de Manila University. Institute on Church and Social Issues. February 14, 1989.

Carvajal, Edgardo J. Executive secretary, Bankers Association of the Philippines. May 14 and July 13, 1990.

Castro, Amado A. Former governor, Development Bank of the Philippines; former dean, University of the Philippines School of Economics. February 14 and May 16, 1990.

Coligado, Arsenio. Former department manager, Money Market unit, Continental Bank. May 15, 1990.

Cristobal, Adrian. Former special assistant for special studies (to President Marcos). June 19, 1989.

Cruz, Bayani. Senior reporter, *Business Star.* January 25, 1990.

Deang, Rey. NOVIB (Dutch aid agency). April 25, 1989.

de Dios, Emmanuel S. University of the Philippines School of Economics. February 2, 1989, and May 5, 1993.

Deuster, Paul. United States Agency for International Development. Metro Manila, April 21, 1993.

Diokno, Maria Theresa. Former executive editor, Ibon Databank. January 23, 1990.

Esguerra, Emmanuel, and Ernesto Bautista. Agricultural Credit Policy Council. September 5, 1989. Second interview with Emmanuel Esguerra, May 5, 1993.

Fabella, Armand. Former ranking Central Bank consultant (co-chair of the Joint IMF-CBP Banking Commission, 1971–72; chair of the Central Bank Advisory Group through the 1970s; chair of the Financial Reforms Committee, convened in 1979); President, Jose Rizal College. June 8 and 12, 1990.

Fabella, Raul. University of the Philippines School of Economics. May 5, 1993.

Faustino, Jaime. University of the Philippines Department of Political Science. April 30, 1993.

Fernandez, Jose B., Jr. Founder of Far East Bank and Trust Company, former president of the Bankers Association of the Philippines, and former governor of the Central Bank (1984–1990). April 6, 1990.

Ferrer, Ricardo. University of the Philippines School of Economics. February 6, 1989.

Fitts, Robert W. First secretary, finance and development, U.S. Embassy to the Philippines. February 8 and May 4, 1990.

Gatmaitan, Antonio P. Former president of Commercial Bank of Manila; columnist and political adviser. September 18, 1989, January 31 and February 14, 1990, and April 20, 1993.

Gonzaga, Leo P. Former correspondent of the *Far Eastern Economic Review.* February 2, 6, and 15, 1990.

Gonzalez, Celia M. Bank economist, Department of Economic Research, Central Bank. April 28, 1993.

Gregorio, Reynaldo J. Executive vice-president, Operations Sector, Land Bank of the Philippines. September 26, 1989.

Lallana, Emmanuel. University of the Philippines Department of Political Science. February 13, 1989.

Lamberte, Mario. Economist, Philippine Institute for Development Studies. January 18 and May 11, 1990.

Laya, Jaime C. Former deputy governor for supervision and former governor, Central Bank (1981–1984). May 21, 1990.

Lim, Joseph. Director, Economics Research Center, University of the Philippines School of Economics. January 15, 1990, and April 30, 1993.

Lindsey, Charles W. Professor of economics, Trinity College. June 13, 1990.

Magno, Alexander. University of the Philippines Department of Political Science. February 13, 1989, May 26, 1990, and April 30, 1993.

Mapanao, Mario. Coordinator, Research and Documentation Office, National Council of Churches of the Philippines. May 20, 1988, and March 8, 1989.

McHale, Thomas. Investment banker. New York City (by telephone), November 28, 1989.

Mendoza, Amado M., Jr. University of the Philippines–Manila. December 12, 1989, and March 7, 1990.

Miller, Matt. Correspondent, *Asian Wall Street Journal*, August 17, 1989, March 15 and April 5, 1990.

Miranda, Feliciano L., Jr. Managing director, Central Bank Supervision and Examination Sector. May 17, 1990, and April 28, 1993.

Miranda, Mariano G., Jr. Assistant vice president, corporate banking, Banque Nationale de Paris. October 5 and 17, 1989.

Montes, Manuel. University of the Philippines School of Economics and East-West Center, Honolulu. February 6, 1989, and September 9, 1990.

Nañagas, Vitaliano N., II. President, Philippine Deposit Insurance Corporation. April 23, 1993.

Nemenzo, Franciso. President, University of the Philippines–Visayas. February 13, 1989.

Neumann, A. Lin. Former president, Foreign Correspondents Association of the Philippines. January 30, 1991.

O'Connor, David. Ateneo de Manila University Department of Economics. February 1 and June 10, 1989.

Orosa, Ramon. Former president of Philippine Commercial and International Bank and International Corporate Bank. April 30 and May 4, 1991.

Ortaliz, Wilhelm G. Former director, Bureau of Industrial Coordination, Ministry of Industry. April 26 and May 18, 1989.

Planas, Charito. Former director, Chamber of Commerce of the Philippines. May 10, 1989.

Putzel, James. St. Anthony's College, Oxford University. August 28, 1989.

Quisumbing, Agnes R. University of the Philippines School of Economics. October 15, 1989.

Ramos, Emerito M., Sr. Former chairman, Overseas Bank of Manila. February 24 and March 17, 1990.

Regalado, Iñigo, Jr. Former deputy governor and general counsel, Central Bank; director of Philippine National Bank, April 23, 1993.

Roxas, Sixto K. Founder and former president of Bancom Development Corporation. February 1 and March 8, 1990.

Soriano, Clark. Research director, Institute for Popular Democracy. September 1, 1989.

Tan, Edita A. Professor of economics, University of the Philippines. September 29 and October 4, 1989, June 4 and August 8, 1990, and May 5, 1993.

Tan, Vicente T. Formerly majority owner of Continental Bank, president of Victan and Company, and chairman of the executive committee of Philippine Trust Company. May 15, 1990.

Tatad, Francisco S. Former minister of information (under President Marcos). June 13 and August 22, 1989.

Tenorio, Vyvyan. Business correspondent. March 15 and April 5, 1990.

Tetangco, Amando. Central Bank representative to the IMF. April 22, 1993.

Tiaoqui, Ramon. Former managing director, Central Bank Supervision and Examination Sector for Thrift Banks and Rural Banks. April 26, 1993.

Tiglao, Rigoberto. Business correspondent, *Far Eastern Economic Review.* February 9, June 21, and September 14, 1989, March 26, 1990, and April 1, 1990.

Turner, Melvin R. First secretary, finance and development, U.S. Embassy to the Philippines. April 21, 1993.

Valenzuela, Carlota P. Former deputy governor, Supervision and Examination Sector, Central Bank. March 22, April 25, and May 9, 1990.

Valenzuela, Manuel R. President, Cordym Philippines, Inc.; formerly employed by First United Bank, United Coconut Planters Bank, and Metropolitan Bank. March 30, 1990.

Virata, Cesar E. A. Former finance minister and prime minister. May 24, 1991.

Yap, Josef, and Zingapan, Maria Socorro. Research economists, Philippine Institute for Development Studies. April 12, 1991. Second interview with Josef Yap, May 5, 1993.

Subject Index

Author Index